Macintosh®
Crash
Course

Macintosh®
Crash
Course

Glenn Brown

AP PROFESSIONAL

Boston San Diego New York
London Sydney Tokyo Toronto

AP PROFESSIONAL
1300 Boylston St., Chestnut Hill, MA 02167

An Imprint of ACADEMIC PRESS, INC.
A Division of HARCOURT BRACE & COMPANY

United Kingdom Edition published by
ACADEMIC PRESS LIMITED
24–28 Oval Road, London NW1 7DX

Brown, Glenn (Douglas Glenn)
        Macintosh crash course / Glenn Brown.
            p. cm.
        Includes index.
        ISBN 0-12-135910-7 (acid-free paper)
        Macintosh (Computer) I. Title.
    QA76.8.M3B74   1995
    004.165--dc20   95-30515
                                                        CIP

Printed in the United States of America
    95 96 97 98   IP   9 8 7 6 5 4 3 2 1

Contents

Prevention

Tools of the Trade

Solutions

Hardware

The Information Highway

Appendices

Foreword

by Steven Bobker, Editor-in-Chief, Software Solutions, former Editor-in-Chief, MacUser and Windows User.

Macs crash. It happens. Macs crash way too often even if you're a cosseted, straight-laced user running only ClarisWorks. But I can safely say that no one reading this Foreword is such a Mac user. You're a power user. And you pay for that title. In crashes. And crashes. And crashes.

We (Glenn and I) know who the folks standing there in the aisle in the computer section thinking of buying this book are. Yes, we surely do.

You're the very same folks, when you get to a Macworld Expo, skip the panels on the future of the Mac and how to draw pretty pictures in less than 16.7 million colors, but do pack a clinic session, accurately titled Resolving System Conflicts, that Glenn and I have presented too many times to count. The first we did the session was in Boston many years ago. It was scheduled in the very last slot of a long show and given the unusually great weather in Boston that day, we expected maybe 50 people to show. We were off by maybe a factor of 5 or 6. The crowd spilled into the hallway. And we've overfilled every reprise since then. (If you want to come to the show at Macworld Expo, do please come, but do please come early if you want a seat.)

You're not part of our overflow crowds because you're a good Scout and want to Be Prepared. You're there because, well, you need to be.

You don't run a Mac with only the fonts and extensions approved by Apple Software and Apple Legal. You run a Mac that shows more icons at startup than there are countries in the United Nations. And you want to keep it running for longer at a stretch than it currently does. The run-without-crash range we've heard about spans the whole time spectrum from minutes to hours; not one of you can honestly say your mean-time-between-crashes is measured in days.

That's why you need this book. In the chapters that follow, Glenn distills his years of solving Mac system problems into a readable and usable compendium of tools and techniques you can use to resolve your system conflicts.

When your Mac crashes, who do you turn to? When your Mac was new, still fresh out of its box with that luscious new computer smell still lingering in the air, you probably tried Apple. Why not? If anyone should be able to it should be Apple, right? If you had the patience to wade to one of the most interminable voice mail inquisitions in history and then had the even greater patience to outlast the insipid New Age hold time music, odds are you got no help. You were told, I'd safely bet, to disable each and every non-Apple extension you had. If, and only if, you did that could Apple even attempt to help you. They didn't particularly care that their advice meant your third-party large screen monitor wouldn't work, nor would your trackball or third-party mouse. And if you dared mention those little problems, you were told, well, that's the problem. You dared buy non-Apple-brand items.

So much for Apple tech support. You tried it, and even if you didn't hate it, it didn't solve your problem. Third-party tech support is even more of joke. Yes, there is some excellent support available, and no, it's not the rule. In fact, it's the exception. The only thing I've ever observed about third-party tech support is the larger the company the lousier it is. (Apple is very, very large.) The converse is true: the best tech support comes from the smallest companies. Once you try third-party tech support, the odds are its days later and you're just about where you started. Your Mac still crashes. And while that's a fact of life, it's neither productive nor fun. OK, next step.

The next logical move is get someone with a lot of Mac knowledge to help you. What you're looking for is the humanoid equivalent of the computer-based expert system; you input the problem (verbally, visually, or in combination) and the system supplies a solution that works.

We usually call people like that consultants and depending on their skill or luck or just plain niceness, they cost anywhere from $0.00 to tens of dollars per minute. Nothing beats a good consultant, especially if said consultant is free. If you hire Glenn it'll cost you a lot. If you can hire Glenn. Glenn is very busy helping people, writing books, and working full-time in some mysterious job for the Canadian National Revenue (IRS-equivalent). He's tried to explain to me what he does, but somehow my mind can't associate him with duty and tax collection, so I really don't know what he does.

Anyway, knowing Glenn has not affected my taxes, and reading this book won't affect yours. Even if you're Canadian. I have his promise.

This book is like a consultant in a box (or book , if you insist). Read it carefully, use the tools it provides and your mean-time-between crashes will increase, usually dramatically. If you enjoy your Mac now, you'll enjoy it a lot more after reading *Macintosh Crash Course.*

Of course, you being you (and remember, we know who you are), you're going to add something you shouldn't add or do something you shouldn't do. You'll do that soon. And you'll do that more than once. Glenn and I do wish you good luck, but I can also suggest something far more efficient than mere luck. Keep a copy of *Macintosh Crash Course* within 24 inches of your Mac and as soon as you crash, before you even call your Mac those nasty names you've been calling it lately, reach for this book and look up what you've just done. Then after seeing what the fix is, slowly, calmly restart your Mac while holding down the Shift key and clean up after yourself. I figure after one or two good crashes *Macintosh Crash Course* will have paid for itself.

So far I've pretty much asked you take all I've said about this Glenn Brown person on faith. Who is Glenn Brown and why should anyone trust him on the subject of Macs and how to make them run as long as possible between crashes?

If appearances count, Glenn is a "normal" guy, and certainly not a propeller head. In fact, I never even seen him with a plain beanies, much less one with a propeller; and he does come from the far north; Canada, to be precise. He doesn't, at least in public, wear a pocket protector.

He calls himself an amateur magician, but if you've ever had the privilege to see him perform, you know that amateur is a misnomer. Glenn has the quickest hands and best sense of showmanship that I've ever seen in a Mac person. With the exception of Harry Anderson of Night Court renown, of course. But while Glenn may not be as famous, nor as reliably funny as Harry, he's much better at diagnosing and fixing what ails Mac software. If you ever get to meet him, do tell him your Mac problems. He's always interested in helping out and maybe finding out something new himself. Just don't surprised if, as Glenn works on your problem, a quarter pops out of your ear, or a rabbit out of your pocket. It's all part of fixing your Mac.

Reading this book is less exciting and less stressful than having Glenn do the job, but after you finish the book and practice with the tools provided on the CD-ROM, you'll be able to fix your Mac. Glenn originally intended to put a few feats of his magic art on the CD-ROM in addition to the hundreds of Mac tools, but they kept popping off. Maybe he'll have that system conflict licked by the second edition.

Dedication

There are way too many people to thank for putting up with me while I wrote this book. My friends — Darcy, Pat, Rocco, Martine — have put up with a lot; they've asked that I never write another. Steven Bobker came through big time, providing technical editing, advice, and more. Thanks, guys.

This book is for my friends and family, especially Mom and Dad.

Introduction

The *Macintosh Crash Course* is not a prescription for disaster. In fact, just the opposite. This book is designed to help you get control of your Mac, to prevent and fix problems, and preferably before they happen. The book will also introduce you to the world of shareware utilities (and more) for your Mac. The book is intended for all Mac users, from novices to power users.

Macintosh Crash Course is an outgrowth of the *Resolving System Conflicts* sessions that Steve Bobker and I have done for the last five years at Macworld conventions in San Francisco, Boston, and Toronto. Steve kindly agreed to write the Foreword for this book. I've also interviewed him (see Chapter 10), and he has provided advice and technical editing.

Interviews

You may think I am an expert, a guru of Macdom. To be honest, I'm not — I just fake it well. I don't even *own* a pocket protector. With this book, I wanted to include some background on and the opinions of those people that I feel are *truly* expert. Throughout the book you'll find interviews with some of the people who have made the Mac the way it is today; I am pleased that I was able to get some of the very best to give their opinions. These interviews include some personal information on the individual or group, a bit of background on their company, and their views on their area of specialty.

CD-ROM

Another vital part of the the book is the accompanying CD-ROM — you'll find all sorts of commercial demos, along with almost all of the shareware covered in the book. Unfortunately, there was no way that I could fit all of this great software a floppy (there are over 175 megabytes of software on the CD-ROM; check out Appendix E for a complete listing).

Shareware

A lot of the software covered in this book, and included on the CD-ROM, is shareware. Shareware is software that authors write and freely distribute, relying (some say naively) on users to send them money if they use it. Having been involved in writing and distributing shareware (as part of MagiMac, who wrote *INITInfo*), I can tell you the return is meager (we had 44 registered users, but thousands of downloads). What is the solution? Some authors limit the time you can use their programs, others use the carrot approach, offering more features on registration; the most common is that registered users receive a key that turns off the "guilt" screen (the one that reminds you to pay if you're using the software). Whatever the means used, I recommend that you pay the fees for the shareware that you use — for one, you'll be surprised at the level of support you may get, and shareware authors often include free upgrades for those who pay their fees (compare that with the thousands of dollars it takes to keep just the basic desktop publishing software current!). Variations on the shareware theme include:

- CharityWare (the author asks that you contribute to a favorite charity if you use the software),
- DemoWare (two types: the software is a limited or disabled version of a piece of commercial software, intended to show you how it works; or functional software that includes advertising information on the company that distributes it),
- FreeWare (the author doesn't ask a fee, but retains all rights), and
- Public Domain Software (the author gives up the rights to the software, making it freely available for others to use or modify as they wish; sometimes the author even includes the source code).

In all cases, please remember that it doesn't matter how you get the software — downloaded from a BBS, from a user group, from a commercial shareware provider like EduCorp, or even from a disk included with a book (like this one) — you haven't paid for the software. If you find yourself using a piece of software for a few weeks or a month, send the author the shareware fee. Who knows? Maybe your contribution will be the one that encourages the author to keep going and do another version or another program.

For the record, I have asked and received permission for all of the software on the CD-ROM; in return, each of the shareware authors will be receiving a copy of this book.

Icons

What Mac book would be complete without cute icons in the margins? This book is no different; I wanted to make it easy to spot some of the pitfalls and tips. Here's what to look for:

 CD-ROM: This icon signifies that the software is on the CD-ROM included with the book.

 Warning: Watch out! This can crash your Mac. These are warnings for some of the things you shouldn't do; unless you want to crash…

 Fix: How to fix a problem — these are tips on how to fix some of the more vexing Mac problems.

 Shortcut: These tips tell you how to speed up working on your Mac.

 System-Specific Information: These icons indicate that the information given is specific to a particular system version.

 For Wireheads Only: Tips for those advanced users who want to get their hands dirty.

How the Book Is Organized

The chapters are intended to progress logically, starting with *Prevention,* the things you should do to prevent problems, including specifics for those with Systems 6, 7, and 7.5. *Tools of the Trade* deals with software you can use to make your Mac work better or faster, tools that can help you diagnose and repair problems, and software to protect you or your Mac. *Solutions* gets to the meat of the book — how to fix problems; system conflicts, hard drive problems, and more. *Hardware* starts with SCSI (a black art if ever there was one…), tools to diagnose your ailing Mac, and a chapter on the PowerBook. PowerPC owners aren't left out either — there is information throughout on your Macs, and much of the shareware on the CD-ROM includes native versions. *The Information Highway* tells you how to find out more by getting on-line, and dicusses some of the networking tools included on the CD-ROM. The *Appendices* include a Glossary of the terminology used in the book, a listing of all of the conflicts I know of with the shareware included on the CD-ROM (and more), Sources (who makes all this stuff), the hardware and software used to make this book, and a description of what you'll find on the CD-ROM.

Where Do We Go From Here?

Diagnosing a problem with your computer is one of the most frustrating exercises I can think of. Here are the steps I take when trying to bring my Mac back to life:

- Disable extensions, and, if the problem goes away, isolate the conflict (Chapter 12).

- If your Mac won't boot, try booting from the Disk Tools disk, or, even better, the emergency disk from either Norton Utilities or MacTools Pro (Chapter 16).

- Scan your hard drives for problems using Disk First Aid, Norton Disk Doctor, or MacTools Pro (Chapter 16).

- Check your SCSI cabling, addresses, and termination (Chapter 16).

- Scan for viruses using an anti-viral tool like SAM or Disinfectant (Chapter 9).

- If you have a CD-ROM, make sure the disk is ejected before rebooting (holding down the mouse button during startup should force all disks to eject).

- Re-install your System (Chapter 12).

- Delete the preferences file for the application or extension having problems (Chapter 12).

- Zap the PRAM (Chapter 2).

- Before you call Technical Support, make sure you have a good idea of exactly what your System configuration is. Running one of the reporting tools covered in Chapter 8 is a good place to start.

- Check online to see if there is an update, or if others can help you with your problem (Chapter 20).

- If you're getting out of memory error messages, open the application in the Finder and increase its memory allocation (Chapter 2).

- Have an arcane error message you can't decipher? Try one of the diagnostics covered in Chapter 8.

- If you're getting application not found error messages, use TechTool to rebuild your desktop (Chapter 17).

- If you're running out of memory, and your System file has suddenly grown in size, turn on 32-bit addressing in the Memory Control Panel (Chapter 2).

- Running out of hard drive space? consider using one of the compression tools covered in Chapter 7.

- If you're using System 6, adjust your System Heap and Open Files Count (Chapter 4).

- If you're having problems printing, check out some of the suggestions in Chapter 15.

Ideally, this book should have all the answers; I sure wish I had them. Lately, it seems like I need someone else to write this book, so I can read it, fix my System, and get back to work <vbg> (on-line slang for "very big grin"). In any case, I'm sure there's something here for all Mac users.

Prevention

1 Loading Extensions

Extensions are the bane of the Mac: they make it easy for us to customize things the way we want them, and they are our biggest source of problems. There is no topic more important — other than the location of the power plug and the on/off switch.

Just what are extensions? Extensions (known as INITs if you use System 6, but otherwise no different) are typically small programs that load into your Mac's memory at startup, either performing a function for you (a screen saver, a clock) or staying resident until you call them up (screen capture, fax). The way some extensions run can be changed by accessing them as a control panel. To make things really confusing, not all control panels have INIT (or extension) code in them. Some, like Apple's Map Control Panel, don't load anything into memory until you open them. I have yet to run into a conflict with this type of control panel. On a DOS machine, similar programs are called TSRs (terminate and stay resident applications); the difference is that because of better memory management on the Mac, we can run 25, 50 or more extensions and control panels, while typical DOS users run ten TSRs if they're good.

When you start up your Mac, you'll typically see a row of icons contruct itself across the bottom of the screen; with one of the commercial startup programs, you can specify that they "wrap," creating more rows. The number of rows of extensions is seen by many as a sign of a power user, the reality is that most power users realize that the more toys they run, the longer their Mac takes to boot, the slower it works, and the more often it crashes.

Managing Extensions and Control Panels

The first thing you need to know is how these useful little gems load. The load order is (1) Enablers (2) Extensions folder, (3) Control Panels folder, and (4) System folder; each loading alphabetically. I managed to load 150 extensions on a Quadra 700 at a Macworld session a few years ago; the Mac ran fine until I tried to run one of those pesky applications... If you want to change the loading order, just rename the file with a prefix to change its position relative to other extensions. As an example, Apple's General

Controls Control Panel could be renamed "aGeneral Controls" or "zGeneral Controls" if you wanted it to load before or after other control panels. A space or two works well if you want an extension to load early; the tilde character (~) works if you want to force an extension to load after others. If you want a control panel to load before an extension or extensions, then you'll have to move it to the Extensions folder, and leave an alias in its former place in the control panels folder so you can still access it as a control panel. Once you start playing with changing the loading order of extensions and control panels, you'll really start to appreciate the value of any of the commercial extension loading programs, which allow you to drag items up and down a list to change their order. I'll review some of these later in the chapter.

Why would you want to change the loading order of extensions? Good question. Extensions often make changes or patches; if one extension makes a change to a memory area that another was counting on, then the second may crash, and you'll see a message similar to Figure 1-1. The cure can sometimes be as simple as changing their loading order.

Figure 1-1: I've never expected a crash...

The more extensions and control panels you run, the more likely you are to run into a conflict. The results of an extension conflict can take may forms: your Mac can crash at startup, your favorite application can crash or exhibit weird symptoms, or the conflict can be cosmetic, such as an incorrectly drawn menu bar. The worst conflict is one that isn't readily apparent or duplicatable — this can be a real bear to track down.

Tracking Down Conflicts

If you suspect you may have an extension conflict, the easiest way to find out is to boot up without extensions: just hold down the Shift key when booting until you see the message shown in Figure 1-2.

Figure 1-2: Starting your Mac without extensions

Note: this is a feature Apple has built into the Mac operating system since System 7; System 6 users see Chapter 4.

 If your problem goes away with all of your extensions turned off (presuming that it is one that you can duplicate), then in all likelihood you have an extension conflict. Now the fun begins: you need to isolate the problem file to see if you can cure the problem. The easiest way is by performing a *boolean search*. (This is an outright lie: the easiest way is to have someone tell you the cure; the second easiest is to use one of the commercial extension managers, which can automate this process for you.)

1. Turn off half of your (loaded) extensions (manually or even better with one of the programs covered later in this chapter) and restart your Mac.
2. If the problem still exists, go to step 3; if the problem goes away, go to step 4.
3. You now know that one of the loaded extensions is part of the problem, so go back to step 1 and continue narrowing the search.
4. You now know that one of the loaded extensions is not the problem, so turn the first half of your extensions back on, turn off the second half, restart your Mac, and go to step 2.

Eventually, you should come down to one extension that, when disabled, seems to cure the problem. If you can live without it, then disable it and get back to work. If you can't live without it, reverse the above process, adding back extensions along with the errant one, until you find the two that don't like each other. In this situation, the first thing to try is reversing their load order; if that doesn't work, you'll have to disable one or the other. See Chapter 12 for a more detailed description of the boolean search process.

Controlling Extensions

The preceding material assumes that you know how to turn on and off extensions and control panels. These programs can be disabled by simply dragging them out of the System folder, or by moving them from their correct folders to ones named "Extensions (disabled)" or "Control Panels (disabled)". The actual wording isn't important, just as long as the name is different. This happens to be the method used by most of the extension programs currently available.

There is a better way: there are good shareware and commercial programs for managing extensions available (including the demos and shareware on the CD-ROM included with this book), and Apple has included version 3.0 of Extensions Manager with System 7.5. Here's the lowdown on some of them:

Extensions Manager
Ricardo Batista's Extension Manager is a simple program that allows you to turn extensions on and off, and to create sets of extensions to allow trouble-free computing different circumstances. The program consists of two parts: an extension that loads first, and a control panel that allows you to select the set to be used at your next startup. If you want to select a startup set when booting, hold down the Spacebar until the control panel appears (see Figure 1-3).

Extensions that are highlighted are active or enabled; those that are in normal text are disabled. All one has to do is to double-click on an item to

Figure 1-3: Extensions Manager 2.0.1

change its status. Extensions Manager allows you to view your startup items in logical groups: Extensions, control panels, System Folder; and it also allows you to control programs in your Startup Items, Apple Menu Items, and Fonts folders. With System 7.5, Apple has included a simplified version of Extensions Manager, with an improved interface.

 This new version 3.0 (see Figure 1-4) only works with System 7.5, so users of earlier systems should stick with 2.0.1 or one of the other utilities covered in this chapter. Extensions Manager 3.0 no longer allows you to control programs in your Startup Items, Apple Menu Items, and Fonts folders, so the loss isn't so bad…

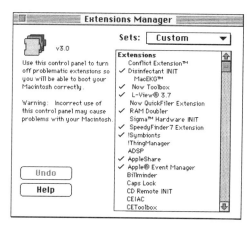

Figure 1-4: Extensions Manager 3.0

 ### IconWrap II
Ken McLeod
Apple Computer, Inc.
Internet: ken@cloudbusting.apple.com (preferred)
AppleLink: THE.CLOUD
eWorld: TheCloud
Shareware fee: Freeware

Want to have your startup icons neatly wrap into rows, but you still haven't sprung for one of the commercial utilities? IconWrap II may be the answer. This tiny extension tries to convince those extensions that load after it to wrap correctly. Ken's only request is that if you wish to contact him, please do so in e-mail.

Extension Kit™
Richard Harvey
P.O. Box 118332
Carrollton, TX 75011
America Online: Banana6000
Shareware fee: donation

Richard Harvey's Extension Kit™ expands on the functionality of Extensions Manager, allowing you to define up to ten "kits" (sets of extensions) that can be keyboard selected at startup, and includes an important feature that all others have (so far) overlooked: the ability to print out a chart of your startup kits. Figure 1-5 shows the opening screen.

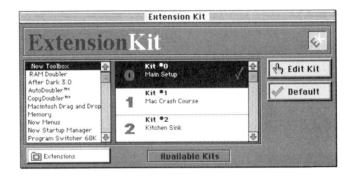

Figure 1-5: Extension Kit™

Selecting Edit Kit brings you a straightforward dialog (Figure 1-6) that allows you to add or delete extensions and control panels from the selected kit.

Figure 1-6: Extension Kit Setup dialog

ExAminer

Mike Weasner
2567 Plaza Del Amo #209
Torrance, CA 90503-7329
America Online: MWEASNER
AppleLink: MWEASNER
CompuServe: 70307,243
Shareware fee: $10.00

Mike has been programming on and off since 1966. He started out with FORTRAN for a few months and then after a 14 year break, began programming in BASIC on an Apple][Plus. In 1985 he began programming on the Mac, first in BASIC and then later in C and Pascal. ExAminer is only his second shareware application and is the most successful. He says that it has been a thrill to receive registrations from many different countries — shareware works. In his real job, he manages Macintosh and Intel-based computers and networks at a large company.

ExAminer offers a much easier to understand interface than Extensions Manager, and allows control of Apple Menu Items, Fonts, and Startup Items, along with extensions, control panels and items in the System folder (Figure 1-7). It requires System 7; version 1.3 (on the CD) is a *fat binary,* with support for 680x0 Macs and native support for PowerPCs. It also includes balloon help, and Apple Guide help for those running System 7.5.

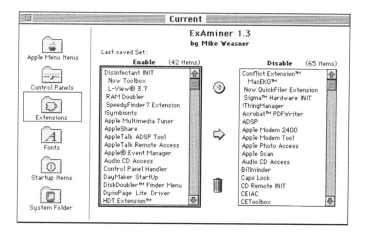

Figure 1-7: ExAminer

INIT-Scope
David P. Sumner
1009 Walters Lane
Columbia, SC 29209
Shareware fee: $15.00

David is a Mathematics professor at the University of South Carolina who programs in C and assembler. He's the author of numerous articles for popular computer magazines; a book *Unleash Your Pocket Computer* (Addison Wesley) a decade ago, and a chapter in the book, *Tricks of the HyperTalk Masters* (The Waite Group). He is also the author of several commercial software products for the Tandy Model 100 computer.

INIT-Scope is for those who really need to know exactly what's going on when their Mac starts up. This control panel (see Figure 1-8) runs under both System 6 and 7, and can tell you which traps are patched, which low-memory global variables are changed, what resources are loaded, and more, about each of your INITs (extensions).

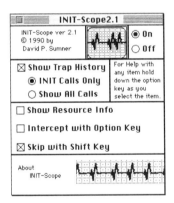

Figure 1-8: INIT-Scope

Symbionts
Kevin Hardman
c/o Nivek Research
108 Kramer Court
Cary, NC 27511
Internet: symbionts@hardman.pdial.interpath.net
Shareware fee: $20.00

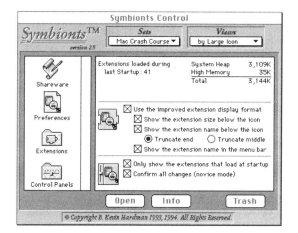

Figure 1-9: Symbionts 2.5 Preferences

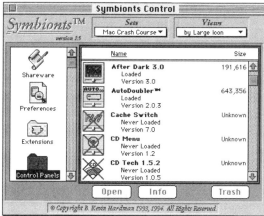

Figure 1-10: Symbionts 2.5

In my opinion, Symbionts is the star player of the shareware extension products, with features that rival those offered by many of the commercial programs. It changes the startup display, with each extension's icon appearing on-screen, and then popping up as it displays the amount of memory used by the extension. It makes your startup display look even more impressive (if you're impressed by that kind of thing), not only by taking more space, but by showing icons for those extensions that normally don't reveal themselves. It alsomakes it clear exactly what each of the icons represents, by allowing you to have the name of the extension shown below its icon, and in the menu bar, if you so choose.

Unchecking "Only show the extensions that load at startup" (see Figure 1-9) gives you control of Apple Menu Items, Startup Items, and, under System 7.1 or greater, the Fonts folder. Like the products already covered, Symbionts allows you to create sets of extensions that you can select at startup. Symbionts' installer installs itself as an extension and a control panel; for System 7.1 and newer it installs as a script resource ("scri") so that it can load before everything else. Symbionts allows you the standard access to its control panel at startup if you hold down the Spacebar. One nice touch is engaging the Caps Lock key, causes it to pause at the end of the boot process to let you know how much memory your extensions are using. Clicking on an item toggles its status; those that are not loaded are shown crossed out (Figure 1-10).

Commercial Products

There have been, and there continue to be, a lot of commercial products out there to help you manage your extensions — products like Aask, init cdev, INIT Manager, INITPicker, and On Cue II have all added to the grand scheme of things. The dust has settled somewhat, leaving two products worthy of your consideration: Now Software's Now Startup Manager and Casady & Greene's Conflict Catcher 3. What do these products offer that their competition doesn't? Plenty:

- the ability to create sets (OK, so everyone does this one…)
- the ability to change the loading order of extensions and control panels by simply dragging them up or down a list (this is a feature that all of the commercial packages have offered)
- the ability to force extensions to wrap correctly, showing multiple rows of icons on your screen (not that there's anything wrong with that…)
- the ability to temporarily disable extensions that crash at startup
- the ability to create "links", so that you can specify which of your extensions don't like each other (more on this one later…)

and the biggie:

- the ability to automate the binary search process, helping you isolate conflicting extensions when you have a duplicatable problem (we'll try this later in the chapter…)

Now Startup Manager
Now Software, Inc.
921 S.W. Washington St. Suite 500
Portland, OR 97205-2823
Telephone: 503 274-2800
Fax: 503 274-0670
America Online: Now
AppleLink: NowSoftware
CompuServe: 71541,170
eWorld: NowSoft
Internet: support@nowsoft.com
Suggested retail (part of Now Utilities): $89.95

I should preface my comments here by stating that I've used Now Startup

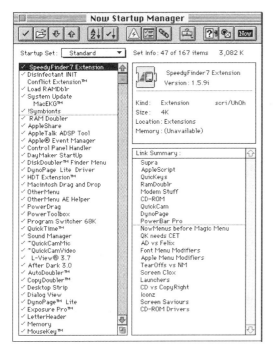

Figure 1-11: Now Startup Manager 5.0.1

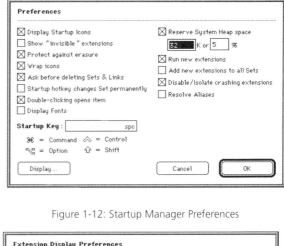

Figure 1-12: Startup Manager Preferences

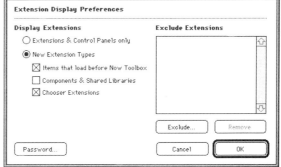

Figure 1-13: Startup Manager Display Preferences

Manager since before it was released (I was a beta tester), that the original author (Jörg Brown) is a friend, and that I don't have any shares in Now Software. Until the release of Conflict Catcher 3, Now Startup Manager was the program I used; I liked the interface, I liked the power user features, and I had gotten used to the program's idiosyncrasies. As you can see in Figure 1-11, I also run way too many extensions.

Here's what the icons across the top of the control panel do (from left to right): the check mark turns items on and off (you can also double-click on item's check mark to toggle its status), the open folder opens an item (double-clicking on an item opens it), and the up and down arrows move items up and down the loading order list (click-dragging an item does the same thing). The AZ arrow will sort items in their loading order (regardless of whether or not they are active), and the check mark arrow sorts only the active extensions at the top of the list, in loading order. This last view is handy, if you just want to view active extensions and control panels (it is the view shown in Figure 1-11), but it has a downside: if you add a new extension to your System folder, Startup Manager will load it after your list, instead of in its correct alphabetical order. The fix is to force Startup Manager to re-sort the list by clicking on the alphabetical sort, then back to the active items only sort. The lightning bolt triangle calls up a dialog to start the conflict isolation process, the checkbook allows you to create or modify startup sets, and the chain icon calls up the links dialog. The question mark/drive allows you to select the startup disk, the question mark/switch allows you to toggle hot help, the buttons brings up preferences (see Figure 1-12), and clicking on Now will tell you about the program and its authors.

The Preferences dialog shows one of Startup Manager's unique features: the ability to reserve System heap space. Memory management (see Chapter 2) is much improved with System 7; users of System 6 should be sure to have this turned on. The ability to show "invisible" extensions is one you should not turn on, unless you're familiar with all of the file types in your System. The risk here is that you might turn off needed files that have little risk of conflicting. Clicking on Display gives you the dialog shown in Figure 1-13.

My recommendation is to select "Extensions & Control Panels only" until you are really comfortable with all of the files in your System folder. The dotted line above RamDoubler in Figure 1-11 indicates items that load before Startup Manager. If you toggle the status of one of these items at bootup, Startup Manager forces a restart to turn the item on or off. There is

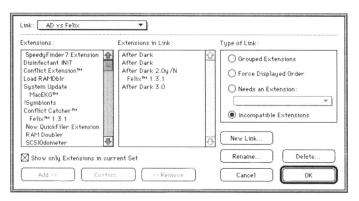

Figure 1-14: Startup Manager Links

little point in turning off components and shared libraries (other than the memory saved); this option does allow you to view what is being loaded, so you can do cleanup on outdated items later. The same is true for Chooser items; turning one off is unlikely to fix a problem, and you may find your printer or fax modem not working the next time you try to use it...

Startup Manager supports the same link types that Conflict Catcher 3 does, and adds the ability to create a dependency that isn't linked. An example is QuicKeys, which needs CEToolbox to run — I don't want to create a group, which would turn CEToolbox off with QuicKeys — so I tell Startup Manager that QuicKeys needs CEToolbox to run. Figure 1-16 shows the Startup Manager Links dialog.

Conflict Catcher 3

Casady & Greene
22734 Portola Drive
Salinas, CA 93908-1119
Telephone: 408 484-9228
Fax: 408 484-9218
AppleLink: D0063
America Online: CasadyGree
CompuServe: 71333,616
Suggested retail: $99.95

The recent release of Conflict Catcher 3 has raised the standard for extension loading utilities. From the time you start up with Conflict Catcher 3 loaded, its influence is evident — as you can see from Figure 1-15, CC3 can show you the names of extensions as they load, and also display the name of the current startup set (as can Symbionts).

Conflict Catcher was the first program with the capability of automating your search for conflicting extensions. Here's how it works: if you have a problem that you suspect may be an extension conflict (preferably a problem you can duplicate), you start the process by clicking on the Conflict Test in Conflict Catcher 3's main dialog (Figure 1-17). CC3 will walk you through the binary search process, automatically disabling extensions, telling you when to restart, and what to do, until you either tell it to stop or (even better) it identifies the problem for you. The improved conflict testing (Figure 1-16) allows you to suggest to Conflict Catcher 3 what extensions you think may be causing your

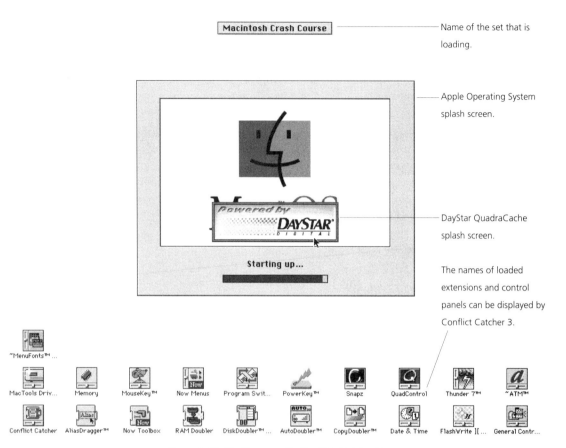

Name of the set that is loading.

Apple Operating System splash screen.

DayStar QuadraCache splash screen.

The names of loaded extensions and control panels can be displayed by Conflict Catcher 3.

Figure 1-15: Starting up with Conflict Catcher 3

grief; other unique features include the ability to scan for damaged startup files and the use of the date installed in performing its tests (unless you tell it otherwise, CC3 will start testing with the most recently installed extensions).

Conflict Catcher 3 offers several ways for you to look at the files it controls. Clicking on the view pop-up allows you to select one of six views: *by Date Installed* shows the files in the order they were added to your System, *by Enabled* lists the active files first in their load order, *by Folder* shows them as they appear in your System folder, *by Kind* shows aliases and other file types, *by Load Order* displays them in the order they load, *by Memory Use* sorts them by the amout of RAM they use, and *by Name* displays all startup items alphabetically. Clicking on a file in the list displays information about the file

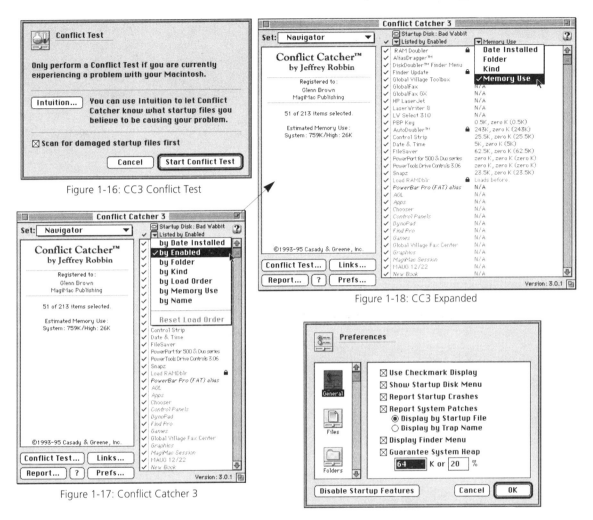

Figure 1-16: CC3 Conflict Test

Figure 1-17: Conflict Catcher 3

Figure 1-18: CC3 Expanded

Figure 1-19: Conflict Catcher 3 Preferences

and Shift-clicking on a file will lock it (making it on for all of your sets). The last feature is handy for those extensions, like AutoDoubler or RamDoubler, that you may want to keep on all the time.

Maximizing the Conflict Catcher 3 window, either by clicking on the button in the upper right-hand corner, or by dragging the window larger displays a second column of information about your startup items (see Figure 1-18), which can be configured to show the date installed, folder, kind, or memory use.

Conflict Catcher 3's Preferences dialog (Figure 1-19) shows off some of the flexibility this program offers: Files allows you to specify whether or not CC3 should display components, shared libraries, Chooser extensions, and aliases; Folders allows you to have CC3 control fonts, Control Strip modules, startup, shutdown, and Apple Menu items; Color allows you to assign colors to various startup items, making it easier to distinguish between them; there are also settings for Icons, Sets, Testing, and Security. If you're concerned that CC3 may be involved in a problem, it even has the ability to turn off its own startup features.

Figure 1-20 shows my favorite feature: Links. (I'm a bit biased here, I suggested the feature to both Casady & Greene and Now Software while MagiMac was developing INITInfo Pro and DiagnoSYS.) This feature allows you to tell Conflict Catcher 3 that certain extensions should be grouped (if one is turned on or off, so are the rest), incompatible (if one is turned on, the others are turned off), or should load in a forced order. I've exported my current links, and included the file on the CD-ROM.

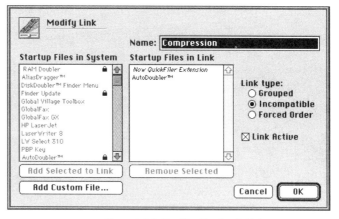

Figure 1-20: Conflict Catcher 3 Links

Conflict Catcher 3 is unique in the tools it offers network administrators: it supports aliases (also good for RAM disk users), the import and export of links so that administrators can maintain standard sets of startup items, and complete System reporting.

Interview: **Jeff Robbins**

Jeff is the author of Conflict Catcher 3, and a member of the team writing Apple's next operating System, currently code-named Copland.

How long have you been programming and how did you get started?

I've been programming since I was 14 (I'm 25 now, that makes about 11 years); I started on an old TRS/80, then an Apple][Plus. I started working for a computer store when I was 14 — they were the first local Apple dealer, and had a Mac 128. My first computer was a TI-99/4A

What is your educational background — are you formally trained, or did you teach yourself?

I have my BSC in computer science from the University of Iowa (with a minor in business), I also have an MBA from the University of Illinois.

What programs have you written (or been involved in the development of)?

Conflict Catcher (versions 1/2/3), Innovative Utilities; Spaceway 2000 (co-authored with john calhoun); the freeware utility AutoFlush (the functionality of AutoFlush is now rolled into System).

What language(s) do you write in?

C, C++ , Pascal, 68k assembly, PPC assembly.

What software tools do you use?

Metrowerks, MPW, THINK C, Resourcerer.

Please describe the equipment you use (what computer, how much RAM, etc.)

My main development machine is a PowerPC 8100/80av with 32 megs of RAM and 2.1 meg Quantum Empire drive.

What is your favorite piece of software (excluding that written by you or your company...)

Metrowerks.

What do you do for a living?
I work for Apple Computer, working on systems software on Copland project, specifically the Copland microkernel.

Where do you live, are you married with children, how old are you, (etc.)
I grew up in Highland Park (a suburb of Chicago), and married Laura last April; we live in Sunnyvale.

Why do extensions conflict?
There can be a number of reasons that extensions may conflict: the startup file may be poorly written or buggy, the startup file may be outdated or incompatible with your System software, the startup file code or data may be corrupted, or two or more startup files may be fighting for the same resources.

Conflict Catcher 3 is a pretty major upgrade — what were your objectives with this release?
I had a number of objectives: to do no harm (to make sure that when installed CC3 cannot ever be the cause of a problem;, to make sure that CC3 would always do everything it does 100% of the time, to give it a more appealing interface; make it easier to use, with more usablity features; and to give the user more information about their System (so that, instead of saying "What are these things?", the average user could see a description of their startup items).

How is conflict testing improved in Conflict Catcher 3?
A number of ways:
- *the algorithm has been improved and speeded up*
- *the tracking of the date things are installed (CC3 will start with the most recently installed items when starting a test)*
- *Intuition: a feature that allows the user to have CC3 start with the extension that he or she feels may be causing the problem*
- *the saving of tests, with the ability to resume them later*
- *automatic reordering: when CC3 finds two conflicting extensions, it can automatically reorder then to see if that fixes the problem, and if it does, it will automatically create a link forcing that new order*
- *if there is a crash during startup, CC3 will offer to go straight into a conflict test. More importantly, it will use the knowledge of where in the boot process the crash occurred to start the testing process intelligently*

Can you explain the line at the top of Conflict Catcher 3's list (when viewed by load order)?

The manual isn't quite correct on this one; items above the line cannot be re-ordered by dragging them. The manual states that items above the line load before Conflict Catcher 3. The best way of determining which items load before CC3 is to expand the dialog and view by memory use.

Are there any Easter Eggs in Conflict Catcher 3?

Try typing "play" when you have "About Conflict Catcher" open (see Figure 1-21). The game controls are left and right arrows; spacebar fires. Because the game uses icons from your System, it takes only 3K of space!

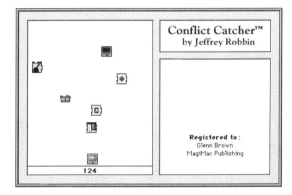

Figure 1-21: The game in CC3's About box.

Which Is Best?

In balance, I'd have to say Conflict Catcher 3 offers more power, ease of use, and features than Startup Manager. A perfect example is how it deals with duplicate items: when Startup Manager finds extensions in both active and disabled folders, it puts the extra into a Duplicate Items folder; CC3 not only finds them, but offers to delete the inactive file for you. Until the release of Conflict Catcher 3, I would have said that Now Utilities users had little reason to buy another program — CC3 has changed that; it is significantly better, in almost every way.

The Future

This is the only program area in which I feel comfortable advising what I'd like to see in the future — these programs control how our Macs run, how they look, they even control how often they crash. I started this list before Conflict Catcher 3 was released, it almost seems that Jeff was able to read my mind. There are still a few features I'd like to see:

- The ability to select sounds, pictures or movies to run at startup or shutdown (CC3 allows you to assign sounds to sets).
- Time or voice controlled startup sets (CC3 allows you to have sets startup by circumstance, i.e., you can have your PowerBook automatically load a particular set when running on battery power).
- The ability to use the Caps Lock key to call up the program at startup (this is a feature of INITPicker that has been added to Conflict Catcher 3.0.2).
- Assignment of sounds to startup (I now use Dubl-Click's ClickChange to assign a bell to tell me when all of my extensions are loaded).
- Control of your Preferences folder, allowing diagnosis and backup to prevent prefs corruption, and the ability to identify and delete outdated or obselete prefs.
- Automated conflict testing (the capability to test and recognize whether or not a problem still occurs).
- Tools to analyze and track system performance (how much are my extensions slowing my Mac down). See Chapter 17 for coverage of MicroMat's PowerScope, which does this.
- Export/import of links as a standardized text file (this is an idea that we pioneered with DiagnoSYS: a rules text file format, so that links could be written and freely distributed, for use with the extension manager of your choice).
- AppleScript support.

Who knows — maybe some bright programmer will read and implement these, and we'll have the next great application!

2 Managing Memory

For some reason, I've forgotten what I was going to say… (just kidding). Understanding how your Macintosh handles memory is very, very, *very* important. The good news is that it is a lot easier to understand than on a PC. Then again, the meaning of a "-108" error message isn't clear to everyone (this is the Memory Manager Error message "Memory Full Error").

A vital distinction to make here is that we are talking about the random access memory (RAM) installed in your computer, not the size of your hard drive. Your hard drive stores information, even when powered down; RAM only stores information when your computer is on — it "forgets" everything when you shut down or restart. I also won't be covering video RAM (VRAM), the amount which determines how many colors your monitor can display on-screen and at what resolution. What I will be covering are the settings in the Memory Control Panel, RAM disks, applications memory, parameter RAM (PRAM), Quadra Cache, and a couple of exciting products to enhance your Macintosh's use of memory: OptiMem and RAM Doubler.

The Memory Control Panel

Let's start by looking at the Memory Control Panel. Figure 2-1 shows the Memory Control Panel from System 7.5; the one in System 7 is virtually (no pun intended) the same.

Disk Cache

Disk caching means a part of your RAM is set aside to hold frequently accessed information. Because RAM is much faster than your hard disk, using it tends to speed up things, particularly if you open and close applications regularly. As shown in Figure 2-1, the default setting is 96K. Like it says, your disk cache is always on: the minimum is 32K. My

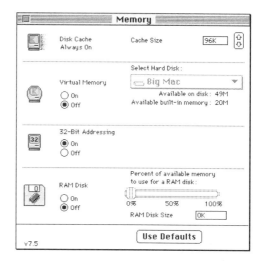

Figure 2-1: System 7.5 Memory Control Panel

recommendation here is simple: if you're running System 7, you should have a minimum of 8 megabytes of RAM (if you don't, set the book down, and go out and buy more RAM!) — you can run System 7 with 4 megabytes of memory, but not very well. Now that we've got that out of the way, I recommend 256K of disk cache if you're running with 8 megs, and up to 512K if you're running 16 megabytes or more. Except in the rarest cases, assigning Disk Cache above 512k does no good, and eats precious RAM. An exception is the PowerBook 100 with 4 megabytes of RAM, where a setting of 1 megabyte helps.

Virtual Memory

Virtual memory means the system is "fooled" into thinking that part of your hard drive is RAM. There are a couple of disadvantages of virtual memory: your hard drive is much slower than RAM, and Apple's virtual memory scheme is inefficient. An example: you have 20 megabytes in your Mac (as shown in Figure 2-1), and you want to run as if you have 40 megabytes. Apple's scheme requires that you set aside 40 megabytes of your hard drive to use 40 megabytes of virtual memory. A better alternative is Connectix's Virtual, which allows you to set aside only the additional hard drive space you require (in this example, 20 megabytes). An even better (and certainly much faster) alternative is to buy more RAM, or to use one of the commercial products (OptiMem or Ram Doubler) covered later in this chapter.

There are a couple of special cases that I should mention: Adobe's Photoshop uses its own virtual memory scheme (Adobe recommends that you run with Apple's virtual memory turned off); and those lucky users with PowerPCs should run with virtual memory on (the optimal setting is your memory size plus one megabyte).

32-Bit Addressing

The Apple Operating System requires 32-bit addressing in order to "see" more than 8 megabytes of RAM. Turning it off gives you 24-bit addressing, and your Mac can no longer "see" installed RAM over 8 megabytes. This situation results in the single most-asked problem question about the Macintosh: *"I've just installed more RAM in my Macintosh, and all of a sudden my System has grown to 12 megabytes…"* The answer is simple: go to the Memory Control Panel, and turn on 32-bit addressing. When in 24-bit mode, any memory above 8 megabytes will be added to your System (when viewing the "About This Macintosh…" dialog). The only circumstance that you may need to turn off 32-bit addressing would be to run older software — I don't believe there is any current software that is not "32-bit clean" (capable of running when 32-bit addressing is on). Those with a Mac II, IIx, IIcx or SE/30 running System 7 or better need Mode32 7.5 (see "Connectix" at the end of this chapter).

RAM Disks

A RAM disk is the opposite of virtual memory: it allows you to set aside part of your memory (RAM) as a virtual disk. The advantage is that RAM is much faster than your hard drive; the disadvantage is that it is much more volatile: in all but very special cases, anything not saved from a RAM disk is lost on crashing (or rebooting). Still, for those with the need for speed, a RAM disk can offer significant advantages. Another good use for a RAM disk is by PowerBook users — this may allow you to load your main application (usually a word processor) into the RAM disk, and thus reduce hard disk access, significantly increasing your battery life.

RamDisk+
Roger D. Bates
P.O. Box 14
Beaverton, OR 97075
Telephone: 513 591-9223
America Online: RogerB2437
Shareware fee: $35.00

Want to use a RAM disk? You're going to want more than the tools Apple gives you. On the CD-ROM is one of the best, commercial or otherwise: RamDisk+. This great utility can automatically create a RAM disk, copy files into it, and automatically copy changed or new files back to your hard drive. For those without a hard drive, it can even switch control to a RAM disk and eject the startup floppy . If you don't have a hard drive, you need one. Run (don't walk) to your local dealer (if there's one left), and buy a hard drive for your Mac. Figure 2-2 shows RamDisk+'s Control Panel.

Figure 2-2: RamDisk+ Control Panel

The copy back feature has an added bonus for registered users: you can specify the timing used for copying back modified files to your hard drive. Clicking on "Setup" allows you to specify the size and name of your RAM disk (Figure 2-3), and clicking on Selections allows you to specify the files or folders to be loaded (or files within a folder that should be excluded from loading) automatically (Figure 2-4).

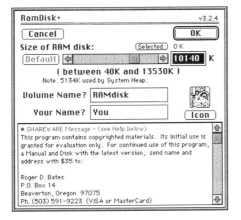

Figure 2-3: RamDisk+ Setup

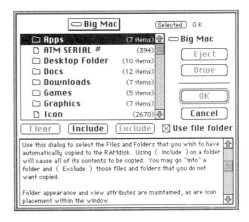

Figure 2-4: RamDisk+ selections

WriteThrough

Stuart Cheshire
29C Escondido Village
Stanford, CA 94305
Telephone: 415 497-2399
Internet: cheshire@cs.stanford.edu
WriteThrough is freeware

Stuart is a Ph.D. student in Networking at Stanford. He's also a PC programmer turned Mac programmer four years ago when he started work on Bolo for the Mac. WriteThrough is unsupported (what do you want for nothing? — Stuart wants to finish his degree); for a complete story read the doc file on the CD-ROM.

WriteThrough addresses the problem with some programs writing their data to disk in chunks and the Mac caching the blocks in its disk cache. When the file is closed the data is finally written to disk, causing a big slowdown. It would be much better if the data were written continually to disk, instead of in one big burst at the end. WriteThrough is a little INIT which sets the File Manager "don't cache" bit for disk writes of 1K or more. One surprising side effect is that it not only amortizes the disk time over all the writes, but it also makes it considerably faster. This may not make much difference to people connecting over modem, but for people on Ethernet it makes a huge difference.

Stuart wrote the program because he has a IIci, with 17MB RAM. The standard advice is to set the disk cache to minimum, but on a IIci video memory shares main memory, and slows down the machine by about 30%. Setting the disk cache to 384K is a well-known trick to fill up the remaining space in that memory bank and avoid the 30% slow down, but it also cripples write performance. That's why he wrote WriteThrough.

WriteThrough works with System 7.5, but it may not be necessary. Apple has fixed the bugs (features) in their disk cache, so it now gives acceptable performance across the whole range of write sizes. Although WriteThrough will still improve performance another 30% for large writes (16K or more) it will actually slow down writes in the 1K to 8K range, so on balance you're probably better off without it.

Application Memory

Another common complaint goes something like this *"I've got 20 megabytes of memory, and my applications are still running out…"* The problem may be simply that you haven't assigned enough memory to the application. This can happen as the document you are working with grows in size. The way to find out if this is your problem is to select About This Macintosh from the top of the Apple Menu in the Finder. Each of your running applications will be shown, with a bar graph depicting how much of their reserved RAM is currently being used (Figure 2-5).

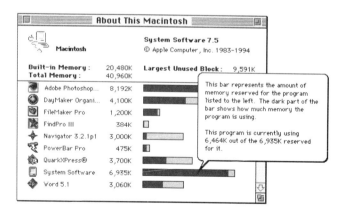

Figure 2-5: About This Macintosh dialog box

Figure 2-5 illustrates a great use of Balloon Help: turning it on and pointing to each application's memory bar will show you the exact memory figures. If the dark part of the bar is over 90%, then you might want to consider raising the memory partition for the application. Just get info on the application (highlight the application's icon in the Finder and press command-I), and you'll get a dialog like that shown in Figure 2-6.

System 7 introduced expanded Memory Requirements fields in the Info dialog: the *Suggested size* is that which the developer recommends, the *Minimum size* is just that, and the *Preferred size* is the amount of memory the application will "grab" if it is available when it is launched. You can adjust the minimum and preferred figures. I recommend that you always leave the minimum as set, and adjust the preferred figure as needed.

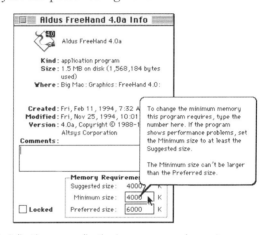

Figure 2-6: Adjusting an application's memory requirements

About
Michael Hecht
SAS Institute Inc.
SAS Campus Drive
Cary, NC USA 27513
Internet: hecht@vnet.net
About is freeware

Mike is a 32-year-old Senior Systems Developer (aka "Programmer") who's been programming professionally for 10 years (on the Mac for the last 6) using the languages PL/I, Pascal, Forth, C, C++, AppleScript, and most recently Perl. He's been programming the Mac as an amateur since its inception in 1984.

Like the About This Macintosh dialog, but wish it did more? So did Michael Hecht — so he wrote About, an application that greatly expands the functionality of the About box. When you first run it, it seems to look just like the regular About box, with an arrow pointing to the active application. A quick look at the menus reveals a lot more power: you can change the size of the icons, use it as an application switcher (just click on the application you want to switch to), option-click to hide or show applications (like Word and FileMaker Pro in Figure 2-7); System 7.5 users can even drag and drop documents onto the About box to launch them. Those with Apple's Drag 'n Drop Extension installed can do this, too.

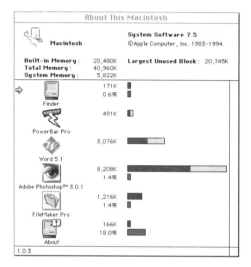

Figure 2-7: About 1.0.3

Try turning off Group System Software and turning on "by Partition" in the View menu to get a snapshot of your memory. Figure 2-8 shows some memory fragmentation caused by Word 5.1; the gray bars represent "holes" in memory.

One note of caution: I've discovered that dragging files to the trash on my PowerBook means that I occasionally drop a file intended for the garbage onto About; this can result in a crash if the process doesn't like the document you've dropped on it.

About shows you how you are using your memory, but it doesn't help you much when you run out. NowMenus (part of Now Utilities) includes a few

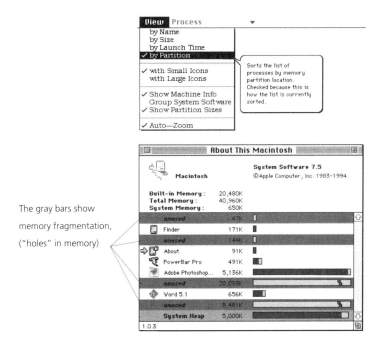

The gray bars show
memory fragmentation,
("holes" in memory)

Figure 2-8: About showing memory allocation

memory utilities: the Preferences dialog (Figure 2-9) allows you to have Memory Sizer open automatically when you need to temporarily reduce the memory allocated to an application in order to get it to run.

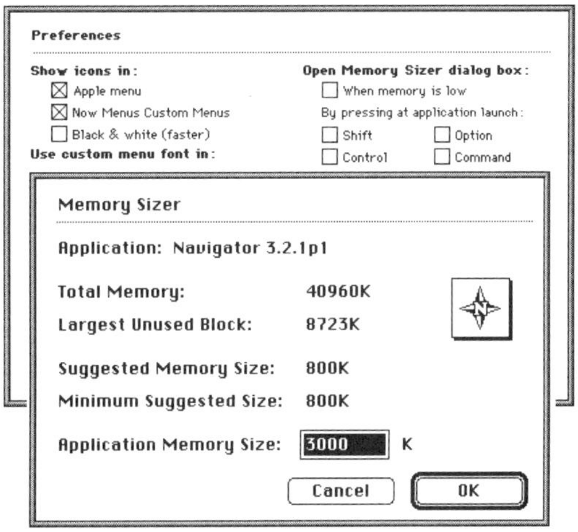

Figure 2-9: NowMenus Preferences; Memory Sizer

Power users will appreciate NowMenus' Memory Viewer (Figure 2-10):

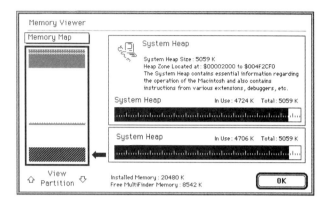

Figure 2-10: NowMenus' Memory Viewer

UnFinder

 Eberhard Rensch
Spitalhofstr. 3
D-94032 Passau
Germany
CompuServe: 100010,604
 Shareware fee: $5.00

Eberhard is a computer science student at the University of Passau who has been programming since 1982. His favorite language is C++, but he's also done programming in C, Pascal, Assembler (680x0, Z80 etc.), and other languages. For the past three years he has had a small business, selling his larger software products.

If you're tight on memory, UnFinder offers a simple fix: it allows you to quit the Finder to free up a bit more memory for your applications. Just select the application(s) you want to run, and drop them onto UnFinder — it will quit the Finder (releasing up to 350K of memory), launch your application(s), and finally quit itself. The downside is a short delay when you have to run the Finder, and the inability to use Control Panels (when the Finder is quit).

PRAM

Parameter RAM (PRAM) is the area in your Macintosh where all sorts of settings are saved, including time and date, mouse, keyboard repeat, and startup drive. Occasionally, these settings will get corrupted; the cure is to "zap" or reset your PRAM. The key command is easy enough to remember for System 7 users: command-option-p-r while starting up; System 6 users should use Shift-Option-Command while opening the Control Panel. Even easier (and better) is MicroMat's freeware utility TechTool, which allows you to save or zap your PRAM settings. TechTool is on the CD-ROM; see Chapter 18 for a complete description.

Quadra Caching

The Quadra class Macintoshes (those equipped with 68040 processors) were the first class of Macintoshes to allow the addition of high-speed cache RAM. (The Mac IIci was the first Mac that had a special slot for the addition of a cache card.) Adding a cache card results in about a 20% performance improvement (at least, it did in mine). There is a downside, however: with or without an additional card, some applications do not run well with the Quadra's memory caching enabled. Apple ships a Control Panel that allows you to turn off the Quadra's caches after a restart. I much prefer the solution offered by the QuadControl Control Panel (see Figure 2-11) shipped with my DayStar cache card — it allows you to set individual

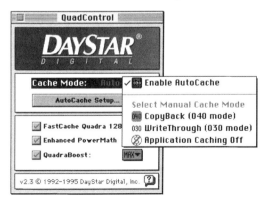

Figure 2-11: DayStar QuadControl

preferences to disable or reduce the level of cache depending on the application being run.

SpeedSwitch '040
Daniel Schwartz
Articulate Systems Inc.
600 West Cummings Park Suite 4500
Woburn, MA 01801
Internet: dan@cs.brandeis.edu
SpeedSwitch is Jerryware

Have a Quadra, but not a DayStar card? Want to turn off the cache without having to reboot? SpeedSwitch '040 (Figure 2-12) may be the answer.

Figure 2-12: SpeedSwitch '040

Commercial Memory Enhancement Software

Let's turn our attention to a couple of products that make your Mac's use of memory so much more efficient, you may not need to buy more.

OptiMem
Jump Development Group Inc.
1228 Malvern Avenue
Pittsburgh, PA 15217-1141
Telephone: 412 681-2692
America Online: JumpDevgrp
AppleLink: RThornton
CompuServe: 71321,1527
Suggested retail: introductory street price under $60.00

Wow! I'm impressed with the latest version of OptiMem (2.1 as of this writing). If you like to tweak your system to try and wring out that last ounce of performance, then this one's for you. Unlike RAM Doubler, OptiMem doesn't require the latest Mac, just that you be running System 7. There's good news for power users, too, because OptiMem works fine with RAM Doubler.

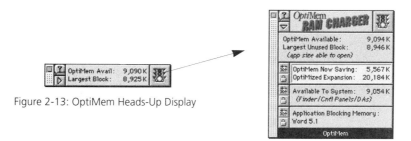

Figure 2-13: OptiMem Heads-Up Display

Figure 2-14: OptiMem Control Panel

OptiMem makes your Mac's memory a little more intelligent; it opens applications in smaller memory partitions, which it dynamically resizes as needed. This helps reduce memory fragmentation problems. The first thing you notice when running OptiMem is a new Heads-Up display (Figure 2-13). The Heads-Up display works like a gas gauge for memory. Clicking on the diamond in the lower left-hand corner expands the display into the full Control Panel (Figure 2-14).

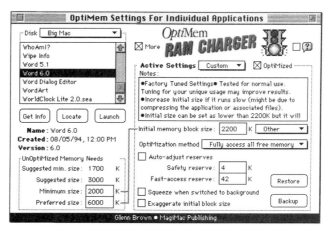

Figure 2-15: OptiMem Settings

Clicking on the traffic light in the upper right-hand corner calls up OptiMem's applications settings. If you click on More, you'll get the expanded dialog shown in Figure 2-15. The applications settings include those for a number of major applications. The Notes box gives suggestions on how to fine-tune the way OptiMem works with each application.

One program notorious for being a RAM hog is Adobe Photoshop; here are the Notes from OptiMem (reprinted with permission):

- Factory Tuned Settings

- Tested for normal use.

- Works with an Initial memory block size set to Adobe's suggested Minimum size (or with v3 you can reduce the initial size to 3820K).

- If you have over 24,000K of memory and wish to use Photoshop OptiMized, you should use Adobe's Piggy Plug-ins Patch to keep Photoshop from taking a large amount of memory when it first opens. (Copy "Piggy Plug-ins Patch" from the Photoshop "Optional Extensions" folder into the "Plug-ins" folder.)

- For a good percentage of Photoshop use, when doing simple tasks with only a few moderate sized documents, you should be happy with Photoshop OptiMized. On the other hand, when working with memory intensive operations, and/or very large documents you can get better performance with Photoshop unOptiMized and using a large Suggested size.

- When used with some scanners or other third party plug-ins you may have varying results. These can check memory and refuse to run if they don't find a certain amount free in the initial Photoshop memory block. If so, increasing the initial block size might get them working.

- Starting with Photoshop version 2.5, Adobe has taken special measures to cater to image processing work requiring very large amounts of memory. In order to deal with dozens (and even hundreds) of megabytes efficiently, they have found it necessary to depart from much of the normal Mac application methodology of memory management. This can circumvent some of the dynamic memory OptiMization which OptiMem offers an application. (Photoshop 2.0, however, seems to be very Mac-normal in its memory management and use with OptiMem.) In particular, with later versions, memory which is no longer used after closing a document is not released until later, after other operations are performed.

So, when Photoshop is OptiMized, it does start out in a smaller partition and it grows dynamically as you open documents. But it doesn't give memory back right away, to use in other apps, when you close a document. Adobe says they hold on to it because the user might do something which needs it again, right away. So, you only get two thirds of the benefits of OptiMem with Photoshop. (There are some combinations of operations that get Photoshop to release some of the unused memory that it is holding but we have not determined a sequence that does this consistently. Users have reported that Opening a JPEG file or Copying a area will cause it to release some unused memory.)

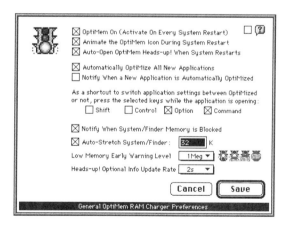

Figure 2-16: OptiMem Preferences

OptiMem is particularly useful when running in tight memory situations — it will warn you when you start to run out of room (Figure 2-16).

The following article, written by Jump Development, explains some of the technical issues involved, and will be of particular interest to those interested in running OptiMem and RamDoubler together.

Not Just More Memory — Better Memory

Summary

There has been much interest in — and some confusion about — the new category of Macintosh software ushered in last year with the introduction of OptiMem, The Software Memory Upgrade. More details about OptiMem's features and benefits are provided elsewhere. This note goes into some depth to address questions raised about the differences and similarities between OptiMem and the alternatives for getting more useful memory on the Macintosh (such as System 7's virtual memory and RAM Doubler by Connectix).

- OptiMem is very different from other methods of getting more usable memory for your Macintosh. Where OptiMem optimizes allocation of the logical memory space but does not expand it, the alternatives do the opposite: they expand the logical memory space but do not optimize the use of it.

- Optimizing memory, rather than simply expanding it, provides a unique and important benefit. With OptiMem, applications work as if their previously fixed memory partitions can grow and shrink dynamically. So they only use the amount of memory which is actually needed at any given moment. This is especially beneficial to users who run several programs at a time or have a widely varying mix of documents and applications.

- OptiMem works well in conjunction with all methods of expanding the logical memory space (including RAM Doubler and virtual memory). Users who are already using RAM Doubler or VM are amazed by the increased memory, and optimization benefits they get when they use OptiMem in addition.

• For Macs without a PMMU, and already at their physical memory barrier, OptiMem is the only alternative for more useful memory. Since OptiMem is designed to work with all Macintosh hardware and does not require any special processor support (such as the virtual memory mapping PMMU available on 68030 and 040 processors) it will optimize any Mac running System 7-including 68000 Macs like the Plus, SE, or Classic; Macs with third party accelerators; and the new Power Macs.

• Unlike the other memory upgrade methods, OptiMem works on a per-application basis-so you can easily specify optimization for some applications and not others. This allows you to use any combination of optimized and unoptimized applications simultaneously. Other software methods require you to disable the product and restart the computer in order to use any software which doesn't work well with it.

Introduction to Software Memory Upgrades
First let's clarify some terms used. The logical memory space in a Macintosh is what is seen by the user (for example, in the About This Macintosh window), or by the application software. This logical memory space is usually equivalent to what is provided by the physical or hardware memory (often referred to as RAM). The logical memory is most easily expanded by installing additional physical memory and maintaining the usual one-to-one mapping between physical and logical space. Providing a logical space that is larger than the physical memory requires a selective mapping of blocks of physical memory into the logical space. This differentiation of logical and physical memory access and the mapping between the two spaces is commonly called virtual memory. (The resulting logical space is also called the virtual address space.) As can be imagined, the constant address lookup and translation necessary to support such a scheme has considerable processing overhead. Therefore, it is only used on Macs that have special memory mapping hardware in their processors, to minimize this overhead. With the standard Mac virtual memory, the extra blocks of logical memory (which are not mapped to physical memory at a given point in time) are stored on disk and swapped with other blocks in physical memory when the processor

must access them. However, virtual memory can be implemented using other methods of storing the swapped-out blocks, such as the in-memory compressed buffers used by RAM Doubler. Using these terms, we define the fundamental difference between OptiMem and other methods of getting more useful memory as this: OptiMem optimizes allocation of the logical memory space but does not expand the logical space. The alternatives do the opposite: they expand the logical memory space but do not optimize the use of it. This might be confusing when examining virtual memory techniques for implementing a larger logical memory space. The virtual memory manager (as provided by the system or by a third party product like RAM Doubler) uses a block replacement strategy to minimize swapping data. This could be described as optimizing the allocation of physical memory, but is more commonly called a memory policy or a paging algorithm. An important thing to notice is that this applies to the allocation of physical memory rather than the logical space, dealt with by applications, that OptiMem optimizes.

The Benefits of OptiMem Technology

Optimized applications open using minimum sized initial partitions, but are not limited to them. They use additional memory only where and when they need it (for example, when opening or expanding documents, printing and checking spelling), and each application has access to all the free memory on the machine. When an app releases memory no longer being used (for example, when closing a document or finishing printing), it is immediately available for reuse by other programs-including optimized applications that are already open.

Since OptiMem optimizes the logical memory space, in contrast to expanding it, OptiMem is compatible with and works very well with the other methods for getting more usable memory (such as virtual memory and RAM Doubler). Jump Development Group has done a lot of testing with OptiMem and RAM Doubler and finds they work extremely well together, without any downside. The technologies are entirely different. RAM Doubler uses virtual memory techniques to expand the logical memory space, and then OptiMem is happy to optimize allocation of the increased logical space provided. And, in fact, the two together give you much more useful memory than either one alone. So, the two products really complement each other.

OptiMem provides the reduction of initial application partitions and dynamic resizing of apps, while they remain open, so you get more into the memory you have. RAM Doubler compresses your in-memory data and maps in additional virtual address space, so you have more to allocate in the first place. Since OptiMem works on any Mac running System 7, it is able to provide benefits for all Mac users, including those unable to use virtual memory expansion for one reason or another. (Virtual memory and RAM Doubler can only be used on machines with the memory management hardware.) OptiMem is the only way to more useful memory for millions of Macs, including all the 68000 machines like the Pluses, SEs, and Classics-or for any Mac which is already at the limit of its physical memory capacity. Even Macs with third party accelerators and Power Macs can benefit from OptiMem. The owners of many Macs with memory limitations have held off upgrading to System 7 because of the additional memory demands. Now, with OptiMem, these people can upgrade to the latest system and application software, keep multiple major applications open at the same time, and still have enough memory to work productively.

No memory upgrade is 100% compatible in all situations (yes, even adding physical memory can cause problems for some configurations of hardware and software). Unlike the other techniques, OptiMem applies its improvements on a per-application basis. That means it can be turned off for some applications while it continues to optimize others. This allows you to use any combination of optimized and unoptimized applications simultaneously. Virtual memory and RAM Doubler require you to stop what you're doing, close/quit all of your work and restart the computer with the expanded space completely disabled in order to use any product which doesn't work well with them.

Interview: Robert Thornton

Robert is the author of OptiMem.

How long have you been programming and how did you get started?

I took my first programming course in college in 1969, and found we were made for each other. I was a student of architecture and in the following few years got involved with a variety of computer applications in architecture, finally focusing on 3-D graphics as a design modeling medium. Computers have been my life since 1973.

What is your educational background?

I have been teaching myself about computing every day for over 23 years, but have also had the benefit of many good professors and research colleagues. After half a dozen computer courses in college, I spent 7 years in graduate school at Cornell and Carnegie Mellon Universities, working in the areas of high-performance 3-D graphics, computer-aided design, and interactive systems, in addition to the full computer science curriculum.

What programs have you written (or been involved in the development of)?

OptiMem (and now OptiMem RAM Charger) is my first mass market product. My previous software has been for research projects or for large custom or semi-custom systems involving 3-D design, animation, and image/document management.

What language(s) do you write in?

On the Mac, C, and 68000 assembly language. But I have used many algorithmic languages (Unix C, Pascal, Modula, Bliss, Algol, Algol-68, PL/1, X/PL, FORTRAN), "symbolic" languages (Lisp, Snobol4, APL), object-oriented (Smalltalk 80, Simula, C++), and assembly languages (PDP-11, VAX, IBM 360, several specialized high performance graphics processors).

What software tools do you use?

Mostly Apple's development tools: MPW, ResEdit, and MacsBug. Also, two excellent third-party products: TMON and Resorcerer.

Please describe the equipment you use (what computer, how much RAM, etc.)

My everyday Mac is a Quadra 610 12/540 with a 17" color display.

What is your favorite piece of software? (excluding that written by you or your company…)

I have enjoyed Hiro Yamamoto's Super Boomerang for many years . Super Boomerang started as shareware (I registered the day I first tried it); it is now part of Now Utilities. In particular the concept of ready access to recently used files and the direct-open submenu which gives you ready access to them.

Do you have other interests you'd like mentioned in a bio?

I enjoy music (especially blues), bicycling, racquetball, and restoring old cars and old houses (but there just hasn't been time in recent years).

What do like to do when you're not programming?

Lots of reading (mostly computer related), writing and designing marketing materials and packaging.

What do you do for a living?

Since my company is in the start-up phase, there is some doubt as to whether I've been earning a living for several years. But I have not held a job outside of the computer industry for over 20 years.

Where do you live, are you married with children, how old are you, (etc.)

I'm 43 years old and live with my wife and daughter in the east end of Pittsburgh, overlooking Carnegie Mellon University.

How did Jump Development get started?

After spending many years developing software that only a small number of people would use and enjoy, I wanted to do something that could really make a difference to a lot of people. I began working on some ideas for document browsing. I chose the Mac since it is clearly the best tool for a person applying the computer in a creative endeavor. Since that's the kind of endeavor I'd like to contribute to on as broad a basis as possible, I believe that the person who appreciates the creative boost of the Macintosh will probably be best equipped to benefit from my craftsmanship. The need for dynamic memory allocation in my document browser led to the idea for OptiMem.

How big is your company?

We are seven people.

What are the top questions your tech support people field, and more important, what are the answers?

1. What do the memory bars in the About This Macintosh window tell me? The System Software bar changes all the time and the application bars never change.

    The About This Mac window is a little confusing because the Finder doesn't define exactly what it is displaying here. You might guess that the System Software bar represents the size of the System Heap data structure, but that is only part of the story. It actually shows the combined total of "high" memory allocated by the system and extensions at startup, the memory used by any background-only applications, the memory used by the Finder, any memory allocated on behalf of any application outside of its initial memory block, and the System Heap (which grows and shrinks on demand). That means that any memory that OptiMem allocates dynamically, outside of an application's initial partition, will be included in the System Software bar. Likewise, the bars for the individual applications only show the size of their initial memory block, so they do not grow or shrink to show memory provided by OptiMem from outside of the initial block. You can see the total amount of memory allocated dynamically in the OptiMem Heads-up display, or for an individual application, in the OptiMem Settings window.

2. Why does the Finder sometimes close control panels and other windows or refuse to perform an operation because there is "Not Enough Memory"?

    This is a confusing situation that can occur even when there is plenty of free memory. It is usually an operation that requires some amount of memory from the System Heap that is temporarily unavailable. The System Heap can grow when more is needed but it must stay in a single continuous block of memory. So, if there is a block of memory being used right next to the system heap, it blocks the system heap from expanding. It is often a temporary situation, for example when the Print Monitor is running, so simply retrying the failed operation again will often succeed. OptiMem is not able to eliminate this situation but it does provide a couple of ways to reduce it or work around it. There is an option in the OptiMem Preferences window called Auto-Stretch System/Finder that regularly checks the free space in the System Heap and tries to keep it above a minimum amount. Also, the OptiMem Heads-Up display shows how much memory is available to the system and which application, if any, is blocking its growth. This helps you recover quickly or even avoid running out in the first place.

3. How can I tell if OptiMem is helping me?

    With the original version of OptiMem, you had to work a little to figure out just what OptiMem was doing for you at any given moment. Now, with OptiMem RAM Charger, the Heads-Up display shows you three values that sum up the benefit that OptiMization is providing at the moment. First, the OptiMem Now Saving value indicates how much memory was saved in your currently open applications by using smaller initial block sizes than would have been used if not OptiMized. Second, the OptiMized Expansion value indicates how much dynamic resizing of application memory you are taking advantage of. Third, the OptiMem Available indicates the total amount of free memory that is currently available to any Optimized application (this is often much more than the Largest Unused Block that is usually all you are able to access in opening additional applications).

What are some of the problems you've experienced in developing OptiMem?

The biggest difficulties are in working well with other software products that are not well-behaved or don't play by Apple's rules. (Such problems are sometimes found in the system software itself.) From the beginning I knew OptiMem must not only play by the rules but go out of its way to accommodate other software that didn't. Thus the unique design that optimizes each application individually. (You can even run some applications unoptimized at the same time that others are being optimized.) The result has been a surprisingly small number of conflicts, which have had easy work-arounds. OptiMem also fixes a number of bugs in the system software which we found (some which crash the system).

How does OptiMem work with (and without) RamDoubler?

RamDoubler uses virtual memory mapping techniques to expand the amount of address space available to the system. However, it does not alter the way this expanded space is assigned to applications. OptiMem does the opposite: it does not expand the space but makes a fundamental breakthrough in the way the space (expanded or not) is allocated to open applications and documents. So, whether you use expanded memory or not, OptiMem will help you get more into memory, and get more flexibility, productivity, and reliability out of your Mac. OptiMem's biggest benefit is enabling applications to vary the amount of memory they use dynamically, up and down, while they remain open. No other product can offer this. The flexibility this provides in helping you keep open more applications and documents, is the real magic of OptiMem. Finally, since OptiMem technology is fundamentally processor-independent, it can be used with any Mac running System 7, from the Mac Plus to the Power Mac.

What functionality does a RamDoubler user gain by using OptiMem?

Automatic adjustment of the size of optimized applications, according to your current needs, while they remain open. There is less triggering of virtual memory swapping in some situations, and thus increased speed. You are able to pack more applications and documents into your expanded memory. Several types of feedback are provided, about how memory is being used, so that you can anticipate and avoid problems or recover more quickly when they do occur. Applications don't have to run out of memory when their initial blocks become full and there is free memory elsewhere. Several types of crash-causing system bugs are eliminated.

Why does memory on the Mac tend to fragment? What can users do to reduce RAM fragmentation?

Fragmentation refers to the total of your free memory being broken up into smaller pieces when allocated blocks are locked in a specific location and cannot be relocated. This problem is of particular concern on the Macintosh because you need a single, large continuous block of memory for an application in order to open it, and the partitions are fixed in location so fragmentation occurs readily. Using OptiMem reduces the problems of fragmentation in several ways. First, the initial block size of an OptiMized application is often smaller, you will be able to open it under more fragmented conditions than before. Then, the additional memory allocated for applications outside of their initial blocks is generally in much smaller blocks so they can fill in the cracks, where ever possible. Since the smaller blocks are often relocatable, OptiMem is able to move them in order to repair existing fragmentation.

Other than the obvious (not enough RAM installed or assigned to the app) what are some of the reasons for getting an "out of memory" error message?

A common "Not Enough Memory" problem that Mac users see is when the Finder does not find enough free memory in the System Heap. In such a case, Finder windows or Control Panels might be forced to close, or commands might not be completed. This can happen even if there is plenty of free memory, if it is not accessible in the System Heap. This is discussed in detail above. Another confusing situation arises when opening an application. Most users have gotten messages that there is not enough memory to open an application even though the amount of memory required must be free. This happens because the application's memory must be available in a single continuous block of memory, and free memory in a Mac is often fragmented into smaller blocks. So, for example, if you want to open an application that requires 1200K and you have 2000K free, it will still not be able to open if the 2000K is currently fragmented into two 1000K blocks. The "Largest Unused Block" reported in the About This Mac window is the size of the largest free memory fragment that can be used for an opening application's initial block of memory. OptiMem is effective in reducing these problems, as described above in the discussion of fragmentation. There is a similar problem when opening applications that we are seeing more and more of, as applications become bigger and more complex and the system provides more shared services to applications. What happens is that the Largest Unused Block is big enough for the application to open but then additional resources that must load into the System Heap are unable to do so because all memory is then full or the System Heap is blocked from growing enough. The latest "oversized" versions of some of the most popular applications can have this trouble regularly. This can be confusing, even to very experienced users, due to the limited form of feedback provided. OptiMem RAM Charger provides the Auto-Stretch System/Finder option and additional feedback that help you avoid these problems and work around them if they happen.

Of course one of the most frustrating "Not Enough Memory" situations is when you are working in an application that cannot open another document or complete an operation because its partition is full — even though there is plenty of free memory elsewhere. OptiMem is very helpful in reducing this type of error since most optimized applications will not run out until all memory in the whole machine is in use.

Do you see any value in assigning a larger memory partition to the Finder or to PrintMonitor?

Increasing the System 7 Finder's application partition will only benefit very unusual situations. The common "Not Enough Memory" problems that are seen with the Finder are due to a limitation in the System Heap and will not be affected by increasing the Finder size. For the same reason, OptiMization does not benefit the Finder and is not offered by OptiMem. The PrintMonitor, however, is a candidate for increased partition size or OptiMization. The system will adjust the PrintMonitor size on a semi-automatic basis, but if your particular configuration or use causes it to happen often, many users will benefit from OptiMizing it.

Is there any need for System 7 users to adjust the size of their System Heap (as they used to have to for System 6)?

The System Heap, beginning with System 7, is able to grow and shrink according to need. Therefore, there is no straightforward way to set a specific size for it like there was in System 6 and, theoretically, there is no need to do so. However, as described above, the implementation of this automatic growth has some inherent limitations, so there are times when there is not enough System Heap memory and it cannot be grown, even when there is plenty of free memory elsewhere. OptiMem RAM Charger provides an option (called Auto-Stretch System/Finder and controlled from the Preferences window) which attempts to keep a specified amount of free memory accessible to the System Heap on a continuing basis.

Where do you plan to take OptiMem in its next release?

At the lowest level we will make any adjustments necessary to work well with the next major release of the Mac OS, including additional Power Mac native code to interface with additional native code in the future system software. Although the recent release of OptiMem RAM Charger makes significant advances, we continue to strive for improvements in the following three important areas:

1.   Simplicity of configuration and use.

2.   Enhanced feedback to help avoid and work around memory problems.

3.   Further improve memory savings for an even wider range of applications.

Connectix

It has been suggested by many that the wizards at Connectix know Mac memory better than Apple's engineers; products like Mode32, Virtual, Maxima, and RAM Doubler attest to that. In order to get a better idea of Connectix's recommendations for these products, I went straight to the source: Brian Grove, Manager of Memory Products for Connectix. This chapter concludes with an interview with Jörg Brown, one of the authors of RAM Doubler.

Mode32 7.5

Connectix
Connectix Corporation
2600 Campus Drive
San Mateo, CA 94403
Telephone: 415 571-5100
Toll-free: 800 950-5880
Fax: 415 571-5195
America Online: Connectix
AppleLink: Connectix.CS
CompuServe: 75300,1546
eWorld: RAM Doubler
Internet: support@connectix.com

Mode32 7.5 is freeware

For those with a Mac II, IIx, IIcx or SE/30 running System 7 or better, then you'll need Mode32 7.5. All those using Mode32 1.2 should upgrade to 7.5, regardless of whether or not they are using System 7.5. (The upgrade makes a number of important fixes.) Mode32 allows these Macintoshes to run in 32-bit mode which they normally can't do, and gives them access to memory above 8 megabytes. If don't have one of these, then you don't need Mode32 7.5 because your Mac has 32-bit addressing in ROM, can't run in 32-bit mode (this applies to all the Macs with a 68000 processor), or is always in 32-bit mode (this includes PowerPCs, PowerBook 500 and AV Macs). Connectix Corporation, proving they know Macintosh memory better than Apple itself, has made Mode32 freeware.

Mode32 lets you temporarily boot in 24-bit mode by holding down the Escape (Esc) key at startup.

Virtual

Connectix was the first company to create virtual memory for the Macintosh back in System 6; Virtual 1.0 was Connectix's first product. Virtual 3.0 (actually 3.0.1 as of this writing) is Connectix's latest version of virtual memory. When you assign virtual memory using Apple's Memory Control Panel, you'll need as much disk space as the total amount of memory you're asking for (so if you want to "stretch" your 20 megabyte Macintosh to 40 megabytes, you'll need to set aside 40 megabytes of space on your hard drive).

Connectix Virtual is an enormous improvement: it only requires that you set aside the extra space that you need (so "stretching" your 20 megabyte Macintosh to 40 megabytes will only require 20 megabytes of space on your hard drive). Connectix recommends Virtual for 68030 Macs that need to more than double their memory; it requires that your Mac have a PMMU (Paged Memory Management Unit), and is not compatible with the 68040-equipped Macs.

Maxima

Maxima (version 3.0 as of this writing) is a powerful RAM disk, with one big advantage: it doubles the size of the RAM disk (it takes 4 megabytes of RAM to create an 8 megabyte RAM disk, and so on). It is recommended for Macs with more than 8 megabytes of memory (16 is even better). Maxima works with Power Macs, with 68030 or 68040 Macs, and with Mac II's with the 68851 PMMU installed (if you have an accelerator card, it must work with virtual memory). Maxima also works well with RAM Doubler: you can use Maxima to double your RAM disk size, and RAM Doubler to double your remaining memory. This could leave you in the enviable position of having 16 megabytes of physical RAM, 16-megabytes of available RAM, and a 16 megabyte RAM disk!

RAM Double

RAM Doubler is a system extension that does what it says: it doubles the amount of RAM available for use on your Mac. Here's how it works:

- First, it reassigns free memory assigned to applications that is not currently in use. That's the light part of the bars in the About This Macintosh display (refer to Figure 2-5 on page 28).
- When that's not enough to double memory, RAM Doubler looks for parts of memory that are in use (the dark part of the bars in Figure 2-5), but contain code that is unlikely to be needed again (such as code used to boot the computer or launch an application).
- Finally, if RAM Doubler needs to compress too much memory in order to double (compromising performance), it occasionally stores some compressed information (typically in a file less than 300K) on

the hard drive using techniques similar to, but much faster than Apple's virtual memory.

The bottom line is a true doubling of application memory, with little or no negative affect on performance (at most 3 to 5%, which is imperceptible to the human eye). To use RAM Doubler, you need at minimum 4 megabytes of RAM, an PMMU (built into the 68030, 68040 and PowerPC Macs), and System 6 or newer.

I talked to Brian Grove about using OptiMem and RAM Doubler together — his comment on OptiMem was that it doesn't give you much of a (RAM) advantage, and it extracts a performance hit. He recommends OptiMem for 68000 and 68020 Macs and for those with less than 4 megabytes of RAM (RAM Doubler will not work with the 68000 or 68020 because it requires a MMU).

 If you want to see when RAM Doubler is "doing its thing" hold down the Esc key when booting to turn on RAM Doubler's activity indicator (a small white dot in the upper left-hand corner of your screen). If you want the indicator to always be on, see below ("RAM Doubler 1.5.1 Indicator Patch").

What software doesn't run with RAM Doubler? Because RAM Doubler occasionally uses virtual memory techniques, it requires that you turn off Apple's virtual memory (in the Memory Control Panel). Because it uses the MMU, RAM Doubler is not compatible with Connectix Virtual or Apple's virtual memory. Programs that don't work with virtual memory won't work with RAM Doubler. Also, RAM Doubler is best suited for use with multiple applications, rather than for assigning a lot of memory to a single application (see the next page for notes on using RAM Doubler with Adobe Photoshop).

Technical Notes: Using RAM Doubler with Adobe Photoshop

This information on RAM Doubler compatibility with Adobe Photoshop was provided by Connectix Technical Support, and is reprinted with permission.

Connectix RAM Doubler has been tested and is compatible with Adobe Photoshop — versions: 2.0, 2.5, 2.5.1, 3.0, and 3.0.1. The current version of RAM Doubler is 1.5.1; the RAM Doubler 1.5.1 Updater is on the CD-ROM.

RAM Doubler is compatible with Photoshop and Photoshop's proprietary virtual memory scheme (scratch disk usage). You can allocate up to all your free physical RAM (see examples and the formula listed below to determine the amount) to Photoshop when RAM Doubler is installed. Photoshop's performance should be unaffected if you follow these guidelines.

Example #1: Macintosh with 68020, 68030, or 68040 processor.
Adobe (in the *Adobe Photoshop 3.0 Getting Started* manual) recommends a minimum of 6MB of application memory for Photoshop 3.0 ("application memory," as defined by Adobe, is the amount of physical memory left over after the system has started).

In this example, we will use a Quadra 610 with 8MB of RAM and RAM Doubler installed. With RAM Doubler installed, the total memory becomes 16MB. Application memory in this case, as defined by Adobe, is 6MB.

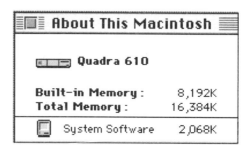

In this configuration, we can set Adobe Photoshop 3.0 to use all the available application memory. This amount can be determined by this simple formula: Built-in Memory (amount) *minus* System Software (amount) = application memory

For this Quadra 610, the amount would be 8MB – 2MB or 6MB of application memory. You can then set Photoshop 3.0 to 6MB, which is the minimum amount recommended by Adobe. With Photoshop using 6MB and the System Software using approximately 2MB, this leaves 8MB (when subtracting Photoshop and System Software from Total Memory) for other applications to run. Feel free to open more applications (such as Adobe Illustrator, QuarkXpress, and Microsoft Word) using the extra memory RAM Doubler provides.

Example #2: Power Macintosh

Adobe (in the *Adobe Photoshop 3.0 Getting Started* manual) recommends a minimum of 11MB of application memory for Photoshop 3.0 ("application memory," as defined by Adobe, is the amount of physical memory left over after the system has started).

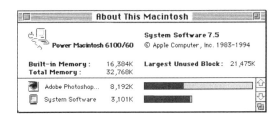

In this example, we will use a Power Macintosh 6100 with 16MB of RAM installed. With RAM Doubler installed, total memory becomes 32MB. In this configuration, Adobe Photoshop 3.0 can have a memory allocation up to the total amount of physical RAM installed minus System Software usage. In this Power Mac that amount is 11MB, the recommended amount of application memory for Photoshop 3.0. But with RAM Doubler installed, you'll notice that Photoshop only uses 8MB, not 11MBs.

Since Photoshop 3.0 is a Power Mac native application, RAM Doubler uses File Mapping to reduce the RAM memory demands. File mapping is a memory reduction technique for Power Mac native applications that is built into Apple's ROMs, but is only active if RAM Doubler or System 7 virtual memory is turned on. Evidence of the memory savings is shown when you do a "Get Info" on the native application.

The memory saved by RAM Doubler on Power Mac native applications can be used to open more applications or to work with larger graphic documents.

Summary

RAM Doubler helps you be more productive by running Adobe Photoshop with other applications. Just set Photoshop to use available application memory (Built-in memory minus System Software) and use the extra memory RAM Doubler provides to keep other applications running.

Even if you decide to add more RAM later, to handle larger documents or improve performance, RAM Doubler will double that memory as well. 16MB becomes 32MB, 32MB becomes 64MB, and so on, with RAM Doubler installed. If you do not have enough memory for Photoshop to work on the documents you need, it's a good idea to install more physical RAM.

Known Incompatibilities

One optional Photoshop plug-in for the Quadra/Centris 660AV and Quadra 840AV is called "AV DSP Power" and is distributed by Adobe. This plug-in accelerates some Photoshop functions by using the DSP chip included with the 660AV and 840AV models.

However, this plug-in does not function with extended memory (more total memory than real RAM). As a result, when this plug-in is used and you are running under an extended memory environment (such as RAM Doubler or System 7 virtual memory), a freeze or crash will occur. The solution is to disable extended memory or remove the AV DSP Power plug-in.

A severe performance degradation can occur if you increase the amount of memory allocated to Photoshop beyond the amount of application memory available with RAM Doubler installed. In the aforementioned case of the Quadra 610, there is 6MB of application memory available (determined by subtracting System Software amount from built-in memory amount). Photoshop can be set up to 6MB; however, if it is set to use 7MB or more, a performance degradation can occur. The best solution is to keep Photoshop set to the amount of application memory available. If you need more memory for Photoshop, you should consider installing RAM SIMMs.

RAM Doubler 1.5.2 Indicator Patch
Ross E. Bergman
Internet: hyjinx@isr.harvard.edu

RAM Doubler 1.5.2 Indicator Patch is freeware

If you want RAM Doubler's activity indicator to default to "on", try this patch. As with any patch, please make sure you apply it to a copy of RAM Doubler.

By the way, Connectix doesn't recommend modifying RAM Doubler with ResEdit or by using a utility such as this one. If you want the indicator functionality, just hold down the Esc key after you see "Connectix RAM Doubler installed." If you hold down the ESC key earlier, you will disable RAM Doubler.

Interview: Jörg Brown

Jörg is the author of HierDA (the shareware predecessor to Now Menus), as well as Now Menus, Startup Manager, RAM Doubler, and Connectix's new Speed Doubler. My first recollection of Jörg is getting a chuckle out of the documentation he had built into HierDA. The last line was "If you call me at home, I will kill you". Jörg has since explained that this wasn't that unreasonable, given that he didn't have a home telephone at the time. Jörg loves too drive way to fast (the last time I saw him in Boston, he had driven out from the west coast in a leisurely 24 hour drive), and has a passion for Mountain Dew. I'd tell you about his apartment, but then he'd hafta kill me…

Jörg has been programming computers since the age of 10, on a Southwest Technical 6800 kit computer. By the age of 13 he was attending college, and at the age of 17 he became the youngest to ever graduate with an electrical engineering degree at Colorado State University. Despite 7 straight-A semesters, he managed to flunk out of 2 of 3 computer science courses, and for almost a year after graduation, his highest-paid position was for a local pizza delivery business. From there things only got better: in the years since he was finally able to land a real job, he has written code for 5 Eddy-award-winning products: THINK Pascal, THINK C, Now Utilities, Now Contact, and his most recent joint effort, RAM Doubler. Jörg is well-known among the Macintosh programming community not just for his coding ability but for his creative driving skills, which have led to his license being revoked in 5 states. He laments, "I miss delivering pizzas."

What language(s) do you write in?
C, by far. C++ is interesting but mainly its a hallmark of bad programming design. Assembly is fun, but when you write in assembly, nothing ever ships.

What software tools do you use?
Metrowerks, with MPW in the background for its set of tools.

Please describe the equipment you use (what computer, how much RAM, etc.)
A Power Macintosh 8100/80 with 40 megs of RAM doubled to 80.

What is your favorite piece of software (excluding that written by you or your company…)
Metrowerks, Marathon, Malph. They know what they're supposed to do, and they do it well; all are designed efficiently and cleanly.

Do you have other interests you'd like mentioned in a bio?

Exploration of any kind — boating, hiking, spelunking.

What do like to do when you're not programming?

When I'm not programming, I like to sleep. Sleep is a poor substitute for caffeine, but absence makes the heart grow fonder....

How did Connectix get started, and what products has your company released?

Connectix got started as a company designing a network system capable of transmission speeds in excess of 1 gigabit per second. Hence the name. Our Founder, Jon Garber, got distracted with putting a virtual memory system on the Macintosh, and we've been doing utilities ever since: Virtual, Maxima, Hand-Off, Optima, MODE32, CPU, CDU, and RAM Doubler. Jon is a hardware guy so it seems logical that we'd eventually go back to hardware, and that's how we got to doing QuickCam. It's fun to watch the company metamorphose.

How big is your company (how many people do you employ, annual sales, whatever)?

Connectix is currently 35 people, but we have 15 openings currently. Connectix is currently running at around $30 million per year. That's up from 2 million per year, which is where it was when I joined in September 1993.

Why do extensions conflict and what can users do to reduce the resulting problems?

Why do extensions conflict? That's like asking why are bears Catholic... It's their nature. Imagine if you put 40 different add-ons onto your car's engine. Every extension has bugs, and extensions have a tendency to magnify the impact of bugs in other extensions. It's really a wonder that Macs boot at all sometimes, what with systems like yours that have 40+ extensions at all times. More to the point, I think it's because there are no real guidelines on how to write extensions. It's only vaguely covered by Apple, and until recently (my Patching Traps chapter in Dave Mark's new book), there was no real information on it. Even at MacHack, there are rarely sessions on the subject.

What are some of the problems you experienced in writing Now Startup Manager?

Having all the best ideas stolen by Conflict Catcher. Of course, the Startup Manager interface came mainly from INITPicker, so I guess I deserve it.

Do you think the protected mode offered in Copland (Apple's current code name for System 8, now slated for release in 1996) will alleviate the problems of conflicting extensions?

Copland won't ship in 1996. Bet your house. Protected mode is BS. The system will find ways to crash just fine without Protected mode, and you'll want to turn PM off so that you can run your old INITs. Fact is, Apple breaks its rules just as often as anyone else; if Apple focused some effort on cleaning up its own system software rather than focusing on writing as much more system software as possible, you'd see the reasons for protected mode vanish. You'd also see system software run a lot faster.

What are your thoughts on using OptiMem and RAM Doubler together (I use OptiMem as a "gas gauge" to let me know when things are getting tight)?

Power users may well know how to properly use these both at once, but normal people don't. Users who have both are quite dissatisfied with the combination, even if they like each individually. A MacWarehouse bundle of the two (or was it Tiger Software?) generated phenomenally high return rates. Yes, you and I know how to make it work. Other people use both together and wonder why everything is slow.

What are some of the problems you've experienced in developing RAM Doubler?

I think I've answered this before: mainly, a lot of developers assumed that they didn't have to worry about VM environments, either Apple's or Virtual 3.0. It took a long time to convince them how wrong they were, and there are still programs which test for VM and say "please turn off extended memory to run this program." The Microsoft bundle helped to change that situation, due to the shear numbers involved, but there are still quite a lot of programmers who refuse to learn about extended memory environments and the small changes they could make that mean all the difference for RAM Doubler users.

Why does RAM Doubler require two reboots to reactivate itself after its been disabled?

The basic problem is that RAM Doubler loads before anything else does, so if an INIT Manager of some sort loads and wants to turn RAM Doubler off, the INIT Manager has to restart the machine to make it happen. There are also some programs that will allow you to turn off RAM Doubler's invisible files, which means that RAM Doubler the extension is forced to re-create them in order to work properly. This becomes an interesting contest of wills in some cases, as INIT Managers keep turning off the invisible files RAM Doubler keeps creating.

Where do you plan to take RAM Doubler in it's next release?

We plan to take it to Windows. (Note added in page layout: I now have RAM Doubler for Windows running on my office PC laptop). *It's funny; on Windows machines the problem really isn't memory, per se — there's more than enough RAM to go around, and if you install more, you still can't launch more programs because the real problem lies in things called "heaps": user heaps, GDI heaps, etc. Heaps are limited by old Windows versions to 64K each, and they fill up rapidly. So, in order for RAM Doubler to work at all, we had to solve that problem first. And it turns out, I think that problem will be more important to solve than the RAM-Doubling problem. As for a RAM Doubler/Mac 2.0 release, I have no idea what we'll do. One of the biggest lessons I learned at Now Software, from the 4.0 release of Now Utilities, is that it doesn't pay to mess with a product when its sales are escalating rapidly. We tend to think of RAM Doubler as last year's hit, but users don't know that, and the sales numbers are still going up, month to month. Our first priority is making sure that the current RAM Doubler continues to work what with Apple constantly changing the system around, and with new models of Macintosh being released constantly. We're very proud of 800-line tech support for our software, and the free update for Power Macintosh support. The big companies say you have to charge for these things. We know better — and our customers seem to like it just fine our way.*

3 File Synchronization and Backup

A quick quiz: do you have a backup of the data on your hard drive? No? Well slap yourself — put this book down, and make one now. There are three important ways you can prevent data loss as a result of a crash: (1) backup, (2) backup, and (3) backup. Those without a backup can rely on one thing: it isn't a matter of if their hard drives will fail, but *when*.

There are lots of things to consider when devising a backup strategy: How important is your data? How much of it do you need to back up? How often should you back up? How many backup sets should you have? You should also consider what software and means you will use to make a backup, and what media you will backup to.

The rule of thumb is simple: How much can you afford to lose? You may not need to have copies of your applications backed up, because you can reload them from your original floppies (but you'd better have backups of those floppies in case they go bad). You can probably live without a backup of your games folder (then again, do you really want to risk loosing that 711 million score in your Looney Labyrinth log?) (Okay, I admit a small addiction — I've resolved not to play again until I finish this book…) One thing is certain: if you work on your Mac, there is data on your hard drive that you had better back up. It is a proven scientific fact that hard drives fail at a ratio inversely proportional to the length of time since their last backup.

All storage media — hard drives, floppies, micro opticals, Syquests, tape, DAT — are subject to some risk of failure. For this reason, you should consider more than one copy of your essential data, even if it is only copied to floppies. Given enough time, you can do what back up software does yourself manually, but the added convenience and peace of mind make one or more of these programs a good investment.

For this book, I chose a conservative approach: a complete set of all of the files is kept on both my 540C and my Quadra 700 (fortunately, both have 500-megabyte hard drives). These two drives are synchronized at least twice daily using Leader Technologies' PowerMerge. Twice a week, I use

Retrospect to back up all of the files to my 230-megabyte APS MicroOptical drive, and the backup disks are alternated — I keep one set at the office, and one set at home. I also use Retrospect to make biweekly backups to the APS MO of all non-application files on both of my Macs.

In this chapter, I'm going to cover shareware and commercial utilities for synchronizing drives, along with commercial applications for backing up your hard drive. The chapter concludes with an interview with Larry Zulch, the president of Dantz Development.

File Synchronization

File synchronization is simple in concept; the execution can be a bit complex. Basically, the idea is to make two directories on two different disk drives the same, regardless of whether changes have been made to files on either or both drives since the last time the software was run. I used to use PowerMerge to sync my Duo 230 to my Quadra 700 over AppleTalk (all that you need to set up an AppleTalk connection is two AppleTalk connectors and some telephone wire); I now connect my 540C via SCSI using an APS SCSI Doc and a standard SCSI cable. If you have a PowerBook with a SCSI port, an APS SCSI Doc should be part of your "kit." Made in typical first-rate APS quality, this device allows you to use a standard SCSI cable to connect to your PowerBook in regular or SCSI docking mode. SCSI docking allows you to have another Mac treat your PowerBook drive as if it were an external drive. The biggest users of file synchronization software are PowerBook and portable hard drive users, but synchronization also qualifies as backup.

MacUpdate
Richard E. Fiegle
P.O. Box 5062
Kokomo, IN 46904-5062
America Online: RFigleaf
CompuServe: 76350,761
Shareware Fee: $5.00

Richard is a 27 year old manufacturing engineer at Delco Electronics in Kokomo, Indiana. He graduated from GMI Engineering and Management Institute in Flint, Michigan with a BS EE/CS and has taught introductory computer courses at Indiana University in Kokomo.

MacUpDate is a file synchronization and folder reconciliation program that can also serve as a simple backup utility. It works with System 6.0.5 and up. One thing to remember with all backup utilities is that the clocks on your Macs should be reasonably close to each other; if not, you could end up replacing newer files with older ones. When you run MacUpdate, you'll get a modified file dialog (Figure 3-1) that allows you to select the two directories you want to synchronize.

Selecting What to Synchronize from the MacUpdate menu allows you to tell it to check or skip aliases, folder icons files, invisible files, System-related files, and applications. One great feature of MacUpdate is its ability to automatically synchronize directories at startup, at a specified time interval, or daily.

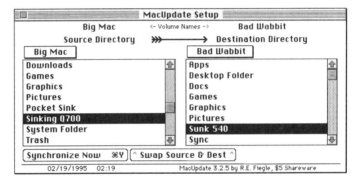

Figure 3-1: MacUpdate Setup

 Be very careful when using the Delete Folders/Files option; MacUpdate will delete folders and files on the destination drive that are not on the source drive. Two-way synchronization also requires caution, because only the latest version of any document will end up in both locations. In most cases, this is exactly what you want.

Synk

Randall Voth
46058 Fiesta Avenue
Chilliwack, BC V2P 3S4
Canada
Telephone: 604 795-4746
Internet: hvoth@sfu.ca or: hvoth@cln.etc.bc.ca
Shareware fee: $5.00 US/$7.00 Cdn. (free for those who registered BatteryMinder)

Randall publishes his wife's piano teaching material; their company is Pure Light Music. For him, programming computers has always been a dream and is now officially a reality. His next two projects are to write a 3-D Outliner for the Macintosh and subsequently use it to write a series of fantasy novels. The only thing that could sidetrack him is perhaps a large sum of money.

Synk is the first of the shareware synchronization programs to ship as a fat binary (it includes code for both PowerPCs and 680x0 Macs). It requires at minimum System 7, and includes balloon help, the ability to use the trash for deleted files (so you can have a look at what is being deleted, before it's too late.), and a Collisions folder for files updated on both drives after the last sync (you decide whether to keep either or both). If you're running BatteryMinder, it provides a Sync menu for direct access to Synk's functions. (Randall waives the shareware fee for Synk for those who register BatteryMinder). Synk's rules feature gives you the ability to ignore aliases, folders, and/or applications, plus up to five rules defined by file name ending, type, or creator (see Figure 3-2).

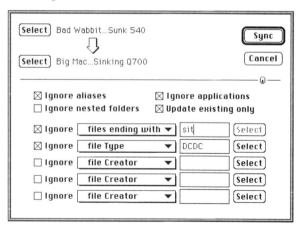

Figure 3-2: Synk options

SwitchBack

David Davies Payne
Glendower Software Limited
12 Grosvenor Terrace
Wadestown, Wellington
New Zealand
Internet: dave.davies-payne@strongbow.otago.ac.nz
Shareware fee: $30.00

David is the Technical Director of Glendower Software Limited and Consultant Programmer to the University of Otago in Dunedin, New Zealand. He has been programming the Macintosh since 1989, first in Pascal and C, and later in C++. Much of his work with Macs has involved the development of medical instrumentation. While currently an intern, he is looking at the field of radiology as a career that can happily merge his interests in technology and medicine.

Like MacUpdate, SwitchBack is a file synchronization utility that can be used for light backup duty — it offers more functionality to go along with the higher shareware fee. The impressive feature list includes auto start, auto-mounting and unmounting of remote volumes, background copying, collision detection, detection of network time discrepancies, error logging, a progress status bar, and the ability to work with DOS diskettes. SwitchBack

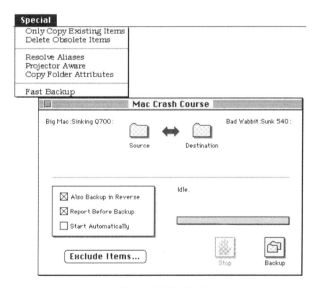

Figure 3-3: SwitchBack

works with System 6.0.4 or greater; System 7 users have additional features, including alias resolving, balloon help, AppleScript aware, and support for Drag and Drop (see Figure 3-3).

Synchronize!
Hugh Sontag
Qdea
6331 Hilton Court
Pine Springs, MN 55115
Internet: Qdea@eworld.com
Registration fee: $29.95

Hugh has been programming the Mac since it came out in 1984. He was the first one in his company to buy one. He's used FORTH, Pascal, and C in programming the Mac. Nothing pleases him more than having people use and appreciate the software he writes.

Synchronize! is distributed as a demo, which also happens to be the commercial version of the software. When users register, they receive a unique serial number that enables full access to all the advanced features of

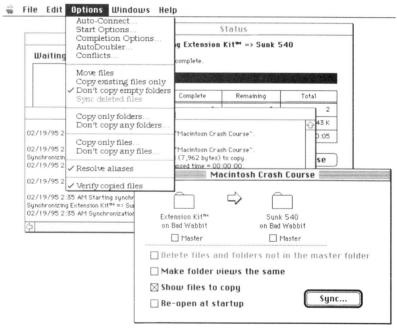

Figure 3-4: Synchronize dialogs

the program. As new versions become available on-line, existing users can upgrade for free by downloading the new version. The serial number they purchased will continue to work with new versions. Crippled demos are not my favorite, but this one provides some functionality, and does give you a good idea of the program's impressive feature set (the demo version works only with folders less than 400K).

Synchronize! features completely automatic operation, including the capability to automatically connect and disconnect AppleTalk Remote Access and file servers; to synchronize deleted files; conflict checking; bi-directional background copying, at user-definable speeds; an activity log; AutoDoubler support; and file verification. It requires System 6.0.2 or greater; under System 7 it supports balloon help, Apple Events, and AppleScript. Figure 3-4 shows some of its dialogs.

Apple File Assistant
Apple Computers
20525 Mariani Avenue
Cupertino, CA 95014-6299
(408) 996-1010
Apple bundles File Assistant with selected PowerBooks

Apple's File Assistant (Figure 3-5) offers one feature that no one else does: it can synchronize more than one folder (regardless of where they are located)

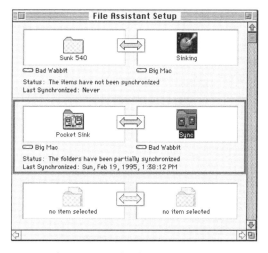

Figure 3-5: Apple File Assistant Setup

at the same time. It requires System 7, and includes balloon help, Apple Guide help (if you're running System 7.5), and support for drag and drop. Certainly worth trying if it came with your PowerBook.

PowerMerge
Leader Technologies
4590 MacArthur Blvd., Suite 550
Newport Beach, CA 92660
Telephone: 714 757-1787
Fax: 714 757-1777
Technical Support: 505 822-0700
America Online: LeaderTech
Suggested retail: $129.00

PowerMerge is the utility I use to keep the files on my 540C and those on my Quadra 700 synchronized — it is a big step up from all of the other synchronization utilities covered so far in this chapter. PowerMerge provides detailed control and feedback about what it will do for you. The dots in the

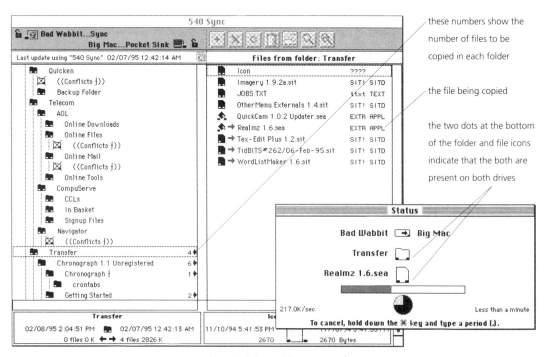

Figure 3-6: PowerMerge at work

bottom corners of the icons in Figure 3-6 indicate which side of the synchronization has the file; the numbers and arrows to the right indicate how many files will move in which direction from each folder. The icons across the top (grayed because no file is selected) allow you to specifically include, exclude, make neutral, or discard a file; begin an update, find a conflict, and find the next document to be moved. The folders marked "((Conflicts ƒ))" are folders containing files that were updated on both sides after the last reconciliation; the X through folder icons indicates that I have told PowerMerge not to synchronize the folders. Advanced settings (Figure 3-7) allow you to specify how the program should treat files that have been created, deleted, moved, or renamed on either side.

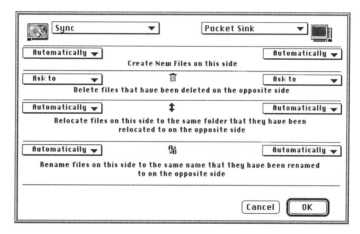

Figure 3-7: PowerMerge advanced settings

Backup-Related Utilities

Here are a few utilities that can help you with your backup strategy — AutoClock to make sure your Macs' clocks are accurate, CopyDoubler for quick 'n dirty backups, and a couple of floppy cataloging programs: AutoCat and Disk Wizard. If you want to automate the synchronizing of your Macs, check out Chronograph in Chapter 10.

AutoClock

Jean-Pierre Gachen
Résidence Beaucastel
4, avenue François Mauriac
F-64200 Biarritz, France
Fax: +33-59 22 18 20
CompuServe: 76667,3075
Internet: jpg11@calvacom.fr

AutoClock is freeware

Jean-Pierre is a 29-year-old living in France. When he was 15 he started programming (BASIC, 6502 assembly language, and later PASCAL) as a hobby on his first computer — an Apple][+ with 16KB RAM — with which he learned a lot by himself. Later he studied computer science at the French University of Bordeaux for 5 years (pre-doctorate level). He practiced a lot of high-level languages (FORTRAN, COBOL, PROLOG, LISP, SCHEME, FORTH...) and assembly languages (Z80, 8086, 680x0, 8086...) on a variety of computer systems during these years and later. AutoClock was written in C (first version in 1991), but he is now mainly using C++ for everything he writes (on Macintosh and PC/Windows).

With all of the file synchronization and backup programs, it is crucial that your Macs' system clocks be reasonably close. You can imagine the disaster if

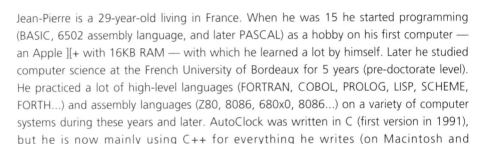

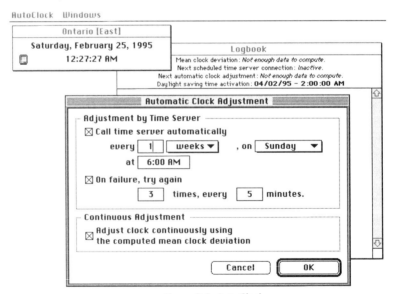

Figure 3-8: AutoClock

one or the other was out by a day or a month — older files could end up overwriting newer ones, all because of incorrect dates. AutoClock (see Figure 3-8) is a freeware extension/application combination that helps you keep your Mac clocks accurate by allowing you to: set the clock by calling a time server; set the clock manually from an accurate source; and generate a log of your clock changes, calculate the accuracy of your Mac's clock, and use those calculations to maintain its accuracy.

CopyDoubler

Symantec
10201 Torre Avenue
Cupertino, CA 95014
Telephone: 408 253-9600
Tech Support: 503 465-8420 (free for 90 days)
America Online Keyword: SYMANTEC
CompuServe: GO SYMANTEC
CopyDoubler is part of Symantec Norton DiskDoubler Pro; the suggested retail is $109.00

CopyDoubler is a utility originally developed by Dave Heller at Salient Software, it is now sold as part of Norton SuperDoubler. This simple utility speeds up Finder copying and trash emptying so much, it should be bought by Apple and built into the operating system. Not only does it speed up copying, but allows copying to run as a background process, so that you can continue working while files are being copied.

How does CopyDoubler qualify as a backup utility? By virtue of its Fast Replace feature (see Figure 3-9), which only copies new or changed files. This allows you to copy a group of files from a folder to a backup drive, make changes to those files, later drag the same group of files to the same backup directory, and have CopyDoubler only copy the new or changed files. As you can see from CopyDoubler's preferences (Figure 3-11), there is more, too: it can verify disk writes, copy AutoDoubler or DiskDoubler files compressed or expanded, schedule copies, and even ring a bell when its finished!

CopyDoubler provides a progress dialog, and, because it can run in the background, you can have it cue up multiple copies (note the 2 more copies remaining in the lower left-hand corner of Figure 3-10). When I want to do a quick and dirty backup, CopyDoubler is the tool I use.

Fast Replace can be used for fast backups

Figure 3-9: CopyDoubler Fast Replace

The diamond in the corner expands the dialog to update copy information

Because CopyDoubler allows background copying, you can have several copies waiting in line

Figure 3-10: CopyDoubler in action

Once you've had background copying, you'll never go back!

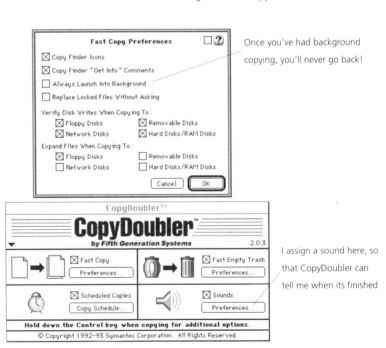

I assign a sound here, so that CopyDoubler can tell me when its finished

Figure 3-11: CopyDoubler Preferences

AutoCat

Olivier Lebra
8, rue Paul Bounin
06100 Nice
France
Telephone: (+33) 93 98 40 91
Internet: olebra@ifaedi.insa-lyon.fr
Shareware fee: $10.00

Olivier is a 21-year-old French student who studied in Montreal at Concordia University. He got his first Mac, an LC, for Christmas three years ago. He now has a Duo 270c with Minidock, which he likes because it allows him to use two screens. He started to program the Mac two and a half years ago with THINK Pascal and now programs with Symantec C++ 7.0. Next year he plans to become an engineer specializing in computer science. Olivier learned to program at INSA (National Institute of Applied Sciences in France). He is self-taught on the Mac, using Inside Mac, New Inside Mac, and a few French and English books. Olivier acts as a Mac evangelist at his school — he is the only one of 115 students in his department with a Mac.

What do you do if you've decided to store files off-line (multiple copies, of course — we're talking about backup here), and you want to find that memo you wrote three months ago to Aunt Lesley? The solution may be a cataloging system, to keep track of what you put where. AutoCat and Disk Wizard (which follows), both allow you to keep track of what is on your floppy disks.

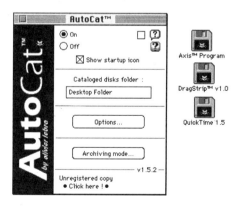

Figure 3-12: AutoCat Control Panel

AutoCat is a control panel (see Figure 3-12) that automatically creates a catalog of the files on your floppy disks (or on any other removable volume) when they are ejected. With AutoCat, you have only to write the name of your disks on their label. To find a file, you can use the Finder's "Find..." command as though your file was on your hard disk.

When you eject a disk, AutoCat creates a folder with the same name as your disk. Into this folder AutoCat puts aliases to all the files on the disk. AutoCat maintains the hierarchical directory structure of your disks; it copies folders from the disk and, instead of copying files from the disk, makes aliases of the original files and puts them in their respective folders. You can quickly catalog a series of disks — in the Archiving Mode, each disk you insert is cataloged and is immediately ejected.

Disk Wizard
François Pottier
4 rue Colette
94210 La Varenne
France
Internet: pottier@dmi.ens.fr or: pottier@clipper.ens.fr
Shareware fee: $10.00

François is a student of theoretical computer science in Paris. He is starting his Ph.D. thesis on the theory of modern languages. He first discovered the Macintosh around 1986 — back then he was amazed by MacPaint. He started playing around with a 512K Mac (which now sleeps in his attic), first in BASIC, then in Pascal, C, and C++. He says more elegant and powerful languages exist (such as Caml-Light) but they have no Toolbox interface. He entered the shareware field by chance. One day he wrote a quick hack to display a picture in the background. He thought it could be useful to others, so he sent it out into the wilderness (that is, Internet). He immediately started receiving lots of electronic mail about it, urging him to improve it. So he worked on it, and when it was elaborate enough he turned it into shareware. François says shareware is a very cool hobby, because it puts you in touch with people from all over the world. It doesn't pay for a living (unless you're Andrew Welch) but it can buy you an extra hard drive every now and then. He likes it, and wants to thank the Mac community for their support!

Disk Wizard is a combination of an application and an extension that keeps track of the contents of disks as you eject them. The application (Figure 3-13) lets you search for files.

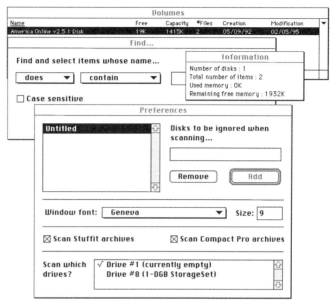

Figure 3-13: Disk Wizard Setup

Backup Programs

Now we get to the real thing: programs dedicated to backing up your hard drive. I'm going to start with the backup utilities shipped with MacTools Pro (Central Point Backup) and Norton Utilities for the Mac (Norton Fastback), and end with Dantz Development's products: DiskFit and Retrospect.

Central Point Backup

Central Point Software/Symantec
175 W. Broadway
Eugene, OR 97401
Customer Service: 503 690-8090
Technical Support: 800 491-2764 (billed to credit card)
America Online Keyword: CENTRAL
CompuServe: GO CENTRAL
Suggested retail: $149.00

As you can see from Figure 3-14, Central Point Backup may have all you need — it offers full backups, along with incremental, differential, and update backups. To briefly explain the difference: an incremental backup updates all files that have changed since the last backup, a differential backup updates all files that have changed since the last full backup, and an update backup uses Finder format and amends the same media. Clicking on Options allows you to set the type of backup you wish to perform (Figure 3-15). Other options include settings for compression, password protection, encryption, and expert settings for virus scanning and cleaning, verification, and logging.

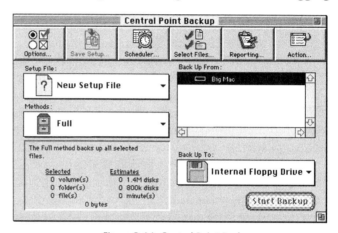

Figure 3-14: Central Point Backup

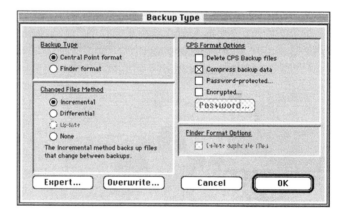

Figure 3-15: Central Point Backup options

Norton FastBack
Symantec Peter Norton Group
10201 Torre Avenue
Cupertino, CA 95014
Telephone: 408 253-9600
Tech Support: 503 465-8420 (free for 90 days)
America Online Keyword: SYMANTEC
CompuServe: GO SYMANTEC
Suggested retail: $149.00

An interesting observation: for the most part, MacTools Pro does more hand-holding than Norton Utilities — this seems to be reversed with their backup products: Norton Fastback offers a much simpler interface. Fastback offers a number of features, including the ability to create self-extracting backups, the ability to schedule automatic unattended backups, spanning of disks, and support for DiskDoubler and AutoDoubler files. Like Central Point Backup, it supports a variety of media: floppy disks, mounted drives or volumes, disk cartridges, network drives, or tape drives (Figure 3-16).

Figure 3-16: Norton Fastback

DiskFit Direct / DiskFit Pro

Dantz Development Corporation
4 Orinda Way, Building C
Orinda, CA 94563
Telephone: 510 253-3000
Fax: 510 253-9099
Tech Support: 510 253-3050
America Online: Dantz
AppleLink: DANTZ

CompuServe: 72477,1322
Suggested retail: DiskFit Direct $49.00; DiskFit Pro $125.00

DiskFit Direct is a "bundled" version of DiskFit that is shipped with a number of disk drives (including my new APS 230 MO). As you can see from Figure 3-17, it just doesn't get any easier than this. DiskFit Direct can back up or restore files to (and from) floppy disks, Syquest or Bernoulli cartridges, optical disks, or any other removable media. The one new term you need to learn when using Dantz products is "SmartSet," their term for a backup set. DiskFit Direct cannot back up to a tape drive or another hard drive.

DiskFit Pro does all of the above, and adds more flexibility, with the ability to back up to another hard drive or a file server, set backup reminders, and create automatic duplicates.

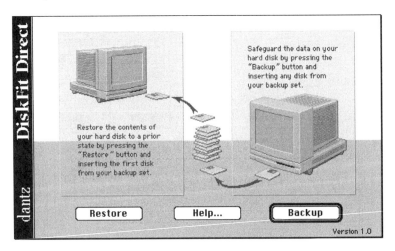

Figure 3-17: DiskFit Direct

Retrospect / Retrospect Remote
Dantz Development Corporation
(see above for address information)

Suggested retail: Retrospect $249.00; Retrospect Remote $449.00

Retrospect (Figures 3-18 and 3-19) is Dantz's flagship product, and is widely regarded as the best backup software you can buy for your Mac. It offers unattended local or network backup to any tape, cartridge, or optical drive. Retrospect Remote is Dantz's product for backing up an entire network to a single storage device.

To be honest, I only have one thing left to say about backing up: do it!

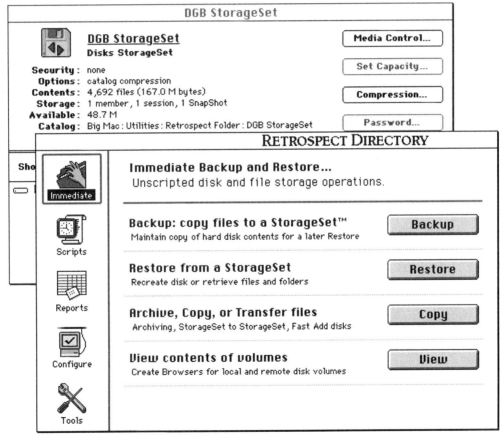

Figure 3-18: Retrospect

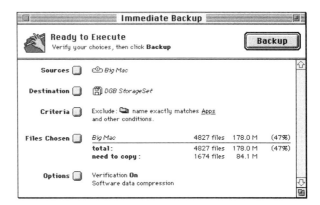

Figure 3-19: Retrospect Backup options

Interview — Larry Zulch

Larry is president of Dantz Development, the developers of DiskFit, DiskFit Pro, Retrospect, and Retrospect Remote.

How long have you been programming and how did you get started?

I (Larry) don't program. My brother Richard Zulch, VP Engineering at Dantz and principal author of the products in the DiskFit and Retrospect family, started programming in the 70's when he was in high school and "boot" meant a seemingly endless process of toggling front–panel switches in hex and clicking load.

What are your educational backgrounds — are you formally trained, or did you teach yourselves?

I went to UC Davis and got a degree in Econ; Richard went to UC Santa Barbara and got a degree in Electrical Engineering with an emphasis in Software Design.

What programs has Richard written?

Richard wrote BoxBack and MegaCopy for Iomega for their Bernoulli Boxes for Mac, and then DiskFit, Network DiskFit, TapeFit, Retrospect, and Retrospect Remote.

What language(s) do you write in?

C, and now C++

What software tools do you use?
MPW, Steve Jasik's debugger, and Meson, an internally developed object framework.

Please describe the equipment you use (what computer, how much RAM, etc.)
Richard uses a PowerMac 8100/110 with 64MB RAM, a 21" monitor, GBs of hard disk, a DAT drive, and an HP UPS good for almost an hour. He also has a PowerBook 540C, and a few other Macs. Larry has a PowerMac 7100/66 with Apple 21" monitor and 24MB of RAM and a Duo 250 and no UPS.

What is your favorite piece of software (excluding that written by you or your company...)
Me: Hard question. Perhaps the engine control code in my new Honda Accord, since it just works and makes my car work better. Or maybe the Finder, since it concretizes metaphor so ably. The third choice would be the Magnifying Glass DA, since the same code which worked on my first 128K Mac still works on my PowerMac.

What do like to do when you're not programming?
Richard: be with family and friends; Me: bicycle and be with friends.

Where do you live, are you married with children, how old are you, (etc.)
Richard is married and has two children, Matthew, 5, and Samantha, 2. He will be 35 in September 95. I am not married and will be 38 in October 95.

How did Dantz get started?
In 1984, one of my friends got a Mac 128 with ImageWriter. Richard was at HP in Colorado, working in their Telecom Division, and I would send him things produced on the Mac and extol its virtues. He was impressed, and we talked and he decided to move back to California and start a company with me. We didn't even know what products we'd create, just that the Macintosh had a great deal of potential. We applied to be "Certified Developers" and were approved, so we got three Macs through the developer program, each with an external 400K disk drive as well as the internal 400K drive. This wasn't enough storage, so we looked around and bought an Iomega 5MB Bernoulli Box that connected to the serial port on the Mac. It was great, but there was no backup software with it! So, as practice, Richard wrote our first product, BoxBack, and for still more practice, we decided I

should try to sell it to Iomega. They saw it, and liked it, and bought unlimited rights to the object code forever for $12,000 and a couple of SCSI Bernoulli Boxes (that should work with the soon-to-be released Macintosh Plus.) At that time, that was a lot of money and we were very happy, and Dantz was started.

What products has your company released?
DiskFit Direct, DiskFit Pro, Retrospect, Remote 10-Pack, Remote 50-Pack, Retrospect Remote

How big is your company (how many people do you employ, annual sales, whatever)?
50 people, over $9 million annual sales. We were number 190 on the Inc. Magazine 500 fastest growing private companies in the US in 1994.

What are the top five questions your tech support people field, and more importantly, what are the answers?

1. How do I tell Retrospect that I want an incremental backup?
    An "incremental backup" means a backup of all files that are new or modified since the last time you backed up. A "full backup" means a backup of everything that meets the selection criteria. Retrospect automatically performs incremental backups when appropriate: the first backup to a "StorageSet" (the set of backup disks or tapes) is full, and subsequent backups are incremental. Retrospect keeps track of which files have changed and which haven't.

2. What is the best backup strategy?
    This depends on how many days of work you are willing to risk and how safe you want to be. For many people, daily backups make sense, for others, biweekly or weekly. Of course, with weekly backups, you can lose a week's worth of work! The other important issue is whether or not to make multiple backups. With just a single backup, there is still a chance of losing data if something happens to both your hard disk and the backup (such as a fire, theft, or even a power surge at the wrong time.) In general, rotating between two backups and getting one off-premises periodically is the best strategy.

3. Why should I use scripts and how do I set them up?
    You should use scripts when you want to have your backup automatically occur on a regular basis, even when you aren't there. Backing up is a good activity for times when you aren't trying to work on your computer. Setting up a script is easy. In

Retrospect's directory, click on the Scripts icon and the Edit button. Click New in the window that appears to create and name a script. You'll see an overview window. Click on Sources and pick your hard disk (or whatever disk you want to back up), then Destinations to pick a StorageSet (your set of backup disks or tapes) or to create a new one. Skip over Criteria and Options for now and click Schedule. You can Add a "Day of Week" scheduler, for example, that will schedule your backup for, say, Tuesdays and Fridays at 10 pm. Click the close box, and Save. That's it!

4. Can I run a script just by opening a file in the Finder?
    Sure. Once you've created a script, click the Scripts button in the Retrospect Directory and then the Run button. Select the script and click OK. Then select "Make a Run Document" and Save the file wherever you want. Now, whenever you double-click on that file, Retrospect will run the script you've chosen.

5. What do "Remotes" do and how are they different from Retrospect Remote?
    Remotes are control panels (CDEVs) that are installed on Macintoshes on a network. They allow any copy of Retrospect installed on any one Macintosh to back up all the Macintoshes on the network to a single storage device, preferably something high capacity, like a DAT drive. Remotes are available separately and work with any copy of Retrospect. When we sell Retrospect and ten Remotes together in one package, we call it Retrospect Remote.

What are the main differences between DiskFit and Retrospect?

The primary difference is that DiskFit "maps" your hard disk to one or more disks called a SmartSet. When a file is changed, added, or deleted on the hard disk, that file is changed on the SmartSet the next time you run DiskFit. So there is always a one-to-one correspondence between the files on your hard disk and those in the SmartSet. Pros: this allows DiskFit to keep all backup files (that aren't too big to fit on a single disk) in Finder readable format, to use a consistent set of media—you don't have to keep adding disks each time you back up, and to keep operation very simple. Cons: DiskFit only works with disks such as floppies, MO, SyQuest, and Bernoulli, not tape. There is no history of files, and backup files can't be compressed or encrypted. Because each disk in a SmartSet may contain files that must be updated, it is not very practical to use DiskFit in an unattended fashion.

Retrospect works quite differently. It backs up all selected files to a set of disks or tapes — a StorageSet — and then automatically performs incremental backups to that StorageSet thereafter, adding the new or changed files to the end of the previous ones. Pros: Retrospect supports any backup media, including tape, disks, optical, file on a server, or another hard disk. Files can be compressed or encrypted, and multiple versions of a file are kept. Because all of the incremental backup files are stored together, they typically fit on a single piece of media, so unattended backup is practical and useful. Cons: Retrospect does not store files in a Finder readable format, more storage media is required each time you backup, and operation is somewhat more complex.

The upshot is that DiskFit is a good, easy-to-use utility for personal backup to disks. Retrospect is more powerful and is useful for anyone who wants maximum versatility and speed.

What do you think the future holds for backup media? Please comment on the pros and cons of media types (tape, DAT, Syquest, MO) and where you think they're headed.

Hard disks are getting larger very rapidly and the amount an average user stores is increasing just as quickly. Add to these factors the increasing time investment required to set up a Macintosh, and you can see that the days of backing up by dragging a few files to floppies in the Finder are just about gone. The challenge for backup media is to match the increasing capacity and performance of hard disks.

Tape, which initially was unpopular on the Macintosh, mainly because Apple's tape drive was not very good, has become very important since nothing else can match its capacity, low media cost, and performance. By far the most popular kind of tape drive on the Macintosh is DAT (Digital Audio Tape) which started as a consumer format but now has special mechanisms and tape formulations just for computer use. DAT performance is very well matched to the Macintosh file system (unless you have relatively large files, the gating factor for backup performance is the Mac file system even on high-end Macs) and has capacities up to about 8 gigabytes per tape.

Other kinds of tape drives includes DC 2000, which promises lower cost drives with performance and capacity approaching DAT, and DLT (Digital Linear Tape) which has higher capacity, performance, (and cost) than DAT. Some DLT drives can hold 40 GB on a single tape, and transfer data many times faster than the fastest Macintosh can supply it. Tape storage is very reliable. As long as tapes are kept cool and dry, they last for years and have proven to have very low error rates. In the future, the performance, reliability, and capacity of tape drives of all kinds will continue to increase, and prices will drop. Ah, the wonders of advancing technology.

MO (Magneto-Optical) drives are very popular for those who need their backup storage device to also be useful for "ad hoc archiving", that is, using the Finder to drag files from, say, a current project off a hard disk to free up space. The older, high-capacity 5 1/4 inch drives are giving way to 3 1/2" drives which will soon achieve capacities close to those of their 5 1/4" brethren. MOs performance is not equal that of the better tape drives because MOs require three disc [note spelling for optical only] rotations to write a single track of bits. And while the drive mechanism prices are roughly comparable with DAT drives, the discs used in MO drives are 30-100 times (yes, 30x to 100x) as expensive as DAT media on a per megabyte basis. This can really add up, particularly with large hard disks or network backups.

A new technology holds a great deal of promise for backup: second generation CDR drives. First generation CDR drives allow you to create a CD-ROM disc but don't allow the creation process to be interrupted, which makes them inappropriate for backup, since interruptions occur constantly as the file system hunts for files or delays sending one for just a fraction of a second. With a first generation drive, the slightest interruption ruins the CDR disk for good. [This is because CD ROMs and CDR are written in a continuous spiral from hub out.] Second generation drives, just now appearing on the market [actually coming out in June/July '95] allow the writing process to be interrupted so they are suitable for backup. The same drive that makes CDR discs can also be used as a 4x CD-ROM drive. The costs for these drives are comparable to those of MO.

Magnetic media cartridge drives, such as SyQuest, Iomega Bernoullis, and Iomega Zip drives keep improving their performance and capacity at ever lower prices. The fastest, such as the SyQuest 270, works at hard drive speeds; the least expensive, the Iomega Zip drive, has a suggested retail price of $199, and each $20 cartridge holds 100MB!

What do you think the future holds for backup software?

The challenges for backup software are to get more automatic and easier to use while continuing to meet user's varied needs. The area of most rapid change will be in network backup: the potential benefits of being connected to a network are only starting to be exploited by backup software.

4 System 6

Raise your hands if you still use System 6 — we keep asking for a show of hands at Macworlds, and the System 6 response has dropped to 1% or less. We may even stop talking about it. In any case, for those of you still out there, this short chapter covers some of the specific problems you may run into when running System 6.

The biggest difference between Systems 6 and 7, at least from the perspective of this book, is that System 7 improved greatly on System 6's poor memory management. My recommendation for most System 6 users is to upgrade to System 7 if you can — users who must run System 6 for a particular application may want to consider using SwitchBoot.

SwitchBoot
John Mancino
Decision Maker's Software, Inc.
1910 Joslyn Place
Boulder, CO 80304
AppleLink: D0391
CompuServe: 70337,2143
SwitchBoot is freeware

One solution if you have an old application or an old Mac that insists on System 6 is to switch between disk drives; one with System 6 installed, and the other with System 7. Installing this extension allows you to select which drive to boot from — holding down the "s" or the Caps Lock key during startup gives you a dialog of currently bootable drives to select from.

System Heap

The single biggest problem for System 6 users is the System heap. This is the memory area where fonts, desk accessories (DAs), control panels, and INITs load. One sign of System heap problems for System 6 users is a memory error -108. Don't worry — there are utilities on the CD-ROM to help.

Open Files and O/S Events

The things to be aware of when dealing with your System heap are the open files count and the maximum number of O/S events. These are actually contained in tables within the System heap. The Maximum Open Files uses something called File Control Blocks to store information on every file that your Mac opens; the result is a number that specifies the maximum number of files you can have open at one time. Applications, fonts, and DAs all count as files — it's amazing how fast this number can build when you're running MultiFinder. The commercial font utilities Suitcase and MasterJuggler both have the ability to adjust the open files count, or you can use BootMan. The maximum number of operating system events is just that — the maximum number of things that your Mac can handle at once.

FCB Inspector

Maurice Volaski
8201 Henry Ave Apt J23,
Philadelphia, PA 19128-2216
America Online: fluxsftwre
Internet: volaski@contra.med.buffalo.edu
FCB Inspector is freeware

Maurice and I have "known" each other for quite some time. We've never physically met, but we've talked to each other many times, on-line and by telephone. When we needed someone to write the external Gestalt calls so that the HyperCard stacks we wrote (INITInfo Pro, DiagnoSYS) could examine the user's Macintosh, we went to Maurice — he did a great job for us.

FCB Inspector (Figure 4-1) works under both System 6 and System 7, allowing you to look at the files your Mac has open, and close those that aren't essential to your System.

Figure 4-1: FCB Inspector

 Be sure you know what you do before you start closing open files, because there is always a risk that the file you close will be the next one your Mac needs (if so, you'll crash). The reason I've included FCB Inspector in this chapter is that it also allows System 6 users to adjust their Mac's maximum number of open files.

 The cryptic information beneath the Close button gives you FCB information about the highlighted file; a complete list of the fields is given in the documentation on the CD-ROM.

 While FCB Inspector works just fine under System 6 and 7, there is little point in System 7 users using the rest of the software covered in this chapter — System 7's improved memory management has obsoleted both Bootman and HeapTool (neither provide any benefit for System 7), and HellFolderFix does not work with System 7.

Bootman™
Bill Steinburg
America Online: BillS
AppleLink: X02542
CompuServe: 76703,1027
Bootman™ is freeware.

Billy has written a number of commercial Mac products, including Pyro and PBTools.

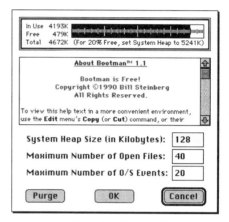

Figure 4-2: Bootman™

Billy's freeware Bootman is the solution for many System 6 users: as you can see in Figure 4-2, this elegant little utility allows you to adjust your System heap along with the maximum number of open files and the maximum number of O/S events. For most System 6 users, the recommended 20% setting will be just fine; I recommend that MultiFinder users also set the maximum number of open files to 100, and the maximum number of O/S events to 40. When running MultiFinder, Bootman shrinks to the "thermometer" (the top of the dialog) to give you a gauge of how things are going. The one downside to Bootman is that it requires a reboot for changes you make to take effect.

HeapTool

Kerry Clendinning
P.O. Box 26061
Austin, TX 78755-0061
AppleLink: KerryC
CompuServe: 76424,2214
Shareware fee: $13.50

Kerry works for a commercial software company in Austin, Texas, producing Unix tape backup software. His software experience is primarily communications, wide area telecommunications, and relational database design, with a total of 10 years' experience programming in C, SQL, and assembly. He received a BSCS degree from the University of Texas at Austin, and began working on Macintoshes in 1989.

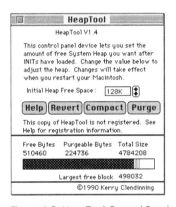

Figure 4-3: HeapTool Control Panel

Like it says in Figure 4-3, HeapTool is a control panel that allows you to set the amount of free System heap *after* INITs have loaded. (A note for System 7 readers: under System 6, extensions were called INITs or initialization routines. Technically they still are called INITs because they contain INIT code, but most refer to them by Apple's new designation: extensions.) I've emphasized the "after" for good reason: this is what makes it worth the shareware fee to those who run lots of INITs. By adjusting the System heap after other INITs have loaded, HeapTool becomes a good choice for those who regularly change their setup with an INIT manager — you can change your setup at boot time, and HeapTool will adjust your System heap without requiring a further reboot (usually by holding down the spacebar to call up your favorite startup utility).

HellFolderFix
John Jeppson
CompuServe: 76174,2007

HellFolderFix is freeware

Ever had a folder that looked empty, but that you couldn't trash? You may have been stuck with the Folder from Hell. This simple System 6-only utility (Figure 4-4) may be able to repair the problem for you.

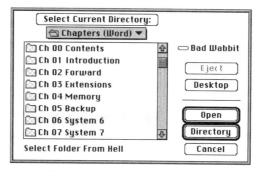

Figure 4-4: Fixing the Folder from Hell

Please read the documentation on the CD-ROM before using HellFolderFix; the author recommends a number of steps, including a complete backup, before running HellFolderFix.

5 System 7

The Mac was always a great machine. But the jokes about System 6 and memory finally reached the level of a loud, constant roar. Even Apple heard and heeded them. And so, after much effort, System 7 was born.

System 7, with much improved memory management, brought a new level of stability to the Mac. It also drastically increased memory requirements — Apple recommends four megabytes, and me and virtually everyone who works with it recommend eight megabytes if you want to use any of the tools and toys that make a Mac fun to use.

Better memory management wasn't all System 7 improved. We also got (you'll note my list doesn't include publish and subscribe, which never really caught on, or balloon help, which most leave off unless learning a new program):

- Aliases: see later in this chapter for tools to help you with aliases
- Apple Menu: a menu with access to everything on your hard drive; NowMenus (part of Now Utilities) or MenuChoice (shareware on the CD-ROM) are programs that give you hierarchical Apple Menu access
- Application switching (Chapter 6 covers a couple of great products for application switching: DragStrip and PowerBar Pro)
- Print spooling with PrintMonitor
- The trash only empties when you tell it to; utilities covered in this chapter make it even better (under System 6, the trash would empty if you restarted or shut down).
- TrueType fonts (see Chapter 16 for more on fonts).

There's even more. There are changes that have made things easier for those of us who tend to run way too many things: better organization of the System folder, with subfolders for extensions, control panels, preferences, and more; the ability to temporarily reboot without extensions or startup items loaded by holding down the Shift key at startup; and the ability to force applications to quit by pressing Command-Option-Escape. This key combination will force a reluctant application to quit, but I recommend against using it unless you have to. It may leave your Mac's System in a fragile state, so a reboot is a good idea after forcing an application to quit.

Shareware Products

While it took quite a while for the commercial software industry to come out with utilities to help System 7 users with their new systems; shareware authors filled the void quickly (and continue to do so).

CommentKeeper
Maurice Volaski
8201 Henry Avenue, Apartment J23
Philadelphia, PA 19128-2216
America Online: fluxsftwre
CommentKeeper is freeware

One of the fixes that was originally slated for System 7 was to save the Finder's Get Info comments during a Desktop rebuild. Earlier versions of the Finder did this, and the feature that was lost with System 6 was to have been fixed with System 7. Somehow, it missed the cut, so Maurice wrote the CommentKeeper extension to get around this problem. The only time you need to have it active is when you do a Desktop rebuild. See Chapter 15 for more on why, how, and when to do a desktop rebuild.

DeskTop Remover
Adam Stein
Insanely Great Software
126 Calvert Ave. E.
Edison, NJ 08820
Telephone: 908 548-5107
America Online: AdamStein
CompuServe: 71140,2051
Desktop Remover is freeware

Insanely Great Software was founded in 1988 by Adam Stein while he was a freshman in high school (he's currently studying entrepreneurial management at the Wharton School of Business at the University of Pennsylvania). The company name came from Steve Jobs, who often called things he really liked "insanely great." They aim to make your experience with them one worthy of their name: from product quality to technical support. They also aim to bring you the advantages of a small company without sacrificing the professionalism of a large corporation. So you'll be able to talk to him personally whenever you'd like (try talking to the president or author in large companies like Microsoft or Claris!), but you'll also be able to order by credit card 24 hours a day, 7 days a week, from toll-free 800 order lines. (As well as fax, e-mail, and regular mail!) And they ship within 24 hours, so that you won't have to wait for your products any longer than necessary! They even ship your order out Airborne Express if you desire. International customers can get express shipping as well — with product usually arriving in less than a week. Desktop Remover was written in Think Pascal.

Here's a utility for those System 6 users who take my advice, and move up to System 7. When you do, you'll still have left on your hard drive the invisible System 6 desktop file. Unless you're switching back and forth between operating systems, there's no reason to keep that file, so why not let DeskTop Remover get rid of it for you, and free up some space on your hard drive?

Kill FinderZooms

Jonathan Jacobs
2374 Euclid Heights, Blvd. #407
Cleveland Heights, OH 44106-2745
Telephone: 216 368-3574 (lab)
Internet: jxj24@po.cwru.edu
Kill FinderZooms is freeware

Jonathan is a graduate student in Biomedical Engineering at Case Western Reserve University in Cleveland, Ohio — he's back in school several years after getting his Master's degree in electrical engineering. His area of research is the neural basis of adaptive behavior (basically; can we find physical changes/activity in the nervous system that indicate what a subject — in this case a big, squishy sea slug — is going to do?). They use a lot of computer power (Macs and clones) in their lab for data acquisition, data analysis, modeling, graphics, mathematical computing, frame grabbing and movie making. After spending all day at his Mac, Jonathan goes home for more. He first started programming on the Mac in the spring of 1994; after a false start he wrote a set of applications to convert sounds between the Mac and an engineering tool called MATLAB (Internet users can find the SoundEdit<->MATLAB suite on sumex). After that, he started to write interface tools for the Mac, including Kill FinderZooms and WhoAmI? (see Chapter 6).

Want to get every last ounce of performance out of your Mac? The animated "zoom" effect you get when you open a window may look pretty, but it does slow things down a bit. Run Kill FinderZooms, and your windows will pop open a little faster than before.

MenuChoice
Kerry Clendinning
P.O. Box 26061
Austin, TX 78755-0061
AppleLink: KerryC
CompuServe: 76424,2214
Shareware fee: $15.00

The Apple Menu was one of the best additions that Apple made with System 7 — the only thing missing was hierarchical access (see Figure 5-1). There are a number of commercial utilities that give you hierarchical access: HAM,

Figure 5-1: Hierarchical menus with MenuChoice

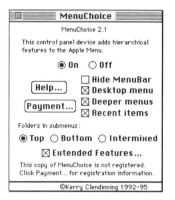

Figure 5-2: MenuChoice Control Panel

SuperMenus, and NowMenus, but none of them offer what Kerry has built into this shareware utility: the ability to go beyond the Apple operating systems' five-menu limit ("Deeper Menus" in Figure 5-2). This feature does not work with System 7.5, at least not on my Macs. Mind you, if you have System 7.5, then you also have Apple Menu Options. MenuChoice also can show a hierarchical menu of all the items on your desktop, including all mounted volumes, mount AppleShare volumes, show a menu of recently opened applications and documents, and even hide the menu bar for you.

Alias Utilities

Aliases are a great feature of System 7; I have hundreds on my hard drive (276 to be exact). An alias is a icon that acts as a pointer to another file — it can be a document, an application, a folder, even a hard drive. Double clicking or dropping something onto the alias has the same effect as doing so to the original file. You can have as many aliases as you want, and you can trash an alias without having to worry about the original file being lost. One down side is that aliases can "forget" what they are supposed to be pointing to, and deleting a file does not delete its aliases, so you can end up with orphaned aliases. Although there are still not commercial utilities to help you manage all your aliases, there are some commercial-grade shareware utilities on the CD-ROM.

Alias Director
Laurence Harris
1100 W. NC Highway 54 BYP, Apt 29-J
Chapel Hill, NC 27516-2826
Telephone: 919 933-9595
America Online: LHarris
CompuServe: 76150,1027
Shareware fee: $10.00

I've "talked" to Larry via e-mail on several occasions — I've often asked him why he hasn't commercially released his programs (they are certainly good enough). His answer is simple: he does quite well on shareware, and doesn't want the hassles associated with commercial release. This doesn't mean that he doesn't want or need your fee...

Alias Director is a powerful tool for creating and managing aliases. Dropping a file onto Alias Director gives you a dialog (Figure 5-3) that allows you to select where the alias should be put: on the desktop, in the Apple Menu Items folder, or in any location you care to stipulate. Those with limited screen space can even have desktop aliases without the space an icon would take. You can also use modifier keys to configure how Alias Director should act (see Figure 5-4). Holding down a character key will have it put the alias in the first menu location that starts with that letter — in both cases Alias Director does its magic without even bringing up the dialog box.

The program also includes the capability to update aliases or multiple aliases, and to check your hard drives for unattached aliases. Having said all these wonderful things about Alias Director, you'd think I'd recommend it, right? Well you'd be wrong — Larry has written an even better utility called File Buddy that does everything that Alias Director does, and a lot more. The only down side is a little higher shareware fee. I presume you'll all be sending

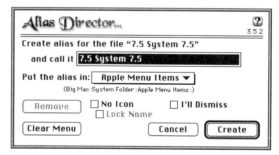

Figure 5-3: Alias Director

Figure 5-4: Configuring Alias Director's drop keys

Larry a check, because you'll all be using this one. See Chapter 13 for a complete description.

Alias Zoo
Cliff McCollum
Blue Globe Software
P.O. Box 8171
Victoria, BC V8W 3R8
Canada
CompuServe: 76170,601
Internet: cmccollu@sol.uvic.ca
Shareware fee: $15.00

I'm sure Cliff and I share a love for Victoria (I was raised there, my parents have retired to Victoria, so I get to visit every once in a while).

AliasZoo (Figure 5-5) is a utility for maintaining and updating the aliases on your hard drive. It supports PowerTalk, drag 'n drop, and obviously requires System 7. AliasZoo can reconnect aliases, delete orphaned aliases, or connect aliases to new parents. During the scanning process it can mount and scan network or local volumes, try to connect using AppleTalk Remote Access, or request removable disks.

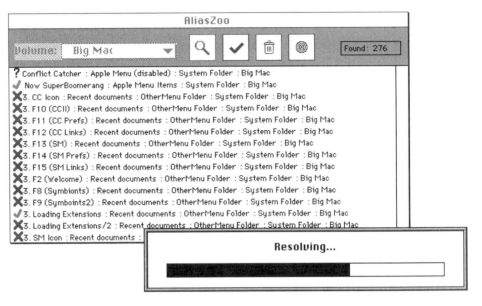

Figure 5-5: AliasZoo resolving aliases

TrashAlias

Maurice Volaski
8201 Henry Ave Apt J23,
Philadelphia, PA 19128-2216
America Online: fluxsftwre
Internet: volaski@contra.med.buffalo.edu
TrashAlias is freeware

As I mentioned earlier, when you delete a file or folder under System 7, any aliases pointing to that file or folder are left orphaned. TrashAlias fixes the problem, by automatically deleting the alias when you delete its parent. The TrashAlias Control Panel (Figure 5-6) allows you to have the program adjust for other alias and trash tools — it comes preconfigured to work with the Finder (when most aliases are created and deleted) and the shareware utilities AliasMaker and Trash Chute. You can add your own by clicking on

Figure 5-6: TrashAlias Control Panel

the Add App... button. There is no need to add TrashMan to the list, because it uses the Finder to do its work.

Trash Utilities

Unlike the dearth of commercial alias tools, there *are* commercial tools to help you manage your trash. Norton Utilities for the Mac includes Unerase, which allows you to recover files that have been accidentally erased and MacTools TrashBack goes even further; both are covered in Chapter 13.

Trash Chute
Melissa Rogers
P.O. Box 20723
San Jose, CA 95160
America Online: AFLBear
Trash Chute is freeware

Melissa has retired from programming after working with some of the best: Darin Adler, Chris Derossi, Dean Yu and others. She says she could never be as good as them; now instead she works in project management where she still works with their likes. Even better yet, she gets to ask them all about their code, figure out how long it will take to ship, and do what she can to help them ship it.

Miss the way the trash used to work in System 6? Trash Chute empties the trash for you — drop it in the Startup Items folder and it will empty the trash when you start (or restart) your Mac. Place an alias next to the trash for things you're sure you want to get rid of.

Melissa asked that I make sure that everyone who uses this understands that they should be especially careful when dropping an alias on Trash Chute, because it will resolve the alias and delete the original.

TrashMan

Dan Walkowski
140 Pasito Terrace #512
Sunnyvale, CA 94086
Internet: walkowsk@taurus.apple.com
Shareware fee: $10.00

TrashMan is a combination of a background application and a control panel (Figure 5-7) that allows you to "age" your trash — you set the duration in days, hours, and minutes — before it is automatically deleted.

Figure 5-7: TrashMan Controls

Interface Tools

One of the things that makes the Mac great is the fact that we can customize the interface to our hearts' content, adding extensions and control panels until our Macs take hours to boot, only to crash a minute later (gee, maybe that's a bit negative — still, I'll leave it in, because it makes a valid point: the more extensions and control panels you run, the slower and less stable your Mac becomes).

7Tuner

Jerry Du
Dragonsoft
603 E. Minor Drive #101
Kansas City, MO 64131
Telephone: 816 943-1835
America Online: Dragonsoft
CompuServe: 74471,3403
Shareware fee: $15.00

Dragonsoft is a small (three member) team writing shareware. Jerry Du is a graduate student who writes in Pascal, SuperTalk, C, and C++.

7Tuner modifies a copy of your Finder, so you have no risk of an extension conflict with it. Most of the 7Tuner's options (see Figure 5-8) are self-evident: the ability to select command keys for the Finder (I particularly like Command-m for "Make Alias"), to select from modified folders and icons, new colors for your windows, and cool new cursors and pointers. Two options are not self-explanatory — Cool Options allows you to have an alias with the same name as original file, speed up your mouse, set keyboard equivalents for your mouse, eliminate the window zooming effect, and eliminate the Finder rename delay for Systems 7.0 to 7.1. System 7.5 Aid offers three options: show machine name in the "About this Macintosh..." box, change the startup

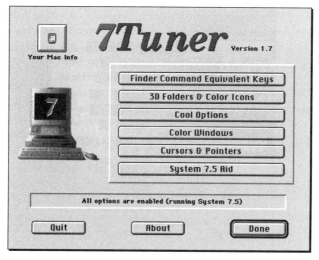

Figure 5-8: 7Tuner Options

"Welcome to Macintosh" to "Welcome to Power Macintosh," and add a corrected machine icon to "About this Macintosh" (see Figure 5-9). For those using About (Chapter 2), these programs work just fine together.

Figure 5-9: About box modified by 7Tuner

Finder Preferences 7
John Carlsen
CompuServe: 74766,1164

Finder Preferences 7 is freeware

John has been programming in APL, C, and C++ for 24 years, mostly for scientific modelling in optical physics research. Two years ago he left the research lab to do research in philosophy. He plan to publish interactive electronic works on philosophy, and to develop some Macintosh applications which help people keep their ideas and thinking explicit and consistent.

Apple's 31-character limit on file names beats the heck out of DOS (FILENME.CRP); the only problem is that viewing a file by name ends up showing you a truncated view (LONG FOLDER NAME WIT... instead of LONG FOLDER NAME WITH 31-chars). Finder Preferences 7 is a set of 67 files, each one a modified view — you can not only view full 31-character file names, but also select from regular or generic icons, sizes or files or files and folders (watch out for this one: calculating folder sizes will considerably slow your Mac), modified or deleted kind, date, label, and version fields. There are a few caveats, so be sure to read the docs carefully.

Warp7Utilities
Mark Crutchfield
P.O. Box 6456
Kingwood, TX 77325
America Online: MarkC23041
Shareware fee: $12.00

Mark has a BSC in Mechanical Engineering from the University of Houston; for the past 10 years he's been the owner and president of AD-STAR Graphics & Signs, Inc. in Humble, Texas. Although he's written engineering applications in FORTRAN and BASIC, he just started Mac programming a little over a year ago when he picked up a copy of Dave Mark's wonderful *Learn C on the Macintosh*. He started Warp7Utilities as a learning exercise, which has evolved into a much larger project. He currently uses the THINK C compiler.

Registering Warp7Finder removes three limitations of the demo: it removes the four-link limit in the Application Substitution feature (Figure 5-10), it removes the six-alias limit in the Alias Manager feature (Figure 5-11), and it enables the Other Destination button in the Alias Manager.

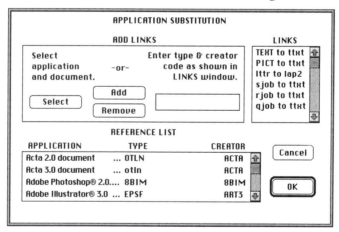

Figure 5-10: Warp7Finder Application Substitution

Select Options (Figure 5-12) is my favorite part of Warp7Finder; it includes options to speed up the Finder (eliminate the 2-second rename delay, disable zoomrects, fast copy), to adjust the Finder's memory, or to adjust and preload the Finder (recommended for those with a slow hard drive and spare memory).

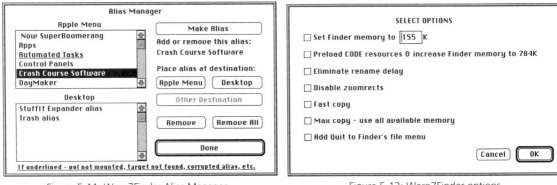

Figure 5-11: Warp7Finder Alias Manager   Figure 5-12: Warp7Finder options

Commercial Utilities

There are lots of utilities to customize the way your Mac looks — programs like 7th Heaven, I like Icon, Icon 7, Icon Mania, and Wiz Tools. The balance of this chapter covers three of my favorites: ClickChange, Open Sesame, and Now Utilities.

ClickChange
Dubl-Click Software
20310 Empire Avenue, Suite A102
Bend, Oregon 97701
Telephone: 503 317-0355
Fax: 503 317-0430
Suggested retail: $89.95

Want to go crazy with the Mac interface? ClickChange is the answer. In one control panel (Figure 5-13), you can select new, animated cursors (my favorite is the pencil as an editing tool — it just makes sense); icons instead of text in your menu bar (including animated Apple Menu and Help icons); a menu bar clock; 3D buttons; new scrollbars, including

The menubar icons and clock were added using ClickChange

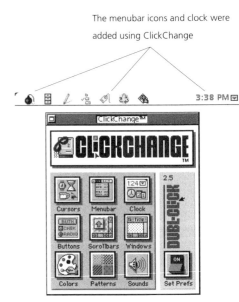

Figure 5-13: ClickChange Control Panel

those with double arrows at each end; new look windows (including ones that look like Windoze); new color schemes and background patterns; and sounds that can be assigned to system events. For many of the modules there are also editors, so you can create your own look. Cool!

Open Sesame!

Charles River Analytics Inc.
55 Wheeler Street
Cambridge, MA 02138
Telephone: 617 491-3474
Fax: 617 868-0780
America Online: OpenSesame
AppleLink: OPENSESAME
Internet: sesame@cra.com
Suggested retail: $99.00

Ever wish your Mac could anticipate your every wish, that it could do things for you before you knew you wanted to do them yourself? Open Sesame is a program that will do just that. It incorporates a learning agent, that watches what you do, anticipates your next move and offers to do it for you. It can be a number of things, including: opening or closing items, emptying the trash, shutting down, hiding, showing, or arranging items, rebuilding your Desktop (unless you tell it otherwise, Open Sesame will offer to rebuild your Desktop every 30 days), adding or removing items from your Apple Menu, Startup Items folder, or Desktop (see Figure 5-14).

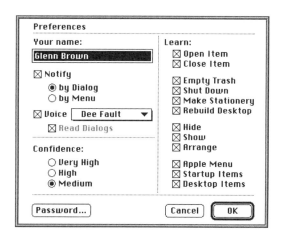

Figure 5-14: Open Sesame preferences

Now Utilities

Now Software, Inc.
921 S.W. Washington St. Suite 500
Portland, OR 97205-2823
Telephone: 503 274-2800
Fax: 503 274-0670
America Online: Now
AppleLink: NowSoftware
CompuServe: 71541,170
eWorld: NowSoft
Internet: support@nowsoft.com
Suggested retail: $89.95

Now Utilities is the best utility set you can buy for a Mac running System 7. I've covered Now Startup Manager in Chapter 1; and you can read about Now QuickFiler in Chapter 7, Now Profile in Chapter 8, Now Save in Chapter 9, Super Boomerang in Chapter 13, and Now WYSIWYG Menus in Chapter 14. That just leaves Now Scrapbook, Now FolderMenus, and Now Menus for this chapter.

Now Scrapbook

Now Scrapbook is an application that replaces Apple's scrapbook. What does it give you? Multiple catalogs (text, graphics, sounds, movies), Clipboard Editor (see Figure 5-15, which shows the Clipboard Editor working on a screen capture of Now Scrapbook), and multiple views (standard, detail, and thumbnail).

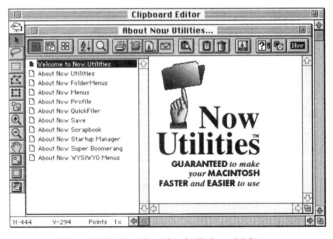

Figure 5-15: Now Scrapbook Clipboard Editor

Now FolderMenus

Now FolderMenus (Figure 5-16) is functionally the same as InLine Software's PopUpFolder: it gives you hierarchical access to items within your folders. Folders are shown with small diamond character to indicate that they have contents, just click and hold on the icon to navigate down the hierarchy. One minor limitation is that the diamonds are hard to see if you've customized the folder icons on your desktop. The easiest to see in Figure 7-19 are those on the Pictures folder, and on Bad Wabbit (my 540C's hard drive). Viewing the diamond makes no difference to the functionality of FolderMenus.You can use the same technique with drag 'n drop, too: just drag an item onto a folder and hold to navigate down.

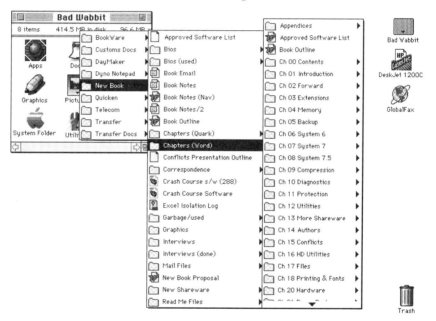

Figure 5-16: Now FolderMenus

Now Menus

This is the one component of Now Utilities that I cannot live without. Now Menus started life as Jörg Brown's shareware cdev hierDA. This System 6 control panel gave us all hierarchical menus (and a good laugh: the doc file ended with "If you call me at home I will kill you." Since he didn't have a home phone at the time, Jörg thought this was only fair). The first and most obvious thing Now Menus does is give you the ability to tailor your Apple Menu, with custom fonts (I've used Bookman in Figure 5-17), dividers, the ability to rearrange items, and (of course) hierarchical access to your Apple Menu. It also gives you configurable pull-down and pop-up menus (like the icon to the right of the Special menu in Figure 5-17), Sticky menus, and the ability to add command keys to itself or the Finder. My three favorite command keys: Command-m to create an alias, Command-8 to toggle screen resolutions, and F5 to hide the currently active application. The last two illustrate a little-known trick: you can assign the same command keys to different actions, so that they act as a toggle between the two. Adding custom menus is easy; just drag an item or folder into the setup screen. You can also add separators, recent files /folders /applications, active applications, the menu bar, Now Utilities (displays all the Now components), a find command, and the memory viewer and sizers mentioned in Chapter 2.

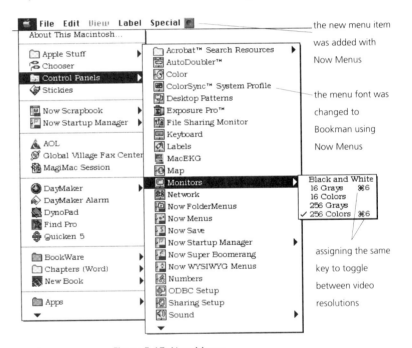

Figure 5-17: Now Menus

6

System 7.5

System 7.5. Unless you buy a new Mac, it's not free. In fact, it costs more than Windows. So why should anyone buy it? Does it offer enough new features? Does it work well? Is it safe? That's what this chapter is all about: System 7.5 along with System 7.5 Update 1.0 — which is also known as System 7.5.1 and which adds some nice new features to System 7.5.

When I started writing this book, I was running System 7.1. System 7.5 came preinstalled on a new 540C, but I left 7.1 on my Quadra, so that I'd be sure all of the book's shareware would run. Then, after a nasty crash on the Quadra, I gave in, and installed 7.5 there — guess what?— everything ran. It was a pleasant surprise to learn that very little breaks with Apple's latest. In this chapter, after a quick look at System 7.5 (and System 7.5.1) to see if there are compelling reasons to upgrade, I look at some shareware and commercial enhancements, and conclude with an interview with Dr. Mac himself — Bob LeVitus.

System 7.5 has its critics. There are those who accuse Apple of releasing what they call a shareware operating System on the basis of a few of the new components. I am not one of the critics — I think the additions, while evolutionary instead of revolutionary, are well worth the cost of upgrading.

The cost of upgrading is more than just the cost of the software. If you haven't yet upgraded your memory, you'll likely have to: System 7.5 carries hefty memory requirements. The basic installation requires 4 megs (and 8 on a PowerPC!); adding QuickDraw GX and PowerTalk doubles those numbers.

The 7.5 upgrade has a lot to offer — there are improvements to performance, new toys to customize your Mac with, updates, improved compatibility with DOS files, special features for new users and PowerBook owners, and files for those with special requirements.

Performance

Apple has addressed an number of performance-related issues with System 7.5; the longest-standing was bringing something that offered the functional equivalent of DOS' batch files.

AppleScript

AppleScript gives you the ability to record and replay your actions, but don't be fooled: unless you're a programmer, you're unlikely to use anything but canned scripts. AppleScript does give programmers the ability to control the actions of other (scriptable) applications remotely; which should result in some powerful scripts in the future.

Clean Install

With Systems 7.0 to 7.1, you could reinstall your System, and the Installer could leave corrupted or damaged resources, pressing Shift-Command-k at the main installer screen (instead of Install) gives you a dialog that allows you to chose between updating your existing System folder or installing a new System folder. The fix for System 7.0 to 7.1 users is to boot off of the DiskTools disk, trash the System and Finder (after first copying out any resources you want to save), and then do a System install.

CPU Energy Saver

For those with Macs that you can turn off with the keyboard (Centris, Quadra, and later), this control panel (see Figure 6-1) allows you to shut down automatically. In theory, this can save energy; in reality, our spouses could use this to shut *us* down.

Extensions Manager

As described in Chapter 1, Apple has included version 3.0 of Extensions Manager with System 7.5. My advice is to stick with one of the superior commercial alternatives: Conflict Catcher 3 or Now Startup Manager (see Chapter 1).

SCSI Manager 4.3

For those with Macs that can handle it (Quadras and newer), SCSI Manager 4.3 improves SCSI performance.

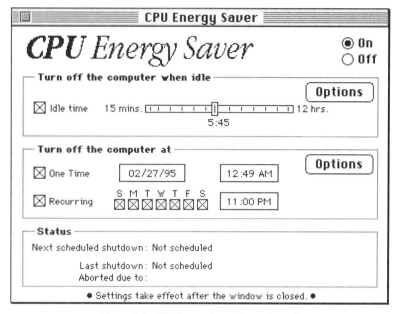

Figure 6-1: CPU Energy Saver Control Panel

Universal Enabler

Tired of the System enablers required by System 7.0 to 7.1? So am I. With System 7.5, Apple built them all into the System.

Customizing

I love toys to customize your Mac, and System 7.5 has lots of them. One hole in System 7 that was quickly filled was the lack of hierarchical (pop-out) menus — Apple include their own version, and lots more in the new System.

Apple Menu Options

Here's another case of Apple using the sincerest form of flattery: this control panel gives you hierarchical access to your Apple Menu Items. It's nowhere near as good as Now Menus, but worth installing while you wait for your copy of Now Utilities to arrive in the mail.

Audio CD Player

As I write these words, I'm listening to Buddy Guy's "Slippin' In" CD. Clicking on the small diamond under the normal button opens up a track listing (see Figure 6-2). After you've keyed them in, Apple's new Audio CD Player can remember CD titles and tracks (it keeps a small database on your hard drive). To be honest, it looks sexy, but I prefer CD Menu (Chapter 10).

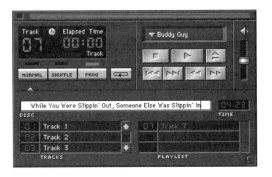

Figure 6-2: Audio CD Player

Menubar Clock

Steve Christensen (who just happens to work for Apple) is the author of SuperClock!, a freeware utility that gave us all a menubar clock. (Actually, SuperClock! was CharityWare: if you wanted to, Steve suggested a donation to The Lucile Salter Packard Childrens' Hospital at Stanford, 725 Welch

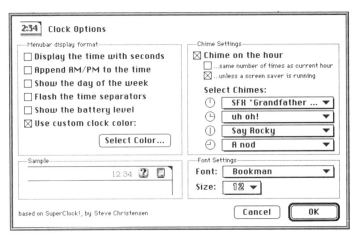

Figure 6-3: Date & Time Clock Options

Road, Palo Alto, CA 94304.) With System 7.5, Apple has included SuperClock as part of the Date & Time settings (see Figure 6-3).

WindowShade

WindowShade (Figure 6-4) was a freeware control panel written by Rob Johnson that Apple licensed for System 7.5. The only difference between the shareware and the 7.5 version is that the shareware version also allowed you to use a single click to hide or show a window (surely this has to qualify as one of Bob LeVitus' *Stupid Mac Tricks:* this meant that trying to select the window would toggle it open and closed).

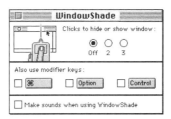

Figure 6-4: WindowShade

Stickies

Stickies is Apple's electronic version of 3M's yellow Post-It™ notes — little notes that you can leave on-screen (Figure 6-5). PowerPC users should avoid the version of Stickies that shipped with System 7.5, there is a fix in the 1.0 update to System 7.5. Stickies expects to find itself inside the Apple Menu Items folder; it won't run from a subfolder (which is where I put most of the Apple's desk accessories)(See Chapter 7, Figure 7-20; this is a technique I use to reduce Apple Menu clutter).

Figure 6-5: Stickies

Updated

Some of the changes in System 7.5 are more evolutionary than others — an improved Find File and QuickTime 2.0 fall into this category.

Improved Find Command

With System 7, Apple gave Mac users a Finder that could actually find things; with System 7.5, they licensed some of the code Bill Monk used to create Find Pro for ZiffNet/Mac. In the Find File dialog box (Figure 6-6), clicking on More Choices expands the dialog box to allow you to add search criteria. Clicking on the Find button gives you Items Found — a listing of what you've found and where it is. What Apple didn't implement from Find Pro is the ability to act on files after you've found them (the Open, Open With..., Show, Get Info, Alias, Copy..., Move..., To Desktop, and Trash buttons in Figure 6-7). By itself, this utility makes signing up for ZiffNet worth it (Find Pro is a ZiffNet exclusive). See Chapter 13 for more file finding utilities.

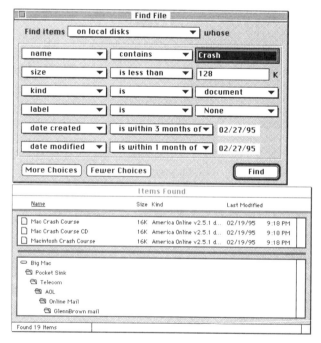

Figure 6-6: Find File

Figure 6-7: Find Pro

QuickTime 2.0
Apple has included version 2.0 of QuickTime with System 7.5.

Compatibility

With System 7.5, Apple has acknowledged that many of us work in cross-platform environments, making it easier than ever to read DOS disks and files on our Macs.

PC Exchange
The first problem in dealing with DOS has always been getting the files into your Mac. Prior to System 7.5, unless you were running Apple File Exchange, then putting a PC disk into your Mac would result in a message asking if you wanted to format the disk. The solution was to buy one of the commercial extensions — Access PC or DOS Mounter — that allowed your Mac to directly read PC disks. For System 7.5, Apple licensed technology

from Insignia Systems (the makers of Access PC) to give us PC Exchange (Figure 6-8).

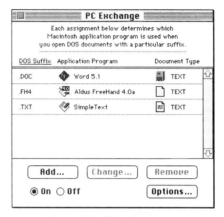

Figure 6-8: PC Exchange

Macintosh Easy Open

Once you've moved files onto your Mac's hard drive, the next step is to find an application to open the document. In many cases, you may have the Mac equivalent (such as Microsoft Word), but if you don't, Easy Open (Figure 6-9) should be able to automatically translate the document into a form that one of your applications can read.

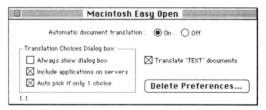

Figure 6-9: Macintosh Easy Open

If you notice that your Mac is rebuilding the desktop every time you start your Mac, Macintosh Easy Open may be the culprit. The cure is to boot once with all extensions except for Easy Open disabled, and allow the desktop rebuild.

MacLink Plus

Also included with System 7.5 is Dataviz' MacLink Plus (Figure 6-10), which includes more translators to help you read documents from Mac or PC applications that you don't have; it requires Macintosh Easy Open to run.

Figure 6-10: MacLinkPlus Setup

For the New User

Apple hasn't forgotten the new user with the System 7.5: Apple Guide is arguably the single best new feature in the upgrade.

Macintosh Guide

The Macintosh Guide (Figure 6-11) is a great tool for new users — even power users can find new tricks hidden in the Guide. The second best part is that it is truly interactive — when you ask for help, it prompts you along the way (note the circle around the current date in Figure 6-12). The best part is when you show it to Windoze users — Bob looks pretty goofy next the Apple Guide, and it is our job as Mac users to point these little things out to the unconverted masses.

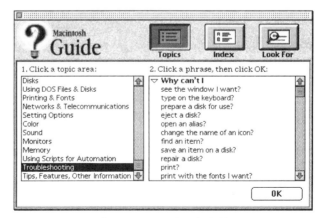

Figure 6-11: Macintosh Guide

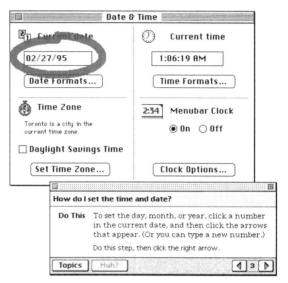

Figure 6-12: Macintosh Guide in action

General Controls

Apple has moved a few things out of the General Controls Control Panel (Date & Time and Desktop Patterns are now separate control panels), and added a few things for the novice, as shown in Figure 6-13.

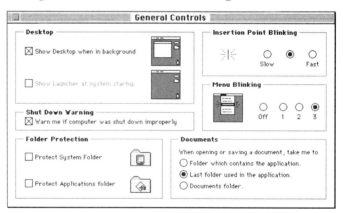

Figure 6-13: General Controls Control Panel

Launcher

Apple's Launcher (Figure 6-14), which was first introduced on the Performa series, allows you simple access to applications, documents, and control panels on your hard drive(s). To install an item, you have to drag an alias of it into the Launcher Items folder within your System folder. Launcher is a great tool for new users, although power users may prefer one of the two products covered later in this chapter (DragStrip and PowerBar Pro).

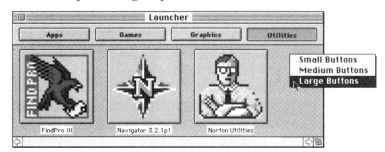

Figure 6-14: Launcher

Apple made major improvements to the Launcher with version 2.7 (included with System 7.5 update 1.0); the biggest is support for drag 'n drop — just drag an item (an application, file, or folder) onto the Launcher, and an alias of it will automatically be put into the Launcher Items folder. To remove an item, just hold down the Option key and drag it out of the Launcher. Buttons are resizable — just hold down the Command key and click on the Launcher to get the pop-up shown in Figure 6-14. If you want to have multiple categories ("apps", "games" etc. as shown in Figure 6-14), just create folders within the Launcher Items folder, and begin the folder name with a bullet character (Option-8). This isn't in the 7.5 manual, but it is in the Apple Guide.

PowerBook

There are a few goodies in System 7.5 for PowerBook owners, too: Control Strip and File Assistant help to make life easier with a small screen. Other improvements include the ability to defer printing or e-mail until you connect, an improved RAM disk, and new command keys for sleep (Shift-Command-zero) and spinning down your hard drive (Shift-Control-Command-zero).

Control Strip

Control Strip (Figure 6-15) is a cool new add-on that Apple started shipping with the 500-series PowerBooks, and have included with System 7.5. Just click on either end to expand the strip, and Option-click to relocate it on your screen. System 7.5 ships with a number of Control Strip modules, there are plenty available as shareware and the latest version of PBTools includes a Control Strip module (see Chapter 18 for descriptions of the shareware Control Strip modules on the CD-ROM). To activate a new module, all you have to do is drop it into the Control Strip Modules folder in your System folder and restart your PowerBook. For more on Control Strips and PowerBooks, turn to Chapter 18.

Figure 6-15: Control Strip

File Assistant

System 7.5 includes Apple's File Assistant utility for synchronizing files or folders between your PowerBook and desktop Macs — see Chapter 3 for details.

If You Need Them...

There are some features of System 7.5 that not all users will need to install right away. As I mentioned at the beginning of the chapter, QuickDraw and PowerTalk come with stiff memory requirements (8 or 16 megabytes for 680x0 Macs and PowerPCs, respectively), and have not yet been widely accepted. Other new features, like ColorSync and MacTCP, also have specific requirements.

QuickDraw GX

QuickDraw GX is a new screen imaging technology that offers a number of features: support for extended character sets, drag 'n drop printing, the ability to create stand-alone documents, and support for additional printing capabilities. The downside is that there are very few applications that support QuickDraw GX; unless you have one of them, I'd recommend against it for now.

PowerTalk

PowerTalk is Apple's new communications technology that integrates a number of telecommunications features into the operating system. Features include a Key Chain to access network servers and other services, a mailbox for all incoming and outgoing mail (fax, voice, e-mail, and documents), Catalogs to store information about users and groups, and digital signatures (DigiSign). A digital signature isn't an electronic version of yoru signature, but an encryption means that ensures that documents that you "sign" cannot be modified, and can only be read by their intended recipients.

ColorSync

ColorSync maintains consistent colors between your monitor, scanner, and printer. Unless you are involved in color publishing, you're not likely to need it.

MacTCP

Unless you're attached to a TCP/IP (Transmission Control Protcol/Internet Protocol) network, you're unlikely to need MacTCP. Those who have a dial-up connection to the Internet also need MacTCP.

System 7.5 Update 1.0

If you're using System 7.5, make sure to get update 1.0, which updates you to System 7.5.1. The 1.0 Update is free, and is available from on-line services and your local Mac user group. After installing the update, the first thing you'll notice is Apple's new Mac™ OS logo (see Figure 6-17).

What do you get with this upgrade? Lots of bug fixes and enhancements, including:
- The Power key on your keyboard can now be used to turn your Mac off as well as on, but don't worry: you get a chance to change your mind (see Figure 6-16).

Figure 6-16: 7.5.1's Power key dialog

Figure 6-17: Starting up with Apple's new Mac™ OS logo

- Improvements to Apple Guide, Apple Menu Items, File Sharing, General Controls, Launcher, Macintosh Easy Open, and WindowShade.
- Updates and fixes for SimpleText, Find File, Jigsaw Puzzle, PowerTalk, MacTCP, and LaserWriter.
- One of the major pains with System 7.5 is that the installation automatically installed foreign keyboards, and a keyboard shortcut (Command-Option-Spacebar) would switch you to a foreign keyboard. Keyboard version 7.5.1 has the keyboard shortcut disabled by default (you can still turn it on if you want, by selecting the option in the control panel).

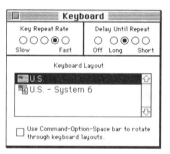

Figure 6-18: Keyboard version 7.5.1

- Stickies 1.0.1 fixes a problem that could cause a crash when it opened with collapsed notes windows (if you had a Power Mac with

RamDoubler installed, opening Stickies with a collapsed note guaranteed a crash).
- PowerBook 150 Update extension, EM Sound Update, and Mount IDE Drive were all replaced with 7.5.1.
- Power Mac improvements, including an updated Threads Library (for developers), updated Math Functions Library (improves math performance), and native QuickDraw.
- specific fixes for PowerBook Duo docks, 150 and 500 models, Quadra 700, Quadra 840AV and Macs with IDE drives installed.

System 7.5.1 Problems
Along with the improvements come a number of problems, including:
- MacTools TrashBack (see Chapter 16) needs to be updated to version 4.0.2 or better.
- Norton Partition 2.0 (formerly part of Norton Utilities, now discontinued) does not work with System 7.5.1.
- Files on your CD-ROM may disappear with file sharing and RAM Doubler 1.5.1 installed; the cure is to upgrade to RAM Doubler 1.5.2 (an updater is on the CD-ROM).
- StuffIt SpaceServer 3.5 needs to load after General Controls 7.5.1, otherwise files may become invisible.

Shareware

There's not a lot of System 7.5-specific shareware available yet, but there are a few gems on the CD-ROM.

AliasDragger
Leonard Rosenthol
Aladdin Systems
165 Westridge Drive
Watsonville, CA 95076
Telephone: 408 761-6200
Fax: 408 761-6206
AOL/AppleLink: ALADDIN
CompuServe: 75300,1666
Internet: aladdin@well.com
AliasDragger is freeware

Apparently, System 7 Pro introduced a number of undocumented new features. One was the ability to create an alias by Control-dragging a file. The only problem is that you need an extension (like this one) to enable the feature. Once installed all you have to do is hold down the Control key and drag a file to wherever you want the alias. Once you've installed and used this, you'll never go back.

AETracker
C.K. Haun
RavenWare Software
22045 McClellan Road
Cupertino, CA 95014
AppleLink: C.K.HAUN
CompuServe: 75300,1001
GEnie: C.Haun1
AETracker is Fredware

AppleEvents were a great addition to the Macintosh System — finally a means to automate applications externally, with power that equals or exceeds the DOS batch file capability. Only one problem — how do you tell exactly what's going on? AETracker (Figure 6-19) is a fully configurable tool that logs AppleEvent activity on your system.

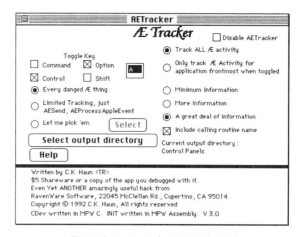

Figure 6-19: AETracker Control Panel

Jon's Commands
Jon Pugh
1861 Landings Drive
Mountain View, CA 94043
Internet: jonpugh@netcom.com
Jon's Commands is freeware.

Jon began using a 512K Mac in the hospital after a car crash and hasn't stopped since. He's written a lot of freeware and shareware programs and gotten rid of the 512 after several upgrades. He's an Apple alumnus and has been involved with AppleScript programs lately. His real wish is to be a ski bum, though. He's basically a Mac hack since the 512 days; an Apple alumnus who has worked at a number of other places. He's programmed in just about everything, although he likes Object Pascal and C++ most. He describes himself as large, loud, obnoxious, a dad, and a husband. He has only two hobbies; skiing and hacking. He loves them both almost as much as he loves his family. If you want to find more of his stuff, check out his Web page for a list of his software: ftp://ftp.netcom.com/pub/jo/jonpugh/homepage.html.

Jon's Commands is an AppleScript Scripting Addition that gives you a great starting point if you want to learn AppleScript. To examine any of these commands, just drag it onto the Script Editor; to install one, just drop it into the Scripting Additions folder. The Scripting Additions folder is in your Extensions folder, which is in your System folder. Complete documentation is on the CD-ROM.

One of the nice touches in the About This Macintosh box was the fact that it identified your Mac, and even showed an iconic representation of it. Unfortunately, this somehow got lost in the 7.5 upgrade; both Mac Identifier and WhoAmI? will fix the problem for you.

Mac Identifier
Maurice Volaski
8201 Henry Ave Apt J23,
Philadelphia, PA 19128-2216
America Online: fluxsftwre
Internet: volaski@contra.med.buffalo.edu
Mac Identifier is freeware.

WhoAmI?
Jonathan Jacobs
2374 Euclid Heights, Blvd. #407
Cleveland Heights, OH 44106-2745
Telephone: 216 368-3574 (lab)
Internet: jxj24@po.cwru.edu
WhoAmI? is freeware.

Commercial Utilities

One of my favorite techniques used to be to leave a collection of aliases on my desktop for drag 'n drop launching: Word to open text documents, Photoshop to open graphics, and ResEdit to open just about anything else — I even left an alias of the Apple Menu Items folder on my desktop so that I could add items to the Apple Menu easily. This solution has its drawbacks: your screen can quickly get cluttered, you can't attach documents, and worst of all, a desktop cleanup could mess up your carefully arranged icons. There are two commercial utilities that I've just started using that make life a lot simpler for me: PowerBar Pro and DragStrip.

PowerBar Pro
Trilobyte Software
6982 Devon Drive
Middletown, Ohio 45044
Telephone: 513 777-6641
Fax: 513 779-7760
America Online: Trylobyte
AppleLink: flying.phone
CompuServe: 73740,2472
Suggested retail: $25.00

About two years ago, I was sitting in a restaurant with Cliff Joyce. He and I started discussing the design of a new Finder replacement/desktop launch utility that his company (Dubl-Click) was considering. I spent the next few hours giving him a laundry list of suggestions. About a month later, he showed me the beta of Scott Johnson's PowerBar, with almost every one of those suggestions incorporated! Dubl-Click never did publish PowerBar (a mistake if you ask me), but, by the time you read this, Trilobyte will have published the newly updated PowerBar Pro.

PowerBar Pro (Figure 6-20) is a combination of an optional extension and a startup application. What you get are two bars: a Launch Bar and a Process Bar. You can drop documents onto Process Bar or Launch Bar applications to open them, and click on an application in the Process Bar to switch to it. The Launch Bar is the component I use the most; dragging a folder, document, control panel or application is all it takes to configure it, and you can have multiple Launch Bars. PowerBar Pro ships with a set of twenty-five applets (see Figure 6-21), icons that can be dragged to your Launch Bar for instant access to various functions (sound volume, sleep, empty trash, etc.).

Figure 6-20: PowerBar Pro

Figure 6-21: PowerBar Pro's commands

DragStrip™
Natural Intelligence, Inc.
725 Concord Ave.
Cambridge, MA 02138
Telephone: 617 876-7680 x1203
Toll-free: 800 999-4649
Fax: 617 492-7425
America Online: ChrisEvans
Internet: evans@natural.com
Suggested retail: $39.95

Christopher Evans is Director of Software Development at Natural Intelligence in Cambridge. He is also author of QuickCode Pro, the acclaimed procedure editor enhancement for 4th Dimension and DragStrip, the ultimate desktop and file organization utility for Macintosh, both of which are available from Natural Intelligence.

DragStrip is very similar to PowerBar, but there are two big differences. Where PowerBar has twenty-five custom commands, DragStrip supports additions (it ships with six, including the Compact Disk Player is shown in Figure 6-22). DragStrip creates pop-up menus of documents you've launched by dropping them onto it — I like this unique feature, although I have to admit I'd like it better if the pop-up list included all files opened.

Figure 6-22: DragStrip

Which is the best? Hard to say; I'd like to see a combination of Launcher's groups, PowerBar's commands, and DragStrip's pop-up document lists.

Interview: Bob LeVitus

I've known Bob for about 6 years; ever since I started speaking at Macworld Expos, we've been paired up on panels. When I was working for Maxa in California, Bob asked if I'd like to write a book with him. The book, *Customizing Your Mac for Fun & Productivity* (published by Brady Books in 1993) was an outgrowth of the *Customizing Your Mac* panels that we did at Macworlds. Using CompuServe, we wrote the book together — Bob in Texas, and me in L.A (Bob's CompuServe address is 76004,2076). Bob has recently started working for Power Computing as a product evangelist.

How long have you been in the computer business and how did you get started?

I test–drove a Mac 512 in 1985 and loved it but waited until 1986 to buy my first one, a Mac Plus which was delivered on the first day Pluses were available. I paid full retail for it — $2495 if I recall correctly. I was running a market research company out of my spare bedroom when I pitched a project to the publisher of MACazine, Chuck Abrams. He didn't want the research but he hired me as Editor-in-Chief. And that, in a nutshell, is how I got my start in the computer business.

What is your educational background — are you formally trained, or did you teach yourself?

I received a B.S. in Marketing from California State University in 1977. (FWIW: I flunked FORTRAN Programming the first time I took it!) From 1977 to 1986 I worked in marketing, first at an advertising agency in Los Angeles (Kresser/Craig), then as Director of Marketing for a pay television outfit (SelecTV), and finally as part-owner of a market research concern (L & J Research). I was fascinated by computers the entire time but never considered owning one until I saw the Mac. As far as the Mac goes, I'm totally self-trained. When I first became interested I joined my local user group (LAMG) and spent a lot of time online in CompuServe's MAUG forums; between the two, I learned a lot.

What products (including books and magazines) have you been involved in?

- *Webmaster Macintosh (w/Jeff Evans) (AP Professional) 1995*
- *Webmaster Windows (w/Jeff Evans) (AP Professional) 1995*
- *Macintosh System 7.5 for Dummies (IDG Books) 1994*
- *Guide to the Macintosh Underground (w/Michael Fraase) (Hayden) 1993*
- *Customizing Your Mac (w/Glenn Brown) (Brady) 1993*
- *Dr. Macintosh's Guide to the On-Line Universe (w/Andy Ihnatko) (Addison-Wesley) 1992*
- *Dr. Macintosh, Second Edition: How to Become a Macintosh Power User (w/Laurie Miller Love) (Addison-Wesley) 1992*
- *Stupid Windows Tricks (w/Ed Tittel) (Addison-Wesley) 1992*
- *Stupid Beyond Belief PC Tricks (w/Ed Tittel) (Addison-Wesley) 1992*
- *Son of Stupid Mac Tricks (Addison-Wesley) 1991*
- *Stupid PC Tricks (w/Ed Tittel) (Addison-Wesley) 1991*
- *Marvelous Macintosh Games (Prima) 1991*
- *Phenomenal PC Games (w/Ed Tittel) (Prima) 1991*
- *Stupid Mac Tricks (Addison-Wesley) 1990*
- *Dr. Macintosh, 1st Edition (Addison-Wesley — out of print) 1989*
- *MACazine (1987-1989)*

Software (HyperCard Stackware) projects
- *Macintosh Bible: STAX Edition 1989*
- *STAX Sound Effects Studio 1989*
- *STAX Helper 1989*

Please describe the equipment you use (what computer, how much RAM, etc.)

Power Macintosh 8100/80; 72MB RAM; 500MB Apple (Connor) internal hard disk; 4GB APS (Micropolis) external hard disk; APS (Toshiba) quad-speed CD ROM; APS (Deltis) magneto-optical 230 cartridge drive; APS (WangDat) DAT tape drive; US Robotics Courier HST v.32bis modem; Kensington Turbo Mouse

Trackball; a pair of 17" (Digital) Trinitron monitors; Connectix QuickCam; LaCie SilverScanner II; NewGen TurboPS/400p printer.

Do you have other interests you'd like mentioned in a bio?
Rock and roll music; playing my Stratocaster; travel.

What do like to do when you're not writing books?
Read murder mysteries (someday I'll write one!), play with my kids and dogs, go to movies, attend live music shows, eat fine food, drink fine beer.

Where do you live, are you married with children, how old are you, (etc.)
I just turned 40, and live in central Texas by choice, having (thankfully) fled Los Angeles in 1989. I have been married since 1984 to the wonderful Lisa LeVitus (nee Satenspiel). I have two wonderful kids: Allison (age 6) and Jacob (age 3). We also have three totally cool dogs: Max (a Vizsla), Sadie (another Vizsla), and Briar Rose aka Rosie (a Welch Springer Spaniel puppy). (Don't know what a Vizsla is? There's a great picture of one in the New Grolier Multimedia Encyclopedia. Check it out!)

Do you think there are compelling reasons for Mac users to upgrade to System 7.5?
Yes. It's the most stable version and it offers many valuable extras, including Macintosh Easy Open, PC Exchange, AppleScript, a better Apple menu, a better help system, Stickies, and more. It's well worth the cost.

What are your thoughts on PowerTalk and GX?
I don't use them at present but reserve the right to do so someday. If third-party developers create compelling applications that use these technologies, I'll turn them back on. Until then, they are turned off on my Mac (using Conflict Catcher II, of course).

What should users do to reduce the "bomb effect" on their Macs?
Increase the RAM allocation of most programs, and only run control panels and extensions you can't live without.

How many extensions are you running, and when was the last time your Mac crashed?
Right this second my Extensions folder contains 91 items, though many of them —

like shared libraries, printer drivers, and Comm Toolbox items — are inert and don't load at startup. My Control Panels folder contains 42 more items, all of which load at startup. Put another way, on my 17" monitor I see 2.5 rows of icons at startup. My system software — which includes the RAM consumed by extensions, and control panels — requires about 9 megabytes of RAM.

The last time I crashed was about an hour ago. I frequently go an entire day without a single crash or freeze. (Did I say frequently? "Every so often" or "occasionally" would be more accurate.)

Do you think the protected mode offered in Copland will alleviate the problems of conflicting extensions?

I sure hope so. I'll be writing Macintosh System 8 for Dummies *later this year so I'll know before most people. I'll let you know...*

What is your favorite piece of software? hardware?

Software: Toss up between Now Utilities and QuicKeys. Both save me a ton of time and effort every time I turn on my Mac. Hardware: Power Mac 8100/80. (Power Macs rock! If you're considering one, go for it! You won't be sorry!)

How about a Top 10 list of extensions?

10. Popup Folder
9. Reminder (Now Up to Date)
8. QuickContact (Now Contact)
7. QuickTime
6. Conflict Catcher II
5. Thunder 7
4. Now WYSIWYG Menus
3. Now SuperBoomerang
2. Now Menus
1. QuicKeys

Tools of the Trade

Compression
Diagnostics
Protection
Shareware Utilities
Outstanding Authors

7

Compression

CN U RD THS (Can you read this?) Compression software is easy to understand — it removes redundant, duplicate information, reducing the amount of space a file takes, and puts the redundant information back when you need it. However, before we look at some specific programs, let's have look at some of the terminology involved. The language of compression is full of jargon, since it was invented by serious nerds. You don't need to understand it, but you do need to know what the words you'll come across mean.

- **Lossy vs. lossless compression** — Lossless compression means compressing and restoring files where both the original and restored files are identical. Lossy compression involves some degradation of the file when it is restored. Using lossy compression on a 24-bit graphics file can result in a file significantly smaller than the original, with an almost imperceptible loss of picture quality. As the amount of lossy compression increases, tell-tale banding of color (particularly in gradient fills) starts to appear in the graphic. The best use for lossy compression is for previewing or cataloging high-resolution graphics files, where the larger, high-resolution file is stored off-line.

- **Archival compression** is designed for just that, the archiving or long-term, remote storage of files. Much of the first compression software was written for archiving and backup. The other common use of archival compression is for cutting telecommunications costs by reducing the size of files for transmission. The downside of archival compression is that you need to run decompression software to expand a file before you can use it. Shareware versions of two of the best — StuffIt and Compact Pro — are on the CD-ROM.

- **On-the-fly compression** solves the problem by automatically expanding files as they are needed, and recompressing them when your Mac is idle, using a software mechanism not unlike that used by a screen saver. On the CD-ROM is a demo version of Now Utilities, which includes Now's compression utility QuickFiler. I have to admit to a bias in this field: I've been a beta tester for DiskDoubler since

137

version 1, and I'm proud to count Lloyd Chambers among my friends. The compression software I use to give me more space is the combination of AutoDoubler and DiskDoubler. As with all products in this category, there is a price to pay for the increase in available hard drive space: a performance hit that is inversely proportional to the speed of your Mac. The faster your Mac, the faster on-the-fly compression utilities can work. I have found the slowdown to be noticeable on 68030 or lesser machines — for 68040s and Power PCs, the speed loss is minimal.

- **Driver level compression** operates at a lower level than the other programs in this category, by compressing all files at the driver level. Basically, this means that these programs require that you reformat your hard drive to use them. The downside is that when things go wrong with your hard drive, this software adds a layer of complexity for your disk utility to unravel. I had some bad experiences with driver level compression (Golden Triangle's Times2, which is no longer available), but I have no reason to believe those problems exist with the Mac version of the most popular PC compression utility (Stacker).

Filename Extensions

I know, I know— Macs don't (normally) have to conform to the DOS file-naming conventions (eight alphanumeric characters, a period, and a three-character extension). However, many of the services we find Mac files on (BBSs, the Internet, commercial services) are run on computers other than Macs, so compressed files follow the following naming conventions (you may see these as all caps, there's no difference to the software):

Extension	Format
.arc	Arc (PC, Atari compression format)
.bin	MacBinary
.cpt	Compact Pro archive
.gz	GZIP (UNIX compression format)
.hqx	BinHex file
.pit	PackIt archive
.pkg	AppleLink (also Newton file)

.sea. . . . . Self-extracting archive
.sit . . . . StuffIt archive
.uu . . . . UUEncoded (Internet)(UUEncoded is also a Unix
format; it just happens to be the one most commonly
used on the Internet.)
.z . . . . (UNIX compression format)
.zip . . . . Zip (PC Compression format)

Compact Pro
Bill Goodman
Cyclos
P.O. Box 31417
San Francisco, CA 94131-0417
CompuServe: 71101,204
Shareware fee: $25.00

Bill is an electrical engineer (he did some chip design at Intel back in the mid-70s, and worked at Tandem Computers, and also at Sun Microsystems when it was first starting up). He has been writing software since 1976; shareware Mac software has been a full-time job since 1990. His software is written predominantly in C, although he has converted some parts to assembly language.

Compact Pro started life as Compactor; somewhere along the road it was changed to Compact Pro (Figure 7-1). "Pro" is a good description of the shareware found on the CD-ROM, too: there are English, French, German, and Japanese versions, plus a utility called ExtractorPC, which allows you to

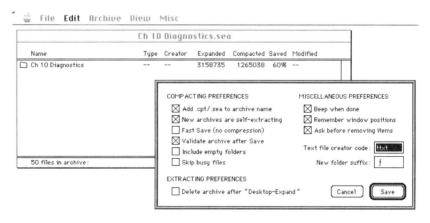

Figure 7-1: Compact Pro

expand compressed Mac files on a PC. There is also the Smaller Installer Toolkit, a tool for developers to make their own installers with compression. Compact Pro offers compression speed and efficiency as good as or better than the commercial competition. The current version (1.5.1) is a Fat binary, with native support for Power Macs and 680x0 Macs.

Other features include the segmenting of files (this allows you to have large files or archives split into smaller pieces, usually floppy-sized, that can later be recombined back to recreate the original), encryption (the scrambling of files so they can only be read or used by those with the correct password; available only to registered users because the U.S. government forbids the export of most encryption technology outside of Canada and the USA), support for self-extracting files, the ability to work in the background, and the ability to encode and decode BinHex4 files. Some networks encode non-text Mac files using BinHex4 so that they can be transmitted and stored as text files. If you are on the receiving end of such a file, all you'll see on screen is apparently random characters. Open your telecommunications data file in a word processor, select the characters (they usually begin and end with a colon), save the file in text format, and then decode the result with Compact Pro. It's surprising to see what looks like garbage text turn into an application, complete with custom icon!

Compression is usually an essential part of backing up. Selecting "Add only if modified on or after: date" in the Add dialog provides a simple means of using Compact Pro to perform an incremental backup, by only adding files to an archive that have been changed since the date of your last backup.

StuffIt Lite
165 Westridge Drive
Watsonville, CA 95076
Telephone: 408 761-6200
Fax: 408 761-6206
AOL/AppleLink: ALADDIN
CompuServe: 75300,1666
eWorld/GEnie: AladdinSys
Internet: aladdin@well.com
Shareware fee: $30.00

Raymond Lau originally wrote StuffIt as a shareware program; Aladdin Systems still makes shareware and demo versions of their software available. StuffIt Lite (Figure 7-2) is anything but; it and the two companion programs on the CD-ROM offer formidable compression tools. Features of StuffIt Lite include acceleration for the Power Mac, drag 'n drop support for those with System 7.5 or better, support for AppleScript, BinHex, and self-extracting archives, file segmenting, and encryption (for registered users only).

The Palette (see Figure 7-2) gives direct access to the most commonly used functions, and even supports drag 'n drop. The Add Match dialog (see Figure 7-3) goes beyond that offered by Compact Pro, giving you greater control of what files should be added to a backup archive.

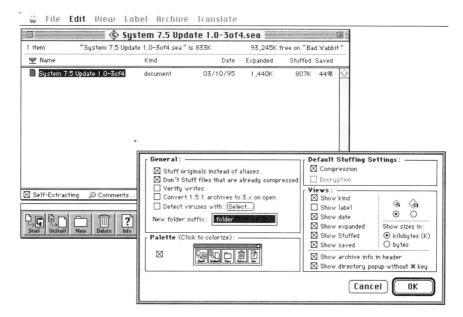

Figure 7-2: StuffIt Lite

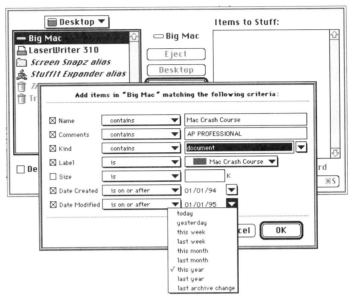

Figure 7-3: StuffIt Lite Add Match dialog

DropStuff
Aladdin Systems
(see above for address information)

Shareware fee: $30.00

Confused by the interface? Want things as simple as they can be? DropStuff and StuffIt Expander make things as easy as physically possible. Just drop a

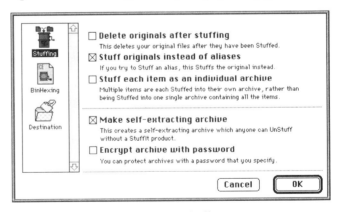

Figure 7-4: DropStuff

file, files, or folder onto DropStuff to compress it (see Figure 7-4). The companion program for expansion is StuffIt Expander.

StuffIt Expander
Aladdin Systems
(see above for address information)

StuffIt Expander is freeware, DropStuff with Expander Enhancer is shareware ($30.00)

Drop just about any compressed file (or files) onto StuffIt Expander to expand it (see Figure 7-5). I leave an alias of StuffIt Expander on my desktop for easy access — even better if you're on-line: you can tell StuffIt Expander to "watch" your downloads folder, so that downloaded files can be automatically decompressed for you. What's the difference between the freeware and shareware versions? StuffIt Expander expands StuffIt, Compact Pro, BinHex, and MacBinary files — Expander Enhancer (the shareware version) adds the ability to expand PC formats (.zip and .arc), AppleLink packages, and Unix formats (GZIP, Unix Compress, and UUEncoded). If you're expanding groups of files, be aware that neither version will automatically expand all self-expanding archives or DiskDoubler archives.

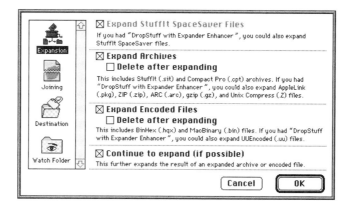

Figure 7-5: StuffIt Expander

Norton DiskDoubler Pro

Symantec
10201 Torre Avenue
Cupertino, CA 95014
Telephone: 408 253-9600
Tech Support: 503 465-8420 (free for 90 days)
America Online Keyword: SYMANTEC
CompuServe: GO SYMANTEC
Suggested retail: $109.00

About five years ago, I phoned a little software company in California to order a program called Partner. It allowed those of us who were impatient for System 7 to edit graphics from within DTP applications, maintaining a link not unlike Publish & Subscribe. The company was Salient Software, and the guy I was talking to (Terry Morse) convinced me to try their latest: DiskDoubler. Well, it wasn't very long before I figured out that the star program was DiskDoubler — this was the first program that allowed you to leave files compressed on your hard drive, and have them decompress automatically when you opened them. I became a beta tester, and somewhere along the road, Terry's partner and the DiskDoubler author (Lloyd Chambers) became a friend. Two years later Salient came out with another big step forward: AutoDoubler, which automatically compressed files when your Mac was idle. In 1992, Lloyd and Terry became rich overnight, by selling the company they had financed with their credit cards to Fifth Generation, and in 1993 Symantec acquired Fifth Generation, having previously acquired Peter Norton Computing.

Enough history — what does DiskDoubler Pro do? It is a set of three main utilities: AutoDoubler, CopyDoubler, and DiskDoubler. DiskDoubler (see

Figure 7-6: DiskDoubler's Menu

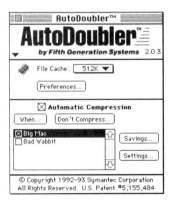

Figure 7-7: AutoDoubler Control Panel

Figure 7-6) allows you to compress or expand files, create archives, create self-expanding archives, and split files or archives.

AutoDoubler is activated the same way a screen saver is — it waits until your Mac is idle, then starts compressing files. (I'm aware that programs like StuffIt SpaceSaver and others provide similar functionality, but DiskDoubler Pro is the one I know, use, and trust, and it is my book!) In many cases, AutoDoubler compressed files open as quickly as their uncompressed counterparts, so the speed hit is virtually unnoticeable, and the benefits are obvious: more space available on your hard drive. The AutoDoubler Control Panel (see Figure 7-7) allows you to specify how long AutoDoubler should wait until it starts doing its thing (When...) and which files shouldn't be compressed. Preferences allow you to specify whether or not backup, modem, or e-mail programs should send files in compressed format, and whether or not DiskDoubler should show a "DD" on icons to indicate that a file is compressed. Clicking on Savings... tells AutoDoubler to calculate the savings gained by using AutoDoubler on your hard drive (see Figure 7-8).

Figure 7-8: AutoDoubler Savings

DiskDoubler Pro ships with DiskTester, a utility for testing your hard drive's integrity before you start using compression, and AutoDoubler Internal Compressor, which allows resource compression of files on your hard drive, including files within your System folder. The advantage of resource compression is that these files don't need to be expanded to run, so they usually open faster. There are a few applications (QuarkXPress and MacEKG are the only two I know of) that won't run when internally compressed.

Figure 7-9 shows AutoDoubler Internal Compressor in action, indicating AIC compressed files with a bullet (•). The crossed out files are ones that AIC will not compress, usually because the file is already resource-compressed.

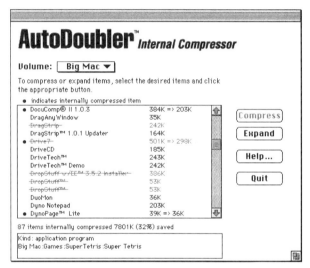

Figure 7-9: AutoDoubler Internal Compressor

  A note for PowerPC users: you shouldn't use AIC to compress native applications — not only will you not save any space, but the resulting file will likely crash. (PowerPC users can run AIC compressed 680x0 files without problems.) Lloyd tells me that a future release will fix the problem by preventing AIC from compressing native applications.

Interview: Lloyd Chambers

About five years ago, I called a little company in California to order their new program, a DTP utility called Partner. Terry Morse convinced me to also try their new program, DiskDoubler, and it quickly became evident to me that this was Salient's star program. I volunteered to become a beta tester and have tested every major release since. I met the author, Lloyd Chambers, after one of Steve and my Macworld sessions. Lloyd is one of the genuinely nice people in the Macintosh software business; I'm proud to call him a friend

How long have you been programming and how did you get started?

My first experience with a computer was as a freshman in high school using a Dec PDP 8 minicomputer. It had dual 8" floppy drives, a "dumb terminal" screen, and a line printer attached to it. I learned to program it using Basic. Fortunately, the school obtained some Apple I computers with 32K of RAM. I learned to program these, too, with Basic, but also learned how to program them in assembly language. I remember one program I wrote that inverted the screen as fast as it could. The Apple was so slow in graphics mode (even in assembly code) that you could watch the screen invert. It was a rather bizarre display—the screen was not mapped to memory contiguously as the Macs are today; adjacent portions of memory were mapped about 10 lines apart on screen, leading to a levelor blind effect as the screen inverted. I become so fascinated by that I quit the school band, in which I played the trumpet, and devoted that time to learning and playing with the school computers.

As a freshman at Stanford, I took a few computer courses which used the school's Dec 20 machines. These were big mainframe computers with hundreds of dumb terminals attached. Although much more powerful than an Apple, they were so sluggish in response that they were really a let down. Fortunately, I become friends through the Stanford Photography Club with Glenn Kroeger, a Phd student in charge of several VAX Unix computers. I obtained accounts on these machines and soon began learning Unix. Not long thereafter, I took a job as a computer operator at a company called Octal (not Octel). There, I backed up and maintained VMS and Unix systems, and learned much more about these systems.

When Apple introduced the Macintosh, I was tempted to buy one, but the high price, coupled with the realization that it was inadequate for my needs prevented me from buying it. I did buy a Macintosh when the Mac II was introduced. Stanford employed a lottery system to determine the place in line for delivery. I chose a reasonable number, but still had to wait for several months. A color monitor, which I had ordered, was in such short supply, that Apple gave everyone who had ordered them a gray-scale monitor, and months later, supplied the color one. It was a good deal; I got to keep both of them. Too bad Apple doesn't use this philosophy today!

My introduction to the Mac rapidly converted me to a Macophile. It was so much easier to use, and was actually faster compiling code than the Unix machines and Sun workstations I was using (due to Lightspeed C now known as THINK C). Unix boxes rapidly began to look like dinosaurs to me and I began to learn more and more about the Mac. I made a job switch in 1986 to a startup company called Mansfield Systems. I worked on and off there to pay my way through school, going to school one quarter, working the next, sometimes doing both. At Mansfield systems I learned a tremendous amount about programming, as well as witnessing the pitfalls of software development which caused Mansfield Systems to go bankrupt in November, 1989. This experience proved invaluable at Salient...

How did Salient get started?

Salient Software was formed in November 1989 with myself, Terry Morse and a third person who left shortly thereafter. Salient's initial product was Partner, a utility to make it easier to insert and edit graphics in DTP packages. It was interesting enough to establish relationships with vendors, but never became very popular. In January of 1990, I was struck by the crude and frustrating interface of the then-popular StuffIt program and it was then that the important thought came to me: compressing files should be no harder than selecting them in the Finder and choosing a menu command. That was the genesis of the DiskDoubler idea. I was very excited about the idea; Terry was less so, so we initially decided to offer it as shareware. That lasted about two weeks, as encouragement from others and my increasing excitement about the idea caused us to work full time on that idea. We worked hard, and DiskDoubler 1.0 was a smash hit at the March, 1990 MacWorld Expo in San Francisco. In retrospect, this was the only time MacWorld Expo had ever been held in March, and it coincided perfectly with our release of DiskDoubler 1.0 in late February. We sold about 350 copies there, a huge number (to us) which replenished our now flagging bank accounts. Our main source of funds, VISA, was becoming difficult what with credit limits and 19% interest.

What products did Salient release?

DiskDoubler became our bread and butter product, and we discontinued Partner later that year. In May of 1990 we formed a corporation, and Martin Mazner, former editor of MacUser, and Guy Kawasaki, Mac guru, joined our board of directors and also invested in the company. This infusion of cash and experience was crucial in our success.

DiskDoubler went through numerous, rapid revisions: 1.0, 1.1, 2.0, 3.0, 3.1, 3.2, 4.0, 4.1 and today stands at 4.1.1 as Symantec Norton DiskDoubler Pro. Our introduction of AutoDoubler in January, 1992, turned a hot product into a red-hot one and accelerated our sales dramatically.

We agreed to sell Salient Software to Fifth Generation Systems and the sale was made on June 29, 1992. At that time, we had 13 employees and were selling around 8000 copies a month. Fifth Generation Systems was later acquired by Symantec Corporation on Oct 4, 1993. Today, I work for Symantec as part of the Peter Norton Group. I continue to work on the DiskDoubler/AutoDoubler products, but also work on Norton Utilities/Mac.

What is your educational background — are you formally trained, or did you teach yourself?

I majored in Mathematical and Computer Science at Stanford University, concentrating on Computer Science.

What language(s) do you write in?

I write in C, C++ and assembly. Most of my work has been done in C. Today, most of it is done in C++.

What software tools do you use?

I use MetroWerks CodeWarrior for PowerMac code, and THINK C for 68K code. I also use Resourcer and Macsbug.

Please describe your computer equipment.

My home computer is a PowerMac 8100/100 32/1000 CD with a 16" color monitor. Prior to that, I had a Quadra 700 24/1000. My work computer, which is feeling a bit pokey, is a Quadra 950 64/1000 with a 21" color monitor.

What do like to do when you're not programming?

My favorite activites are mountain biking, driving my BMW M5 on the racetrack, and gardening.

Where do you live, are you married with children, (etc.)

I live in the Bay area and am married, with 3 cats and 2 dogs.

Tell me about your patents.

One patent has been issued for the "AD 1" method used in DiskDoubler. Another patent will be issued soon for the "AD 2" method. Two others are pending.

What is your favorite piece of software (excluding that written by you or your company...)

Dunno. Myst, I suppose.

Comment on the pros and cons of file and disk level compression techniques.

1. *choice versus all of it: with file level compression you can choose which files get compressed and which don't. If you don't want or need everything compressed, you don't have the overhead of waiting.*

2. *ability to transmit/store/share files: with disk level compression, you cannot shrink a file for transmission by modem or to store it on a floppy, or to back it up. You still need a file level compressor for these things*

3. *speed. Both methods can be faster or slower than working with uncompressed data. In general, however, file level compression is faster because changing a file usually transforms it first to an uncompressed form which can be accessed more quickly; with disk level compression, everything has to be compressed whenever the data is written*

4. *safety: both methods have their drawbacks. File level compressors can have some compatibility problems, driver level compressors make it more difficult to recover a disk if even a small part is damaged.*

5. *convenience: you don't have to do anything special to use a file level compressor, even on a network or floppy disk. Driver level compressors force you to reformat the drive before using it.*

Describe some of the safety features incorporated into DiskDoubler Pro.

1. *read-after write verify: data that is written to disk is read back and compared to the original. If it's not the same, the operation is halted;*

2. *temporary files: all operations use a temporary file so that if the power fails or the machine were to crash, the original file is unaffected;*

3. *checksums. A checksum is kept on the file. If it is damaged, the damage can be detected and reported.*

8 Diagnostics

So how do you find out what's going wrong with your Mac, and how do you report your Mac's configuration to the technical support person you're talking to, who just happens to be 2,000 miles and two time zones away? In this chapter, we'll look at some of the diagnostic tools available, including tools to help you decipher error messages, perform benchmark testing, gather System information, and tech tools, for those who really want to get "under the hood."

Deciphering Error Messages

Just what is a "-17" error, anyway? The error messages on the Mac can be cryptic, to put it mildly. Fortunately, there is help: on the CD-ROM are two tools, one freeware and one shareware, designed to help you understand just what those messages mean.

Easy Errors
Dave Rubinic
1315 Pieffers Lane
Oberlin, PA 17113-1016
America Online: DaveR9
Internet: udrubini@mcs.drexel.edu
Easy Errors is freeware

Easy Errors (Figure 8-1) is certainly that — a simple freeware application that lists both Macintosh and Newton error messages. Just type in the error code to see Apple's description for the code.

Figure 8-1: Easy Errors

MacErrors

Marty Wachter
2107 Sulgrave Avenue
Baltimore, MD 21209
America Online: AFA Marty
Internet: mrw@falconmicro.com
MacErrors is Boloware

Figure 8-2: MacErrors

MacErrors (Figure 8-2) provides a simple lookup mechanism for Macintosh error codes (now if someone could just tell us what the explanations mean…).

Benchmarking

A *benchmark* is a standard test that can be performed (in this case, on your Mac) to determine relative performance. Here are a couple of tools for benchmarking.

MacEKG

MicroMat Computer Systems
7075 Redwood Boulevard
Novato, CA 94945
Telephone: 415 898-6227
Toll-free: 800 829-6227
Technical Support: 415 898-2935
Fax: 415 897-3901
America Online: MicroMat
AppleLink: MicroMatComp
CompuServe: 71333,166
eWorld: MicroMat
Suggested retail: $150.00

MacEKG is a utility that can perform hardware diagnostics on your Mac at startup or on demand. What makes MacEKG unique is that fact that it can log the results of its tests, and report to you on performance degradation or improvement. MacEKG is covered in detail in Chapter 17 (Hardware).

Speedometer
Scott Berfield
26043 Gushue Street
Hayward, CA 94544
America Online: SBERFIELD
Shareware fee: $30.00

Scott is the Senior Producer, Sony Computer Entertainment of America. He produces video games for a living and has done so for about 10 years (he's currently working on games for the new Sony Playstation machine). A Mac user since March 1984, he has been programming the Mac for about 8 years — but only as a serious hobby for the last 5. He programs in C, but Speedometer 4.01 is written in Metrowerks CodeWarrior C because it was the only effective way to do Power Mac native mode support.

Want to know how your Mac stacks up to the latest? Want to check out how different startup settings and configurations affect your Mac's performance? Speedometer is the tool. This professional-quality shareware tool can perform a complete set of performance diagnostic tests (CPU, Graphics, Disk, and

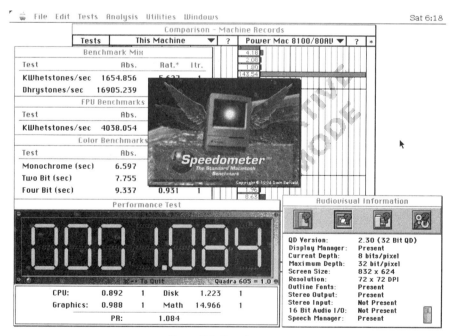

Figure 8-3: Speedometer

Math), and allows you to compare the results to your choice of Macintosh. Speedometer also allows you to import, merge, and print machine records, to annotate results (so you can distinguish between setups), and to print graphs. The performance rating in the bottom left-hand corner of Figure 8-3 show your Mac's performance relative to a Quadra 605.

Reporting Tools

When you call for help, the first thing that a technical support person will ask you for is a Systems listing — what extensions and control panels you are running, what video mode you are running in, whether 32-bit addressing is enabled, ... the list goes on from there. You need is tool to collect all this information for you — which is exactly what these do for you (see Chapter 17 for coverage of Apple's MacCheck).

MacEnvy
Ken McLeod
Blue Cloud Software
Internet: ken@cloudbusting.apple.com
MacEnvy is freeware

Ken works for Apple (please don't send him snail mail, if you want to reach him, use the address shown above), and has made MacEnvy available as freeware.

This elegant little application provides all sorts of information about your Mac, the buttons in the upper right-hand corner of Figure 8-4 allow you to view information about (left to right) hardware and memory (selected); files; SCSI; (second row) video information; PRAM, ports, and settings, and finally, a visual diversion: the game of life. All of the information gathered can be saved in a file.

Figure 8-4: MacEnvy

Now Profile

Now Software, Inc.
921 S.W. Washington St. Suite 500
Portland, OR 97205-2823
Telephone: 503 274-2800
Fax: 503 274-0670
America Online: Now
AppleLink: NowSoftware
CompuServe: 71541,170
eWorld: NowSoft

Internet: support@nowsoft.com
Suggested retail (part of Now Utilities): $89.95

I'm starting to wish I did have shares in Now Software <vbg> (on-line slang for "very big grin'). This is the tool I use when I want to report to someone else on my configuration — usually when I'm talking to a technical support person or when I need to report my setup for beta testing. The Preferences dialog (see Figure 8-5) allows you to set basic, detailed, or omit for a number of items.

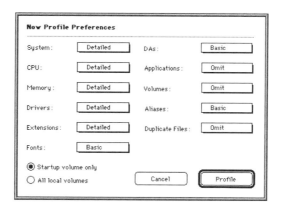

Figure 8-5: Now Profile Preferences

TattleTech

John Mancino
Decision Maker's Software, Inc.
1910 Joslyn Place
Boulder, CO 80304
Fax: 303 449-6207
America Online: JGCMAN
CompuServe: 70337,2143
Internet: mancino@decismkr.com
Shareware fee: $15.00

TattleTech started life as TattleTale. John later added TattleTech for commercial users, then combined the two after resolving a name conflict with Onset Computer Corporation, who has trademarked the name TattleTale™. I don't know of a more complete reporting tool — check out Figure 8-6 to get an idea of some of the things TattleTech can report on.

Some of the information TattleTech can provide is beyond the needs of most users, but it's nice to have a tool that does it all. TattleTech also has excellent integrated help; Figure 8-7 shows the explanations for SCSI devices.

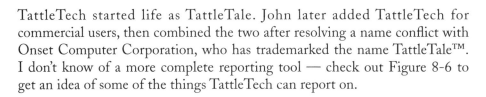

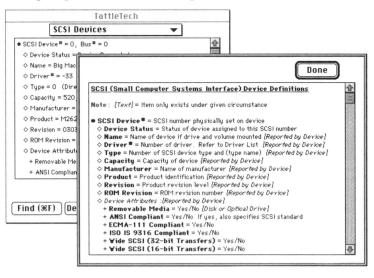

Figure 8-6: TattleTech

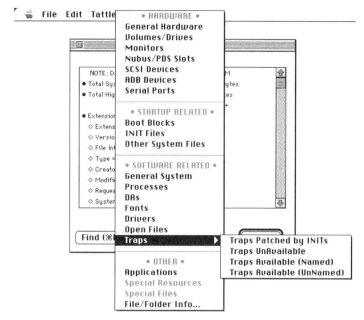

Figure 8-7: TattleTech SCSI help screen

Not only can TattleTech gather a ton of information on your System, but it can also provide detailed reports (Figure 8-8). I had planned to include a printout of my Quadra 700's configuration, but the report exceeded 140 pages! A copy of the report is included on the CD-ROM in the TattleTech folder as "TattleTech Report DGB".

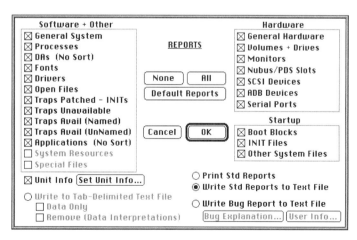

Figure 8-8: TattleTech reporting

Techie Tools

I debated on including TattleTech as a techie tool — it certainly qualifies. I decided against it, because anyone can use it to prepare detailed reports on their Systems. These tools are for those who want to get their hands dirty, and have a look at the guts of their Mac Systems.

Go Gestalt
Paul Reznick
1535 S. Marie
Westland, MI 48185-3874
America Online: PRzeznik
CompuServe: 72154,2710
Go Gestalt is freeware

Apple's *Gestalt* call is one a programmer can use to get information about a user's System. Go Gestalt (Figure 8-9) is a utility that provides us with that information, in a simple, easy-to-read format.

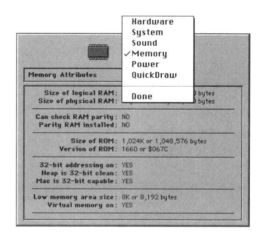

Figure 8-9: Go Gestalt

Open Files

Peter S. Bryant
Ethos Software
P.O. Box 11235
Zephyr Cove, NV 89448
America Online: BryantPS

CompuServe: 74071,3536
Shareware fee: $10.00

Remember back in Chapter 4, when I mentioned the Open Files Count? If you're curious about the files you have open on your Mac, Open Files (see Figure 8-10) is a Desk Accessory (DA) that allows you to have a look at what is running. One thing that surprises many users is the fact that each font is considered by the System to be an open file.

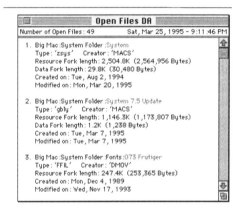

Figure 8-10: Open Files DA

MacSnoop™

Art A. Schumer
Evergreen Software, Inc.
15600 NE 8th Street, Suite A3126
Bellevue, WA 98009
Telephone: 206 483-6576
America Online: ArtSchumer

CompuServe: 76004,557
Shareware fee: $25.00

MacSnoop is sophisticated file and volume editor for your Mac. It is intended for advanced users only; it has the capability of doing real damage to your Mac, so use it with great caution. MacSnoop allows you to directly edit data in the resource or data forks of files on your hard drive. The version on the CD-ROM (1.5.5) works fine on Macs excluding 68040-based ones (like my Quadra). In view of this disclaimer, I would also recommend against its use on a Power Macintosh. Note: the demo will expire 60 days after you first use it.

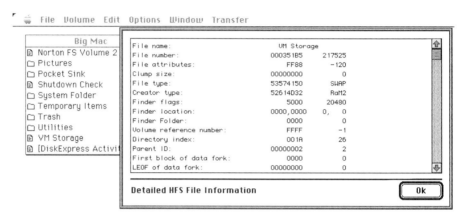

Figure 8-11: MacSnoop™

ProcessWatcher
Hugues Marty
19 rue Franc
3100 Toulouse
France

Internet: hugues@isoft.fr
ProcessWatcher is freeware

Hugues began programming a long time ago on an Apple II, using BASIC and machine language (not assembly at that time). He's now working in a small French company as an engineer, writing software for Unix/Motif and Windows (unfortunately), in C++. He still tries to find time for developing on Mac at home (once a month... ;-); that's why there is not — yet — a 2.1 release of ProcessWatcher). Apart of this, he's now learning Chinese (more complicated than C++)!

Process Watcher is a utility for showing you running processes on your Mac; it requires System 7, and includes balloon help, and support for AppleEvents.

As you can see in Figure 8-12, it can also be used to check out the System 7 support within other apps.

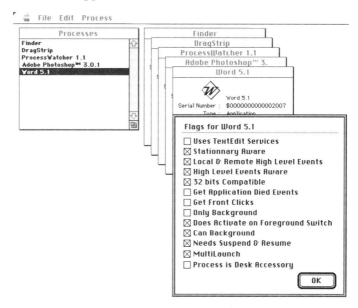

Figure 8-12: Process Watcher

Snitch

Mitchell Jones
P.O. Box 354
Temple City, CA 91780
Fax: 818 287-3067
America Online: MitchJones
CompuServe: 76506,753
Internet: mjones@netcom.com
Shareware fee: $5.00

Mitch has been playing/programming/hacking computers since 1977 when he started with a TRS-80 Model 1; he moved over to the Mac in 1984. He now works as a software engineer for Symantec, working on Symantec Antivirus for Mac. You'll also find him in the credits of the re-make of the Blob in 1989. Mitch is also a musician: he has played the trumpet since 1976 and electric bass since 1987.

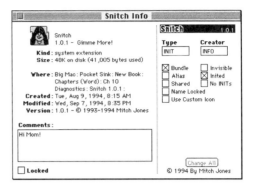

Figure 8-13: Snitch

Snitch is an elegant little extension that enhances the standard get info dialog (see Figure 8-13), allowing you to see and edit a file, folder, or volume's type creator, and other attributes. Good idea!

9 Protection

Bad things might happen, even to good Macs like yours. Aside from being well and truly backed up (see Chapter 3) what can you do to prevent problems? Plenty, as it turns out. In this chapter we look at utilities to protect your screen, your data, and even you. We also look at basic bomb recovery (System crash) tools. Let's start with a product category we all wish we didn't need: virus protection.

Virus Protection

We in the Mac community have been lucky: we haven't really been hit as badly with destructive viruses as those in the PC world. Still, viruses are an unfortunate reality — and a reality we have to protect against. The CD-ROM does not include any of the shareware anti-virus utilities for a simple reason: with every new virus, you need an updated version. I would rather not include a virus utility that may be out of date by the time you use it — the false sense of security could prove disastrous. If you have a source — a user group, a local bulletin board, one of the on-line services — then I recommend one of the excellent shareware or freeware utilities. John Norstad's freeware Disinfectant is as good as they get, and John has a track record of providing on-line updates as soon as there is word of a new outbreak. If you don't have a means of getting regular updates to a shareware program, then I recommend one of the commercial programs: Virex, Symantec Antivirus for the Mac (SAM), and Central Point Anti-Virus are all good, and offer their customers regular updates.

Protecting Your Screen

It used to be that if the same image was left on a video screen for long enough, it could "burn" in, leaving a ghost image. Virtually all computer monitors made in the past five years have built-in circuitry that prevents that

163

problem; so for users of newer Macs, screen-saving utilities can viewed as "eye candy." Some of these utilities also include limited password protection, to keep those unwanted persons from seeing or modifying your work. Remember that the password protection offered by screensavers is rudimentary at best: it can be gotten around by simply rebooting without extensions (i.e., by rebooting and holding down the Shift key).

After Dark
Berkeley Systems, Inc.
2095 Rose Street
Berkeley, CA 94709
Telephone: 510 549-2300
Fax: 510 849-9426
America Online: BrklySystm
AppleLink: D0346
CompuServe: 75300,1376
eWorld: BSI
Internet: mactech@berksys.com
Suggested retail: $49.99

After Dark isn't the first big seller in the Mac screensaver business, but it certainly has taken over, spawning an industry of add-ons. Berkeley now makes After Dark, along with add-on modules More After Dark, Simpsons, Disney, Star Trek, X-Men, ... the list goes on. Berkeley has made it easy for programmers to create their own modules; this has resulted in hundreds of freeware and shareware modules being available from on-line sources. The

Figure 9-1: After Dark 3.0 Control Panel

basic 3.0 engine (see Figure 9-1) gives you the functionality and a number of fun modules — the other packages add graphic modules to the basic package.

Clicking on the Setup button in the control panel allows you to tell After Dark's settings when to blank your screen, how to "wake up," assign a password to protect your Mac from prying eyes, adjust setting for WallZapper (this allows you to have a screensaver graphic as your desktop background pattern) and EcoLogic (which allows you to turn off your Energy Star monitor to save energy). The reason for the oddly shaped screen in Figure 9-2 is simple: After Dark displays whatever your System thinks the screen shape is; this is how my 17- and 19-inch monitors are interpreted.

WallZapper is grayed out because I had the Screen Posters extension disabled for this screen shot

The odd shape represents my 16 and 19 inch monitors as a virtual screen

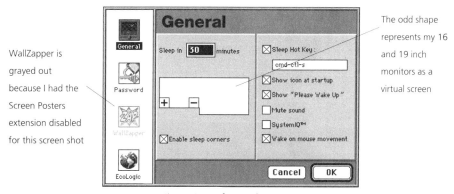

Figure 9-2: After Dark settings

Basic Black
Mason L. Bliss
18 Beach Street
Middleton, MA 02346
Internet: mason@acheron.middleboro.ma.us
Basic Black is freeware

Mason Loring Bliss was born and raised in Middleborough, Massachusetts. This 22-year-old Leo has been a computer nerd since he was 8 years old. He loves being outdoors, volleyball, boats, redheads; he's a cat person and an avid reader. Mason is also a fan of guinea pigs, and has a parakeet named Rick who is rather fond of Pink Floyd. He doesn't listen to Siouxsie, though, which Mason thinks is a shame. Rick is the only parakeet I know of with a membership at a video rental place.

Figure 9-3: Basic Black Control Panel

Basic Black is a simple, efficient screensaver — the control panel occupies 32K in your System folder, and it takes only 4K of memory once loaded (for comparison, After Dark's control panel is 272K; the modules I have on my hard drive occupy 17.2 megabytes). There are two versions on the CD-ROM: a basic version, and one for those with 68020 or newer processors. English and French versions of both are included, as is source code. The control panel (Figure 9-3) allows you to have Basic Black display a bouncing clock, fade to black or (if you have a PowerBook) white, set the sleep corners (move your cursor to this corner to immediately sleep or to prevent sleep), and set the delay until Basic Black kicks in. The unique display of the patches in effect after restart is a nice touch that allows you to fine-tune Basic Black's performance.

BugOff
Herb Otto
America Online: Herbo
CompuServe: 72257,1133
BugOff is freeware

Figure 9-4: BugOff
minimized

I've included BugOff as a screensaver, but this freeware application does a lot more. As well as the screen saving and password protection, BugOff includes a simple network messaging system, folder watching (it can check to see if things have been added to a folder while you are working), auto shutdown, and a simple reminder program. Because BugOff is an application, you don't have to worry about extension conflicts. When running, all you'll see on-screen is a minimized box (Figure 9-4) that lets you read messages or set reminders.

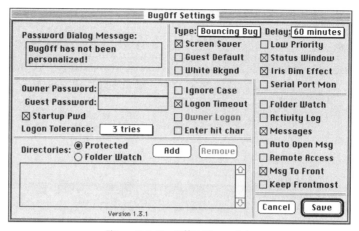

Figure 9-5: BugOff Settings dialog

When you bring BugOff to the foreground by clicking on this box, your menubar will change, giving you access to the program's commands. Figure 9-5 shows the settings dialog box and Figure 9-6 shows the Set Reminder dialog. Pretty impressive for a freeware application!

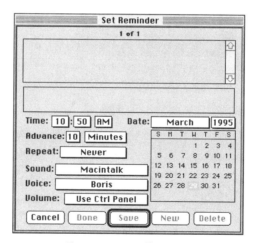

Figure 9-6: BugOff reminders

Eclipse
Andrew Welch
Ambrosia Software, Inc.
PO Box 23140
Rochester, NY 14692
Telephone: 716 427-2577
Fax: 716 475-9289
America Online: AmbrosiaSW
AppleLink: Ambrosia.SW
CompuServe: 73424, 1226
Shareware fee: $10.00

Andrew is the most prolific Mac shareware author I know of — see Chapter 11 for more great Ambrosia Software, along with an interview with Andrew.

As can be seen in Figure 9-7, Eclipse is an elegant shareware control panel that allows you to have the screen dimmed, display a picture, or show the time after a specified period of inactivity.

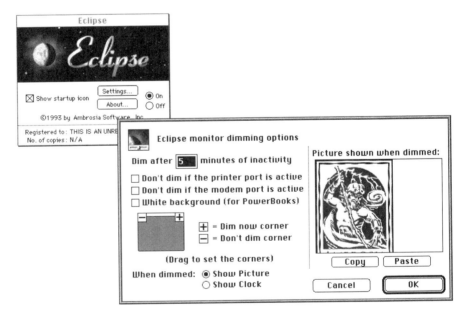

Figure 9-7: Eclipse options

Sleeper
Jon Gotow
St. Clair Software
2025 Mohawk Road
Upper St. Clair, PA 15241
America Online: StClairSW
CompuServe: 72330,3455
Internet: gotow@ansoft.com
Shareware fee: $10.00

Jon did his undergraduate work at Duke University, and has his Masters Degree in Mechanical Engineering from Carnegie Mellon University. He's presently employed as Manager of Software Development at Ansoft Corporation, which has very little to do with his educational background (they write commercial electromagnetic field analysis software for PCs and Unix workstations). Jon received his first Macintosh as a wedding present in 1986, much to his wife's chagrin, and has been programming the Mac ever since. His obsession began with some little Pascal programs written on his Mac Plus for a robotics class at CMU, and grew into a full time vocation as he switched to coding in C and C++. He lives in Pittsburgh, PA, with his wife and three children, where he says he spends entirely too much time playing with his current Mac, a Quadra 840av.

Sleeper (Figure 9-8) takes a unique approach: it offers some of the PowerBooks' ability to sleep to those with desktop Macs. Not only will Sleeper dim your screen, but it can also spin down your hard drives after a period of inactivity.

Figure 9-8: Sleeper

SunBlock

Brian Cyr
415 Long Hill Avenue
Shelton, CT 06484
America Online: Cyrano B
Internet: bcyr%mother@utrcgw.utc.com
Shareware fee: $5.00

SunBlock (Figure 9-9) is screen-saving application that includes simple password protection, and provides 15 selectable screen-saving modules, including a message module that allows you to create your own personal messages.

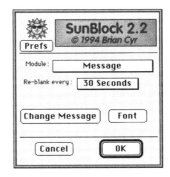

Figure 9-9: SunBlock Control Panel

Umbra

James L. Paul
PumpSoft™
6 Chestnut Street
Bath, NY 14810
Telephone: 607 776-3070
America Online: PumpSoft
CompuServe: 72767,3436
Internet: james@netcom.com
Shareware fee: $5.00

James Paul has been writing software for the Macintosh since 1985, and has been an Apple developer since 1980. He has been employed by MediaLab Technologies and NASA, and is currently doing graphic systems work for a daily newspaper in upstate New York. He writes shareware in his spare time and uses Apple's MPW C++ as his development environment. His software has won awards from Apple Computer and

Macworld Magazine, and has been published under the Hyperpress, MediaLab, and Component Software commercial labels. He is currently working under his own shareware label, PumpSoft™.

With Umbra, James Paul has taken a minimalist approach: there is no control panel, no user interface, and no preferences. Just drop the extension into your System folder and go. Umbra requires at minimum System 7 and one of the newer Apple monitors that can be gamma faded (this reduces the screen brightness). If you want to change the settings (sleep corners, delay, speed, etc.), ResEdit instructions are included in the documentation on the CD-ROM.

Volume/DS Screensaver

Alex Rampell
1186 North Ocean Way
Palm Beach, FL 33480
America Online: LOTTSIM
Shareware fee: $10.00

Alex is an eighth-grade student who programs as a hobby. He started two years ago, and has come a long way since. He started with HyperCard, then moved on to C, which he uses for all of his current programs. Alex learned by reading books on C and by downloading and studying sample source code. He really enjoys doing it, and can't think of anything he'd like to do better for a profession. He was worried that his being an eighth-grader would preclude him from inclusion. Volume/Depth Switcher is impressive — I didn't select it because of the author's age, but I *am* impressed. He's currently working on several utilities for Ziff-Davis.

Volume/Depth Switcher is a utility control panel that also happens to function as a screensaver. Clicking on Screensaver settings in the control panel (Figure 9-10) allows you to set sleep corners, delay, and type for the screensaver (Figure 11). User-definable hot keys allow you to have sound level and screen depth pop-up menus (see Figure 9-12).

Figure 9-10: Volume/Depth Switcher Control Panel

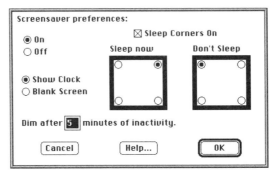

Figure 9-11: Volume/DS Screensaver settings

Figure 9-12: Depth pop-up

Protecting Your Data

We all have data on our hard drives that has some degree of confidentiality — whether it be work-related information, your résumé, or state secrets. The password protection offered by a screensaver is rudimentary at best — certainly not enough to keep a knowledgeable user from browsing your hard drive. My recommendation for those who need industrial-strength protection is a removable drive; Kent-Marsh also makes a commercial product called FolderBolt which does an excellent job of locking folders. Included in this section are programs with various levels of data protection.

KillDF
Tobias Engler
Môhrendorferstr. 6
91056 Erlangen
Germany
CompuServe: 100317,545
Internet: te@syrinx.franken.de
KillDF is freeware

One way to make sure no one can read your personal files is to trash them. KillDF (Figure 9-13) is a little utility that can kill the data fork in a file, and optionally overwrite it with garbage.

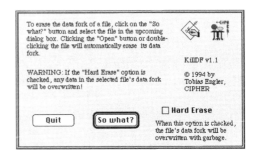

Figure 9-13: KillDF

MacPassword

Art A. Schumer
Evergreen Software, Inc.
15600 NE 8th Street, Suite A3126
Bellevue, WA 98009
Telephone: 206 483-6576
America Online: ArtSchumer
CompuServe: 76004,557
Shareware fee: $49.00

MacPassword (Figure 9-14) is definitely commercial–grade shareware: I registered and used it for years on my office Mac. The shareware version on the CD-ROM offers basic volume and folder password protection; additional functionality (high security protection; screen locking, sound password, and activity options; virus protection) is added when you register. The screen locking in MacPassword is more sophisticated than that offered in the screensavers covered elsewhere in this chapter; it cannot be defeated by simply rebooting without extensions.

Figure 9-14: MacPassword Control Panel

Padlock

John A. Schlack
406 Newgate Court, Apartment A1
Andalusia, PA 19020
America Online: John40
CompuServe: 70252,143
Shareware fee: $5.00

Worried about your kids accidentally deleting files on your hard drive? Padlock (Figure 9-15) is a simple drag 'n drop program that allows you to drop files or groups of files onto it for locking or unlocking. Obviously, Padlock requires System 7 to run. You can drop your work files onto it to lock them, and unlock them en masse later, when you get back to work.

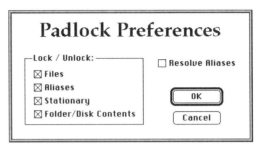

Figure 9-15: Padlock Preferences

Password Key

Carl Powell III
2306 Pembrook Circle S.W.
Huntsville, AL 35803
CompuServe: 76702,457
Shareware fee: $20.00

Carl has been programming computers since 1977. His first (and still favorite) language is BASIC. He currently uses PG:Pro and FutureBasic on the Mac for writing applications. In addition to writing software, he is now the K-12 Sales Agent with National Data Products, Inc. for Apple Computer, Inc. to the schools in Alabama. He formerly worked as a Senior Member of the Technical Staff at Boeing Computer Support Services at NASA's Marshall Space Flight Center in Huntsville, AL. Carl is also the author of *Network Your Mac (and live to tell about it): The REAL Beginner's Guide*, a book written to help the *real* beginning networkers get started without all the detail, bits and bytes usually associated with networking.

Figure 9-16: Password Key

Password Key offers simple protection of your hard drive, and logs all logon attempts, successful or otherwise. While it can be beaten by rebooting without extensions, the log will notify you that an unsuccessful attempt was made, alerting you to the possibility that someone may have bypassed Password Key's protection. As can be seen in Figure 9-16, the protection offered in the unregistered version is non-existent.

ShredIt
Robert Wiebe
Systems Research Group
20-8451 Ryan Road
Richmond, BC V7A 2E8
Canada
CompuServe: 70262,342
Shareware fee: varies (see documentation)

Okay, so you've decided to delete those hot love letters, or the letter telling your boss exactly what you thought — what happens if someone runs a file recovery tool (like Norton Unerase) to get the files back? Don't worry, there is a cure. Overwriting the area on your hard drive where the file existed is the easiest, and the easiest way to do that is with ShredIt (Figure 9-17), a simple drag 'n drop application. (The manual method for preventing recovery of sensitive data is to create another file with the same application, using the same file name and dummy data; then save it in the same location, overwriting the old file.) Just make sure you never want to see the file again, because there's no turning back after you've shredded a file.

Figure 9-17: ShredIt

StartupLog
Brian Durand
Aurelian Software
922 W. Buena #3W
Chicago, IL 60613
Telephone: 312 857-7110
America Online: BriDurand
StartUpLog is freeware

When you suspect someone may be tampering with your Mac, or when you just want to log activity, Brian Durand's freeware control panel StartupLog is ideal. The help feature in the control panel (see Figure 9-18) lists other potential uses.

Figure 9-18: StartupLog Control Panel

Protecting You: Ergonomics

So you've gone to all sorts of trouble to protect your Mac — how about you? Ergonomics are an important factor in your productivity. Without proper screen and keyboard placement, you risk repetitive strain injuries (RSI). Even worse, if you don't take a break every once in a while, you may get grumpy. Remember: the Mac is supposed to be fun. If you *want* to get grumpy, go use a PC for a while.

LifeGuard

Visionary Software
1820 SW Vermont, Suite A
Portland, OR 97219-1945
Telephone: 503 246-6200
Fax: 503 452-1198
Suggested retail: $79.95

LifeGuard (Figure 9-19) is an extension and application (the application works as a DA under System 6, and installs itself in your Apple menu if you're running System 7) that goes beyond the obvious reminders to give you

Figure 9-19: LifeGuard Control Panel

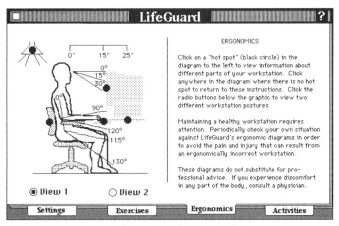

Figure 9-20: LifeGuard advice

advice on how to best set up your computer ergonomically (see Figure 9-20), and what exercises and activities you can perform to reduce the stain of extended periods at your Macintosh.

Mac Life Insurance
Adam Stein
Insanely Great Software
126 Calvert Ave. E.
Edison, NJ 08820
America Online: AdamStein
CompuServe: 71140,2051
Shareware fee: $29.95

Mac Life Insurance is a set of four shareware modules: EyeSaver warns you to break after a specified period of time or keystrokes, FileSaver (Figure 9-21) automatically saves files after a specified period of time or keystrokes, KeySaver (Figure 9-22) saves every keystroke (so that even if your word processor crashes without a save, you'll be able to reconstruct the memo you've been working on all day), and MouseSaver allows you to assign hot keys to common tasks.

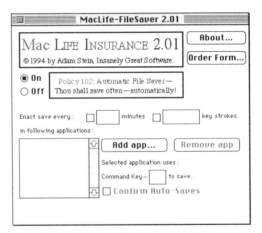

Figure 9-21: Mac Life Insurance – FileSaver

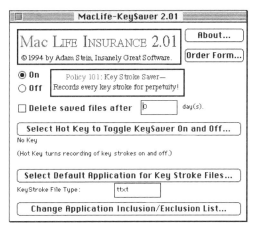

Figure 9-22: Mac Life Insurance – KeySaver

Bomb Recovery

The title here is more apt than what I started with (Bomb Protection). These utilities may help you recover from a crash a little more gracefully — just remember that any crash has the potential to do damage to your System or your hard drive. My recommendation after a crash is to save what you can, reboot, and run your hard drive utility (Chapter 16) to make sure that there is no lasting damage. One alternative built into System 7 is the ability to force an application to quit by pressing Command-Option-Esc. Be aware that this should be a last ditch effort, because some applications hang when you attempt this.

Bomb Shelter
Andrew Welch
Ambrosia Software
P.O. Box 23140
Rochester, NY 14692
Telephone: 716 427-2577
Fax: 716 475-9289
America Online: AmbrosiaSW
CompuServe: 73424,1226
Bomb Shelter is freeware

Usually when you crash, your Macintosh will bring up a dialog box that says

"Sorry, a System error has occurred" with two buttons: Restart and Resume. Most applications don't enable the Resume feature, and this is where the Bomb Shelter extension comes in: it enables the button, forcing the application to quit, and hopefully returning you to the Finder. This allows you to save files from other open applications or RAM disks, and reboot.

Macsbug

Apple Computer
20525 Mariani Drive
Cupertino, California 95014
Macsbug is freeware

Macsbug is a debugger; a programmers' tool that allows them to track software's performance. Fortunately for us mere mortals, it is not only available free from on-line sources, but it offers a useful function. If you have the Programmer's key installed and Macsbug is in your System folder, then hitting the key will drop you into Macsbug. (The Programmers key is one of the two switches on the front or side of you Mac. The one with a small triangle restarts your Mac and the one with a small circle is the Programmer's key.) The first thing you'll notice is the lovely PC-like command line interface (yuck!). I use only four commands: ES (escape to shell, which attempts to return you to the Finder), EA (exit application, which tries to quit the current application), and RS (restart) or RB (reboot).

10 Shareware Utilities

This book wouldn't exist if it weren't for the generosity of the shareware authors whose programs you see described in these pages, and whose hard work you find on the CD-ROM included with it. Shareware exists — make that *subsists* — on the contributions of the few who pay. Unfortunately, many users rarely, if ever, pay the shareware fees on the programs they use. If you find yourself using one of the shareware programs included on the CD-ROM, remember: you haven't paid for it yet. The price of the book does not include shareware fees. If after a few weeks you can't live without it, send the author the fee he or she asks for. Your contribution might just be the one that encourages them to push on with a new version. Some of the best commercial utilities out there started out as shareware: programs like StuffIt Deluxe, Super Boomerang, and a good part of System 7.5 all began life as shareware.

Much of the software in this chapter (and in the book) is generously released by the author as Freeware, which means that the author retains all rights to the software, but does not ask that you send a fee.

In this chapter, I focus on shareware utilities, including those that help you automate your Mac, tools to customize the way your Mac works, some sound utilities, and a few that defy categorization. The chapter ends with an interview with Steven Bobker, whose *Bobker's Dozen* column in *MacUser* more than qualifies him as an expert on Mac utilities.

 One caveat with any of these programs: remember that the more extensions and control panels you add to your Mac, the more likely you are to experience conflict problems (see Chapter 12 for more on conflicts). I strongly suggest you add those utilities that you want to try one at a time — adding them all at once is just asking for trouble!

Automation

The easiest way to speed repetitive operations up on your Mac is to automate them. CE Software's QuicKeys has been the commercial automation tool of choice for most Mac users for years, and with the release of AppleScript, Mac owners finally have a means to automate the Finder and their applications.

Let's have a look at a few shareware tools on the CD-ROM to help you automate your Mac.

Auto Shutdown
Tim Bitson
AnalySYS Software
P.O. Box 35967
Tucson, AZ 85740-5967
America Online: TBitson
Auto Shutdown is freeware

Tim has worked for the past 17 years as an Engineering Specialist for Hughes Aerospace and Electronics. For the past 10 years, he has also moonlighted doing Mac consulting — his specialty is developing data acquisition and analysis programs for business applications. He started programming 15 years ago on the Apple][, and moved up to the Mac, where his primary language is C/C++. Tim has been an Apple Associate for 6 years, and has been using Macs since 1984.

Auto Shutdown is included on the CD-ROM, but users should be aware that Tim no longer supports it. The main reason is that Apple's CPU Energy Saver offers the same functionality; there were also unresolved reports of conflicts with Berkeley Systems' After Dark. See Chapter 21 for another of Tim's programs, Mail Slot.

If you don't have CPU Energy Saver, Auto Shutdown (see Figure 10-1) provides unattended shutdown of your Mac. This allows you to run a BBS session, optimize your drive, or whatever, and have your Mac automatically shut down whenever you tell it to.

Figure 10-1: Auto Shutdown

AppleTalk On

Jon Pugh
1861 Landings Drive
Mountain View, CA 94043
Telephone: 415 691-6643
Internet: jonpugh@netcom.com
Shareware fee: $5.00

AppleTalk On is an application extension that makes AppleTalk a little easier
to work with by turning AppleTalk on whenever you restart or shut down.
Why is this necessary? Starting with the System 7 Tuneup, AppleTalk does
not load into memory if it is off at startup. This means that a restart if
required if you need AppleTalk to print or for your network. AppleTalk On
saves you the PITA (pain in the neck) of that restart. PowerBook users should
also check out Jon's ToggleAT fkey in Chapter 18.

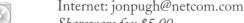

Bring Finder to Front

Brian Bezanson
Manta Software Corporation
1289 129th Avenue NE
Blaine, MN 55434
Telephone: 612 754-8140
CompuServe: 76711,550
Bring Finder to Front is freeware

Bring Finder to Front has a simple purpose — put it into the Startup Items
folder so that after all of your startup applications have loaded, BFTF will do
its thing, leaving you with the Finder, instead of an application, as the
frontmost application.

Quit All Applications

David Giandomenico
4 Waverley Drive
Camberley, Surrey GU15-2DL
England
CompuServe: 100016,1053
Quit All Applications is freeware

David Giandomenico obtained his Bachelors degree in Electrical Engineering from MIT
and his M.S. & Ph.D. in E.E., Solid State Devices from U.C. Berkeley, in 1990. He has

been living in England since 1990. David first started programming back in 1972 with BASIC while at Cal Tech. He added C to his list of programming languages in 1982. He began writing code for the Macintosh in 1990 and has created several utilities. His current Macintosh projects are written in either C and C++.

Okay, you're running six applications, and you want to quickly shut down or restart. Quit All Applications is a simple utility that does just what it says: run it, and all of your active applications will quit. Quit All Applications attempts to quit those applications that will not normally quit when you do a normal shutdown. David recommends putting Quit All Applications into your Apple Menu Items folder, so you can quit everything directly from your Apple Menu.

Quit It
Berrie Kremers
Remise 4
4207 BC Gorinchem
The Netherlands
Internet: Berrie.Kremers@kub.nl
Shareware fee: $15.00

Ever close a document (either by closing a document or by using the Command-w keyboard equivalent), and later realize that even though you've closed the last document, the application is still open? This isn't a problem with working applications like a word processor, a spreadsheet, or a graphics program, but it can be a pain with single-document applications, like a

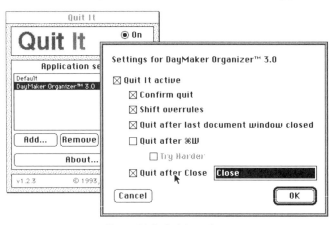

Figure 10-2: Quit It settings

personal information manager. Leave enough of these applications open, and you're bound to run out of memory. Quit It is a control panel (see Figure 10-2) that allows you to force applications to quit when you close the last remaining open document.

Timing

One thing that can make automation more powerful is the ability to have a task run unattended, at a prescheduled time. On the CD-ROM you'll find a number of time-related shareware utilities, including some to make your Mac work, and a couple to remind you or track you while you work.

Chronograph
John A. Schlack
406 Newgate Court, Apartment A1
Andalusia, PA 19020
America Online: John40
CompuServe: 70252,143
Shareware fee: $15.00

Chronograph (Figure 10-3) is a powerful time-based utility in fat binary format. It allows you to play sounds, open files or applications, or launch scripts; these tasks can be assigned once or repetitively. Uses include regular

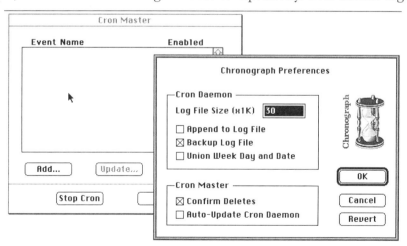

Figure 10-3: Chronograph Preferences

backups, reminders, and checking for e-mail. From the perspective of this book, uses include scheduling hard drive optimization or running of your hard drive utility.

Notify
Steve Stockman
Sonflower Softworks
219 S. Barrington Ave. #3
Los Angeles, CA 90049-3324
Telephone: 310 440-3933
America Online: SonflowrSw
CompuServe: 76507,2646
eWorld: SonflowrSw
Shareware fee: $10.00

Steve now lives in Los Angeles. His day job is working on Norton Utilities for Macintosh, which leaves him little time or gumption for shareware. That's our loss, as he's created wonderful software in the past.

Want a simple reminder program, something that will remind you of meetings or appointments? Notify uses the Notification Manager built into Macintoshes since System 6 to keep you on track. This control panel (see Figure 10-4) allows for repeat messages, multiple alarms for a single event, and can even dismiss itself if your Mac is unattended.

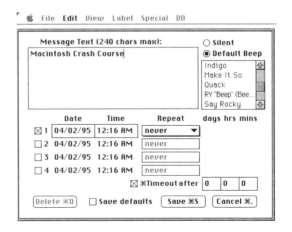

Figure 10-4: Notify reminder

Once Daily

David Giandomenico
4 Waverley Drive
Camberley, Surrey GU15-2DL
England
CompuServe: 100016,1053
Once Daily is freeware

The Startup Items folder that came with System 7 is handy, but it has a flaw. Everything in it runs *every* time you start up. There are operations that you want to set to run automatically, but only *once* a day. That's exactly the purpose of Once Daily — just append the word "daily" to any file in your Startup Items folder that you only wish to run once a day, and this control panel (see Figure 10-5) will do the rest for you.

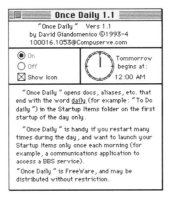

Figure 10-5: Once Daily Control Panel

The Timekeeper

Carl Powell III
2306 Pembrook Circle S.W.
Huntsville, AL 35803
CompuServe: 76702,457
Shareware fee: $5.00

The TimeKeeper (Figure 10-6) is a utility that logs the time you spend on your Mac, with the ability to track up to nine separate user-definable categories at once. I'd use it, but I don't know if I want to know how much time I've actually spent working on this book.

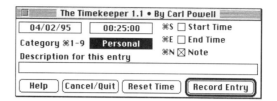

Figure 10-6: The Timekeeper

Keyboarding

Using a mouse is great, especially for editing, but it can get in your way when you're typing. Here are a couple of tools that allow you to use the keyboard instead of the mouse, and one that lets you use the keyboard less.

Key Tools
Dawson Dean
Software Publishing
654 Blair Avenue
Piedmont, CA 94611
America Online: DawsonDean
Internet: dawson@cs.cornell.edu
Shareware fee: $15.00

Dawson recently finished his Ph.D. in Computer Science at Cornell. He's written a variety of Mac software, some commercial and some shareware.

If you're typing away, you don't always want to take your hands off the keyboard just to dismiss a dialog box. Key Tools is a control panel that allows you to use the keyboard in modal dialogs — just press Command and the first letter of the button you want to press, and Key Tools will do the rest. As you can see in Figure 10-7, Key Tools can also insert the date and time, and it can echo text (repeat text typed between mouse clicks). This is easier to do than it is to explain — just try it!

Figure 10-7: Key Tools

TaskMan

Paul Cunningham
Performance Data
P.O. Box 1923
Mango, FL 33550-1923
America Online: TKS Paul
CompuServe: 75020,3540
TaskMan is freeware

Figure 10-8: Taskman popup

One of the few things I like about Windoze is the fact that you can use the keyboard to switch among active applications. TaskMan brings that functionality to the Mac — just hit Command-Tab to get a window (Figure 10-8) with the name and icon of the next process; then Tab will cycle you through active processes. If you hold down the Shift key, you can reverse the direction of the cycling. Pressing Control-Esc opens TaskMan's Process List dialog (Figure 10-9), which allows you to select from active processes.

Figure 10-9: TaskMan Process List

TypeIt4Me

Riccardo Ettore
67 rue de la limite
1970 W-Oppem
Belgium
CompuServe: 72277,1344
Shareware fee: $30.00

The concept for TypeIt4Me (Figure 10-10) is simple, but it works so well that it's no wonder Microsoft has included its functional equivalent within Word 6. TypeIt4Me expands abbreviations on the fly, so that when I type *mcc*, it will automatically expand to *Macintosh Crash Course* (see Figure 10-11). An abbreviation can be longer, too; typing my initials (*dgb*) results in my name, address, phone number, and e-mail address to be typed out. TypeIt4Me is a labor of love for the author — Riccardo has been supporting and updating TypeIt4Me since 1989.

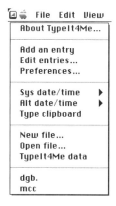

Figure 10-10: TypeIt4Me menu

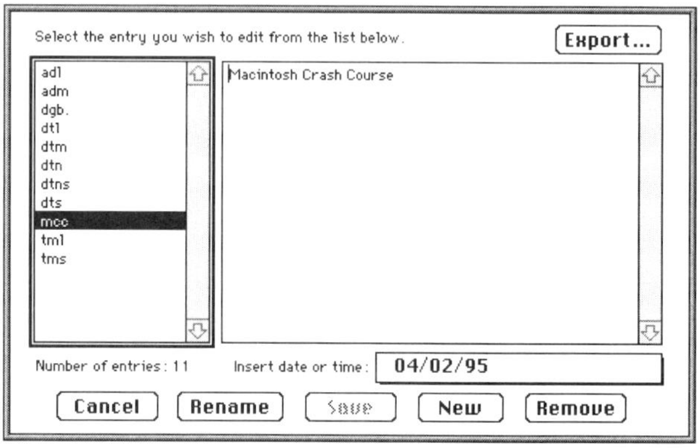

Figure 10-11: Editing an entry in TypeIt4Me

Customization

Customizing your Mac, adding junk to your System folder — that's the easiest way to screw your Mac up. The more you add, the slower your Mac will run, the less memory it will have left to run applications, and the more likely that you'll crash sooner rather than later. Having said all that, what fun would the Mac be without toys, especially ones as useful as the ones on the CD-ROM with this book?

AutoMenus Pro
Mike Conrad
Night Light Software
P.O. Box 2484
Oak Harbor, WA 98277-6484
America Online: NL Software
CompuServe: 73457,426
Shareware fee: $15.00

Would you rather have menus drop down automatically when you move the cursor under them, without having to click to drop them down? That's exactly what AutoMenus Pro (Figure 10-12) does for you. One note of caution for Now Utilities users: AutoMenus Pro and Now Menus tend to fight each other. If you want AutoMenus functionality, select "Menus 'stick' when pulled down" and "No click needed" in Now Menus preferences.

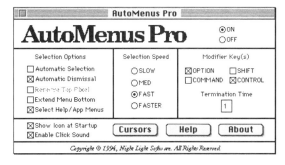

Figure 10-12: AutoMenus Pro

Bail

Robert Thornton
Jump Development Group, Inc.
1228 Malvern Avenue
Pittsburgh, PA 15217-1141
Telephone: 412 681-2692
America Online: JumpDevgrp
AppleLink: RThornton
CompuServe: 71321,1527
Bail is freeware

Ever launch an application accidentally? It happens to me all the time. Even worse, half the time when I try to speed the process up by force-quitting (by pressing Command-Option-Esc), my Mac ends up hung. Bail allows you to quit the launch process by holding down the mouse button or by pressing Command-period. My advice is to set the Bail Delay (see Figure 10-13) to about halfway between Short and Long, otherwise apps will launch before you have a chance to bail out.

Figure 10-13: Bail

Clipboard Master
Bill Woody
In Phase Consulting
337 West California #4
Glendale, CA 91203
Telephone: 818 502-1424
Internet: woody@alumni.cco.caltech.edu
Clipboard Master is freeware

Figure 10-14: Clipboard Master

Bill has been programming on the Macintosh for almost ten years, mostly in C and C++. Prior to founding In Phase Consulting, he worked at JBL Professional where he helped bring to market CADP2, an acoustic simulation package. Bill has also worked for a number of other software companies, including NASA's Jet Propulsion Laboratory, where he created and maintained software for computer animation of the Voyager II encounter with Neptune, and for the first Galileo flyby of Earth.

Ever wish you could have more clipboards, so that when you're cutting and pasting between two documents you could make a series of cuts, followed by a series of pastes in the destination? How about up to nine clipboards? That's what you get with Clipboard Master. A small floating palette (see Figure 10-14) tells you which clipboard you're using.

Décor
François Pottier
4 Rue Colette
94210 La Varenne
France
Internet: pottier@kagi.com
Shareware fee: $10.00

Well, this one certainly falls into the category of eye candy. Décor allows you to assign a picture, or a group of pictures from a designated folder, as your desktop background (Figure 10-15).

Figure 10-15: Décor

Line Up
Richard E. Fiegle
P.O. Box 5062
Kokomo, IN 46904-5062
America Online: RFigleaf
CompuServe: 76350,761
Shareware fee: $10.00

Here's one for the compulsively neat in all of us: Line Up allows you to get control of your desktop windows, by cleaning them up and forcing them into a staggered display you specify the details of (see Figure 10-16).

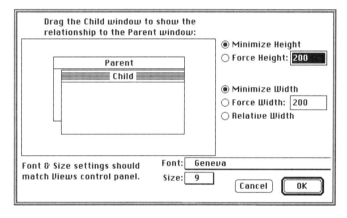

Figure 10-16: Line Up

Scrolling
Ken McLeod
Apple Computer, Inc.
Internet: ken@cloudbusting.apple.com (preferred)
AppleLink: THE.CLOUD
eWorld: TheCloud
Scrolling is freeware

On some of the newer Macs, windows can scroll down so fast in some applications that it is hard to find what you're looking for. Scrolling is a simple freeware control panel (see Figure 10-17) that lets you adjust the scrolling speed of your Mac, giving better control to those lucky enough to have fast Macs.

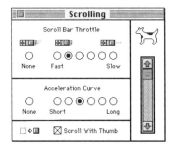

Figure 10-17: Scrolling

Sound Tools

One of the great features of the Macintosh is its integrated sound capabilities. Adding sound to a PC means adding a card (typically a Sound Blaster); adding a CD-ROM with sound (at least for me) can be a three-day nightmare. On the Mac side, we've always had plug 'n play. This section includes two tools: one to allow you menu bar access to your audio CDs, the other to record and convert sound files.

CD Menu
Henrik Eliasson
Sunnerviksgatan 15 A
S-418 72 Göteborg
Sweden
Internet: henrik_eliasson@macexchange.se
Shareware fee: $10.00

Henrik is a 28-year-old physics student at the University of Gothenburg, Sweden, from which he will be graduating in the summer of 1995, after which he will probably continue with Ph.D. studies. He has been programming the Mac for over 4 years, first in Pascal and now for the past 2 years in C (THINK C).

CD Menu is his first programming project made available to the Mac community at large. In the future, he would like to combine his programming skills with his physics knowledge to remedy the lack of good educational physics software. His plans for CD Menu include hot keys for play, stop, eject and track selection; a menu; disc title and track names; and the ability to repeat a disc or to auto-eject it when it has finished playing.

CD Menu gives you a menu bar icon that allows you to play, eject, select tracks, and set the volume level of an audio CD. The control panel (shown on the left side of Figure 10-18) allows you to configure the menu bar, and to set keyboard equivalents for commonly used functions. I've used this elegant tool to listen to countless CDs while writing this book (thanks Henrik!).

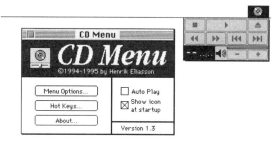

Figure 10-18: CD Menu

Ultra Recorder

EJ Campbell
EJ Enterprises
4096 Sutherland Drive
Palo Alto, CA 943093
America Online: EJC3
Shareware fee: $5.00

EJ is a sophomore at Gunn High School in Palo Alto. He learned to program C on his own. Two books he found especially helpful were *Learn C on the Macintosh* and *Macintosh C Programming Primer*.

Ultra Recorder is an application that expands on your Mac's built-in sound recording capabilities. As you can see from Figure 10-19, it allows you to set compression, recording quality, and file type. It also lets you convert among supported file types (System 7, standard, double-clickable and startup AIFF files, and SoundEdit files).

Figure 10-19: Ultra Recorder

Miscellaneous Utilities

These utilities defy categorization; nonetheless, they all serve valuable purposes. Even better, there are thousands of Mac shareware gems out there — see Chapter 20 for tips on getting on-line and finding more!

LogSpy
Eberhard Rensch
Spitalhofstr. 3
D-94032 Passau
Germany
CompuServe: 100010,604
Shareware fee: $5.00 (or a bottle of beer)

LogSpy is a single-purpose extension: it checks for incoming faxes every time your Mac is started. All incoming faxes are then displayed in a dialog box.

Refreshfkey
Tobias Engler
Môhrendorferstr. 6
91056 Erlangen
Germany
CompuServe: 100317,545
Internet: te@syrinx.franken.de
Refresh fkey is freeware

Tobias Engler a 19-year-old "subcaretaker" at a church in Erlangen, Germany where he's doing his community service. After completing that, he plans to do some studying at the University of Erlangen, maybe some computer science. He likes swimming, playing soccer and badminton, and listening to Rush, Dire Straits, and Bad Religion. Tobias started programming back in 1987 when he got his first Apple, the][+, which was later updated to a][e. In 1991 he got a Mac LC, and, in 1993, a PowerBook 165c. His programming language history is pretty structured (like programming itself): on the Apple][he programmed in BASIC and assembler, on the Mac he has been programming mostly in C (and sometimes assembler), using the MPW environment.

Some programs, including the Finder, can leave artifacts or garbage on the screen. Moving a window over them, then back will usually force a redraw, but Tobias' fkey is much easier — just press Command-Shift-6 to force a screen refresh.

Victoire!

Samuel Caughron
Samat Software
9600 East 150 Highway
Kansas City, MO 64149
America Online: MRCAUGHRON
CompuServe: 76354,3302
Shareware fee: $15.00

Samuel is a 20-year-old student working towards a liberal arts degree at Thomas Aquinas College in Southern California. He started programming in grade school on the Apple][. When his father purchased a Lisa in 1983, he turned his interest to developing Macintosh software. After three rewrites of a PacMan-type arcade game, he abandoned the project and began working on One-Shot Worksheet, which was released by Baseline Publishing with limited success. During the summer of 1992, Samuel wrote Victoire!, which was later expanded and released by Baseline Publishing as Axis the Gamecheater. Still available from Baseline, it adds a number of features including support for more games, and the ability to print hot keys. Samuel is entirely self-taught as a programmer: starting with BASIC, then Pascal, and finally C. He also learned assembly language by debugging with TMON.

I have a simple philosophy when it comes to games: I like those that I can play for a short time, and then get back to work. This means that it is unlikely that I'll ever develop the quick reflexes and skills required to make it to the higher levels, and this is often where all the goodies are. Victoire! offers a means to get the goodies (extra lives, weapons, etc.) using a time-honored tradition: cheating. Install the Victoire! control panel (Figure 10-20), and you too can play like an arcade wizard!

Figure 10-20: Victoire!

Interview: Steven Bobker

I'll never forget the first time I met Steve — he and Gary Ouellet (one of my MagiMac partners) were in a dispute that was close to legal action. I called Steve to see if we could settle things, and we've gotten along ever since. About 6 years ago, I asked Peggy Kilburn (Macworld Conference Director) if she'd like a session on "Resolving System Conflicts", she said "yes", and Steve and I have done the session countless times since. Steve is the only person I know who could have acted as technical editor on the material in this book — his assistance, advice, and knowledge have been priceless. (Thanks Steve!)

How long have you been in the computer business and how did you get started?

I bought a Mac in March 1984 (on a trip to Macy's to look at color TVs; I didn't own a color TV then, and my first had to wait until 1987). I joined every formal and informal Mac group I could and when Felix Dennis and Neil Shapiro began to assemble the original MacUser team back in early 1985, they offered me the position of tech editor. I took to computer magazines like a duck to water, and I still for work computer magazines. And very happily, I can add.

What is your educational background — are you formally trained, or did you teach yourself?

My degree (a real B.S.) was granted by Stevens Tech long ago. I've done graduate work in ocean engineering and human factors (before it was called ergonomics). When still in high school I took an NSF summer course in computer programming and learned Fortran IV and IBM 1620 machine language (right, machine, not assembly: it was an indoctrination program). That's about it for formal computer training.

What products (including books and magazines) have you been involved in?

I've held the positions of Tech Editor, Editor-in-Chief, Chief Scientist, and Chief Visionary at MacUser (1985-88), Editor-in-Chief and Editorial Director at Windows User (1992-93), and Editor-in-Chief at Software Solutions (current). In between I've written for virtually every computer magazine that covers Macs. I also create the editorial copy found in the APS catalogs. Plus I've written several short books for Hayden (How to Get on America Online in 5 Minutes and How to Get on CompuServe in 5 Minutes). Several other book and magazine projects are in progress.

Please describe the equipment you use (what computer, how much RAM, etc.)

Most work is done on a steroided PowerBook 180. It has 14M of RAM RAM Doubled to 28M, and a 500M HD and the fastest modem I can buy. It's always attached to an NEC MultiSync 4FG monitor which I usually run at 832x624 and 256 colors. A Liberty Adapter lets me change resolutions on the fly. Also permanently attached are an Apple Extended Keyboard II (still the best ever), a Logitech MouseMan (best mouse, best software), Kensington TurboTrak 4.0, APS Toshiba 4101 CD-ROM drive, APS HyperDAT backup drive, and an APS Quantum 120 hard drive for overflow from the internal drive and for financial records that I prefer not to keep on the PowerBook.

By the time you read this though, the PowerBook will almost surely be replaced by a 6100 DOS Compatible, one of the greatest computers ever made, and one Apple seems grimly determined to market into obscurity and oblivion.

At work I use a Power Mac 7100/80 with 24M of RAM and a 700M hard drive. My monitor there is a Radius Color Pivot, which is OK, but not, in my opinion, half the monitor my NEC is.

Do you have other interests you'd like mentioned in a bio?

I enjoy reading (and, soon, writing) mysteries and almost any book I can get my hands on. I also enjoy sailing and puttering around the house (that last one is new; old friends will be totally shocked).

What do like to do when you're not writing books?

When not writing, I'm most often reading. I find it relaxing.

Where do you live, are you married with children, how old are you, (etc.)

I'm married to the perfect woman, who I met during a ferocious group argument on CompuServe many years ago. We were living on opposite coasts at the time and the Macs made the whole relationship possible in the beginning.

What System(s) are you running at home?

I run the latest System on my primary machines at work and home. At the moment that's 7.5.1. There are a few other Macs at home (6 I think), and they have older systems on them.

How are Mac users different from Windows users (referring to my favorite ex-magazine, WindowsUser…)

Windows users are a lot like Mac users these days. If you've never used a Mac and take Windows as it is (that is, don't try to change anything) it's a pretty nice system and the hardware is CHEAP. If you've used a Mac, well, Windows is still crude and garish even if it works. From what I've seen of Windows 95 that won't change a whole lot either.

What Windows is though is a de facto standard and as soon as you get away from shareware and basic applications into specialized and niche apps, Windows wins big time. There's so much there and much of it never appears in Mac versions or does so 6 to 12 months later (following Microsoft's lead I guess).

Why do PC users put up with configuration and setup hassles?

Because they haven't used a Mac or because MIS does the setup for them. And speaking of setup, I'm so glad there are now third-party installers for the Mac. Apple's own Installer is so annoying that it could proudly claim to be a Microsoft product.

What does Apple need to do to maintain or increase its market share? Do you think the cloning of the Mac will make a significant difference?

Apple can't increase market share without replacing 95% of its current staff. And even that won't be enough. After they get real marketing people in place they still have to somehow slash prices more without sacrificing quality. I don't think it's a likely scenario.

I do have high hopes for the cheap clones though, especially those from Power Computing. If Apple can increase the market share of the OS by licensing even more cheap clones, they should be satisfied. But I suspect ignorance and greed will prevent that.

What should users do to reduce the bomb effect on their Macs?

You can't eliminate the crashes that are part of the joy of the Mac. You can only learn to be constantly backed up and to deal with and remove conflicts as best you can.

On my Mac at work, I run nothing special (RAM Doubler, QuickMail, Soft Pivot for the monitor, and MouseKey for the Logitech mouse are the only non-Apple extensions), have few fonts (less than 20) and freeze solid 3 or more times per work day. Being pure isn't enough.

How many extensions are you running, and when was the last time your crashed?

At home I'm currently running maybe 44 or so extensions and 100 or so fonts and I crash a lot. Only twice today so far, but it's still before noon. I'm real good about Saving (that's why I love the MouseMan — it has three buttons and I use the right button as a dedicated Save key) and great back up habits. DAT backup is so fast I do a backup frequently.

How about your picks for utilities? the same for extensions?

My top ten utilities and extensions in non–Letterman order:

1. *File Buddy*
2. *Find Pro*
3. *Desktop Strip*
4. *DiskTop*
5. *StuffIt Expander*
6. *Retrospect*
7. *Snapz*
8. *PB Tools*
9. *ApplWindows*
10. *MenuChoice*

Describe the next great utility (existing or not)

The next great utility isn't going to be available in 1995, and maybe not even 1996, but it's coming and sooner than you think. It's a cognitive input device. Voice recognition and command is nice (and here today and too expensive and too slow and too inaccurate), but cognitive input, which will marry advances in voice recognition with artificial intelligence, will solve at least the speed and accuracy problems. Think about it, a word processor that knows you well enough so that you can start thoughts and it can finish them and be right most of the time. I'm serious. I think we'll see the beginnings of that, and on the Mac, within 18 months, and fully developed within 3 years.

11 Outstanding Authors

There are a number of authors whose contributions to this book were outstanding. These people have written a ton of shareware programs, all of which are included on the CD-ROM with this book (for the purposes of this book, one ton = 116 programs). For each author, I've selected a program for coverage in this chapter (many of their other programs are covered in other chapters throughout the book) — to cover all of them would require another book.

Not every program in this chapter relates to the *Macintosh Crash Course* — there are games, utilities, control panels, extensions, and more. Think of this chapter as a short commercial pause.

The wide diversity of this group — from Australia, Belgium, Italy, New Zealand, and the United States — underscores the means that I used to contact these people: the MAUG area on CompuServe (and from there, other services and the Internet). See Chapter 20 for more information on getting on-line.

Installing Fkeys

Some of the programs included on the CD-ROM are fkeys — function key resources that have to be installed before you can use them. Two standard fkeys have been built into the Apple Operating System for years: pressing Shift-Command-1 will eject a disk in your floppy drive, and Shift-Command-3 will take a picture of your screen, complete with an appropriate snapshot sound. You'll find those pictures (named Picture 1, Picture 2, etc.) at the root level of your hard drive with the active System folder on it. You can look at them with SimpleText or any program that can read PICT format files.

One of the catches with an fkey is that you need to install it before you can use it; the good news is that there various skill requirements:

- Install using Suitcase (see Chapter 14 for more on Suitcase).

- Install using fkey/Sound Mover (part of MasterJuggler).
- Install using one of the numerous shareware fkey utility programs (including Carpetbag in Chapter 14).
- If you"re using System 7.1 or later, change the file type to "zsys" and the creator code to "MACS" and put it in your Fonts folder. The easiest way to change a file type is to use File Buddy or one of the other file utilities covered in Chapter 13.
- Even better than the last suggestion is to use any of the font type creators (because the above method adds a system icon that could be a problem if you ever want to trash the fkey.)
- Use ResEdit to copy the resources from the fkey to a copy of your System file. Never use ResEdit to work on a copy of your active System file.

Jason Anderson

Beyond Midnight Software
P.O. Box 471
Devonport, TAS 7310
Australia
Internet: jason_ga@postoffice.utas.edu.au

Jason is a first-year student at the University of Tasmania, where he is studying for a Bachelor of Computing. He has been programming the Mac for a bit over two years now. He started with THINK Pascal, but has recently changed to using CodeWarrior C/C++. He is also the vice-president of the Launceston Macintosh Users' Group, where he has written a simple database to make finding programs in the public domain library easier for its members.

Program	Version	Description
EjectDisk	1.0.3	Allows you to unmount and eject a floppy with a single keystroke.
Volume fkey	1.1	An fkey to adjust the volume level on your Mac.
PictSize	1.1	A utility to show the size (in pixels, inches, centimeters or millimeters) of any PICT in the clipboard.
4-Matter	1.6	A floppy disk formatting utility (see next page).

4-Matter
Shareware fee: $10.00

4-Matter (Figure 11-1) is a disk formatting utility that offers greater speed at erasing disks than the Finder and supports drag 'n drop. It is the only product on the CD-ROM for which Jason asks a shareware fee for, the rest are freeware.

Figure 11-1: 4-Matter

Jan Bruyndonckx

Salvialei, 23
B-2540 Hove
Belgium
AppleLink: WAVE.BEL

Jan is a 31-year-old software engineer who works for Wave Research in Belgium, creating the "killer" application for automated software distribution across networks. He's programmed the Mac since 1984 in a variety of languages, including Pascal, Forth, Modula, but mostly C, and now C++. He also enjoy his holidays: trekking through the Sahara desert, mountain climbing in Nepal, roaming through Thailand or Sri Lanka. When he has the time, and the weather is good, he gets excited by jumping off cliffs... by parasail.

Program	Version	Description
Color SuperApple	1.0	A control panel that replaces the Apple at the top of the Apple Menu with an animated color icon.
Jack in the Trash	1.0	An extension that gives you new graphics for your Trash can.
MenuMail	1.0.11	A paging and conferencing system for networked Macs — a truly great program.
Mithrandir	1.0.1	An extension that can automatically retype words repeated in a document.
SuperApple	1.0	The monochrome version of Color SuperApple.
The Red Queen	1.2	A packet compression utility for speeding up networks (see below).
WindowWarp	2.1.2	This control panel allows windows to warp from screen to screen.

The Red Queen
Shareware fee: $1 per Mac

The Red Queen is a control panel (see Figure 11-2) that speeds network file access by compressing data before it is sent over your network. The amount of speedup you can expect depends on your equipment and LAN configuration; those with slower networks can expect significant results.

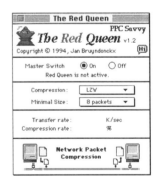

Figure 11-2: The Red Queen

David Lambert

Dejal Userware
P.O. Box 33-1011
Takapuna, Auckland 1309
New Zealand
CompuServe: 100033,2435
Internet: dejal@iconz.co.nz

David works pretty much full-time writing shareware; he's currently working on his latest product (QuickEncrypt 2.0). He's been programming on the Macintosh since 1988, with several years programming home computers before that. His company, Dejal Userware, has been operational since September 1991, with several shareware products released, many of them appearing in numerous books and CD-ROMs. He programs in THINK Pascal; he says he knows that C is more popular nowadays, but he prefers Pascal... besides, it'd be too hard to convert his large library of source code.

Program	Version	Description
Dejal Sound Library	n/a	Like it sez...
Dejal's Quoter fkey	1.6	An fkey for formatting on-line text.
SndCataloguer	1.3	A utility for cataloging sounds.
SndConverter Lite	1.3	A utility for converting sounds.
SndConverter Pro	2.2	A utility for converting sounds (see page 209).
SndPlayer	2.2	A utility for listening to sounds in various formats.
Dejal Desktop Utilities:		
AltClipboard fkey	1.2	Gives you a second clipboard.
AltFromMain Folders	1.1	These extensions allow you to
AltOrMain Folders	1.1	swap different versions of your
AltToMain Folders	2.0b5	System folders.
ClipSize? fkey	1.1	Reports the size and contents of active and alternate clipboards.
DrawDesktop	1.1	A system extension that gives you your desktop pattern during startup.
Hide Menubar fkey	1.1	Hides the menu bar.
LockHD4Session	1.1	Software-locks the startup disk.

Program	Version	Description
Privacy fkey	1.1	A screen blanker.
Volume	1.1	A minimalist volume control panel.
Dejal File Utilities:		
Create Suitcase	1.1	An application for creating suitcase files.
Deleter	1.1	An application for quickly deleting files.
New Suitcase	1.1	An application to quickly create System 7 suitcases.
Resource Leech	1.1	An application for extracting resources from a file.
Dejal Freeware:		
5-6-7 INIT	1.0b1	An INIT for switching between System versions.
Beep fkey	1.0b1	A beeping fkey.
MacCheckers	1.0	A Checkers game.
Message fkey	1.1b1	An fkey for speaking messages.
Say It fkey	1.0b1	An fkey that uses MacinTalk to speak the contents of the clipboard.
Shutdown fkey	1.0b1	An fkey that gives you the choice of shutting down, restarting, exiting to the Finder, or quitting.
SimCity Bank	1.0	Unlimited funds in SimCity.
SndCollector	1.1	A utility for cataloging sounds for a database.
SndRecorder	1.0a3	Allows you to record sounds directly into a snd suitcase.
Vol Setter fkey	1.0b1	An fkey to adjust your System volume.
{ Wrap } fkey	1,1	An fkey for formatting comments in THINK Pascal.
Dejal Text Utilities:		
TextMerge	2.0	A utility for joining text files together.
TextSplitter	2.0	A utility for splitting text files into multiple parts.

SndConverter Pro
Shareware fee: $25.00

SndConverter Pro (see Figures 11-3 and 11-4) is a utility for converting sounds from one format to another, compressing or decompressing sounds, downsampling (reducing the sound quality), and more. It supports drag 'n drop, Apple Events, and includes balloon help.

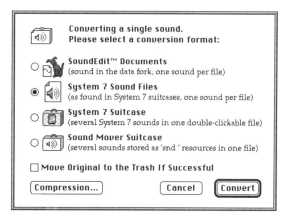

Figure 11-3: SndConverter Pro

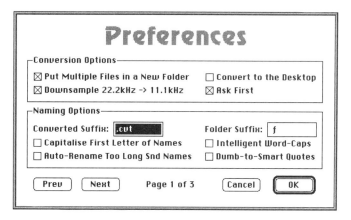

Figure 11-4: SndConverter Pro Preferences

Alessandro Levi Montalcini

C.so Re Umberto 10
10121 Torino
Italy
Internet: Lmontalcini@pmn.it

Alessandro is a 23-year-old Italian physics student. He's been programming since he was 10 years old. His first Mac was a 128K in 1985 or 1986, and he's now using a Power Mac 6100 (along with a Duo 230). He's written many shareware programs (see below — most of them are in his ShareDisk) and he's sold a couple of screensaver modules to Now Software for their NowFun package. His KeyQuencer macro engine recently won the 1994 ZiffNet Shareware Awards in the "System Enhancements" category. As for programming environments, he's currently using both the Metrowerks and Symantec C/C++ compilers, with some assembly language when required.

Alessandro has taken a unique approach to shareware licensing: he sells his titles individually, and also offers a bundle of programs called ShareDisk which he sells for $25. All of his programs are Power Macintosh and System 7.5 compatible. Asterisks mark FAT items that contain native PowerPC code.

Program	Version	Description
Accelerations	1.11	(After Dark module) accelerated balls.
Async Family	1.14	Makes the system beep asynchronous (and more).
Program	Version	Description
Attributor	1.1	Changes any number of resource attributes quickly.
B-Panel	1.17	Displays a message in a window when there's a beep.
Blood	2.0.2	Puts some floating blood spots on your screen.
Bounce!	1.31	(After Dark module) bouncing balls.
CalConvert*	1.2.1	Configurable base converter and integer calculator.
cdevEloper fkey	1.0	An fkey to help those who must build a control panel.
CheckFOpen	1.1	Checks if a file is currently open.

Program	Version	Description
CountPixels fkey	1.0	An fkey to measure distances in pixels.
DBugR	1.2	Installs a floating icon that invokes the debugger.
Depth&Volume	1.0	Changes screen depth and sound volume with a key.
Dotty da Doo	1.11	(After Dark module) cool visual effect.
DragAnyWindow*	3.1	Lets you move any kind of window including dialogs.
Errditor	1.03	Edits your "Welcome to Macintosh" and system alerts.
Global Search	1.03	Searches for an hex or ASCII string in all resources.
KeyClicks	1.0.3	Plays key clicks or funny sounds as you type.
KeyQuencer	1.2.1	Great shareware macro engine.
KQ Macro Editor*	1.2.1	Fat version of the KeyQuencer 1.2.1 macro editor.
List Files*	2.4.1	Creates disk and folder catalogs as text files.
LoopSound	1.0	Plays a sound over and over in the background.
MediaSizer*	1.2.1	Useful when mastering CDs from smaller disks.
MenuBall	2.0.2	Puts a bouncing ball in your menu bar.
NoDesktopCleanup	1.1.3	Adds a confirmation dialog to any menu command.
PowerClicks	1.1	Lets you replace a broken mouse button with a key.
PowerPCheck*	1.2.1	Checks if an application has PowerPC native code (see Chapter 19).
PowerXplorer*	1.0.3	Draws fractal images (requires PowerPC or 68020/881; see Chapter 19).

Program	Version	Description
QuickRedraw	2.01	Refreshes any dirty window or the whole screen.
ResumeToFinder	2.0	Quits to the Finder when a system error occurs.
Set Startup	1.3	Lets you pick an off-line drive as the startup disk.
Shutdown Delay	2.0.4	Gives you time to cancel a shutdown or a restart.
SoundCaser	1.01	Creates fake sound suitcases for the Fonts folder.
SoundSet fkey	1.0	An fkey to change the sound volume.
ST Color Menu	1.4	SimpleText color menu addition for SimpleText.
Startup Player	1.0.3	Plays a sound while other extensions are loading.
Trapper	1.04	Counts all the calls to the Mac's A-Traps.
Verifile*	1.2.1	Calculates the checksum and CRC32 of any file.

KeyQuencer
Shareware fee: $10.00

KeyQuencer (Figures 11-5 and 11-6) is a macro recorder that allows you to have complex tasks performed automatically with a keystroke. Macros can be executed from a text file, from a HyperCard stack, from FileMaker Pro, or by AppleScript. Macros can also be launched over a network. KeyQuencer includes a number of extensions that provide a myriad of functions (Figure 11-7).

Figure 11-5: KeyQuencer

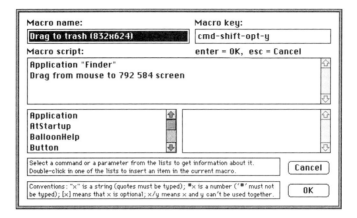

Figure 11-6: A KeyQuencer Macro script

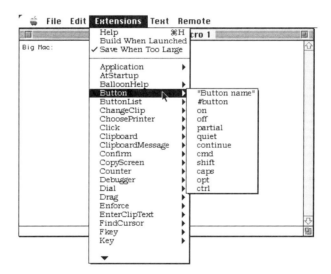

Figure 11-7: KeyQuencer's Macro Editor

Fabrizio Oddone

C.so Peschiera 221
10141 Torino
Italy
Internet: gspnx@di.unito.it

Fabrizio spends most of his time playing his pianoforte, listening to Bach and Beethoven, reading books, thinking, programming the Mac and studying computer science, listed in strict random order, the way he likes them organized. He has apparently conflicting nicknames: "the Optimizer" and "the Sloppy Programmer."

Program	Version	Description
CDIconKiller	1.3.3	Suppresses the display of custom icons on CD-ROMs, floppy disks, and networked disks; speeds up the Finder by a factor of about a zillion. This is the author's estimate; I don't know how much a zillion is, so I can't attest to the validity of his claim…

Program	Version	Description
ChunkJoiner	2.0.1	A utility for joining a group of files into a single piece.
DarkShutDown	2.1	A Darkside of the Mac module for shutting down your Mac.
Disk Charmer	2.3	A disk formatting utility (see below).
FaberFinder	4.1.3	A size-reduced Finder file.
Folder Icon Cleaner	1.1.3	Deletes custom icons from folders (see Chapter 13).
Font Control	1.1.1	An fkey for font adjustments (see Chapter 14).
Forward Delete	1.1.2	An extension that activates the forward delete key on extended keyboards.
SetupPartitions	1.0.5	A hard drive partitioning utility.
µSim	1.0b5	A microarchitecture simulator.

Disk Charmer
Shareware fee: $10.00

 Disk Charmer (Figures 11-8 and 11-9) is a sophisticated disk formatting utility that includes full System 7 support, including balloon help and drag 'n drop support. It can lock out bad sectors, and (for those with System 7.5 installed) includes the ability to format a disk in the background.

Figure 11-8: Disk Charmer

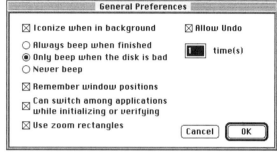

Figure 11-9: Disk Charmer preferences

Maurice Volaski

Flux Software
8201 Henry Avenue
Apartment J23
Philadelphia, PA 19128

I've known Maurice for several years now; he's been involved in coding a number of commercial and shareware products. Maurice wrote the external commands that allowed our HyperCard stack (INITInfo/Pro, and later DiagnoSYS) to "read" a user's System to allow us to compare their setup to our conflicts database.

Program	Version	Description
Beep Saver	1.1	An extension for those who use either Apple's Energy Saver or CPU Energy Saver control panels.

Program	Version	Description
ChooserUser	1.2.1	A control panel that allows system administrators to prevent users from changing a Mac's owner name.
CommentKeeper	1.0	An extension that retains get info comments when you rebuild your desktop (see Chapter 5).
FCB Inspector	1.1	A control panel that allows you to look at your Mac's list of open files (see Chapter 4).
LaserwriterLockout	1.2	An extension that allows system administrators to limit access to network printers.
Mac Identifier	1.1.1	An extension that allows System 7.5 to correctly identify Macs (see Chapter 5).
Movies in the Dark	1.0	An After Dark module that plays QuickTime movies.
SmartKeys	2.1	A control panel that converts text so that it is typographically correct (see next page).
TrashAlias	1.1.1	A control panel that trashes aliases when you trash their "parent" (see Chapter 5).

SmartKeys
SmartKeys is freeware

SmartKeys (Figure 11-10) is a freeware control panel that automatically substitutes typographically correct type for common errors. Most users will be DTPers and those who learned to type on a typewriter (and who've kept the bad habits). The six functions include space (prevents you from typing double spaces), dash (converts double dashes into em dashes), quote (converts straight quote marks to curly), ligatures (converts ligature components into ligatures), kill doubled caps (prevents you from typing two caps in a row), and shifted punctuation (prevents the Shift key from changing the period and comma)

.Figure 11-10: SmartKeys

Andrew Welch

Ambrosia Software
P.O. Box 23104
Rochester, NY 14692
Telephone: 716 427-2577
America Online: AmbrosiaSW
CompuServe: 73424,1226

Andrew is one of the most prolific and successful shareware authors in the Mac marketplace. His work covers a wide range — from useful applications, like Easy Envelopes+ and FlashWrite][, to the whimsical Wacky Lights. What he is best known for now are his arcade-quality games. At a time when everyone said decent arcade games weren't possible on the Mac, Andrew proved them wrong with Maelstrom, his version of the classic Asteroids on an overdose of steroids. Chiral is an original, addictive, thinking person's arcade game, and with his latest, Apeiron, he reinvents another Atari classic: Centipede. I can't wait to see what he and Ambrosia come up with next!

Program	Version	Description
Apeiron	1.0.1	A Centipede-like arcade game (see below).
Big Cheese Key	1.2.1	A control panel that gives you a hot key to cover the game you're playing with a fake spreadsheet.
Bomb Shelter	1.0.1	An extension that activates the "resume" button in crash dialogs (see Chapter 9).

Program	Version	Description
Chiral	1.0.0	An original arcade game.
ColorSwitch	2.3.0	A control panel that gives you a menu (bar item or pop-up) for switching color depth.
Discolor	1.0.2	An extension that "colorizes" mounted floppy disks.
Easy Envelopes Plus	2.6.0	An envelope-printing desk accessory (see below).
Eclipse	2.2.0	A screen-saving control panel (see Chapter 9).
FlashWrite][	1.1.0	A word processor in a desk accessory.
Maelstrom	1.4.1	An Asteroid-like arcade game.
Oracle	2.1.0	A control panel that gives you a saying every day or with every restart.
Snapz	1.0.0	A great screen snapshot utility.
Swoop	1.0.0	A clone of the arcade classic Galaxian.
Program	Version	Description
To Do! DA	3.2.1	A to-do list program as a desk accessory.
Wacky Lights	1.0.1	This extension provides a light show on your extended keyboard.
μLife	1.0.1	The mathematical game Life.

Easy Envelopes Plus
Shareware fee: $15.00

Remember when I said I was going to limit myself to covering one program for each of the authors in this chapter? Well, I lied. I wanted to include Andrew's latest (Apeiron, below), but I wanted also to show the quality in his utility software. Easy Envelopes Plus (see Figure 11-11) is as good as its commercial competition: a full-blown envelope printing utility, with a searchable free-form database.

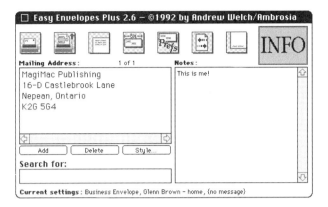

Figure 11-11: Easy Envelopes Plus

Apeiron
Shareware fee: $15.00

Apeiron is Ambrosia Software's latest masterpiece: its take on Atari's classic arcade game, Centipede. Like Maelstrom, Apeiron is a supercharged version of the game it emulates. The idea is to shoot at the centipede that comes marching down the screen, keeping the mushroom patch (the screen) clear of bad guys, and trying to collect coins and other goodies. The overall production of this game — sound, graphics, and pricing — set a standard that commercial game makers should strive for. I couldn't resist a screen shot of the cute animation at the end of each game (Figure 11-12), check out Figure 11-13 for a look at the game itself.

Figure 11-12: Apeiron's centipede

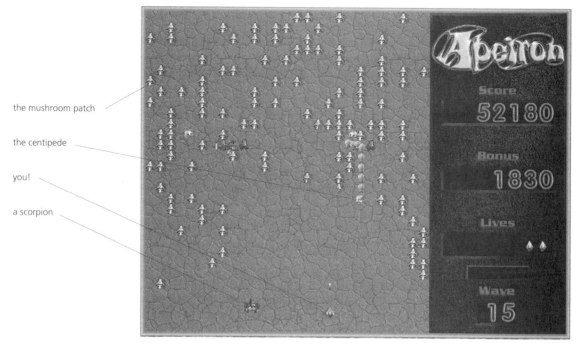

the mushroom patch

the centipede

you!

a scorpion

Figure 11-13: Apeiron

Interview: Andrew Welch

How long have you been programming and how did you get started?

I suppose I've officially been programming for 10 years or so. The first real program I ever wrote was on our old Apple][+ computer: I needed a word processor to be able to type of some of the stories I was writing, and since I couldn't afford to buy one (hey, this was pre-high school!), I wrote one.

What is your educational background — are you formally trained, or did you teach yourself?

My formal education is in Photojournalism, if you can believe it. I never took any programming classes, so everything I've done has been self-taught. This can be somewhat of a hindrance because you don't necessarily get the kind of robust background that you would by a formal education in the field. However I couldn't have done it any other way: once something bores me, I do terribly at it. Short attention spans I suppose. And the courses offered at college would have bored me until my 3rd or 4th year, so I went into another field that interested me.

What programs have you written (or been involved in the development of)?

Oh boy — too many to name and still get 'em all, both shareware and commercial projects. Some of the more popular shareware titles are Apeiron, Maelstrom, Chiral, Eclipse, ColorSwitch, Easy Envelopes Plus, To Do!, and FlashWrite.

What language(s) do you write in?

C, Pascal, and 68K assembler. I'm working on moving towards C++, but the language seems a bit convoluted to me.

What software tools do you use?

Currently I'm using THINK C 5.0.4, even though we own THINK C 7.x. I'm considering either jumping to CodeWarrior soon if Symantec doesn't get a PPC compiler and updated development environment out the door soon.

Please describe the equipment you use (what computer, how much RAM, etc.)

Well Heaphaestus, my home computer, is a PowerBook 540c with 12 megs of RAM, a 320 meg hard drive, and a 19.2 modem. It allows me to do fun things like answer these questions in the bath. At the office, I'm using Hermes, a Quadra 840av with 32 megs of RAM and a 240 meg hard drive. I like that model because I can put the CPU under the desk, out of the way. Computers should be heard but not seen.

What is your favorite piece of software (excluding that written by you or your company)

Aw, no fair excluding the stuff we've done! Well I'd have to say that the piece of software I enjoy most is ClarisWorks. Nicely done stuff.

Do you have other interests you'd like mentioned in a bio?

One word: HOG. I love my 1990 FXRS to death.

What do like to do when you're not programming?

Enjoying a good beer, riding my Harley, traveling, reading, and spending time with friends. Is there anything more?

Where do you live, are you married with children, how old are you, etc.?

I'm 24, unmarried, and though I consider myself a bachelor, some people wouldn't quite see it that way. ;)

How did Ambrosia get started?

Well I'd been writing software under the name "Mark III Software" for a few years, when I got a call from a company's (who shall remain nameless) lawyer. He threatened me because "Mark III" was the name of an old operating system used on their mainframe computers. So whatever, I just came up with a new name (one I like better BTW): Ambrosia. I've always been interested in myth and legend, so it suits me well.

What products has your company released?

Apeiron, Maelstrom, Chiral, Eclipse, Easy Envelopes Plus, To Do!, FlashWrite, ColorSwitch, Oracle, Discolour, and a number of others.

How big is your company (how many people do you employ, annual sales, whatever)?

We're still a small fish: four dedicated employees, myself included.

What are the top five questions your tech support people field, and more importantly, what are the answers?

(this question was answered by Ambrosia's Tech Support Manager, "Cajun" David Richard)

1. Why do I get an Out of Memory message when I print with Easy Envelopes (using a HP Printer)?
    The HP Print drivers need Background Printing ON when printing from a DA, or other program that uses the System Heap for memory space. Background printing sends the print job to the Print Monitor, which has it's own memory allocation.

2. Why does my Maelstrom/Chiral/Apeiron game freeze when I begin to play?
    The Caps Lock key is the pause feature, but it only works during game play. If you start a game with the Caps Lock key down, it will freeze immediately.

3. Why is it that my Screen Snapz are corrupted after taking a screen shot with Snapz?

    Snapz has a conflict with file sharing. Disable File Sharing before taking screen shots.

4. Why does Discolour not show the full color icon?

    Discolor and Apple's At Ease front end conflict. Discolour will not display the improved icon while At Ease is installed.

5. In Maelstrom, sometimes you are left with no asteroids on the screen, but you still cannot proceed to the next level.

    This is a bug that we have not found the answer to. It seems that an asteroid will get caught in "No Man's Land" and the wave cannot end. The only thing to do is to abort the game (ESC key).

What are some of the problems you've experienced in developing and marketing shareware?

Awareness. Shareware's biggest problem isn't that people don't pay for it, but rather that the number of people you can reach is much smaller than with traditional "boxes on shelves." I see this as changing over the years as more people get wired.

Why do extensions conflict and what can users do to reduce the resulting problems?

Extensions conflict because they are very low-level software that are extremely hard to write properly, and test under every possible configuration. It's chaos really. To reduce the number of conflicts you have, always make sure you have the latest versions of all of your extensions, and only use extensions from vendors you find are reliable.

Do you think the protected mode offered in Copland (Apple's current code name for System 8, now slated for release in 1996) will alleviate the problems of conflicting extensions?

Nope. Not unless Apple introduces some kind of an Extension API, which I also can't see happening because you'd have to strike a fine line between comprehensiveness and reliability. It will help somewhat in that if one program goes down, your whole machine won't die, but it won't be panacea from an extension point of view.

What can we expect to see next from Ambrosia?

Lots of cool stuff. :)

Solutions

Resolving System Conflicts: First Steps
Files: Revovery, Repair, and Cleanup
Fonts
Printing

12 Resolving Conflicts: First Steps

Your Mac crashes. Your Mac freezes. The screen goes crazy. Any of the aforementioned occur. You have a problem. What happens when your Mac starts crashing, and just why is it crashing? One of the most common problems is an extension conflict. These wonderful utilities, which do so much for our Macs, can also be our biggest source of grief.

In this chapter, we take a look at how to get control of your Mac, starting with the ways to identify and resolve system conflicts, and ending with a brief look at damaged resources. If none of this solves your problem, try the roadmap ("Where Do We Go From Here?" in the Introduction) of where to look in the book when you're trying to get your Mac back on track.

How do you tell if your current crash was caused by an extension conflict? If you have a problem that won't go away, the first thing to do is to reboot without extensions. This is easy if you're using System 7 or greater: just reboot with the Shift key held down. In some cases, especially if you have a third-party mouse or keyboard you must wait until the smiley face appears. It's a matter of timing. During the startup sequence, you'll see "Welcome to Macintosh," and, then, below that "Extensions disabled." (You should release the Shift key as soon as you see the "Extensions disabled" message. Otherwise, start-up applications won't load.) System 6 users should use one of the INIT managers on the CD-ROM to turn off all of their INITs and cdevs. If the problem goes away once the extensions are disabled, then you have an extension conflict.

The way extensions do their magic is by patching the operating system. Often, an extension presumes that a particular resource is available, and that resource has already been modified by another extension. Another common situation is where one extension sets a register to some value it needs and that value is picked up by another extension which was expecting a zero. Result: crash. There are two possible solutions: changing the relative loading order of the two extensions, or, if that doesn't work, disabling one of the extensions. A simpler scenario has an extension making a change that an application doesn't like, resulting in a crash or other aberration.

Types of Conflicts

There are three types of extension interrelationships: dependencies, conflicts, and loading order. Dependencies are where one extension requires another to work; for example, Now Startup Manager requires Now Toolbox to run. These are easy to discover; they are covered in the program's documentation. The first thing you should do when you read about a dependency in a document file for a new application is to add the dependency to either Startup Manager or Conflict Catcher, if its not already listed. Conflicts are not as easy to diagnose, although you'll often find some listed in program documentation (and more listed in Appendix B).

Load order problems are more difficult to diagnose — if you suspect two extensions are conflicting, sometimes reversing their load order will cure the problem. Fortunately, loading order suggestions are often found in program documentation. (What do you think ReadMe First files are for?) If you suspect an extension conflict, and you don't have either Startup Manager or Conflict Catcher to automate the process for you, then the binary search method is your best alternative.

Binary Search

Here are the steps you should go through to track down an extension conflict, presuming that you have a duplicatable problem:

1. Reboot your computer without extensions.
2. Attempt to duplicate the problem.
   - if the problem isn't fixed then you don't have an extension conflict (see Appendix B for suggestions).
   - if the problem is fixed, then you have an extension conflict, go to Step 3.
3. If you have an extension conflict, reboot your computer with half of your extensions disabled.
   - if the problem isn't fixed, then your problem is with one of the extensions you have turned on — go to Step 5.
   - if the problem is fixed, then your problem is with one of the extensions you have disabled — go to Step 4.

4. Reboot your computer with the other half of the extensions disabled, but the original half enabled.
   - if the problem isn't fixed then your problem is with one of the extensions you have turned on — go to Step 5.
   - if the problem is fixed, then you may not have an extension problem — go to Step 2a. (The other possibility is that the conflict is between two extensions, one in each of the two — enabled and disabled — sets. At this point you can retest, splitting the sample into three to eliminate this possibility, although I'd strongly recommend you run out and buy either Now Utilities or Conflict Catcher 3.)

5. Reboot your computer with half of your remaining extensions disabled.
   - if the problem isn't fixed then your problem is with one of the extensions you have turned on — go to Step 5.
   - if the problem is fixed, then your problem is with one of the extensions you have disabled — go to Step 6.

6. Reboot your computer with the other half of the remaining extensions disabled.
   - if the problem isn't fixed then your problem is with one of the extensions you have turned on — go to Step 5.
   - if the problem is fixed, then you may not have an extension problem — go to Step 2a.

The basic idea behind a binary search is that you are constantly dividing the group in half, until you reach a point where you can reproduce the problem based on the presence of one or two extensions. If it comes down to two conflicting extensions, then the first thing to try is reversing their order. Under System 7, extensions load in the following order: items in the Extensions folder, in the Control Panels folder, and in the System folder. In each area the extensions load alphabetically so you can change the relative load order of two extensions by adding a prefix (such as *aa* or *zz*) to force them to load earlier or later. If you need to load a control panel before an extension, then you must move it into the Extensions folder, renamed so that it loads before the extension. If you want to be able to access the control panel from the Apple Menu, you'll also have to put an alias of it in the Control Panels folder.

Where From Here?

Okay, you identified two extensions that conflict with each other, or one conflicts with an application — what do you do now? The first thing to realize is that you may be only half way through the identification process: what seems to be the errant extension may in fact be innocent. To be complete, you may have to reverse the above process to see if the interaction between your suspect and another extension is the problem.

Once you've identified conflicting extensions, and taken whatever steps you can (reordering or disabling), the best bet is to check with the technical support departments of the companies involved. Often there is a fix available or coming that will resolve your problem. Another source for fixes or updates is the on-line community (see Chapter 20).

Commercial Alternatives

The commercial alternatives to the above process — Startup Manager and Conflict Catcher 3 (both covered in Chapter 1) — simplify the above process, automating it entirely. For most users, merely reading about the process is enough to convince them to use one of them; I don't know anyone who has been able to resist after actually *doing* it.

Commercial History

I can't resist the opportunity to give some of the history of the commercial products in this area. About 8 years ago, I was running Macintosh software in emulation, using a Magic Sac on an Atari ST computer. I got frustrated with the number of times the Atari crashed, and finally broke down and bought the real thing, my first Mac (a IIcx). Imagine my chagrin to discover that the real thing crashed even more. (David Small, the author of the Magic Sac, had written numerous patches that go around crashing problems.) I had convinced my friend Gary Ouellet to buy a Mac at the same time, and he was having the same problem. At the time, Gary was active on CompuServe, and he noticed that while the experts knew about some of these problems, no one kept track of them. He and I started to maintain a listing of conflicts; which grew into INITInfo, which we distributed as shareware document. Geneviève Crabe joined us as the third partner in a company we called MagiMac Publishing (Gary and I are both magicians) — it was her HyperCard wizardry that gave us an interface for all of this information.

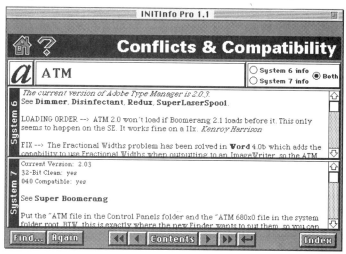

Figure 12-1: INITInfo/Pro

Although INITInfo was popular on-line (the downloads for each release were in the thousands); the return was meager (44 at last count). Baseline Publishing approached us, and asked if we'd like to take the project

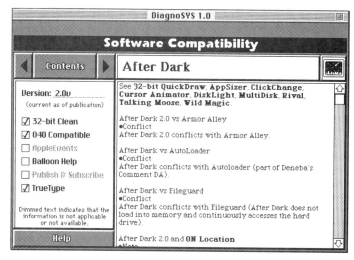

Figure 12-2: DiagnoSYS

commercial, and we did, as INITInfo/Pro (Figure 12-1). We had Maurice Volaski (see Chapter 11) write us a gestalt XFCN that allowed us to gather information on the user's Mac, so that our stack could then filter out information irrelevant to the user. A year later, after the release of System 7, the name INITInfo no longer made sense: INITs were now called extensions. We updated the stack, added some color, and renamed it DiagnoSYS (Figure 12-2).

After a disagreement with Baseline, MagiMac regained the rights to DiagnoSYS. Early in 1993, the Maxa Corporation purchased the rights to use the DiagnoSYS database in their upcoming Alert product, and hired me as their database manager. Maxa released Alert (Figure 12-3) in the spring of 1993, but had severe money problems (they went bankrupt).The rights to several products, including Alert, were sold to Central Point Software, which does not plan a further release.

Figure 12-3: Alert!

Help!
Teknosys, Inc.
3923 Coconut Palm Drive, Suite 111
Tampa, FL 33619
Telephone: 800 873-3494
Fax: 813 620-4039
AppleLink: TEKNOSYS
CompuServe: 73237,2370
Suggested retail: $149.00

Help! is a product that Teknosys released about the same time as we released DiagnoSYS. Like the products mentioned earlier in this chapter, Help! compares a user's System configuration against a database of known conflicts, and presents suggestions as to potential problem areas (see Figure 12-4). Teknosys' real advantage is staying power: they now have a knowledge base that exceeds 10,000 items. My recommendation for anyone considering Help! is to subscribe to their database updates at least twice a year. In the fast-paced Mac software market, new releases and updates happen so fast that the information Help! bases its recommendations on must be regularly updated to be useful.

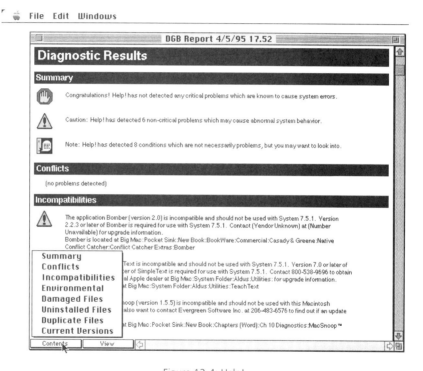

Figure 12-4: Help!

Damaged Resources

There are times when a problem defies you. You've tried everything, and still nothing works. The problem may just be damaged resources. The first thing I try is to delete the preferences file (usually found in the Preferences folder within your System folder) for the application or extension that seems to be having a problem. Remember to make a backup of the file before you trash it, in case there are settings or other information that you may later need. Your System and Finder can also get corrupted with use. As I mentioned in Chapter 5, reinstalling the System and Finder with versions 7.0 to 7.1 involves rebooting with a floppy disk (Disk Tools will do), and trashing the System and Finder files in your System folder, before reinstalling. Otherwise, the damaged resources may not get replaced. Those using System 7.5 can press Command-Option-k to have the installer do a clean install. The last possibility is that the application or extension is damaged itself. The cure is easy; just reinstall from your original disks.

Be sure to check out the latest version of TechTool (Chapter 17). As of version 1.0.7 (on the CD-ROM), it can check for damaged system files (see Figure 12-5).

Figure 12-5: TechTool finds a damaged System file

13 Files: Recovery, Repair & Cleanup

Files — what would we do without them? There is a problem, though: they're not always where you want them, they don't always do what you want, and sometimes they get lost or even worse, damaged. This chapter covers utilities to do all sorts of things with files: clean, change, find, recover, and repair. I've divided the chapter into four sections: Cleaning/Repair Tools, Dialog Enhancements, File Utilities, and File Recovery. I conclude with File Troubleshooting, a table that summarizes the features of the file tools covered in the chapter.

Cleaning/Repair Tools

This collection of shareware utilities fixes, repairs, and cleans — removes and generally makes your Mac a better place. You might not need all of them, but you should have at least some primed and ready to help your files if trouble strikes.

BundAid
Jim Hamilton
2904 Jubilee Trl.
Austin, TX 78748
America Online: JimH16
CompuServe: 71640,235
Internet: hamilton@io.com
BundAid is freeware

Born and raised in New York City, Jim studied Electrical Engineering at The Cooper Union in New York and, upon graduation in 1984, immediately headed for the warmer climes of Austin, Texas. After spending several years doing microprocessor design to support his hobby of Macintosh programming, he took up Mac programming as a career in 1990 to support his new hobby of playing duplicate bridge. He is currently employed by Saber Software Corporation designing and developing network-management software. Most of his work is in C/C++, although he still does just a bit of work in 68000 assembler.

The bundle bit is a resource that tells the Mac operating system which application must be opened when you double-click on a document. (technically, it is a 'BNDL' resource, found in the resource fork of a file). Have you ever seen the message "The document 'life story' could not be opened because the application program that created it could not be found"? This means one of two things: you are missing a needed application, or your bundle bits need repair. Another sure sign of incorrectly set bundle bits is the display of documents or applications with generic icons. The problem can be repaired in a number of ways: rebuild the desktop by holding down Command-Option while booting, run Norton Disk Doctor or MacTools Deluxe (both covered in Chapter 16), or run BundAid (Figure 13-1). I recommend the latter as the first alternative, because it is much faster than a desktop rebuild. Another good alternative is to use MicroMat's TechTool (Chapter 17).

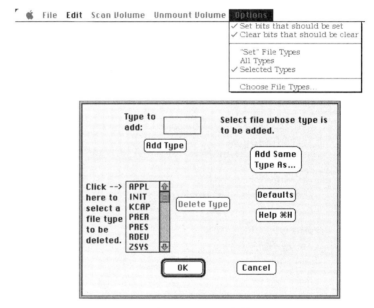

Figure 13-1: BundAid

Cleaning Lady

Joe Zobkiw, President
TripleSoft, Macintosh Software Development
172 Charles St., Suite A
Cambridge, MA 02141-2118
Telephone: 919 782-3230 (voice/fax)
America Online: AFL Zobkiw
CompuServe: 74631,1700
Internet: zobkiw@world.std.com

Cleaning Lady is freeware

Joe is a professional Macintosh software developer and author who tries to stay as busy as possible, without going over the edge. He likes to mountain bike, take evening walks with the wife and the pup, and buy expensive toys.

Do you leave icons, documents, and aliases on your desktop for easy access? Have you carefully placed them just where you want them, only to have an accidental desktop cleanup mess up your work? If you have, then Cleaning Lady is the answer to your problem. This little extension warns you (see Figure 13-2) before you clean up your desktop.

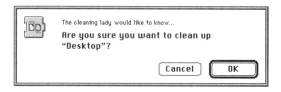

Figure 13-2: Cleaning Lady

DirtyDesk

Dave Ely
Palace Productions
4567 West 159th Street
Lawnsdale, CA 90260
America Online: Ely.D
CompuServe: 72170,2373
Internet: david_ely@qm.symantec.com

DirtyDesk is freeware.

Dave is a software engineer who has been working on the Macintosh for about five years. Until recently, he worked for Symantec in the Peter Norton Group, primarily on

Norton Utilities 2.0 and 3.0 but he also helped some on SAM. Prior to Symantec, he worked for Davidson & Associates, working on Kid Works 2, New Math Blaster Plus and AlgeBlaster Plus. He's now self employed doing contract work and looking for new ideas which he can turn into his own product. Late one night, Dave wrote DirtyDesk in just a couple of hours because he finally became frustrated after one too many incidents where his desktop was rearranged by mistake. After he'd written it, he passed it on to some colleagues who liked it and convinced him to release it to the world. Since then, he's heard from people all over the world who are using it.

DirtyDesk has different solution to the same problem Cleaning Lady solves: this extension removes the "Clean Up Desktop" and "Clean Up All" commands from the Special menu in the Finder, graying them out when they would normally be available (see Figure 13-3).

Figure 13-3: DirtyDesk in action

Folder Icon Cleaner

Fabrizio Oddone
C.so Peschiera 221
10141 Torino
Italy

Internet: gspnx@di.unito.it
Shareware fee: $5.00

Folder Icon Cleaner (Figure 13-4) is another of Fabrizio's utilities (see Chapter 11); this one recovers the extra space taken on your hard drive by

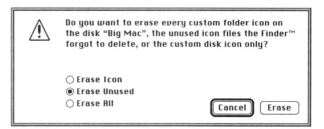

Figure 13-4: Folder Icon Cleaner

folder icons, which are not deleted by the Finder when you delete the folder itself.

Pledge
Brian Hutchison
CompuServe: 70421,3557
Internet: brian@harpo.ampr.ab.ca
Pledge is freeware

Brian is a consultant specializing in networking, integration, development, and support for Mac and Unix platforms. He's been programming Macs since 1985, using primarily Pascal, 4th Dimension, HyperCard, and C. He says that it is unlikely that he will enhance Pledge further, unless he is beset upon by thousands of feature-craving users — and he thinks that is unlikely at best.

Tired of cleaning out the temp files left in your System folder? Pledge is a simple extension that will automatically do the job for you. All you have to do is edit the file "*RemoveTheseFilesOnStartup" to add the files you wish Pledge to delete at startup.

PowerScan
Jonas Walldén
Rydsvagen 252 c:11
S-582 51 Linkoping
Sweden
Telephone: +46-13-176084 (voice/fax)
AppleLink: sw1369
Internet: jonasw@lysator.liu.se
Shareware fee: $10.00

Jonas is a 22-year-old Swede studying Computer Science and Engineering at the Linkoping University. He's been programming since the first day he used his father's Apple][over 13 years ago. He's also done software development on Apple ///s, PCs, Macs and Unix workstations in various languages such as BASIC, Pascal, C/C++, LISP, and assembly language. Human interface and graphics design are two of his interests — he's been able to incorporate a bit of both in PowerScan. At the moment his studies take all of his time but he plans on releasing more shareware in the future. Those with Internet access can find updates at his Web page: http://www.lysator.liu.se/~jonasw

One look at Figure 13-5 shows you that PowerScan is yet another example of commercial-quality software distributed as shareware. PowerScan is a powerful utility for locating duplicate files on your hard drive. Try this simple exercise: do a find on your hard drive for the files "TeachText" and "SimpleText"; you're bound to find duplicates. The fact that most installers put one or the other on your hard drive doesn't help matters. Imagine how much space you could save if you could just track down all of the other duplicates on your hard drives!

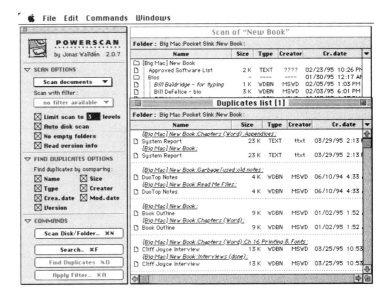

Figure 13-5: PowerScan

Prefs Cleaner
Luc Pauwels
Katholieke Universiteit Leuven
Centre for Computational Linguistics
Maria-Theresiastraat 21
B-3000 Leuven
Belgium
Telephone: +32-16-285092
Fax: +32-16-285098
Internet: Luc.Pauwels@ccl.kuleuven.ac.be
Shareware fee: $15.00

Luc studies computer science and artificial intelligence at the University of Leuven in Belgium. He's currently working at the university's Centre for Computational Linguistics. His professional activities include Unix system administration and software development in C and LISP and his main interests are graphical user interfaces, computational linguistics, and parsing techniques.

PrefsCleaner (Figure 13-6) examines your Preferences Folder and erases all "orphaned" preferences files (preferences files for which the application or desk accessory or whatever created them, can't be found anymore on any of the mounted volumes). Orphaned prefs files can be moved to the Trash folder, enabling you to undo any mistakes.

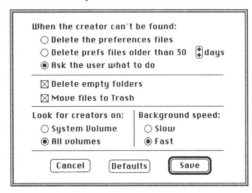

Figure 13-6: Prefs Cleaner

Safety Belt
Justin Gray
Alysis Software Corp.
1231 31st Street
San Francisco, CA 94122
Telephone: 415 566-2263
America Online: Alysis
CompuServe: 75300,3011
Safety Belt is freeware

Safety Belt (Figure 13-6) is a control panel that notifies you whenever temporary files are left on your hard drive. Why do want to know? Many programs will leave temporary files on your hard drive — if you crash, these files can often be your best bet at recovering the most recent version of the data you've lost.

Figure 13-7: Safety Belt

Dialog Enhancements

Here are a few choice enhancements to your System that go right to the heart of your Mac's filing system: the open/save dialog box.

Default Folder
Jon Gotow
St. Clair Software
2025 Mohawk Road
Upper St. Clair, PA 15241
America Online: StClairSW
CompuServe: 72330,3455
Internet: gotow@ansoft.com
Shareware fee: $10.00

Ever go to find a document, and realize you haven't the faintest idea where you put it, or even what you called it? Some applications allow you to specify the default folder that their documents should be stored in, and General Controls version 7.5 gives you the capability to set default folders (see Chapter 6), Default Folder allows you specify default folders for any or all of your applications. Once you've installed this control panel, moving your cursor over the disk name in a file dialog box gives you three new buttons (see Figure 13-8). These buttons give you (from left to right) a Folder Menu, a Link Set Menu, and a Disk Menu. The Folder Menu gives you a listing of recently used folders, the Link Set Menu allows you to set default folders for your applications, and the Disk Menu gives you a pop-up of mounted drives. Sophisticated preferences (see Figure 13-9) allow you to adjust a number of settings, including the number of folders "remembered", command keys and the ability to "rebound" to the last used file.

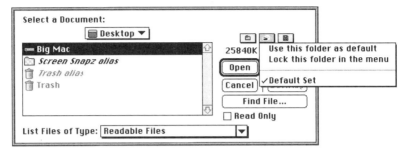

Figure 13-8: Default Folder

Figure 13-9: Default Folder preferences

Dialog View
James W. Walker
3200 Heyward Street
Columbia, SC 29205
America Online: JWWalker
CompuServe: 76367,2271
Internet: walkerj@math.scarolina.edu
Shareware fee: $10.00

James is currently employed as a mathematics professor. He has been programming off and on since around 1972, when he learned BASIC while in high school. These days he programs in C.

If you've ever wished that dialog boxes were bigger, so you could view longer file names, Dialog View is just what you want. This control panel (see Figure 13-10) allows you to change the appearance of the open and save dialog boxes by changing their height, width, the kind of icons used, and the font used in the file list. Figure 13-11 shows a dialog box made wider by Dialog View; the bold typeface indicates a folder.

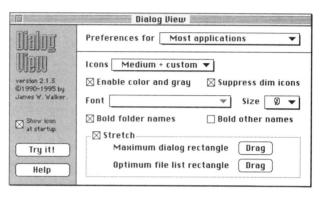

Figure 13-10: Dialog View Control Panel

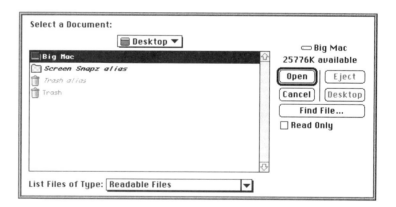

Figure 13-11: Dialog View in action

Super Boomerang
Now Software, Inc.
921 SW Washington St., Suite 500
Portland, OR 97205-2823
Telephone: 503 274-2800
Fax: 503 274-0670
America Online: Now
AppleLink: NowSoftware
CompuServe: 71541,170
eWorld: NowSoft
Internet: support@nowsoft.com
Suggested retail (part of Now Utilities): $89.95

The first thing I did after trying the first shareware version of Hiroaki Yamamoto's Boomerang was to send off a check for two registrations — one for my partner (Gary Ouellet), and one for myself. It was (and is) that good.

The first thing you'll notice with the Super Boomerang Control Panel loaded is that you now have a menu bar at the top of your file dialog boxes (see Figure 13-12) that offers direct access to folders, files, drives — basically everything stored on your hard drives. At the bottom of the dialog, you'll also see a new line, showing the data and time (last modified) and the size of the file highlighted.

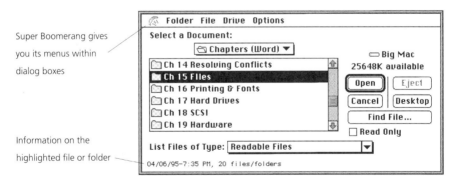

Super Boomerang gives you its menus within dialog boxes

Information on the highlighted file or folder

Figure 13-12: Super Boomerang

Super Boomerang offers all sorts of added features, including an improved find for your Finder, but the one I like the best is the simplest: it adds a hierarchical pop-out to the open menu in applications (see Figure 13-13), showing the most recent documents opened with that application.

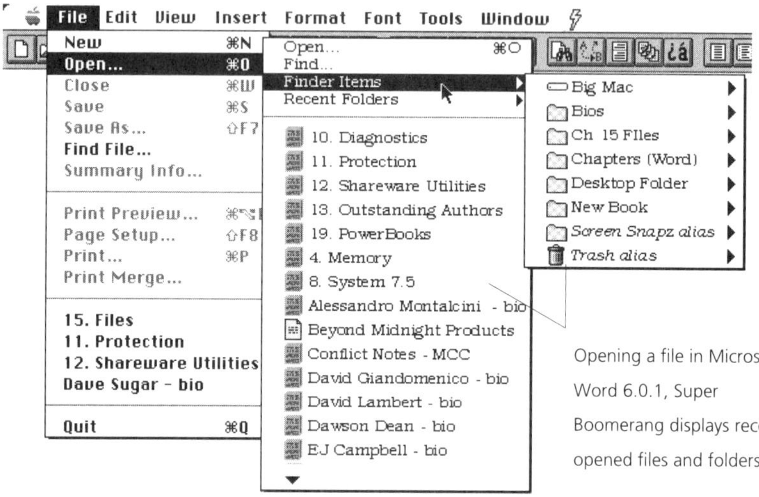

Figure 13-13: Super Boomerang pop-out

Opening a file in Microsoft Word 6.0.1, Super Boomerang displays recently opened files and folders

File Utilities

File utilities — you'd think we wouldn't need them on the Mac. After all, don't we have the superior interface? Earlier versions of Apple's Finder couldn't actually find anything, but that was fixed with System 7. The Find command in System 7.5 (see Chapter 6), which is based on ZMac's excellent Find File utility, improved things, but there are obviously inadequacies that others chose to address. Doing a Get Info (Command-I) on a file gives you some information, but not the whole story. The utilities covered here should help you find your files faster, and tell you more about them than you ever wanted to know.

Attributes
John A. Schlack
406 Newgate Court, Apartment A1
Andalusia, PA 19020
America Online: John40
CompuServe: 70252,143
Shareware fee: $15.00

Attributes is a drag 'n drop utility for getting information on a file; just drop any file onto Attributes to get the information shown in Figure 13-14. Uses include making read-only TeachText documents editable (read the documentation to find out how), hiding files, and altering or locking groups of files. Dragging a group of files onto Attributes will bring up the Batch dialog box (Figure 13-15), allowing you to process groups of files.

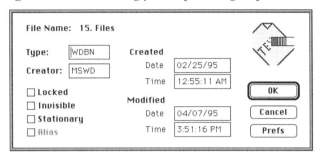

Figure 13-14: Attributes

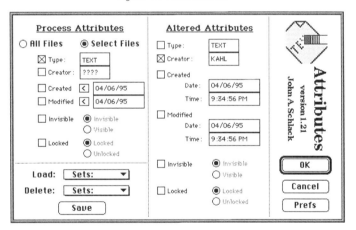

Figure 13-15: Attributes' Batch dialog box

DiskTop
PrairieSoft Software, Inc.
P.O. Box 65820
West Des Moines, IA 50265
Telephone: 515 225-3720
Fax: 515 225-2422
America Online: PrairieSft
AppleLink: PRAIRIESOFT
CompuServe: 72662,131
eWorld: PrairieSft
Suggested retail: $49.95

Gil Beecher's DiskTop is one of the original Mac file tools — it was recently acquired from CE Software by PrairieSoft. The latest update (4.5.2 as of this writing) has brought it up to date, with a new interface, support for aliases, jump-to submenus, and more. DiskTop (see Figure 13-16) lets you examine and manipulate files on your hard drive. Selecting Find from DiskTop (or from the Apple Menu) gives you the search capabilities shown in Figure 13-17.

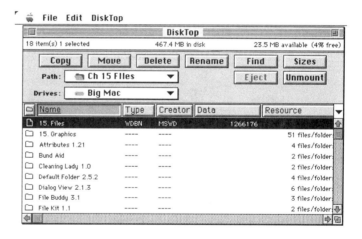

Figure 13-16: DiskTop

DiskTop also includes DT Launch, a file-launching tool that allows hierarchical access to files and documents that you specify (see Figure 13-18), and Microlytics' GOfer, a program that allows you to search for text within files.

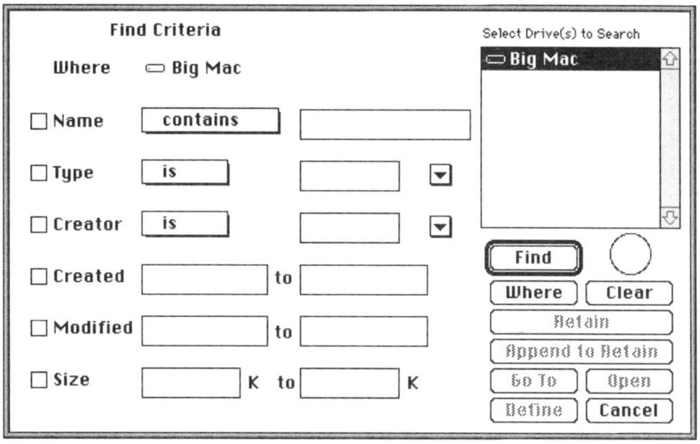

Find Criteria		Select Drive(s) to Search

Find Criteria

Where   ⬭ Big Mac

☐ Name   `contains`

☐ Type   `is`

☐ Creator   `is`

☐ Created   `____` to `____`

☐ Modified   `____` to `____`

☐ Size   `____` K to `____` K

Select Drive(s) to Search

⬭ Big Mac

Find

Where   Clear

Retain

Append to Retain

Go To   Open

Define   Cancel

Figure 13-17: DiskTop Find

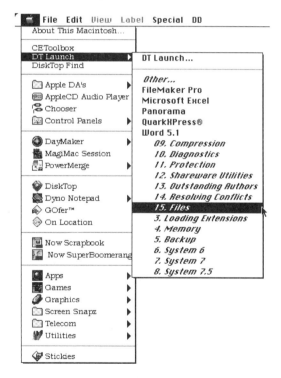

Figure 13-18: DT Launch

File Kit

Dawson Dean
Software Publishing
654 Blair Avenue
Piedmont, CA 94611
America Online: DawsonDean
Internet: dawson@cs.cornell.edu
Shareware fee: $15.00

File Kit is a utility that lets you look at and change system information on files (see Figures 13-19 and 13-20), get information on volumes, open or close files, and compare and delete files.

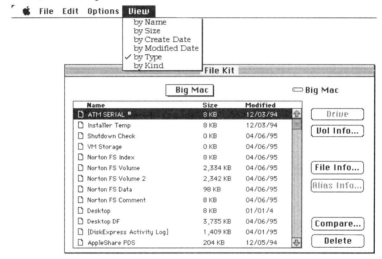

Figure 13-19: File Kit

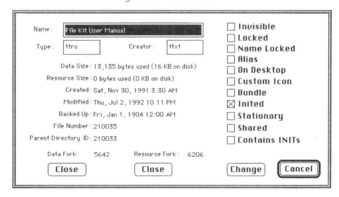

Figure 13-20: File Kit file information

Filename Mapper

Rick Genter
Useful Software Corporation
12 Page Street
Danvers, MA 01923-2825
Telephone: 508 774-8233
America Online: Useful
CompuServe: 73163,2142
Shareware fee: $10.00

Rick has been the President and Chief Technical Officer of Useful Software Corporation for almost 3 and a half years. He's been programming professionally since graduating from Boston University with a Bachelors of Science degree in Computer Engineering in May of 1980. He's been doing Pascal since 1977, C since 1982, C++ since 1988, BASIC since 1972(!), and various assembly and other languages since 1976. Rick has designed and implemented compilers, multitasking/multiprocessing operating systems, cross-platform GUI hierarchies, non-GUI class hierarchies, and embedded control programs. You name it, he's done it (probably).

This one's a bit different — this is a tool for those who do cross-platform development between the Macintosh and Windows. Filename Mapper scans a list of files (that you provide), makes copies of the files using their mapped names in a new folder, and maps their contents as well.

Find Stuff

Dave Sugar
3718 Norburn Road
Randallstown, MD 21133
Internet: udsugar@king.mcs.drexel.edu
Find Stuff is PostcardWare

Dave is a 22-year-old senior majoring in Computer Science at Drexel University in Philadelphia. He has been doing Macintosh programming for about 4 years, mostly using C and C++ (he has been known to use assembly when needed). He worked for a company named Cedrus for about a year where he learned a lot and refined his programming skills. Other things that he does are camping and backpacking. He is a Ham radio operator (N3RRF), and an Eagle Scout of Troop 743 located in Randallstown.

For those users who haven't yet upgraded to System 7.5, Find Stuff (Figure

13-21) offers a number of parameters not available to them (even System 7.5's Find command doesn't let you search by creator).

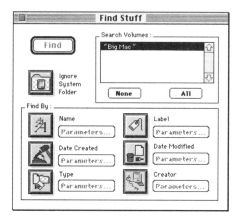

Figure 13-21: Find Stuff

Gumshoe

Shepherd's Pi Software
3408 S. Rusk Street
Amarillo, TX 79109
America Online: RBuckwheat
CompuServe: 75264,3431
Shareware fee: $15.00

You want information on files? You want everything? Then you want Gumshoe (Figure 13-22). Here's a list of some of the things you can do with Gumshoe: make a file or folder invisible, change its creator and type, give it a custom icon, rename it, move it, launch it, change its memory partition, and more.

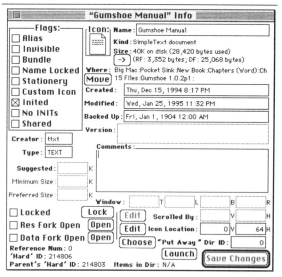

Figure 13-22: Gumshoe

File Buddy

Laurence Harris
1100 W. NC Highway 54 BYP Apt 29-J
Chapel Hill, NC 27516-2826
Telephone: 919 933-9595
America Online: LHarris
CompuServe: 76150,1027

Shareware fee: $25.00

Wow. This is *shareware*? The only way I can describe Larry Harris's tour de force is wow! I've talked to Larry about the reasons he hasn't taken File Buddy commercial — it's not because it isn't good enough (it certainly is), but rather because he's not willing to put up with the hassles of commercial distribution.

Let's have a look at the things File Buddy does. (I guarantee to miss some of File Buddy's functionality here — the best way to find out more is to try it for yourself).

- Complete information on files or groups of files (see Figure 13-23).
- Automatic creation and placement of aliases.
- Disk cleaning (see Figure 13-24): finding duplicates, checking aliases, scanning for empty files or folders or unnecessary preferences.
- Completely configurable drag 'n drop operation (see Figure 13-25).
- Finding files and folders (see Figure 13-26).

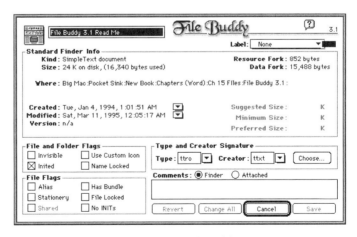

Figure 13-23: File Buddy

Figure 13-24: File Buddy's cleaning options

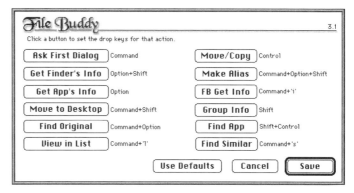

Figure 13-25: File Buddy drop keys

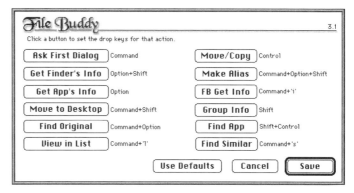

Figure 13-26: File Buddy Find

Once you've found or listed a file, File Buddy gives you the dialog shown in Figure 13-27. Highlight an item in the list, and use the icons at the top to perform one of the following (left to right): show, open, open with…, print, get Finder or group info, make alias, copy, move, move to desktop, mark duplicates, remove non-duplicates, add or remove from list, change names or delete resource fork, find similar, or move to trash. (If you use this — and you will — and don't pay the shareware fee, then my guess is you're too cheap to pay shareware fees.)

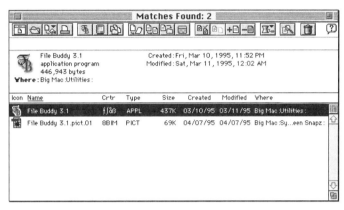

Figure 13-27: Files found with File Buddy

 On Location
Insanely Great Software
126 Calvert Avenue E.
Edison, NJ 08820
Telephone: 800 368-5195
Fax: 908 632-1766
America Online: AdamStein
CompuServe: 71140,2051
Suggested retail: $129.95

Okay, so we've figured out how to massage and keep track of all of the files on your hard drive. How about the files that aren't on your hard drive (SyQuests, MOs, remote drives)? Insanely Great Software has taken over the distribution of On Location from ON Technology. On Location does two things incredibly well: it can index the text within files, so that you can later search for "Memo to Bob" even if you called it MTB95.DOC, and it can index files whether or not they are on-line. I use it to keep track of nine 230 MB MO cartridges (see Figure 13-28) — over 36,000 files, and it can find anything for me almost instantly.

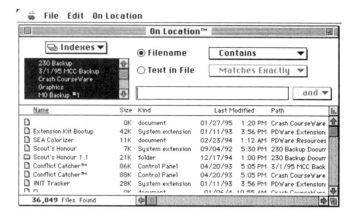

Figure 13-28: On Location

UltraFind
UltraDesign Technology Ltd.
5/39 St.George's Square
London SW1V 3QN
England
Telephone: +44 171 931 0010
Fax: +44 171 630 9105
AppleLink: ULTRA.TEC.UK
eWorld: UltraTec
ftp: ftp.demon.co.uk/pub/mac/ultratec
Internet: find@ultratec.demon.co.uk
Shareware fee: $38.00

UltraDesign Technology Ltd. is a software development company based in London, run by brothers Julian and Steve Linford. Julian holds both an M.Sc and a B.Sc in Computer Science and has programmed Unix, MS/DOS and VAX/VMS mainframe systems for 12 years. In 1993, convinced that the future is Macintosh, he joined up with Steve — an interface designer with 8 years experience in Macintosh — and together they now develop software exclusively for the Apple Macintosh.

After File Buddy, I thought I'd seen it all when it comes to File Utilities, but I was wrong. UltraFind (Figure 13-29) is an impressive utility which allows you to search your hard drives for files or folders, based on type or creator, date and time created or modified, the Finder label , or file size. Even better, it allows you to search for text within files. Once you've located files, you can have them displayed in a Finder view (Figure 13-30), Hierarchic (tree) view (as shown in Figure 13-31), or Path view. Want more information on a file? If you move the cursor over a file, detailed information will be displayed on the bottom the screen (see Figure 13-31). CopyRight-IT is a unique feature that allows you to modify files get info information, adding your own copyright and address information.

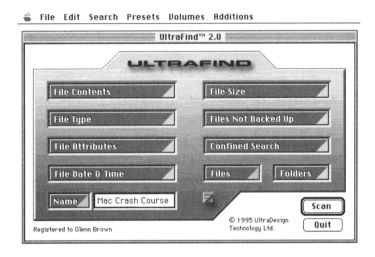

Figure 13-29: UltraFind

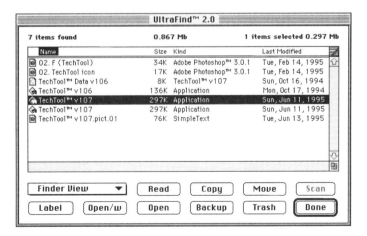

Figure 13-30: UltraFind Finder View

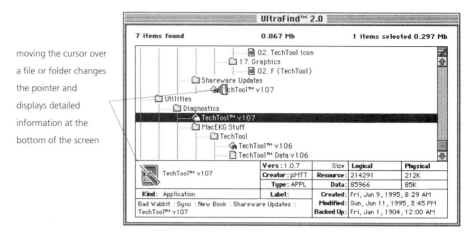

moving the cursor over
a file or folder changes
the pointer and
displays detailed
information at the
bottom of the screen

Figure 13-31: UltraFind info

File Recovery

So what do you do when that file you've been working on all day suddenly won't open? Files occasionally get damaged, through crashes, electrical spikes, or just plain bad luck. There are tools out there to help you, but it's gonna cost ya.

ResEdit
Apple Computer
20525 Mariani Avenue
Cupertino, CA 95014-6299
(408) 996-1010

ResEdit is a resource editing tool Apple has made widely available (check your favorite Mac user group or on-line service). One of the things the latest version does, much to my surprise, is attempt to repair damaged files. Just drag a damaged file onto ResEdit, and cross your fingers — if this doesn't work, then try one of the commercial alternatives.

MacTools Pro

Symantec
10201 Torre Avenue
Cupertino, California 95014
Telephone: 408 253-9600
Tech Support: 503 465-8420 (free for 90 days)
America Online: keyword: SYMANTEC
CompuServe: GO SYMANTEC
Suggested retail: $149.95

One of the modules in MacTools Pro is FileFix (Figure 13-32), a utility to repair damaged files. For more on MacTools Pro, see Chapter 16.

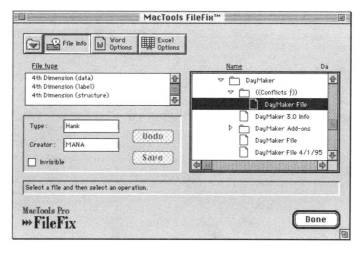

Figure 13-32: MacTools Pro FileFix

Both MacTools Pro and Norton Utilities for the Mac include the capability for recovering files that have been accidentally erased (Figure 13-33). When you trash a file, the operating System doesn't actually erase it, it just "marks" it as gone. As long as that part of the hard drive hasn't been used for storing other information, then these utilities have a chance of recovering your file.

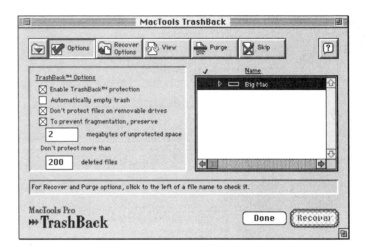

Figure 13-33: MacTools Pro TrashBack

RescueTXT

Abbott Systems Inc.
62 Mountain Road
Pleasantville, NY 10570–9802
Telephone: 800 552-9157
Fax: 914 747-9115
Suggested retail: $79.00

Abbott Systems has the only two dedicated Mac file recovery tools I know of. RescueTXT (see Figure 13-34), offers a simple interface, and does one thing well: it recovers text from files.

Figure 13-34: RescueTXT

CanOpener
Abbott Systems Inc.
(see address information for RescueTXT, above)
Suggested retail: $125.00

CanOpener (Figure 13-35) is a serious tool for recovering data from all kinds of files — it can recover text, pictures, sounds, even movies from damaged files. The description may be short, but all you need is for CanOpener to work for you once, and you'll be sold.

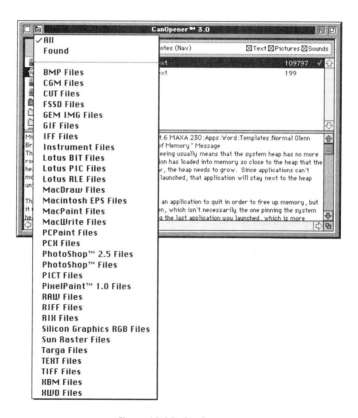

Figure 13-35: CanOpener

RescueTXT

Abbott Systems Inc.
62 Mountain Road
Pleasantville, NY 10570–9802
Telephone: 800 552-9157
Fax: 914 747-9115
Suggested retail: $79.00

Abbott Systems has the only two dedicated Mac file recovery tools I know of. RescueTXT (see Figure 13-34), offers a simple interface, and does one thing well: it recovers text from files.

CanOpener

Abbott Systems Inc.
(see address information for RescueTXT, above)
Suggested retail: $125.00

CanOpener (Figure 13-35) is a serious tool for recovering data from all kinds of files — it can recover text, pictures, sounds, even movies from damaged files. The description may be short, but all you need is for CanOpener to work for you once, and you'll be sold.

File Troubleshooting

There are so many files in this chapter that I thought it would be worth it to summarize with a table highlighting the features of each of the tools:

File	What it does
Attributes	A utility for getting (and changing) detailed information on files
BundAid	Repairs bundle bits
CanOpener	Recovers data from damaged files
Cleaning Lady	Prevents you from accidentally rearranging your

File	What it does
PowerScan	Powerful utility for locating duplicate files on your hard drives
Prefs Cleaner	Erases "orphaned" preferences files
RescueTXT	Recovers text from damaged files
ResEdit	Apple's resource editing tool, can also repair some damaged files
Safety Belt	Notifies you if temporary files are left on your hard drive
Super Boomerang	One of the best, a utility that enhances your dialogs, making files easier to find and work with
TrashBack	Recovers files that have been accidentally trashed
UltraFind	Sophisticated find (and manipulate) file utility

14 Fonts

The first Mac introduced high-quality fonts, easily changed to other high-quality fonts, to personal computing. The Mac is still the choice of graphic artists. While part of this is due to the fact that service bureaus still prefer files from the Mac, a more important reason is that the Mac is simply a better graphics machine. Adding and removing fonts on the Mac is immeasurably easier than on a Windows PC. Still, things have gotten more complicated over the past few years — first with TrueType™, then Multiple Masters, and now QuickDraw GX. This chapter looks at the different types of fonts available, installing them, and utilities for managing them. It concludes with an interview with Jim Lewis, author of theTypeBook.

Fonts

Fonts come in many types. You'll probably need at least some of each. Let's start with a look (Figure 14-1) at the icons associated with different kinds of fonts:

Figure 14-1: Font icons

Bitmapped fonts, also known as screen fonts, are made up of dots, in the same fashion as a paint program draws on-screen. They can show up jagged both on-screen and in your printed output. You need to have fonts three times the value of that you wish to print to get decent output (that is, you'll need 36-point type installed if you want decent 12-point output). This depends upon your printer; my advice is to stick with TrueType™ or PostScript™ Type 1 fonts, and leave bitmapped fonts behind.

PostScript™ fonts use vector graphics. These are fonts drawn and defined by the outlines of the letters. They add new costs; printers with PostScript are most

265

costly than those without. Type 1 PostScript typefaces have hinting (additional information that adjusts for printing at 12 point or smaller sizes); Type 3 PostScript fonts do not. Type 3 fonts have been obsolete for years, any that you find are old. The font icon shown in Figure 14-1 is from an Adobe PostScript font (Adobe Caslon, the typeface used for the body text in this book).

Apple's **TrueType**™ fonts provide decent outline fonts to users who don't want to pay the high prices associated with quality PostScript typefaces. TrueType fonts don't require multiple sizes to be installed and don't require an expensive printer to produce high-quality output on a laser printer. PostScript Type 1 fonts are almost always required for high resolution output on an imagesetter.

A few years ago, Adobe started releasing typefaces in a new format: **Multiple Masters**. These fonts can be adjusted over a wide range, allowing you to tailor a typeface to fit a page perfectly. Imagine a table, with a short, skinny font in the upper left-hand corner, and a tall, fat font the the lower right-hand corner, and you have the concept.

Apple shipped **QuickDraw GX** with System 7.5. When you install QuickDraw GX, your Type 1 typefaces are converted to GX format. This new format offers better control of the letterforms, drag and drop printing, the promise of faster, printer-independent printing.

Installing Fonts

How you install fonts depends on which System you are running:

System 6 users need to use Font/DA Mover to move fonts into and out of their System folders. The current version of Font/DA Mover is 4.1; versions earlier than 3.8 are dangerous to use. System 6 users are best off with either of two commercial utilities: ALsoft's MasterJuggler or Symantec's Suitcase.

System 7.0 (and 7.0.1) gave us the ability to drag install fonts directly, without having to use Font/DA Mover, but the actual fonts are still stored in the System file. To install a font, just drop it onto the System folder. To remove one, quit all other applications (you cannot modify the active System when other applications are running), then double-click on the System file to open it and drag the unwanted files out. If you have to reinstall your System, remember to copy the fonts out before deleting the file.

System 7.1 gave us a fonts folder within the System folder — adding and removing fonts is as easy as dragging them into or out of the folder. Note, however, that there is a limit of 128 active files. If you have more fonts, combine them into suitcases, or use Suitcase or MasterJuggler.

System 7.5 gave the option of adding QuickDraw GX, although few have yet exercised that option.

Font Utilities

Font utilities have been with the Mac for a long time. Although Apple has made some less useful than they once were, many commercial utilities still flourish. I've listed the best here.

Adobe Type Manager
Adobe Systems
1585 Charleston Road
P.O. Box 7900
Mountain View, CA 94039
Telephone 415 961-4400
Suggested retail: varies, often free, and included with many products, including System 7.5

Adobe Type Manager (ATM) is a utility that prevents the "jaggies" (see Figure 14-2) when displaying or printing PostScript fonts. Adobe also make a version called Super ATM, that uses Multiple Master fonts to create substitutes for fonts that you do not have installed. This allows you to view a document created by someone else with fonts you don't have, at something approximating the original — otherwise, font substitution may ruin the look of the document. Adobe recommends that you set aside approximately 50K per font per document (including styles as fonts); for my setup, 256K is optimal. If you assign too little memory to ATM, you'll find that documents with multiple fonts will scroll slowly; if you assign too much, you'll be wasting valuable RAM. Figure 14-3 shows the ATM Control Panel.

without ATM

with ATM

Figure 14-2: Before and after ATM

set aside about 25K for each font or style used in a document; if you need more than 256K, read a good design book

SuperATM uses Multiple Masters to "fake" fonts that aren't installed on your system

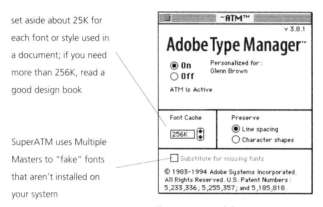

Figure 14-3: Adobe Type Manager

Adobe Type Reunion
Adobe Systems
(See above for address information)
Suggested retail: $39.95

One of the drawbacks to the more sophisticated PostScript typefaces is that each typeface variation (bold, italic, etc.) is considered another font. The naming convention (BFontBold, IFontItalic, and so on) makes for a long and confusing font menu (see Figure 14-4). Adobe Type Reunion unifies font families, giving you (for example) Garamond, with a hierarchical pop-out for the related font styles. If you like this idea, however, you're bound to like one of the two utilities that follow even better.

Figure 14-4: A font menu without ATR

WYSIWYG Menus
Now Software, Inc.
921 S.W. Washington St. Suite 500
Portland, OR 97205-2823
Telephone: 503 274-2800
Fax: 503 274-0670
America Online: Now
AppleLink: NowSoftware
CompuServe: 71541,170
eWorld: NowSoft

Internet: support@nowsoft.com
Suggested retail (part of Now Utilities): $89.95

WYSIWYG Menus improves greatly on ATR's good idea: not only does it unify font families, but it also displays each font correctly in the menus. Your control over fonts goes much further, as you can see in Figure 14-5. Other features let you disable fonts; change their order; change the size, color, and font of display; get information on typefaces; and disable WYSIWYG Menus within specific applications.

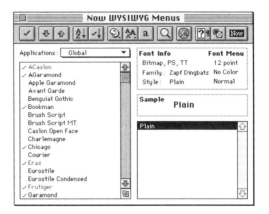

Figure 14-5: WYSIWYG Menus Control Panel

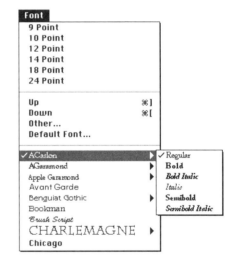

Figure 14-6: WYSIWYG Menus in action

MenuFonts

Dubl-Click Software
20310 Empire Avenue, Suite A102
Bend, Oregon 97701
Telephone: 503 317-0355
Fax: 503 317-0430
Suggested retail: $69.95

MenuFonts (Figure 14-7) is the typographers' obvious choice — it includes display of the font's type (bitmapped, TrueType, PostScript), along with the font ID and the locations where the file is loaded from and of the printer file (PostScript fonts include two parts: the screen font and the printer font). One minor shortcoming is that for those typefaces with hierarchical pop-outs, only the pop-out is stylized or colored.

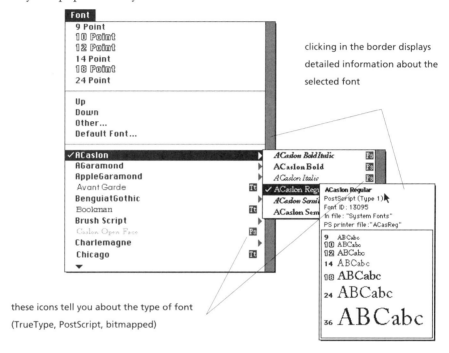

Figure 14-7: MenuFonts

Adding a Font Menu to Microsoft Word

To add a font menu to Microsoft Word 6, so that MenuFonts and WYSIWYG Menus work correctly, try the following:

1. Select Macro… from the Tools menu, then click on the Organizer button to select it.

2. The Organizer (see Figure 14-8) will display two windows, both showing "Macros available in: Normal (Global Template)"; click on Close File (either one will do, I chose the right for this example), then click on Open File.

3. Navigate out of the Templates folder into the Macros folder and load the file "5.1 Upgrade."
4. Copy the AddFontMenu macro to the Normal template, then click on Close.
5. Re-open the Macro… dialog and run the AddFontMenu macro.
6. Wait for a minute (progress will show in the lower left-hand corner), et voila!: Word 6 now has a standard Font menu! (Figure 14-8).

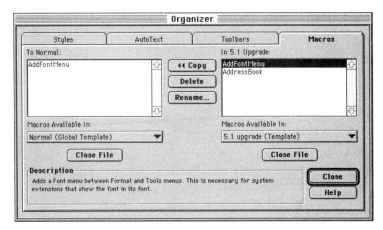

Figure 14-8: Copying the AddFontMenu macro in Word 6

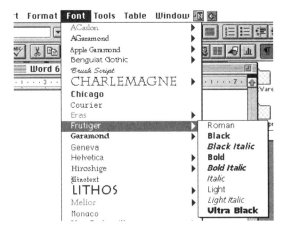

Figure 14-9: Word 6 (with WYSIWYG Menus) after running the AddFontMenu macro

More Font Control: MasterJuggler and Suitcase

ALSoft MasterJuggler and Symantec Suitcase are utility programs for loading fonts and other resources. With Apple's addition of the Fonts folder in System 7.1, there is a reduced need for most users. Those involved in desktop publishing, or with extensive font collections, will still want the control offered, especially the ability to load sets of fonts. Simpler font control is also offered by Conflict Catcher 3 and Startup Manager, which can both disable fonts loaded from the Fonts folder. ExAminer (Chapter 1) can also do the disable fonts trick.

Font Strategy

What type of fonts should you use? For starters, forget bitmapped typefaces. If you print all of your documents on your own printer, then you're probably best off with TrueType fonts: they're cheaper, they work well, and you don't need to use Adobe Type Manager. If you output any of your work on an imagesetter, then you should stick with PostScript fonts. As for QuickDraw GX, until there are more applications that support it, and more importantly (at least for graphic artists) until service bureaus have imagesetters with RIPs that support GX, I'd recommend against it. The RIP is the Raster Image Processor, the hardware that converts your pages into high resolution output.

Shareware Font Utilities

If you think with all these great commercial font utilities that there aren't niches for shareware to fit into, you'd be wrong.

Carpetbag
James W. Walker
3200 Heyward Street
Columbia, SC 29205
America Online: JWWalker
CompuServe: 76367,2271
Internet: walkerj@math.scarolina.edu
Shareware fee: $5.00

Carpetbag is a control panel (See Figure 14-10) that lets you have System resources (fonts, sounds, FKeys, keyboard layouts) installed outside of your System folder. Note that Carpetbag does not support PostScript fonts. For those with System 7.0 or 7.0.1, the folder also includes Laser Path, a control panel that lets you place PostScript fonts in a folder outside of the System folder, and still have ATM and the LaserWriter driver see and use them.

Figure 14-10: Carpetbag

Extensions Manager Fonts Patcher
Bill DeFelice
Connecticut Trimedia Broadcasting
P.O. Box 20
Monroe, CT 06468-0020
America Online: McBill
EM Fonts Patcher is freeware

Active in the area of personal computing for over 16 years, Bill DeFelice has worked with a variety of platforms in many user environments. A certified technician for both Apple and IBM products, Bill provided support for many corporate clients while employed in the retail channel. He presently serves as Senior Computer Technician for the Norwalk Public Schools overseeing the maintenance of over 850 Macintosh computers. He is also the Director of Engineering for Connecticut Trimedia Group integrating Macintosh technology with radio and television broadcast technologies.

These patches modify Apple's Extensions Manager (versions 1.8 and 3.0) so that it can also be used to control System 7.1's Fonts folder.

Font Control

Fabrizio Oddone
C.so Peschiera 221
10141 Torino
Italy
Internet: gspnx@di.unito.it
Shareware fee: $5.00

Here's another from Fabrizio: Font Control is an fkey, that allows you to set fractional widths for StyleWriter or ImageWriter printers, ensures that TrueType fonts are used instead of their bitmapped equivalents, and more (see Figure 14-11).

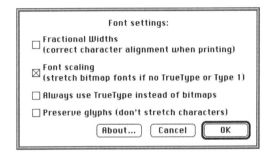

Figure 14-11: Font Control

FontClerk

Robert Chancellor
963 Cedar Street
El Segundo, CA 90245
Shareware fee: $20.00

Font Clerk (figure 14-12) is yet another commercial-grade application hiding as shareware. With this utility, you can convert TrueType fonts from the Mac to Windows and back (they both use TrueType fonts, but each requires a slightly different format). Also included is the ability to create empty font suitcases, get font information, view full character sets, and locate the specific keystrokes required for individual characters.

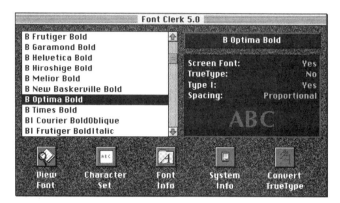

Figure 14-12: Font Clerk

HideFonts
Steven Ting
205 Hewlett Avenue
Merrick, NY 11566
CompuServe: 72267,2035
Shareware fee: $20.00

Steven is the manager of international sales at Ultre division of Linotype-Hell Company. He wrote HideFonts using MPW Assembler and MPW C. Another hack he wrote on the Mac is PrintTimer, which is designed to get a measure of print timing.

HideFonts is a simple extension that allows you to trick applications into thinking you have only a small number of fonts installed, thus speeding their launch time. This is especially useful for service bureaus or others with large font collections who need to load documents for printing (without needing to modify them).

theTypeBook
Jim Lewis
Golden Gate Graphics
2137 N. Candis Avenue
Santa Ana, CA 92706-2422
Telephone: 714 542-5518
America Online: JimXLewis
CompuServe: 71650,2373

theTypeBook is freeware (see page 277 for more details)

Want to know what all of your typefaces look like? Most graphic artists need a tool to show available typefaces to clients, and theTypeBook is the tool. I cannot imagine needing anything else in a font display utility. Just select the typefaces you want to print in the application (see Figure 14-13), and theTypeBook will output pages like the sample shown in Figure 14-14.

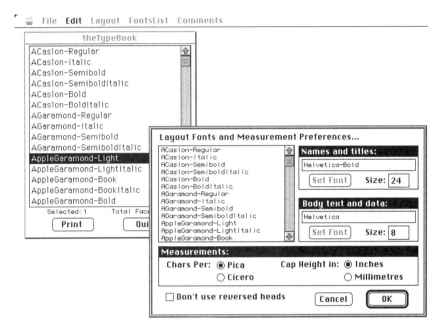

Figure 14-13: theTypeBook settings

This version of theTypeBook is a limited edition freeware program. For a copy of Version 4.0 which includes capabilities for on-screen viewing of all sample sheets, fonts, and characters, and the "Customizer" for adding logos to the page footer, please contact Rascal Software at 805 255-6823 or contact any of the major mail order companies. Please note that technical support is not provided for freeware versions of the program.

FOND: ACaslon Regular Style: Plain ID: 13095 Type: PS

ACaslon-Regular

6 pt. ABCDEFGHIJKLMNOPQRSTUVWXYZabcdefghijklmnopqrstuvwxyz0123456789!?,"¢$&%{}*
7 pt. ABCDEFGHIJKLMNOPQRSTUVWXYZabcdefghijklmnopqrstuvwxyz0123456789!?,"¢$&%{}*
8 pt. ABCDEFGHIJKLMNOPQRSTUVWXYZabcdefghijklmnopqrstuvwxyz0123456789!?,"¢$&%{}*
9 pt. ABCDEFGHIJKLMNOPQRSTUVWXYZabcdefghijklmnopqrstuvwxyz0123456789!?,"¢$&%{}*
10 pt. ABCDEFGHIJKLMNOPQRSTUVWXYZabcdefghijklmnopqrstuvwxyz0123456789!?,"¢$&%{}*
12 pt. ABCDEFGHIJKLMNOPQRSTUVWXYZabcdefghijklmnopqrstuvwxyz0123456789!?,"¢$&
14 pt. ABCDEFGHIJKLMNOPQRSTUVWXYZabcdefghijklmnopqrstuvwxyz01234
18 pt. ABCDEFGHIJKLMNOPQRSTUVWXYZabcdefghijklmno

36 pt. ABCDEFGHIJKLMNOPQR
STUVWXYZabcdefghijklmno
pqrstuvwxyz0123456789!?,"¢$
&%{}*

9/10
This page was generated by "theTypeBook
". A freeware power tool from Jim Lewis.
Customized versions are available in which
the page footer is configured to your specif
ications. A typical layout would include a l
ogo and company address information. Art
work is limited to a height of 32 pts. The c
ombined width of both copy and artwork i
s limited to the printed area. The fee for c
ustomization is $45(US). To order contact
Jim Lewis at the address shown below.

10/11
This page was generated by "theType
Book". A freeware power tool from Ji
m Lewis. Customized versions are ava
ilable in which the page footer is confi
gured to your specifications. A typical
layout would include a logo and comp
any address information. Artwork is li
mited to a height of 32 pts. The comb
ined width of both copy and artwork i
s limited to the printed area. The fee f
or customization is $45(US). To order
contact Jim Lewis at the address show

11/12
This page was generated by "theTy
peBook". A freeware power tool fr
om Jim Lewis. Customized version
s are available in which the page fo
oter is configured to your specificat
ions. A typical layout would includ
e a logo and company address infor
mation. Artwork is limited to a hei
ght of 32 pts. The combined width
of both copy and artwork is limite
d to the printed area. The fee for c

12/13
This page was generated by "the
TypeBook". A freeware power t
ool from Jim Lewis. Customize
d versions are available in which
the page footer is configured to
your specifications. A typical lay
out would include a logo and co
mpany address information. Art
work is limited to a height of 32
pts. The combined width of bot

13/14
This page was generated by "t
heTypeBook". A freeware po
wer tool from Jim Lewis. Cus
tomized versions are available
in which the page footer is co
nfigured to your specification
s. A typical layout would incl
ude a logo and company addr
ess information. Artwork is li

14/15
This page was generated by
"theTypeBook". A freewar
e power tool from Jim Lew
is. Customized versions are
available in which the page
footer is configured to your
specifications. A typical lay
out would include a logo a
nd company address infor

48 pt. AaBbCcDdEeFfGgHh

theTypeBook
A Power Tool from Jim Lewis

Customized/Registered versions are available from
Golden State Graphics • 2137 Candis • Santa Ana, CA 92706
714/542-5518 • CIS 71650,2373 • AOL JimXLewis

Figure 14-14: theTypeBook output

Interview: Jim Lewis

Jim is the author of theTypeBook, and an authority on PostScript.

How long have you been programming and how did you get started?

Wow... since day 1, I've been a hobbyist programmer since 1980. At that time I was working as a Quality Assurance Supervisor for a DEC OEM and systems configuration company. To demonstrate a point to management, I assembled a complete and functioning PDP 11/34 system from equipment scrapped by the test department. The system became my personal office computer for a little over a year. After a couple of months I was a grand master in the original "Adventure" game, after which I installed the RT-11 BASIC software. Learning mostly through books and the occasional question to the software engineers, I began working on a job tracking system which turned out pretty good though it was never adopted outside the QA department.

What is your educational background — are you formally trained, or did you teach yourself?

No formal training or education. I was trained as a telephone, teletype, and crypto repairman in the service. In 1980 I took BASIC and FORTRAN classes but dropped both after only 3 weeks. Far too slow, and too much trouble. If I had come up with a figure I would estimate general training at about 10% and self-taught about 90% with the help of many books and manuals.

What programs have you written?

For the Macintosh, I've been solely responsible for theTypeBook, theFONDler, and the Pica Calculator. To be honest, I don't even know any other programmers... except for the occasional developer's forum Q & A.

What language(s) do you write in?

Symantec LS Pascal, which I may be forced to change in the near future. I also use PostScript which is needed to take advantage of all levels of output devices.

What software tools do you use?

THINK Pascal, ResEdit, Prototyper, LaserTalk, Illustrator, QuarkXPress, Photoshop, DiskTop, Gopher, Vantage, and SuperPaint.

Please describe the equipment you use (what computer, how much RAM, etc.)

I program almost exclusively on my 1987 Mac SE, 4MB RAM, 200MB HD + 44MB SyQuest, LaserWriter Plus. However, at my real job I have access to a wide variety of Mac systems, laser printers, and imagesetters.

What do like to do when you're not programming?

I like collecting classic song recordings from late sixties underground to nineties alternative, landscaping around the house, and riding my '85 650 NightHawk. I'm also restoring my '87 El Camino slowly but surely.

What do you do for a living?

Currently I'm working at a Color/PrePress house providing desktop publishing and output services to a variety of clients. I have been working in desktop publishing since 1987.

Where do you live, are you married with children, how old are you, (etc.)

4.5 miles SE of Disneyland. Not married, no children. 43.

How did your company get started?

Golden State Graphics was started by my sister in 1979 after she received her degree in graphic arts. In 1987 both of us were exposed to the Mac and PostScript output devices at which time I joined with her to help integrate the Macintosh into her work flow. Quickly this evolved into DTP contract work and consulting. After laying low, while I discovered the Mac, my programming interests resurfaced. I bought THINK Pascal and began to create my own solutions to problems for which I could find no other suitable alternative. I believe the first shareware release of theFONDler was in 1990. As we continue to provide DTP services other needs arise; theTypeBook, Pica Calculator and a "yet to be announced."

How big is your company (how many people do you employ, annual sales, whatever)?

My company, Golden State Graphics, is very small. One to two people at any given time. Having shown interest in commercially publishing our software, Rascal Software handles all sales, marketing, and fulfillment aspects, including routine technical support calls.

What are the top three questions your tech support people field, and more importantly, what are the answers?

1. Where can I find, or do you sell, this font called whatever?

   They have seen a sample page from the freeware version somewhere, a local copy shop perhaps, and want to buy a particular font they have seen. We explain that we do not sell fonts, and about the page that they have seen. However, Rascal Software has licensed a small number of fonts from David Rawkoski.

2. Why are some of my fonts not showing up in theTypeBook's list of available typefaces?

   Most frequently this is the result of converted TrueType fonts and the fact that theTypeBook prefers to use the true typeface name known as the "outline name" for each available. Early conversion program(s), particular from IBM to Mac, must create a FOND resource for each face. Unfortunately, the information placed into the data fields was not always appropriate. Specifically, the Offset to the Style Mapping table should be nil if the table is not present or just excess baggage. Or, from converting a linked style variation from a Mac PS font, the base style in the font association table is not set. The Style field of the only font association should be set to zero, indicating that no font styles need to be applied; 0=Plain, 1=Italic, 2=Bold, 3=BoldItalic. These and other problems will be addressed in a forthcoming update to theFONDler.

   On the other hand, it may be simply that their fonts are not properly installed (via accepted methods) or that the font has become corrupt via a media error or system bomb at some point.

3. I get system errors when trying to print more than one page. Why?

   a. *In the case of some QuickDraw printers that must rasterize the image in Mac RAM some of the page layout and font combinations have a memory requirement that exceeds what is available to the print driver.*

   b. *They have received a copy from a friend or associate and are experiencing what I call a print driver conflict. When theTypeBook is launched it checks the name, revision, and device type of the currently chosen (the Chooser) printer. If it is the same as that of the saved printer settings, the old settings are restored... nice huh? Early experience indicated that some print drivers, other than Apple's, erroneously identified themselves. Since there wasn't a reasonable solution to this a manual override has been built into theTypeBook which is required only once when this situation is encountered. By holding down the option key when launching theTypeBook, the old default print record will be discarded and a new one established from the current chosen printer.*

c. *A corrupt outline font has been encountered during printing, perhaps at the system resource level or in the printer language it generates.*

What are some of the problems you've experienced in developing theTypeBook?

Printing presents the biggest challenge. Maintaining compatibility with the wide variety of printers and print drivers, while still taking advantage of some of the features provided by the more sophisticated devices, is challenging. Programmers are left in the dark when it comes to what a printer can do, and how it is done. For myself, information such as support for fixed page sizes, variable page size capability and two-sided printing is required. This information and much more is what PPD files are made of. Even with the release of LaserWriter 8.x, which permits the selection a PPD, there still isn't any way for a Macintosh application to determine the name of the selected PPD or the information contained therein. Apparently, heaven forbids an application programmer from accessing, or even executing, that information. Support for placed EPS graphics in a document is nonexistent and represents a significant programming effort.

Breaking through these barriers is one of the major milestones of a professional quality/level program, one that outputs to anything including PostScript imagesetters.

How do fonts become corrupted, what are the symptoms, and what can users do to avoid or fix the problem?

Question of the decade! I believe that fonts become corrupt for two basic reasons; media errors and, more importantly, they make good targets when the System goes awry. When a font is active, the file it resides in is open and "known" to the System software. If the System becomes confused at the time it needs to write some data, any open file is at risk because the System has a handle on it. Consequently, the best way to reduce the risk of font corruption is to keep the number of active fonts to a minimum. A backup copy of a font library is also highly recommended.

The symptoms vary widely from System bombs and freezes to simply unexpected behavior. System bombs are usually the result of a corrupt font resource file or one of the many resources that make up a Mac font. A corrupt resource file will usually manifest itself immediately when the System tries to get the names of the resources. Corrupt resources do not occur until that particular resource is read into memory and/or used by the System. Aside from a "hard" bomb, users may notice a significant reduction in System performance and/or strange behavior with the cursor or menu functions.

PostScript printer outline files can also become corrupt most frequently due to media errors, but they too are active files at times during the printing cycle. These fonts are tougher to identify as each character is actually an independently executable program. Additionally, fonts are routinely purged from a PostScript printer's memory during which errors can occur. This means, that there is a possibility that one of the fonts used before *the printing problem occurred may be causing the problem in successive outputs even if that font is no longer being used. Power cycling the printer after PostScript errors if often recommended as a first step in correcting suspect PostScript printing problems.*

Should users with PostScript printers replace the TrueType fonts the Apple OS installs and replace them with PostScript equivalents?

Yes, though it isn't absolutely necessary. Most of the PostScript equivalents of that the Apple OS installs are from the same set that is "built-in" on most PostScript printers. This means that the PostScript outline files do not have to be downloaded during printing and provide the fastest printing times. In fact many PostScript printers support an external hard disk mainly for the installation of new fonts in the printer. TrueType versions will print of course, but the outline information must be downloaded each time along with a TrueType to PostScript dictionary for the printer to use for the conversion. TrueType does have the advantage of looking nice on the screen versus PostScript which requires both outline file and Adobe Type Manager to accomplish the same thing.

What are your views on (QuickDraw) GX?

I only have knowledge of the technology and will be adding GX support in future releases. From a service bureau professional's point of view it will end up in the same category as TrueType, and even Multiple Masters. The reality is that the desktop publishing market is driven by the publishing professionals. These professionals are after printed results which typically requires their files are output at high resolution on PostScript imagesetters. In my experience TrueType and Multiple Masters have always added a certain amount of overhead to a job in output times or file handling. Since throughput is money, guess what, most professionals have stuck with the native language of imagesetters, PostScript. If Apple really wants the "whole ball of wax" they will probably have to "give" the GX interpreter to any imagesetter manufacturer who might be interested to keep end user costs at rock bottom, or they will have to come up with a chemical free printer that produces high-resolution film negative color separations, and in registration. I vote for the new printer idea!

From a user's viewpoint I think the font technology is interesting, but is not what I hoped for. I believe that I can derive no direct benefit from it at this point. The desire to modify a font develops only on the extremely rare occasion when all a project's copy must fit in a design area that is otherwise too small. As you might guess, they are many other solutions short of creating a new font. The last published estimate I've read placed the number of digital typefaces available at around 13,000. That was probably six months ago.

I think if Apple wants to improve the fonts used on a Macintosh they should do so from a perspective of accessibility. More people have problems with effectively managing large numbers of fonts than they do finding a font that fits their needs. I would suggest that Apple consider dispensing with the fixed style menu in favor of a dynamic one that would support the 48 style variations available in the FOND resource. An entire font family, from light to heavy, could be installed in a single FOND that in turn would provide a user interface option similar to that of Adobe Type Reunion, only faster. Additionally, the ability to activate and deactivate fonts while a program is running is a significant benefit provided by Suitcase II and MasterJuggler to users of large font libraries (>200) or those with limited disk space. Fifth Generation and ALsoft figured it out... what is one more system event to the Apple OS?

What are the most common PostScript errors?

Certainly "limitcheck errors" in the "path" or "clip" are among the most frequent PostScript errors and are corrected by splitting up paths or clipping paths that are too complex. Too complex can simply mean greater than 256 Bézier points. A single path that crosses over itself and has a fill applied can also cause this error. Another popular error is a "limitcheck" in the "fill." This too can be the result of a path that criss-crosses itself, but more frequently it is the result of a "open" path with a fill applied to it. This allows the fill algorithm to leak outside the intended boundaries of the object. A limitcheck in the fill can also be the result of blend problems such as too many steps, scaling, or color combinations.

The two remaining most common errors are "dict full" and "undefined." In these cases something did not happen that should have. PostScript print files add their own commands and variables to the printer's memory. Dictionaries of commands and variables are created, added too, and destroyed during the print process. Each dictionary is seen as a separate portion of memory that will contain a fixed number of elements. "dict full" means there is no more room in the dictionary for the new command or variable data. There may be plenty of RAM left, however. An "undefined command error" occurs when a PostScript program executing in the printer cannot find a command or variable in the current or previously defined dictionaries. Most of these errors can be corrected by restarting the printer and deleting the cache if that option is available.

What are the most common printing problems?

Aside from the problems described above, by and large most printing problems are the result of a improperly constructed document or one that exceeds the printing capabilities of a given system or program, for example excessive application of scaling factors to objects. Most programs have limitations and the closer a user gets to those limitations the more likely they are to encounter problems.

Where do you plan to take theTypeBook in its next release?

As they would say on CSPAN; "I reserve the right to later extend my remarks." The next release will consist mainly of additional page layouts and layout customization options with, perhaps, additional options to existing layouts. This will probably result in some minor changes to the user interface as well. For the most part, theTypeBook is a complete program. Except for keeping up with Apple's technology and additional layouts only one significant change is being considered. That is the sharing of data between two other font related programs I am currently developing. Of course we will have to wait and see!

15 Printing

You've just spent two days creating it; now why won't your latest project print? Printing problems are among the most frustrating to strike users regularly. They often seem to defy solution, yet when you do solve the problems, and with this chapter you will, the solutions are often embarrassingly simple. Here are the four most common reasons that a document won't print:

1. **Your printer is not selected in the Chooser.**
    This one is easy to fix: go to the Chooser (in the Apple Menu), and select your printer (Figure 15-1). Set AppleTalk on or off as needed, select your printer from whatever list appears, and close the Chooser. If you can't see your printer in the list, then you should make sure that it is turned on, and connected properly (see #2). The Chooser, while highly reliable, sometimes forgets your favored printer after a crash.

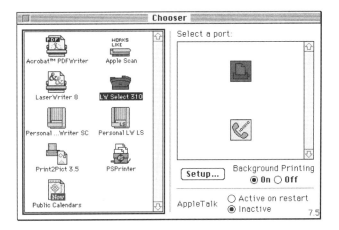

Figure 15-1: The Chooser

2. **Your printer is plugged into the wrong port.**
    I'm amazed at how many times this happens, because almost all of the plugs on the back of the Mac have a unique shape, which makes it difficult to screw up. The serial connectors for the modem port (has a

287

telephone graphic beside it) and the printer port (has a printer graphic beside it) look the same; make sure your printer is connected to the correct one (this will usually be the printer port).

3. **Your document is too large for printer memory.**
   If you get "out of memory" error messages, then your document may be too large — if possible, print small sections or even page at a time. Another solution is to add memory to your printer. Adding memory to your printer may also speed up the printing of complex documents, especially those with multiple fonts. If you regularly print large documents that cause PrintMonitor to resize itself, you may want to increase its memory allocation prevent it from having to quit and resize (you'll find it in the Extensions folder within your System folder).

4. **Your document is too complex, and generates a PostScript™ error.**
   This is a common problem for those using advanced graphics applications like Freehand and Illustrator. Some operations, such as blends and pasting inside, are simple to do but complex to print. Some artists use freehand tools to create very long Bézier paths — these should be simplified or split to reduce output problems (see Figure 15-2).

Figure 15-2: Splitting complex paths in Freehand

5. **Turn off background printing.**
   This ties up your Mac for much longer, but may allow printing of long or complex documents that may otherwise fail to print.

If you're having trouble printing a complex document, go into the LaserWriter Page Setup (Figure 15-3) and turn off all of the printer effects. Then select Options, and turn off all of the options except for Unlimited Downloadable Fonts in a Document (Figure 15-4). This will force your printer to flush each font from memory after it is used, freeing up some printer memory for your document. This tends to slow things down, but if it works, who cares?

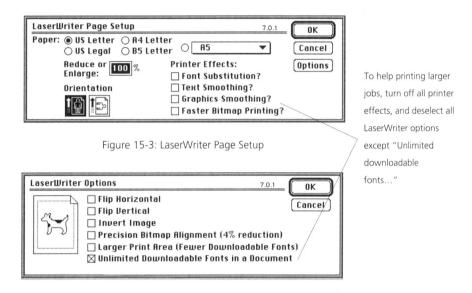

Figure 15-3: LaserWriter Page Setup

To help printing larger jobs, turn off all printer effects, and deselect all LaserWriter options except "Unlimited downloadable fonts…"

Figure 15-4: LaserWriter Options

Printing Software

Here are some tools that should help you in your quest for the perfect page.

EPS Fixer
David Schooley
200 26th Street NW N-203
Atlanta, GA 30309
America Online: DSchooley
Internet: schooley@ee.gatech.edu
Shareware fee: $10.00

David Schooley is a Ph.D. student at Georgia Tech studying how wind and solar energy affect the reliability of electric power systems. David has been programming in various languages since 1981, when he first learned BASIC on a TRS-80 Model I. Since then, he has written programs in FORTRAN, Pascal, C, and C++, and various assembly languages. Besides EPS Fixer and one commercial application, he has also written software to control flight simulators and guided missiles. He has been programming Macs since 1991, which is about the same time he became a Macintosh fanatic.

EPS Fixer (Figure 15-5) is a utility for viewing or creating the PICT preview resources in EPSF (Encapsulated Postscript) files. If the PICT resource is not present there is no screen preview, which can make things difficult in page layout. EPS Fixer can also correct discrepancies between the boundary of the PICT preview and the bounding box information in the PostScript™ file.

Figure 15-5: EPS Fixer

PrintAid

James W. Walker
3200 Heyward Street
Columbia, SC 29205
America Online: JWWalker
CompuServe: 76367,2271
Internet: walkerj@math.scarolina.edu
PrintAid is freeware

PrintAid is a control panel (Figure 15-6) that can alleviate some problems when attempting to background print using printers other than a LaserWriter.

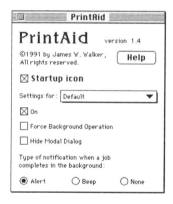

Figure 15-6: PrintAid

PrintChoice

Kerry Clendinning
P.O. Box 26061
Austin, TX 78755
AppleLink: KerryC
CompuServe: 76424,2214
Shareware fee: $14.00

One of the nicest features of QuickDraw GX is desktop printing: you can have icons on your desktop for drag 'n drop printing. The only problem is, you need to have GX installed. PrintChoice is a control panel (Figure 15-7) that gives you a menu bar printer dropdown for selecting printers; even better, it lets you create desktop printer icons, even without QuickDraw GX. (LaserWriter 8.3 also lets you create desktop printer icons.)

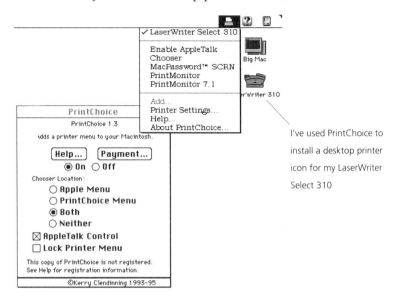

I've used PrintChoice to install a desktop printer icon for my LaserWriter Select 310

Figure 15-7: PrintChoice

Printer Defaults

John Rawnsley
Mathematics Institute
University of Warwick
Coventry, CV4 7AL
United Kingdom
Printer Defaults is freeware

Tired of always changing your printer's default settings? Printer Default (Figure 15-8) allows you to run through the print dialogs, and create new default settings.

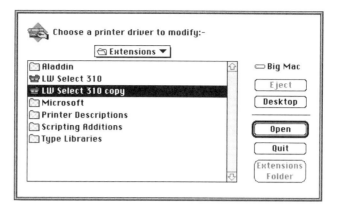

Figure 15-8: Printer Defaults

PrintOne
Scott Silverman
SilverWARE (formerly CRA.Z Software)
P.O. Box 6379
Haverhill, MA 01831
Telephone: 508 521-5262
America Online: Silverwre
AppleLink: Silverware
CompuServe: 74007,2303
eWorld: Silverman
PrintOne is freeware

Scott has been programming the Macintosh since its inception in 1984. He currently programs in THINK C and C++. He wrote the commercial Mac products MacAuto, FetchIt, FolderJump and KopyKat. More recently, he has ventured into Newton programming and has released the commercial product MoreInfo.

PrintOne is a simple extension that gives you a new menu item in most applications: Print One Copy (see Figure 15-9). This means you can often go straight to printing, without having to go to the print dialog.

Figure 15-9: PrintOne

Toner Tuner / Working WaterMaker
Working Software Inc.
P.O. Box 1844
Santa Cruz, CA 95061-1844
Telephone: 408 423-5696
Toll-free: 800 229-9675 (US and Canada)
Fax: 408 423-5699
America Online: WorkingSW
CompuServe: 76004,2072
Internet: Info@working.com
Suggested retail: $24.95 (Toner Tuner), $49.95 (Working Watermarker)

Working Software is another of the small companies that has been making great Mac software since the early days. Toner Tuner is a utility that should pay for itself in about a month — it allows you to decrease the amount of toner that your printer uses for drafts. Here in the great white north, the cartridges for my LaserWriter Select 310 cost about $138.00 each, so I like to make them last as long as I can.

Working Watermaker is a slick utility for placing a watermark ("Draft," "Top Secret," your logo) behind anything you print. The demo comes with a single watermark; the real thing comes with dozens of examples, and the ability to create your own from PICT or EPS graphics.

Toner Tuner and Working Watermaker expand the print dialog, adding new functionality

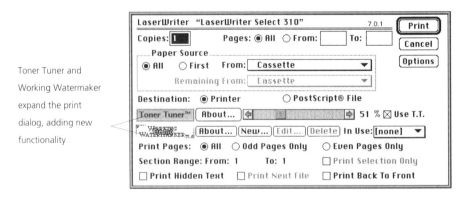

Figure 15-10: Toner Tuner & Working WaterMaker

Interview: Cliff Joyce

Cliff is the president of one of the original Mac companies, Dubl-Click Software, and one of the genuinely nice guys in the business. After one of our Macworld sessions, I was approached by a tall, quiet man who was interested in discussing conflicts and their resolution. He was also interested in my opinions on his software. We've since talked innumerable times, and I've done some beta testing for Dubl-Click.

How long have you been programming and how did you get started?

I've been programming since 1978, although my first commercial product was released in 1984 (a Mac product called Mac the Knife).

What is your educational background — are you formally trained, or did you teach yourself?

I went to art school, and have a Bachelor of Fine Arts degree (in painting and graphic design). I started a graphic design business in my Junior year, and we bought some computerized typesetting equipment. Many of our clients had word processing equipment, and we got tired of rekeying data they had printed from their word processors. Although it's pretty standard now, back then it was a big deal getting these machines to talk to each other. And in the process, I taught myself to program. I also had several Apple]['s, Kaypro's and early S-100 bus CP/M machines — so I learned BASIC and Pascal during that time.

What programs have you written (or been involved in the development of)?

For Macintosh: Mac the Knife, WetPaint, World Class Fonts/LaserType, Brøderbund's Print Shop Companion, Calculator Construction Set, ArtRoundup, PatternMover, BigCaps, FontCharter, ClickChange, ClickTrax, Icon Mania!, MenuFonts, Zonkers. For Newton: GoFigure, Maltin's Movie Guide, several Newton books, and Symantec's Act. Have also written various demos for both platforms. There are probably others I'm forgetting...

What language(s) do you write in?

Assembler, Pascal, C, NewtonScript.

What software tools do you use?

MPW (Mac Programmer's Workshop), Symantec C, NTK (Newton Tool Kit).

Please describe the equipment you use (what computer, how much RAM, etc.)

Main machine: Macintosh Quadra 800, 1 gig drive, 40 meg RAM (RAM Doubled to 80 meg), and a Mac Quadra 610 with 20MB RAM (used while the Q800 is busy building Newton packages; grin). I also use Newton 100, 110, and 120 machines.

What is your favorite piece of software (excluding that written by you or your company…)

There are so many: QUED/M, Finder 7.5.1, NowMenus, RAM Doubler, Touchbase.

Do you have other interests you'd like mentioned in a bio?

Skiing, mountain biking, basketball, daddying.

What do like to do when you're not programming?

The above, and watching Star Trek and movies.

Where do you live, are you married with children, how old are you, (etc.)

Bend, Oregon. Married. 2 kids (girls).

How did Dubl-Click get started?

I started Dubl-Click after my first publisher stopped paying me. Our first product was Calculator Construction Set, our offices were a second bedroom, and our dining room was our assembly/shipping department.

What products has your company released?

WetPaint, World Class Fonts/LaserType, Calculator Construction Set, ArtRoundup, PatternMover, BigCaps, FontCharter, ClickChange, ClickTrax, Icon Mania!, MenuFonts, GoFigure.

How big is your company (how many people do you employ, annual sales, whatever)?

Fluctuates between 3 and 7 people (depending on outside contracting jobs). We have about 1500 square feet of commercial space.

In these days of big mergers, what are some of the problems with keeping a small company like yours independent?

Cost of advertising, materials, labor, and distribution. In the old days, there were several Mac-only distributors who didn't expect as much from each product they stocked — they're all gone, replaced by Windows-mostly distributors who don't see Mac software moving as well as software created for the much larger Windows market. Magazines base their advertising rates on number of readers, and as the readership has grown, so have the ad rates — making it really difficult for small software companies to be heard above the noise. When mail order houses first started, they made most of their money by selling software. Now they make very little margin on the "boxes" they move — their profit center is generally cooperative advertising space. Consequently, it has become very difficult for the little publisher to make it in today's environment because all levels of the distribution chain expect the publisher alone to assume all costs involved with promoting the software titles.

What are the top questions your tech support people field, and more importantly, what are the answers?

In no particular order...

1. *How to use the GetFile/PutFile dialogs; basically, lots of new users who don't read manuals.*
2. *People using very old software (incompatibles). I actually blame technology here; changes in the System and CPUs have created a great need for lots of new versions of lots of software in a very short space of time. Users don't realize that just because something ran a year ago, and was written according to the rules back then, that it might cause problems in today's environment.*
3. *INIT conflicts. We always have to explain how to isolate them by turning half off, then half of those, etc., until found. This is generally only an issue when people are using older versions, or noncommercial software (which has endured the rigors of professional testing).*
4. *Virus protection — turn it off when installing anything. (My recommendation is that you reboot with all extensions disabled before running any installer.) It often prevents vital resources from being installed, resulting in unexplainable crashes later. If you must use virus protection, we recommend Disinfectant.*
5. *Corrupted fonts. This crashes Microsoft Word a lot. The best solution is to replace the offending fonts with fresh copies from your original disks. Also, make sure not to run any utility which alters a font file in any way — or you'll blow ATM's mind, causing crashes in MenuFonts, and most word processors.*

6. *Reinstall the System, and rebuild the desktop files. Many folks install new versions of their System over old system files, never realizing that the old system file never gets replaced. Every year or so, you just have to install a fresh System and Finder.*

7. *A particular problem for us is Adobe's automatic installation of Type Reunion by most of that company's installers (most users never knew it happened). At least one of their products has ATR built into the application itself. Type Reunion and MenuFonts are both competing for the right to change your font menus, and if Type Reunion is installed, MenuFonts doesn't work. Users should choose one or the other — not both.*

What are some of the problems you've experienced in developing MenuFonts?

Font numbering, different font formats from different manufacturers, lack of standard Font menu interface implementations (some programs, such as Microsoft Excel, still don't have font menus — and use scrolling lists instead). Also, "creative" menu implementation by many application developers.

Are there still problems with font numbering, or are all fonts now released with the new font numbering system?

Yes, it's still a problem; although not as bad as pre-Font Folder days, when everyone used Suitcase. However, these conflicts are easily solved by simply moving fonts which share IDs into a single Suitcase file. It is also a big problem with applications that attempt to install fonts into their own resource forks (which Apple cautions developers against). Interestingly enough, Claris' Filemaker Pro has a particular font ID problem with the font used in their main browser window.

What is your advice to users on using TrueType versus Type 1 fonts?

If you're going to use the fonts in a printed piece (one that gets output to a phototypesetting machine), we recommend PostScript™ fonts. Adobe fonts are generally now the standard for most service bureaus, and you can count on the piece printing WYSIWYG without errors if you use Adobe PostScript™ fonts.

If you're a casual user, or never send documents to others for output, I think TrueType is a better solution (doesn't require ATM, simpler installation, works on any printer, always renders on screen— which older PS Type 3 fonts don't). Of course, the overriding factor is price and the style of the font you're looking for — seems like there are more PostScript™ styles available than TrueType.

When do you think users should consider moving to QuickDraw GX, and what are the problems users can expect if they do make the move?

We've had lotsa problems trying to run QuickDraw GX here, and so I don't recommend it yet.

BTW, a general tip for people with lots of fonts: use as few font suitcases as you can, and your System will start up much faster — even with the same number of fonts installed.

Hardware

Hard Drive Utilities
Hardware Tools
PowerBooks
Power Macs

16 Hard Drive Utilities

There is nothing more important to the health and well-being of your valuable data than the place where it resides: your hard drive. Most hardware is just iron, just replaceable parts. It might be expensive to replace it, but it shouldn't be a big problem. Hard disks are another matter. They hold your product and any failure, unless it occurs just exactly as a backup is completed, is going to cost you data and product.

Fortunately, hard drives are very reliable devices, and the tools and techniques covered in this chapter will help you make them even more reliable. Physical failure is extremely rare and often the result of outside events ("I don't have the report; my hard drive got run over by a bus"). Damaged data is the usual source of hard drive problems and, in most cases, far easier to deal with.

Like all complex devices hard drives need regular maintenance to keep them running smoothly. Spending regular time keeping your hard drives in the best possible shape is wise, and in the long run, very cost efficient.

Your hard drives suffer more than any other part of your computer whenever you crash, shut down abruptly (without using a Shut Down command), or even Restart without using the Restart command. Every time something like that happens, there's the possibility of damage to the data stored on the hard drive . Catastrophic damage is rare, but by no means unknown. The tools covered at the end of this chapter can often successfully deal with what appears to be the total loss of a drive.

Far more common is minor damage to the internal structure of the data on the drive. This damage often passes unnoticed. After several small damaging incidents occur, though, the drive may fail and be unrecoverable. The small, unseen problems never get better on their own. The best that you can hope for is that do they do not worsen, but they often do.

I start this chapter with a look at the shareware hard disk upkeep and enhancement products on the CD-ROM. Next I cover commercial hard disk formatters and optimization utilities. The chapter ends with in-depth looks at

MacTools Pro and Norton Utilities for the Mac, two vital utility packages. If you don't own one of these utilities, then I suggest you put the book down, and go get one (or both) right now. My coverage of these packages includes interviews with the development team leaders of both: Dave Camp and Elissa Murphy.

Disk Utilities

It is for good reason that this chapter has very little shareware included with it — any risk to your hard drive, any mistake, and you could be reading the Backup section of Chapter 3 again. What is in this section, however, is good (and safe) stuff.

Disk First Aid
Apple Computer
20525 Mariani Avenue
Cupertino, CA 95014-6299
(408) 996-1010

Versions of Apple's Disk First Aid (see Figure 16-1) since System 7.0 have become more and more robust. You'll find Disk First Aid on the Disk Tools disk included with Apple's System disks. This utility checks your hard drive's directories for damage, and can do several kinds of repair. It can't compete with the commercial offerings, but it often works, and the price is right.

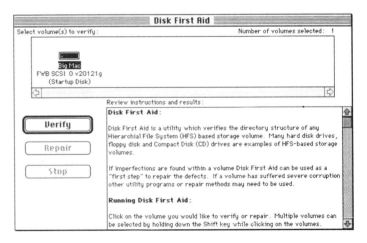

Figure 16-1: Disk First Aid

When using Disk First Aid, you should run it at least five times if it finds damage, because it works incrementally, fixing little bits with each pass.

Disk Bug Checker
Dave Camp
Central Point Software
15220 NW Greenbrier Parkway #200

Beaverton, OR 97006
Disk Bug Checker is freeware

Ever wonder why your Mac boots up so slowly after a crash? It is because the operating System checks all of your mounted drives for damage. There is a bug in the disk check routine that can prevent disks from mounting (you'll see the blinking question mark instead). Disk Bug Checker (Figure 16-2) is a utility that checks for the presence of this bug — if you encounter it, you'll need to use DiskFix or Norton Disk Doctor to remove it.

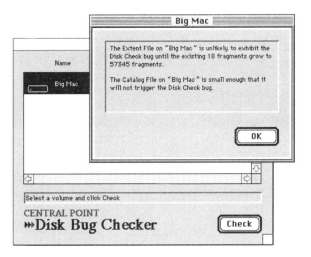

Figure 16-2: Disk Bug Checker

Disk Rejuvenator

Leonard Rosenthol
Aladdin Systems
165 Westridge Drive
Watsonville, CA 95076
Telephone: 408 761-6200
Fax: 408 761-6206
AOL/AppleLink: ALADDIN
CompuServe: 75300,1666
eWorld/GEnie: AladdinSys
Internet: aladdin@well.com
Disk Rejuvenator is freeware

Ever been unable to access your hard drive from a standard open dialog? Ever lost the custom icon for your hard drive? Both of these are symptoms of having a corrupted FinderInfo file. Disk Rejuvenator (Figure 16-3) is a simple utility that can repair the problem for you, although it does need a reboot to do its magic.

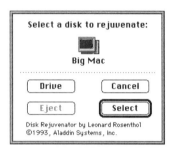

Figure 16-3: Disk Rejuvenator

sAVe the Disk

Michael Thies
Fachbereich Informatik
Universitaet-Gesamthochschule Paderborn
Germany
Internet: thiesana@uni-paderborn.de
sAVe the Disk is freeware

This extension is for those with AV Macs — it can reduce the problem of excessive disk access hits caused by the Resource Manager, the disk cache, and the Sound Manager.

ShowSizes II

Jon Pugh
1861 Landings Drive
Mountain View, CA 94043
Internet: jonpugh@netcom.com
Shareware fee: $20.00

For those with limited hard drive space, ShowSizes II allows you to look at your drive and see exactly what is taking all the space. (No matter how big your hard drives are, trust me, eventually you'll have "limited space.") Using a hierarchical tree (see Figure 16-4), it can display the space each folder takes, as a percentage of its parent folder, of the total disk, or of wasted space. Wasted space is the space wasted by small files stored on a large volume with large file allocation blocks. This is calculated by determining how much space could be saved if the files were stored on a disk drive with smaller block sizes. ShowSizes II is particularly useful for determining which files you should move off your crowded hard drive.

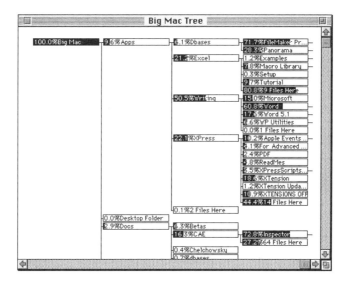

Figure 16-4: ShowSizes

SpaceAlert
Hugo Diaz
32 Whites Avenue #6608
Watertown, MA 02172-4351
Telephone: 617 924-8768
America Online: HugoD
Shareware fee: $15.00

Want to know how much space is free on your drive(s)? SpaceAlert (Figure 16-5) is a configurable display that can show you free space, used space, capacity, and trash for each of your drives, along with logical and physical RAM. One of its handier features is the ability to warn you at a threshold amount you set. Also on the CD-ROM is the companion program SpaceServer, which allows you to find free space on networks without mounting volumes.

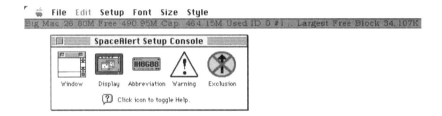

Figure 16-5: SpaceAlert

Hard Drive Formatters

It's a dirty job, but someone has to do it. The software you use to format your hard drive can have a significant impact on your system's performance. While no longer as big a consideration (because of the length of time that System 7 has been a standard), those few stragglers who move up from System 6 still have to make sure that their hard drive formatting utility is System 7 compliant.

Until recently, Apple's hard drive formatting utility did not support partitioning. Partitioning divides your hard drive into smaller chunks, which are treated by the operating system as though they were separate drives. Why bother? There are a number of reasons: effective use of space, speed, and security. The larger the hard drive, the larger the minimum block size. For example, my 520-megabyte internal drive has one partition, so the minimum size for any file with both a resource and a data fork is 8K, regardless of how small the file actually is. Partitioning the drive allowed me to have a smaller minimum file size. I used to have the drive partitioned with a smaller (80 megabyte) System partition; the smaller block size (3K) and the partition's location on the drive allowed for very fast access (4 milliseconds, according to FWB Hard Disk Toolkit.). The downside was that I found it difficult to contain my System folder within an 80-megabyte partition, and changing the size meant reformatting the drive (I just checked; my System folder is 101 megabytes). The last criteria (security) is the easiest to explain: many of these utilities allow you to password protect partitions.

APS PowerTools

APS Technologies
6131 Deramus
Kansas City, MO 64120
Telephone: 816 483-6100
Support: 800 334-7550
Fax: 816 483-4541
APS PowerTools is bundled with APS drives

This is the software that APS bundles with its drives, and it meets the same high standard of quality they have set with their hardware. It supports partitioning, passwords, data caching (the ability to set aside RAM to speed

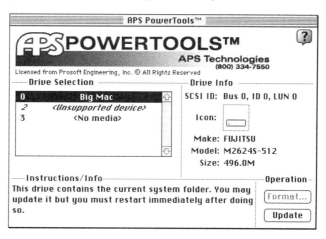

Figure 16-6: APS PowerTools

access times), and can automatically remap bad blocks. As this is being written, I have just updated my hard drive using PowerTools (Figure 16-6) to take advantage of APS's caching capabilities.

Drive7™

Casa Blanca Works, Inc.
148 Bon Air Center
Greenbrae, CA 94904
Telephone: 415 461-2227
Fax: 415 461-2249
Suggested retail: $89.95

Drive7 (Figure 16-7) is a universal formatter, designed to be a System 7–compliant driver that can be used on just about everything (according to the manual, this includes most recent SCSI drives, plus SyQuest 44 /88 /88C /105 /200 /270, Iomega Bernoulli 44 /90 /150, plus various 3.5" and 5.25" optical drives; with support for newer mechanisms added regularly). It includes data caching, partitioning, automatic remapping of bad blocks, password protection, and the ability to lock partitions as read-only. Casa Blanca also makes a utility called DriveCD, which uses caching to significantly improve the performance of CD-ROM drives.

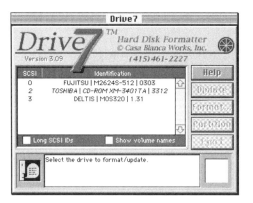

Figure 16-7: Drive7

FWB Hard Disk ToolKit

FWB Incorporated
155 Adams Drive
Menlo Park, CA 94025
Telephone: 415 325-4FWB
Fax: 415 833-4653
Suggested retail: $199.00

In my opinion, FWB Hard Disk ToolKit is the Rolls-Royce of hard drive formatters — not only does it include support for SCSI-2, data caching, partitioning, automatic remapping of bad blocks, password protection, benchmarking, and a customizable on-screen disk access indicator, but it has the best manual I've ever seen. It includes full coverage of the software, and is an excellent reference on hard drives and SCSI in general. Figure 16-8 shows HDT Primer™, the formatting component of Hard Disk ToolKit.

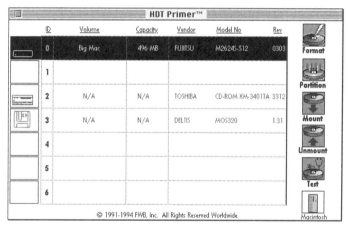

Figure 16-8: HDT Primer

Optimizing Your Hard Drive

Imagine your hard drive as a pie, and the files as pieces. As the operating system writes files to the drive, it tries to maintain as much contiguous free space as it can, so it writes files next to each other. What happens when you update a file that is already saved to disk, but has no free space around it? The operating system writes the file in pieces; the result is file fragmentation. As your hard drive becomes more fragmented, it will start to slow down — not surprising, because it has to work harder to locate files which are now scattered all over the place. The simplest way to correct the problem is to erase all of the files on your hard drive, and recopy them back. There are those who maintain that this is the best way, because the risks of optimization exceed the benefits. I disagree — I think all of these tools are safe, although a recent backup doesn't hurt as a safety net.

Speed Disk
Symantec
10201 Torre Avenue
Cupertino, CA 95014
Telephone: 408 253-9600
Customer Service: 800 441-7234
Tech Support: 503 465-8420 (free for 90 days)
America Online Keyword: SYMANTEC
CompuServe: GO SYMANTEC
Speed Disk is a component of Norton Utilities for the Mac (suggested retail: $149.95)

Speed Disk (in fact all of these utilities) goes far beyond the defragmentation you can achieve by coping files back onto your hard drive. It can display a map of your hard drive, showing you where files are located, and the extent to which your drive is fragmented. In order to ensure data integrity, neither

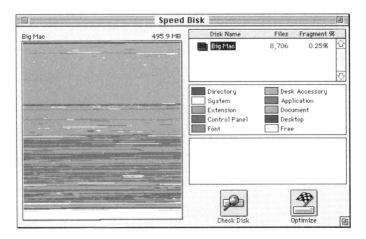

Figure 16-9: Norton Speed Disk

Speed Disk (Figure 16-9) nor Optimizer (Figure 16-10) can fully optimize a disk with open files (both of the Symantec programs can defragment other files when booted from an active System disk). This includes your System and the application itself, which means you need to boot off of another drive or a floppy, which either application can create for you. Speed Disk also includes a Turbo Charge option, which will reorganize the files on your hard drive, placing the most-used files where they will be accessed the quickest.

MacTools Optimizer

Symantec
10201 Torre Avenue
Cupertino, CA 95014
Telephone: 408 253-9600
Customer Service: 800 441-7234
Tech Support: 503 465-8420 (free for 90 days)
America Online keyword: SYMANTEC
CompuServe: GO SYMANTEC
MacTools Optimizer is a component of MacTools Pro (suggested retail: $149.95)

Optimizer offers similar functionality to Speed Disk, but includes what I find to be an easier to understand interface (see Figure 16-10). One nice touch is the ability to list which files are fragmented (Speed Disk can also list fragmented files). I particularly like the RAMboot feature, which can automatically create a RAMdisk, copy the required files to it, and reboot your

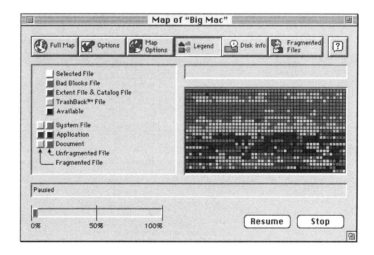

Figure 16-10: MacTools Optimizer

Mac from the RAMdisk, saving you from having to boot from a floppy (System 7.5.1 users need to upgrade to MacTools Pro 4.0.2 or better in order to use RAMboot).

DiskExpress II
ALsoft Inc.
22557 Aldine Westfield
Spring, TX 77373
Telephone: 713 353-4090
Support: 713 353-1510
Fax: 713 353-9868
Suggested retail: $89.95

DiskExpress II (Figure 16-11) works differently than the Symantec products covered in this section — it can operate in the background, activate itself in the same fashion as a screensaver, and perform on-the-fly optimization. I like the fact that DiskExpress II's settings (Figure 16-12) allow you to specify when it should and shouldn't start automatic optimization, so that you can keep it out of your way when you're working. Another major difference is that it can optimize the active startup disk. This is the tool both Steven and I use to defragment our hard drives.

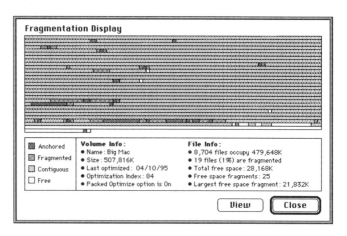

Figure 16-11: DiskExpress II fragmentation display

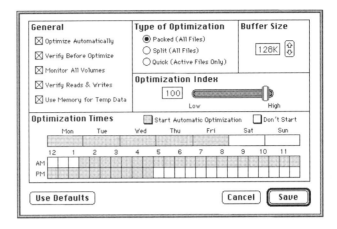

Figure 16-12: DiskExpress II settings

Hard Drive Utilities

Now we come to the big boys — eventually, you're going to need one or both of these products to maintain or repair your hard drive. There is considerable overlap in the two products' feature sets, with MacTools being the easier to use, and Norton aimed at the power user; I recommend both.

MacTools Pro
Symantec
10201 Torre Avenue
Cupertino, California 95014
Telephone: 408 253-9600
Tech Support: 503 465-8420 (free for 90 days)
America Online Keyword: SYMANTEC
CompuServe: GO SYMANTEC
Suggested retail:$149.00

MacTools Pro takes a user friendly approach to fixing your hard drive, offering "hand-holding" throughout the process. MacTools Pro starts up with QuickAssist (see Figure 16-13), which allows you to specify what tests MacTools should perform, either by checking off the problems you are experiencing, or by checking off the actual tests themselves.

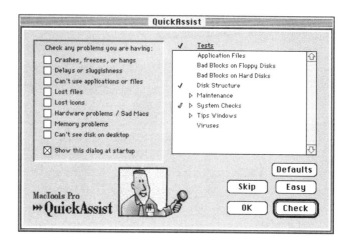

Figure 16-13: MacTools QuickAssist

There are a number of components to MacTools Pro, most of which can be accessed via MacTools Clinic (see Figure 16-14):

DiskFix: this is what this chapter is about, a tool to scan your hard disk and repair the problems it finds.

Optimizer: is a tool for optimizing your hard drive (see above).

MacTools Anti-Virus: scans your disk, or specified files or folders for viruses.

Undelete: allows you to recover files that you've trashed.

FileFix (see Chapter 13): a utility to repair damaged files.

Trashback: an extension that allows instant recovery by tracking recently trashed files.

MacTools Backup: (see Chapter 3): a tool for backing up your hard drive.

FastCopy: a floppy disk utility (see Chapter 17).

DriveLight: a control panel that gives a visual indication of drive (and other) activity. I particularly like the fact that you can specify custom icons for reading and writing different devices.

MacTools Pro includes a number of features that make it easier to use, including AutoCheck, which will scan your disk in the background, searching out and eradicating viruses and hard drive problems; RAMboot, for automatic RAMdisk creation; and SmartTips, which gives explanations of common problems and solutions (see Figure 16-15).

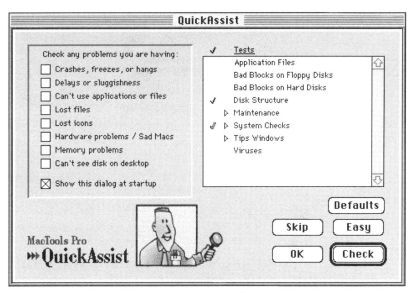

Figure 16-14: MacTools Clinic

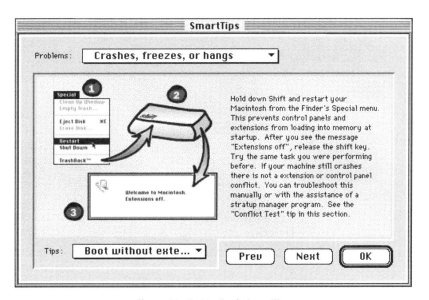

Figure 16-15: MacTools SmartTips

Interview: Dave Camp

Dave is the team leader for MacTools Pro.

How long have you been programming and how did you get started?

I've been programming for 15 years. I learned BASIC on a computer my dad built from a kit. It had great big cards (the size of a MacTools box) with 8K of RAM on each one. Pretty much stone knives and bearskins compared to today's hardware.

What is your educational background — are you formally trained, or did you teach yourself?

I graduated from high school in 1986 and attended a few semesters at University of Texas at El Paso before departing for Oregon. I'm mostly self trained.

What programs have you written (or been involved in the development of)?

MacTools 1.1, 1.2, 2.0, 3.0, and 4.0. Safe & Sound 1.0.

What language(s) do you write in?

Mostly C, and a little assembler where necessary.

What software tools do you use?

I use MetroWerks CodeWarrior Gold (as politically incorrect as it may be).

Please describe the equipment you use (what computer, how much RAM, etc.)

Most of the engineers here at Central Point have some sort of PowerMac (6100, 7100, 8100, or DayStar card) with 21" monitors for editing source code and writing specs, and a minimum of 24MB RAM for compiling and debugging code.

What is your favorite piece of software (excluding that written by you or your company...)

DragStrip and Popup Folder. These utilities do a good job of taming the Mac desktop.

Do you have other interests you'd like mentioned in a bio?

I have no other interests. I'm a geek. Maybe not. We just bought our first house, so I spend my spare time pretending to know how to fix things (other than hard disks). I also have a sizable laser disc collection (I'm into the home theater thing).

Where do you live, are you married with children, how old are you, (etc.)

Aloha, Oregon. About 4 minutes and 3 stop lights away from Central Point in Beaverton. I'm 26 years old, and married.

Why is it better not to repair the active startup disk?

The operating system does not provide a way to perform live repairs on mounted disks. We have found a couple of ways to fix minor volume information block and bitmap damage safely on mounted disks, but otherwise you should always fix serious problems from an emergency disk of some sort.

Comment on the optimization approach used by MacTools.

Our design goals were to make an Optimizer that most importantly was safe. To accomplish this, we made the Optimizer use the DiskFix analysis engine so that the user would get thorough and consistent results. Other optimizers may use different analysis engines than the disk repair programs they come with, which can be frustrating for the user. Secondly, we integrated a file by file integrity checking feature which, if enabled, can alert you as soon as a problem is detected (like a bad block on a floppy disk). The algorithm we used makes a single pass across the disk, which can be more efficient than some of the other algorithms. It determines which files go where ahead of time and then starts placing them from the beginning of the disk to the end of the disk. This combined with optimizing by date means that after the initial optimization, follow-up optimizations will go much faster.

How difficult does file-level compression make disk repair? How about driver level compression?

Not very. File-level compression simply changes the contents of individual files, not the underlying disk structures. Repairing disks compressed with DiskDoubler, Now Compress, StuffIt, etc. is not any more difficult than non-compressed disks. In most cases, driver level compression does not make disk repair any more difficult either. The exception is when you have problems at the driver or partition level. Most driver level compression schemes do strange and not-so-wonderful things to the driver and partition maps which can make data recovery programs have a more difficult time.

What do you think the future holds for hard drive software?

I expect to see diagnostic software become even more user friendly and interactive. Today's Macs are getting even more complex and it is becoming more difficult for people to know all the tricks required to diagnose and repair minor problems.

Norton Utilities for the Mac

Symantec
10201 Torre Avenue
Cupertino, CA 95014
Telephone: 408 253-9600
Tech Support: 503 465-8420 (free for 90 days)
America Online: keyword: SYMANTEC
CompuServe: GO SYMANTEC
Suggested retail: $149.00

Norton Utilities for the Mac is the power users' tool of choice — what it gives up in user-friendliness, it gains in speed and power. Symantec have been aggressive in their acquisition of companies that make disk utilities — first acquiring Norton, then Fifth Generation (some of the functionality of Public Utilities has been rolled into Norton Utilities), and most recently Central Point Software (see MacTools Pro above). I personally like having the choice between the two products, so I hope they continue to market both.

Double-clicking on Norton Utilities brings up a shell (see Figure 16-16), from which you can run the Norton's major components:

Norton Disk Doctor: this disk repair component is the single utility I use most on my Mac (covered earlier in this chapter).
Unerase: allows you to recover accidentally deleted files.
Volume Recover: allows you to recover volumes that are badly damaged or

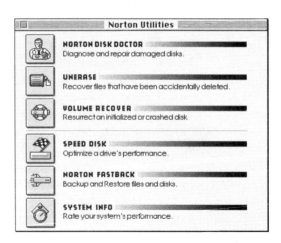

Figure 16-16: Norton Utilities

have been accidentally initialized, by using a backup copy of the Volume Information Block (VIB)(Apple now refers to this as the Master Directory Block).

Speed Disk: a disk optimization utility (covered earlier in this chapter).

Norton Fastback: a backup utility (see Chapter 3).

System Info: a benchmarking utility that allows you to compare the performance of your Mac to other systems.

Whenever I have a crash, a freeze, or an unexplained problem, the first thing I do is to run Norton Disk Doctor (Figure 16-17). This utility scans your hard drive and repairs problems it finds.

Here's an important tip: if Norton reports major problems, you should let it repair them, then reboot and run NDD again, to be sure the problem is fixed. See the Elissa Murphy interview for details.

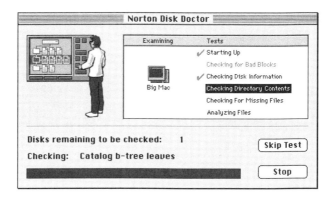

Figure 16-17: Norton Disk Doctor

Here's a tip for speeding up the scan of your hard drives: set Norton Disk Doctor's repair preferences to "fix automatically" and "check directories" leaving the other options disabled — this setting allows me to scan my 525-megabyte Fujitsu internal drive in 45 seconds! If problems are found, reboot and run Norton Disk Doctor again. Elissa also suggests that you run with the other options ("check for defective media", "check files" and "check System Folder") enabled about once a month.

An even better tip from Elissa Murphy: make sure you are running FileSaver enabled, then set the Prevention Preferences to scan at shutdown and after a

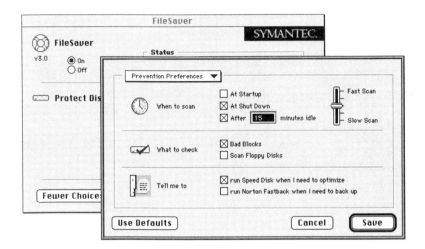

Figure 16-18: FileSaver Prevention Preferences

reasonable mount of idle time (see Figure 16-18) (In my opinion, this tip is worth the proverbial "price of the book." Doing this has made my system much more stable, and I am seeing far less hard drive problems.) The reason for this is simple: big hard drive problems often start out as small ones. In this case, preventive maintenance really pays off. MacTools users can gain similar benefits by enabling the AutoCheck feature.

Rounding out the Norton Utilities toolset are:

DiskLight: a control panel that indicates drive activity (I personally prefer the display options offered in MacTools DriveLight).

Fast Find: a file finding utility.

Floppier: a utility for copying disks and making disk images.

Norton Disk Editor: a power users' tool for editing data directly on your hard drive. This tool is not for the faint of heart — it is designed for advanced users. Unless you know what you're doing, I'd advise against using this one.

Wipe Info: allows you to overwrite files so that they cannot be recovered.

Interview — Elissa Murphy

Elissa is the Macintosh Product Manager at Symantec Software. It was a real treat to talk to Elissa — she really knows her stuff.

How long have you been programming and how did you get started?

I haven't programmed for years, but I have been an overseer for the development of several programs for several years. My position at Symantec is the Product Manager, so my focus is more on the feature sets, implementation of features (on occasion) and market trends.

What programs have you written (or been involved in the development of)?

I've been involved (not on a coding level, but on a product management or development management level) with: Norton Utilities, Suitcase, Public Utilities, DiskLock Mac, Fastback Express, SuperLaserSpool, DiskDoubler, AutoDoubler, CopyDoubler, SuperDoubler, and Norton DiskDoubler Pro. I am responsible for several other products, but no development or revisions of these products has occurred in several years.

What language(s) is Norton Disk Doctor written in?

C and C++.

What software tools are used in the development of NDD?

THINK C.

Please describe the equipment you use (what computer, how much RAM, etc.)

Quadra 950/ 24 megs of RAM /1 gig hard drive /System 7.5 (no PowerTalk) My system needs to be upgraded, but since I have become more product management focused, I have not needed to upgrade my machine.

What is your favorite piece of software (excluding that written by you or your company)

From a marketing point of view, RAM Doubler; from a users' perspective, Lotus Notes, Word, and Norton Utilities (yes I actually use it).

What do like to do when you're not working for Symantec?

Sailing, movies, theater, reading, collecting art, but I'm still pretty much a geek.

Where do you live, are you married with children, how old are you, (etc.)
Single, no kids, 26.

You're young to be where's you're at; how did you get started?
I started at Fifth Generation; I worked as Product Development Manager for Suitcase, Public Utilities, FastBack, Pyro, and others.

What are the main differences between MacTools and Norton Disk Doctor?
Norton Utilities is the premier data protection, repair, and recovery package — it includes all of the tools you need to recover your disk drive; Mac Tools Pro is an award-winning set of tools designed to make data protection, repair, and recovery more convenient and accessible.

Both MacTools and Speed Disk cannot optimize the boot volume, whereas DiskExpress II can (it can optimize on the fly). The Symantec products require that you boot from a floppy, another disk drive, or a RAM disk installed as part of MTP's RAMBoot feature. How would you contrast the optimization approaches used by MacTools, Speed Disk, and DiskExpress?
With both products, we felt that there is a risk to optimizing a disk with files open (if you boot from a disk, then the System and Finder files are open) — both of the Symantec products do significant disk checks before running.

How difficult does file-level compression make disk repair?
Not much; fragmentation may be high, but that's about it.

How about driver level compression?
Driver-level compression adds another variable, but all of the driver level products out there are compatible with both MacTools Pro and Norton Disk Doctor.

Symantec took considerable heat for the problems with SpeedDisk 3.0 (BTW, I think you guys did the right thing). Can you please set the record straight about the specific circumstances that caused problems?
The configuration that had problems required 32 megs of available (free) RAM and a fragmented catalog tree and 32 megabytes of free space on your hard drive; we had only a handful of users with that configuration.

And yet you announced the problem right away, and had an update available on-line within weeks (I was pleased to get my update disks mailed to me unsolicited).

Yes, that was quite expensive, but we felt that it was something that we owed to our users.

Why is it often best to run Norton Disk Doctor twice when errors are found?

It depends on the type of error; certain types of problems cascade into others, so it is best to reboot (and rerun NDD) to ensure that the disk catalog is correctly updated (by the way this is not unique to NDD: you should run MacTools Pro twice or Disk First Aid six times when they find errors). Another problem is that the Master Directory Block (MDB) is stored in your System's cache memory; a restart forces that information to be flushed and replaces that fixed by NDD. By the way, this is not the case when you boot and run NDD off of an emergency floppy, because in that case Norton can dismount the hard disk that you're working on.

What about those problems that NDD cannot repair, but MTP can?

There are very few, but they do exist — the two programs take different approaches. (author's note: this is why Mac power users buy both).

In the past, Norton Disk Doctor has had problems repairing some kinds of b-tree errors. What are b-tree errors and how are these fixed in the latest release?

To quote the Norton Utilities manual: "The catalog b-tree is the central repository of information about files on a disk, and as such is very important. Each file, whether it be a folder, a document, or an application, has an entry within the catalog tree. This entry includes the file's name, the folder it is located in, its location on the desktop, and the location and the length of the files data and resource forks." This was the main focus of the 3.0 upgrade, even though it was "under the hood," so to speak. We incorporated technology acquired from Public Utilities and Norton Utilities. All of NDD's catalog repair tools (including those for repairing the b-tree) were beefed up with the 3.0 release.

What are the top questions your tech support people field, and more important, what are the answers?

1. Upon shutdown, I'm getting a Filesaver scan that is taking too long, telling me that there is something wrong with my drive and I should run NDD to fix it. What is this?
    This is a new part of Filesaver called Prevention. During specific times, Prevention will scan your catalog structure to check for possible damage to your directories before they become serious problems. If Prevention recommends that you run Norton Disk Doctor, you probably should. More information on setting the preferences for this new item can be found on page 9-6 of the manual.

2. Where do the NUM Files get installed?
    The Norton Utilities installation places several files on your hard disk. All applications are located in a folder entitled Norton Utilities. FileSaver and DiskLight, which are control panels, are located in the Control Panels folder in your System Folder. The Norton Fastback Scheduler extension is located in the Extensions folder in your System Folder. Finally, an alias to Fast Find is created and placed automatically in your Apple Menu Items folder.

3. Are FileSaver files and VIF files the same?
    No. VIFs are Volume Information Files and simply contain basic information about the makeup of your drive at a physical level that are used by NDD or the recovery process in the case that your drive is so completely damaged that other methods cannot locate the necessary pointers to access the drive.

4. How are they different?
    FileSaver files contain directory information, the pieces of the logical drive that point to your data. VIFs only contain information about the physical nature of your drive.

When should users use NDD?
Every time you crash your Mac, there is some risk that you have done some damage to your hard drive, so its a good idea to check then. If you're running FileSaver, probably once a month is sufficient, unless you're having problems (symptoms of hard drive problems include long bootups or unexplainable crashes). One way to significantly speed up NDD when checking for directory damage is to run with bad blocks and files off (just remember to turn the option on at least once a month...).

Other than restoring from a backup, what can users do when their hard drive is damaged, and Norton Disk Doctor cannot fix the problem?

FileSaver saves a backup copy of the disk catalog; you can try a volume recover (this is a feature unique to NDD), and NDD will attempt to use the backup copy of the catalog. The next thing to try would be to unerase files, and if that doesn't work, you can call Symantec Tech Support, and they'll walk you through the process of manually recovering your files using the Disk Editor. (Your first call is free, you pay for technical support after 90 days.)

What do you think the future holds for hard drive diagnostic software?

We want to make hard drive utilities more intelligent and invisible, expanding on the proactive approach taken by FileSaver.

17 Hardware Tools

Well, we've covered your hard drive(s), but there's nothing we can do about the rest of our Macs — right? Wrong: this chapter covers the care and feeding of your floppy drives, a couple of shareware video products, running diagnostics to check your Mac, and we return to your hard drive with the voodoo that is SCSI. Two interviews are featured — Jeff Baudin of MicroMat, the makers of MacEKG, and Paul "Doc" McGraw, Vice President of APS Technologies.

Floppy Utilities

It's amazing how quickly your system grinds to a halt if your floppy fails. Keeping your floppy drive healthy and happy is vital. Care, maintenance, and luck all play a role in determining the life of your floppy drive. If you smoke, I suggest you quit, at least around your computer — smoke shortens the life of both floppy and SyQuest drives (APS makes a shield called the SyGuard, which goes a long way toward keeping smoke and dust from your SyQuest). Head alignment also plays a big part in how well your floppy drive can read disks. If your drive is slightly out of alignment one way, and it is trying to read disks from a drive out of alignment the other way, then you're going to have problems reading the disk.

DriveTech
MicroMat Computer Systems
7075 Redwood Boulevard
Novato, CA 94945
Toll-free: 800 829-6227
Support: 415 898-2935
Fax: 415 897-3901
America Online: MicroMat
AppleLink: MicroMatComp
CompuServe: 71333,166
eWorld: MicroMat
Suggested retail: $59.95

329

The only floppy drive diagnostic software I know of for the Mac is MicroMat's DriveTech (Figure 17-1), which combines 3M's drive cleaning kit with calibrated floppies (800K and 1.44 megabyte) and software to test your floppy drives. DriveTech tests relative alignment, the read/write heads, the stepper and eject motors, and can log test results. I test and clean my floppy drives once a month — I recommend that you do the same.

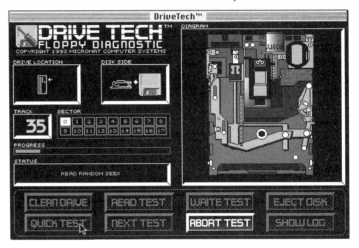

Figure 17-1: DriveTech

DiskSweeper
Jim Speth
Internet: speth@end.com
DiskSweeper is Work-at-Home-ware

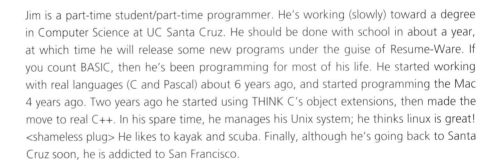

Jim is a part-time student/part-time programmer. He's working (slowly) toward a degree in Computer Science at UC Santa Cruz. He should be done with school in about a year, at which time he will release some new programs under the guise of Resume-Ware. If you count BASIC, then he's been programming for most of his life. He started working with real languages (C and Pascal) about 6 years ago, and started programming the Mac 4 years ago. Two years ago he started using THINK C's object extensions, then made the move to real C++. In his spare time, he manages his Unix system; he thinks linux is great! <shameless plug> He likes to kayak and scuba. Finally, although he's going back to Santa Cruz soon, he is addicted to San Francisco.

Every time you add a file to floppy disk, the System adds an entry to its desktop file. Unfortunately, with System 7, deleting files doesn't shrink the desktop file, and the end result can be an "empty" floppy with much less than the usual space left. There are two solutions: either reformat the disk to recover the space, or run DiskSweeper (Figure 17-2). One small limitation — version 1.0 (on the CD-ROM) doesn't support drag 'n drop for System 7.0.1 (Jim says it's really a bug in the System software that Apple fixed in 7.1; he plans to implement a workaround for 7.0.1 in a future release).

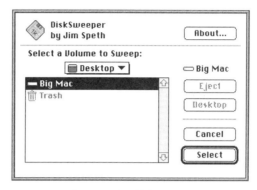

Figure 17-2: DiskSweeper

 EZ Floppy Eject
Coco Chen
Dragonsoft
603 E. Minor Drive #101
Kansas City, MO 64131
Telephone: 816 943-1835
America Online: Dragonsoft
CompuServe: 74471,3403
 EZ Floppy Eject is PostcardWare

This small application (Figure 17-3) ejects the mounted floppy disk, saving you from having to drag it to the trash. This makes it particularly useful for PowerBook owners. Putting an alias of it on your floppies allows you to quickly eject a floppy after using it.

Figure 17-3: EZ Floppy Eject

FLUT

Alex Tang
Internet: altitude@umich.edu
Miguel Cruz (original author)
65 Oakwood Street
San Francisco, CA 94110
Internet: mnc@netcom.com
FLUT is freeware

This software was originally written by Miguel Cruz, and subsequently taken over by Alex Tang. Miguel writes Mac software for a living, but he'd rather not. He recently returned from a 2-year trip through Australia, New Zealand, Asia, and Europe, which he managed somehow to pay for by doing Mac consulting along the way.

FLUT (Figure 17-4) is a sophisticated floppy utility — it can format, duplicate, and analyze disks, edit sectors, and manipulate and recover files or text from files. One caveat: if you're going to use the sector editor, I'd recommend you know what you're doing!

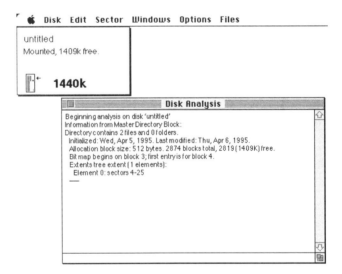

Figure 17-4: FLUT

QuikFloppy
Mark R. Weinstein
#5 Johns Canyon Road
Rolling Hills, CA 90274
Shareware fee: $10.00

This little extension is only of use to those who use Apple's PC Exchange or Insignia Solutions' Access PC — but for them it is great: it uses caching to speed floppy access from 30 to 500 percent!

Floppy Copy Utilities

I'm amazed at how many floppy copying utilities there are out there; you'd almost think this capability wasn't built into the operating system. These utilities can help you get by one of the shortcomings of the operating system — the number of disk swaps required to duplicate a floppy disk. The operating system reads data from your floppy into memory, then writes to the other floppy disk, then reads some more data from your floppy into memory, then writes some more data onto your destination disk... (you get the idea). These utilities allow you to read a floppy in a single pass, then make as many duplicates as you want — I've tried to order them by the number of features offered.

Disk Copy
Apple Computer
20525 Mariani Avenue
Cupertino, CA 95014-6299
Telephone: 408 996-1010

Disk Copy (Figure 17-5) is the utility Apple makes widely available (check with your local Mac user group or your favorite on-line service) for making and using image files. These files allow you to store the exact structure of a floppy disk as a file on your hard disk, for later creation of the floppy — this makes them especially useful for on-line distribution of system diskettes.

Figure 17-5: Apple Disk Copy

QuickFormat
Mike Conrad
Night Light Software
P.O. Box 2484
Oak Harbor, WA 98277-6484
America Online: NLSoftware
CompuServe: 73457,426
Shareware fee: $15.00

QuickFormat (Figure 17-6) offers formatting and duplication of floppies, and includes support for disk images, and the ability to verify information after it has been copied.

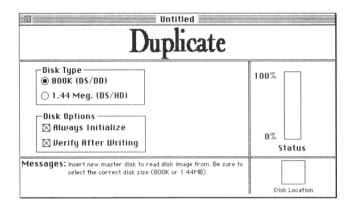

Figure 17-6: QuickFormat

Norton Floppier
Symantec
10201 Torre Avenue
Cupertino, CA 95014
Telephone: 408 253-9600
Tech Support: 503 465-8420 (free for 90 days)
America Online Keyword: SYMANTEC
CompuServe: GO SYMANTEC
Suggested retail: $149.00 (part of Norton Utilities for the Mac)

Norton Floppier (Figure 17-7) ships as part of Symantec's Norton Utilities for the Mac. It includes formatting, support for disk images, write verification, and the ability to make multiple copies.

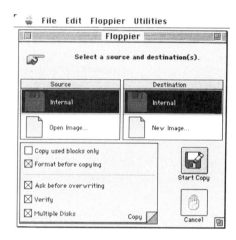

Figure 17-7: Norton Floppier

 DiskDup+
Roger D. Bates
P.O. Box 14
Beaverton, OR 97075
Telephone 503 591-9223
America Online: RogerB2437
 Shareware fee: $25.00

DiskDup+ (Figure 17-8) does disk formatting, and a whole lot more, including sector duplication of 400K, 720K, 800K or 1.44 MB floppies;

automatic creation of disk labels; support for disk images (it can read and write files in Apple's Disk copy format); storage of the original file in memory for faster duplication when making multiple copies; and maintenance of a log file.

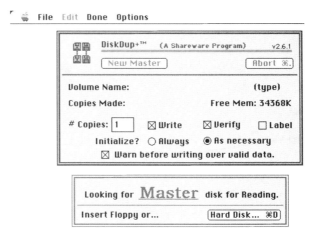

Figure 17-8: DiskDup+

MacTools FastCopy
Symantec
10201 Torre Avenue
Cupertino, CA 95014
Telephone: 408 253-9600
Tech Support: 503 465-8420 (free for 90 days)
America Online Keyword: SYMANTEC
CompuServe: GO SYMANTEC
Suggested retail: $149.00 (as part of MacTools Pro)

MacTools FastCopy (Figure 17-9) is more sophisticated than Norton Floppier; additional features include the ability to copy disks with bad blocks (a great help when trying to recover data from bad disks), compression of image files, use of checksums to determine if a floppy's contents have changed, and the ability to compare the contents of two floppies (Figure 17-10). As with some of the other modules of MacTools Pro, FastCopy needs to upgraded to at least version 4.0.2 for System 7.5.1 compatibility.

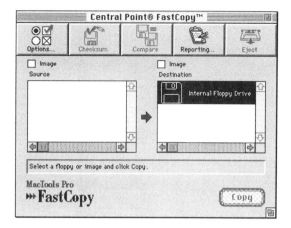

Figure 17-9: MacTools FastCopy

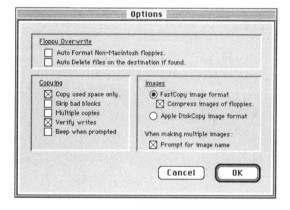

Figure 17-10: FastCopy options

 ### ShrinkWrap

Chad Magendanz
4415 NE 5th, Apt. G104
Renton, WA 98059
ShrinkWrap is freeware

The best floppy tool in this chapter doesn't actually use your floppy; it makes it so you don't have to. ShrinkWrap can create virtual disks on your desktop, allowing you to install software without the hassle of making floppy disks. Great idea! Unfortunately, this is another one that I missed for the CD-ROM.

Figure 17-11: ShrinkWrap

Video Shareware

For those who can use them, these shareware utilities are worth their weight in pixels.

Blind Monitors
Jacques Lövi
Rue des Romains, 50
L-2444 Luxembourg
Luxembourg
CompuServe: 100477,2436
Shareware fee: $10.00

Those lucky enough to have two monitors attached to their Macs will want to try Blind Monitors (Figure 17-12). Eventually, everyone with two monitors is going to get caught with one monitor off or disconnected — one slip of the mouse, and you've lost your cursor on the second (disabled) screen. The cure is Blind Monitors, a little application that allows you to tell your Mac what you already know: that your second screen is disabled.

Figure 17-12: Blind Monitors

Monitor Expander

Petur Petursson
Mice & Men
P.O. Box 7238
107 Reykjavik
Iceland
Fax: +354-169-4991
America Online: MenAndMice
CompuServe: 100045,2425
Internet: me-registrations@rhi.hi.is

Shareware fee: $25.00

Have you noticed the black border around the edge of your monitor? You can adjust your monitor's overscan, but that will result in some distortion. A better solution is Mice & Men's Monitor Expander (Figure 17-13), which allows you to use that space, effectively giving your monitor multiple resolutions. The only catch is that it requires System 7 and a compatible video card. The two video cards supported are Apple Macintosh II video card (Toby card) and the Apple High Resolution Video Card (HRVC).

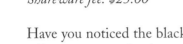

Figure 17-13: Monitor Expander

Hardware Diagnostics

I was once involved with a company that made Macintosh hardware diagnostics — the demise of Maxa (they made Snooper) and Apple's withdrawal of TechStep have left an uncrowded market segment.

MacCheck

Apple Computer
20525 Mariani Avenue
Cupertino, CA 95014-6299
Telephone: 408 996-1010
Suggested retail: $99.00

Apple's MacCheck (Figure 17-14) performs a set of basic hardware tests, along with a hard drive diagnostic (similar to that in Disk First Aid); my recommendation is to read on.

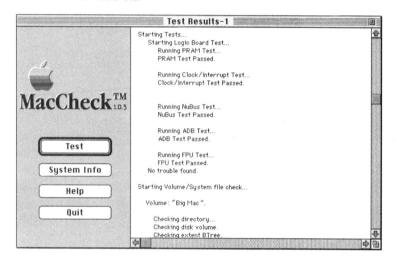

Figure 17-14: MacCheck

MacEKG

MicroMat Computer Systems
8934 Lakewood Drive #273
Windsor, CA 95492
Toll-free: 800 829-6227
Support: 415 898-2935
Fax: 415 897-3901
America Online: MicroMat
AppleLink: MicroMatComp
CompuServe: 71333,166
eWorld: MicroMat
Suggested retail: $150.00

MacEKG is a complete, automated diagnostic system for your Mac — it tests RAM, logic, video, hard drive performance; performs component tests of five important integrated circuits (ICs): VIA1, VIA2, SCC, SCSI, and PRAM; and can announce the results in a sexy voice. MacEKG is a control panel (Figure 17-15) that loads from your Extensions folder (so that it will load early in the boot process). It can be configured to perform it's diagnostics at every startup, daily, or weekly. Even better is the fact that it tracks

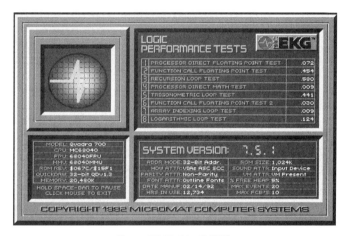

Figure 17-15: MacEKG™

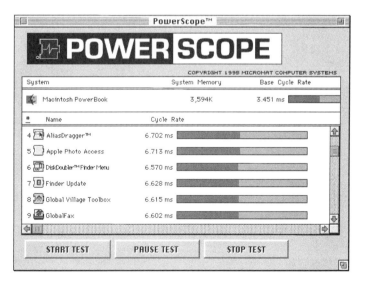

Figure 17-16: PowerScope™

performance in a log, and reports changes in your Mac's overall performance. MacEKG also has a Reactivator feature, to help test for intermittent or heat-related problems, by automating repetitive testing.

The recent release of MacEKG version 3.0 has brought with it a new diagnostic: PowerScope™ (Figure 17-16). This utility runs a series of tests on your computer to determine the exact amount of processing power each of your extensions extracts from your Mac (scary stuff, kids).

TechTool
MicroMat Computer Systems
(see above for address information)

TechTool is freeware

TechTool (Figure 17-17) is the only utility I know of that can not only zap your PRAM, but it can also save and restore it. If you want to be sure your desktop is rebuilt correctly (sometimes a problem under System 7), it can do that for you, too; I even used it to justify AppleCare for my Duo 230 (I used TechTool to establish that the date of manufacture was within a year of the date I was applying for warranty service). It can also provide complete System information (including the ability to identify a damaged System file), and tell you whether or not you've been spending too much time on your Mac.

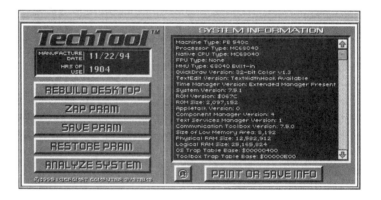

Figure 17-17: TechTool

Interview: Jeff Baudin

Jeff is the Technical Director of MicroMat Systems. We met several years ago at a Macworld Expo — he's always been willing to offer help and assistance, even when I worked for a company that competed with his.

How long have you been programming and how did you get started?

Hmm...my first dabble of programming was in Junior High. Our math class had a terminal tied to UC Berkeley. We did simple BASIC programming that was horribly complex considering what little work the computer actually did. That was back in 1977. I really didn't get into it until about 1983, with my powerful Commodore 64.

What is your educational background — are you formally trained, or did you teach yourself?

High school grad is it. I guess I went to the programming school of hard knocks. A lot of reading and trial and error.

What programs have you written (or been involved in the development of)?

By myself, I've written only a few "known" programs. "The Phoenix," back in '87 was a game done in BASIC, based on the 2001 movies. I also wrote MicroRX, a repair/reference program in 1989. I've also done a few little utilities like DateCheck. The real stuff was coded by Bob Sanders. I design and specify the program, do all the art, sounds, and interface elements like icons and dialogs. These include MacEKG, DriveTech, TechTool, PrintShuttle.

What language(s) do you write in?

We use C, assembler, Forth, and HyperTalk.

What software tools do you use?

CodeWarrior and THINK C, primarily.

Please describe the equipment you use (what computer, how much RAM, etc.)

I use an 8100 with 24 megs of RAM. I use 2 QuadraLink cards giving me a total of 10 serial ports, so that I can experiment with some of the serial devices we've been designing. All that is tied to a 50-conductor trunk line going to our PBX. Did I mention we're making phone stuff now?

What is your favorite piece of software (excluding that written by you or your company...)

Mine is HyperCard. I've yet to find something it can't do. I'm really happy that Apple is putting a LOT of work, effort, and marketing behind it.

Do you have other interests you'd like mentioned in a bio?

I like going to this insane place called BattleZone. It's an indoor paintball arena. It's not like the army men you usually see playing paintball outside. It's this crazy cyber-punk thing where everyone is dressed in these black, armor-plated suits. It reminds me of the scene in Terminator II, where they show the war of the future. Without the HK's, of course...

What do like to do when you're not programming?

Gee...I spend most of my time in front of the computer. Playing with my kids and trying to get our new house put together. I have this "frontier" in my backyard that I'm still trying to figure out how to garden.

Where do you live, are you married with children, how old are you, (etc.)

I live in Windsor, CA (about 50 miles north of SF) with my wife, Rebecca and our three kids. I'm 32.

How did MicroMat get started?

I started MicroMat in 1989 as a Mac-only repair place. We started making stuff that other people wanted, so we became a manufacturing company.

What products has your company released?

We've released: MicroRX, MacEKG, MicroProbe ADB, MicroProbe, PowerCheck, DriveTech, and PrintShuttle.

A lot of people suggest that computers, like most things electronic, either work or they don't. Components that work fine one minute can fail the next. How do you respond to such people?

There are a number of things MacEKG can catch, bad memory is one. As you know, the Mac does a power-up self test. Problems can occur as your Mac warms up — some components degrade or fail once they've warmed up.

How does a user know when to use MacEKG?

Inexplicable crashes, and especially freezes, can be indicative of hardware problems.

How did MacEKG start out?

MacEKG started as an "exercise" tool, meant to exercise your Mac. If you can make problems occur in an automated format, then they are easier to find. As a diagnostic tool, MacEKG is not always meant to find the problem; sometimes it can help diagnose a problem by showing where the problem isn't.

How does EKG differ from its competitors, from a design or philosophical perspective?

MacEKG is the only program that does real chip tests. After doing a lot of research with chip manufacturers, we wrote assembler code to "talk" directly to the chips. Also, we designed MacEKG with intelligence, when other tools precluded predictive maintenance, we were able to look at previous results to assess performance trends.

What do you think of TechStep? Even though it was very expensive, it seems a shame that Apple has discontinued this technician's diagnostic tool.

It's a shame they discontinued it. Steve Martin wrote the code for it; it really just activated the code in the Mac ROMs to suck information from the Mac it was attached to — there was no need for it to be so expensive.

What are the most common hardware failures you see?

First has to be floppy drives.

How about problems that MacEKG can identify?

First would be cycle-sucking INITs. A good example was the old Global Village ADB modem, which patched both the ADB and serial chips (this product is no longer made). Other examples include some networking and shareware products. Second would be hard drive failures — the most common problems are directory problems, stiction, controller errors.

How does MacEKG identify hard drive problems?

MacEKG does a basic read test.

In your opinion, should users leave their Macs on all the time, or turn them off when they plan to be away for a specified period?

Patience is probably the biggest factor (it can take a while to reboot…). I see no problem with people turning their Macs on and off. We have a Mac II that we use for testing, it is on and off all day, sometimes 100 or 200 times a day, and it has yet to fail.

Where do you plan to take MacEKG in its next release?

Version 3.0 will run in native mode. We're also adding an INIT analyzer (see PowerScope in Figure 17-16) that will allow the user to analyze the performance hit taken by the extensions you are running.

What is the average life expectancy of a 1.44 meg floppy drive?

Two years.

How often should users clean their drives?

3M recommends every 40 hours; I recommend once a month, more often if you are having problems (slow reading or mounting of floppy disks are good signs).

What are the common causes and symptoms of drive head alignment problems?

The main cause would be poor design; Apple attaches the drive head to a worm gear in a very fragile manner. Other causes include people trying to remove jammed floppies, and having a floppy hit the upper head after an incomplete eject (the disk is ejected, but the head isn't parked correctly).

What are some of the problems that DriveTech can identify?

The two main problems are the need for cleaning, and head alignment problems. DriveTech also tests the drive controller.

How does DriveTech identify head alignment problems?

DriveTech ships with a digital alignment disk that allows the software to determine head alignment.

What are your plans for DriveTech?

Version 2.0 will be native, and include a number of new techie features for hardware technicians.

SCSI

To say SCSI is a black art is an understatement of epic proportions. SCSI (Small Computer Systems Interface) is a standard for daisy chaining peripheral devices (like drives, CD-ROMs and scanners) to a computer; it happens to be the means Apple has chosen for hard drives until recently. Apple has now shipped some computers with less expensive IDE (Integrated Drive Electronics) hard drive mechanisms.

How can you tell if you have a SCSI problem? Good question — the symptoms vary wildly: unexplainable crashes, long disk accesses, corrupted files, fried motherboard... Testing for a SCSI problem is usually easy — just disconnect your SCSI devices, and see if the problem goes away. This doesn't always help if the problem requires one of your SCSI devices.

Let's look at some simple rules that should be applied to your SCSI chain:

Unique SCSI ID
You can have no more than 7 devices; each device with a unique SCSI ID — numbers can be from 0 to 6; 0 being the last device in the chain (this is usually assigned to your internal hard drive), and 6 being the first device in the chain. Your Mac is always device 7. Just to confuse matters, the SCSI address has no bearing on the device's physical location in the chain — the external drive attached to your Mac can have any address between 1 and 6, just so long as you don't have another device with the same address. A close look at the back of most drives will reveal a changeable SCSI ID number; some devices use dip switches — you'll probably need to consult the manual to learn what the various settings mean.

Cables
SCSI cable is limited to a total length of 6 meters (19.6 feet). You can start by subtracting one foot for cabling inside your Mac — this means that if you have three devices each connected using a 6 foot SCSI cable, then you'll need new, shorter cables before you add another device to the chain. One of the most important things you can do is to get good quality SCSI cables, preferably all from one vendor.

Termination

Let's start with the basics: you need termination at the beginning and at the end of the chain. Simply put, terminators are resistors put at each end of the chain to tell your computer where the chain begins and ends — without them, things probably won't work. All Macs equipped with internal hard drives are terminated on the motherboard, so all you need is one for the end of the chain. Here are a few exceptions, just to confuse things:

- If you have a Mac IIfx, you'll need to use special black terminators.
- If your SCSI bus is very short (18" or less), then you only need to terminate one end.
- If the cable length between two devices is greater than 10 feet, then you should add an additional terminator at the 10-foot point.

My recommendation for those with more than one SCSI device is to consider active termination. An active terminator is a powered terminator that ensures adequate power for your SCSI chain, thereby reducing problems caused by mixed cables or complex chains. I added an APS active terminator to my Mac about six months ago, and I haven't had a SCSI-related problem since!

SCSIProbe

Robert Polic
c/o SyQuest Technology
47071 Bayside Parkway
Fremont, CA 94538
America Online: RedPat
Internet: D6055@applelink.apple.com
SCSIProbe is freeware

This is the "one that got away" — one of two pieces of shareware (actually freeware) for which I could not get permission to include on the CD-ROM (I have the express permission from the authors for inclusion of all of the shareware on the CD-ROM). The reason? Simple — I was unable to reach him (so I cannot attest to the veracity of the above e-mail addresses). In any case, SCSIProbe is widely

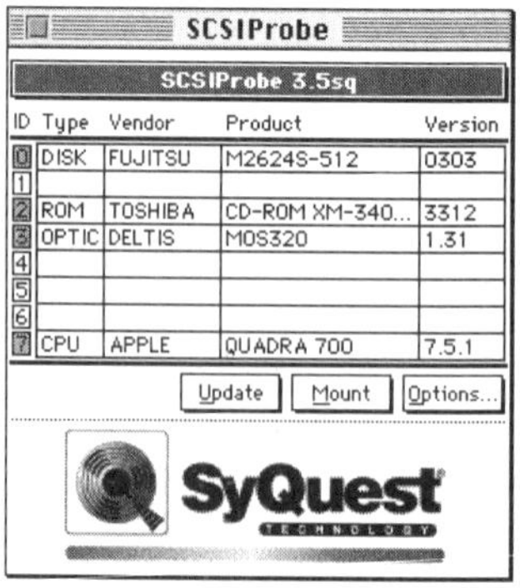

SCSIProbe				
SCSIProbe 3.5sq				
ID	Type	Vendor	Product	Version
0	DISK	FUJITSU	M2624S-512	0303
1				
2	ROM	TOSHIBA	CD-ROM XM-340...	3312
3	OPTIC	DELTIS	MOS320	1.31
4				
5				
6				
7	CPU	APPLE	QUADRA 700	7.5.1

Update   Mount   Options...

SyQuest TECHNOLOGY

Figure 17-18: SCSIProbe

available from user groups.

SCSIProbe is a simple Control Panel (Figure 17-18) that is a boon for those with removable devices (SyQuests, Micro Opticals), or for those with drives that are reluctant in mounting. SCSIProbe can almost always mount reluctant devices, and it gets around device driver conflicts by flushing them from memory when the device is ejected.

Interview: Paul "Doc" McGraw

Doc is the Executive Vice President of APS Technologies.

How long have you been in the computer business?

I guess I "entered" the computer business in 1985 when I became an affiliate of Jerry Daniel's MacUnderground. I operated a Safehouse and wrote for the organization. Subsequently, I took over operation of the organization in 1986 under the company name Buck, Wheat and Associates. We published electronically and developed a number of software tools for electronic publishers. Among B,W&A's products was a weekly information product centered on the Mac called MacWEEK. *There was also a short experiment in conjunction with* Playboy *magazine called* Playboy On-Line. *We eventually sold the name* MacWEEK *to Patch Communications and their product survives today as the weekly industry "rag."*

...and how did you get started?

I bought a Mac in 1984 after suffering with a CPM machine for 2 years. I bought it to produce newsletters. It's a hobby that kind of got out of control.

What is your educational background — are you formally trained, or did you teach yourself?

Educationally, I'm a disgrace. I have only one degree (as well as no high school diploma) after lots of years in school (and yes, it's quite a long story). The good news is that the one degree was a Doctorate in Dentistry so no one's ever asked to see the other diplomas. As a practical matter, I'm self-taught as it comes to computers though I was Apple certified as a technician in 1986 and became an Apple Developer in 1987 and was the founding president of the Kansas City Macintosh User's Group in 1987 (88?).

What products have you been involved in the development of?

Those mentioned above including ufilm reader and maker, Courier and Agent, Safehouse, The Electronic Publisher's Survival Kit and a variety of information products. On the hardware side, I've had involvement in virtually every product APS has ever developed or sold.

Please describe the equipment you use (what computer, how much RAM, etc.)

I use a Duo 280c with a Dock II and a Sony 16" monitor. It has an 800 MB internal drive and 24 MB of RAM. It has a PowerPort Mercury modem, a bright red trackball and the word "MOM" in neon blue on the top cover (OK... just kidding....) It has 7 SCSI devices attached and three or four serial devices at any one time.

What is your favorite piece of software (excluding that written by you or your company...)

Leaving those out is certainly easy.... I guess it depends on when you ask. Right now I'm quite taken with Visioneer's PaperPort product (which is both hardware and software). I guess if you have to ask over the long haul, I've liked and used QuarkXPress and Nisus the longest and most consistently. I love the current incarnation of Quark though I am not particularly thrilled with the company. Conversely, I'm not as happy with the current incarnation of Nisus as I'd like to be but am immensely fond of the company.

What is your favorite piece of hardware (two questions actually: your favorite of APS' hardware, and your favorite from another manufacturer...)

I have a number of favorite APS products. I particularly like the DAT drives and the 270 MB SyQuest drives in the small SR 1000 enclosure. I like the SCSI Sentry a lot as well. Of the non-APS hardware, I guess I like the PowerBook Duos, the Visioneer PaperPort, and the PowerMac 8100/110 the best.

Do you have other interests you'd like mentioned in a bio?

Nothing particularly interesting unless you're into dentistry, fountain pens, watches, or electronic gadgets.

What do like to do when you're not running APS?

Spend time with my 6 year old daughter, play tennis and sleep — not necessarily in that order.

Where do you live, are you married with children, how old are you, (etc.)

I live in Lee's Summit, MO, a suburb of Kansas City — Missouri, not Kansas, dammit. I have a wife who's a practicing periodontist (if you don't know what that is, you're probably either better off or desperately in need of her services.) We have a 6-year-old daughter named Lauren and a goofy Airhead....er, I mean Airedale terrier named Lucy. Her stage name is Jennifer, and anyone can write to her at jennifer@apstech.com.

How did APS get started?

My partner, Paul Mandel and I began doing research on the Mac hard drive business a couple of years before we started APS. We spent over 2 years evaluating drives, enclosures, drivers, business models, distribution and database systems, suppliers, etc. The day we took our first order, we had systems in place to build a drive, test it, ship it, support it and handle any return which might occur. We had systems to take and process an order, accept a credit card, verify it and account for it.

What products has your company released?

So many that I can't begin to recite them all. Of note, the APS DAT and HyperDAT, SCSI Sentry, DAterm™, the SR-2000 enclosure leap immediately to mind.

How big is your company (how many people do you employ, annual sales, whatever)?

APS has 200 employees and fits (just barely) in 56,000 square feet. Our 1995 calendar year revenues will exceed $105 million.

What are some of the problems you've experienced in developing for the Mac marketplace?

Mac people don't like to read manuals — even when they'd save a lot of time and aggravation. Apple never met a standard it wouldn't like to (and usually does) violate. Apple eats its young; doesn't understand its own market; makes insanely great hardware — apparently by accident, and is the source of all life in this market — at least for now.

What should a user look for when considering a hard drive?

Good design, good construction, reputation, solid mechanisms, reasonable business practices, a solid business model including adequate warranty accruals. The problem is that it's hard for a user to cut through the hype and advertising BS to figure out *which drive vendors pay $22 for their enclosure, power supply, power cord and SCSI cable, and which spend whatever it takes to deliver a solid product that'll deliver minimal trouble over years of life.*

(Warning: serious plug ahead) Whenever I'm asked which manufacturer to consider, I recommend APS. The quality is evident from the moment you open the box — these guys think of everything: a good quality SCSI cable, built-in active termination, great documentation, solid construction, good design... Have a look at APS's active terminator, and compare it to their less expensive competitor; you'll see what I mean: APS's device is pass-through (you can attach a device on the other side), the appearance and plastics are first-rate, and the price difference ($10.00) is small.

What is stub length, and why is it important when considering a hard drive?

Stub length is the length of the extension or "stub" which extends off the main SCSI line to a SCSI device. In an external drive, the stub length is the distance from the SCSI cable connection in the back to the actual drive mechanism (depending on the internal cable configuration.) SCSI specifications for stub lengths require that they that don't exceed 10 cm or about 4". Whether or not violations of this spec actually affect your SCSI chain or not depends on a variety of factors. As a practical matter it's fair to say that SCSI chains that adhere to specification on all devices, cables, and terminators are likely to perform the most reliably and efficiently. Those which fall out of spec begin to be problems, particularly as the number of non-spec conditions multiply. It's not always easy to determine just where stub lengths violate specification. Some designs, particularly some modular stacking designs, have significant stub-length violations as do some external case designs which don't use an internal "Y" SCSI ribbon cable in favor of a cheaper configuration that runs a stub off the main SCSI line to the drive. This is easier to diagram than to describe, but suffice it to say that the difference is significant. How and whether those affect operation in a particular case depends on the specific situation and the balance of the SCSI configuration.

There are a lot of new removable storage technologies out there: SyQuest (multiple formats), MO, DAT; with high-density read/write lasers on the horizon ... where to you see storage technologies going in the next few years?

Smaller, faster, cheaper — and you can quote me. People need to begin to think of *storage (at least to some extent) in terms of dollars rather than MBs. This is because the cost per MB will continue to go down for quite some time with occasional plateaus. We find that en masse, customers buy storage in units of about $300, $500, and to a lesser extent $1000. They buy however many MBs they can in those ranges and multiples.*

I'd ask you to comment on the ZIP drive, but I'd doubt I'd be able to print the answer…

Not so! I think the Zip drive is a really interesting product. Whether the market will adopt a standard that's only 100 MB and whether the unit's performance and features will make it a long-term survivor or not remains to be seen. Initial demand seems to be strong.

Why is SCSI such a black art, and why are there so many weird exceptions to the rules?

I believe that there are fewer exceptions than it may seem, but as I indicated earlier, SCSI chains which are entirely in spec tend to work more predictably, consistently, and reliably. Add good active termination scheme and it becomes pretty predictable.

Describe active termination, and why it reduces SCSI errors.

Passive termination uses a pair of resistor sets that "dampen," if you will, "eccentric" signals on the SCSI chain that fall outside a desirable range. The "eccentric" signal must rise or fall considerably before the resistors have much effect — hence the term passive terminator. Active terminators use one of a couple of technologies to more "actively" control signal voltage outside of the ideal range. Traditional analog active terminators use a resistor/diode network. APS uses IC technology to deliver what we call Digital Active Termination. The action is essentially the same, but the digital circuit monitors the changes on the SCSI chain constantly and responds more rapidly to smaller changes in signal strength than might be expected in the case of analog active termination.

The actual phenomena eliminated are referred to as "ringing," "overshoot," and "undershoot." The presence of any of these conditions on a SCSI bus will likely result in a SCSI signal that is either not understood by the peripheral device or by the host. In either case, the condition requires a "retry," reducing performance. When multiple retries do not solve the problem, the result is often a bus error. Because the performance of newer high-speed SCSI buses is critical, maintaining ideal conditions on the bus require active termination in many cases. In fact, new specifications require active termination for higher speed SCSI applications.

Do you think FireWire (Apple's proposed SCSI replacement) will become the next standard? If not, what do you think will replace SCSI in the next few years

No. PCI and Serial SCSI appear more likely successors today.

What new areas does APS plan to get into in the next year?

More and bigger drives, more and better backup alternatives, more CD offerings, CDR, higher capacity SyQuest and 3.5" MO.

18 PowerBooks

I'm on my second PowerBook (my first was a Duo 230; I now have a 540c), and I have to admit, it's a bit of a love/hate relationship. PowerBooks bring with them a whole range of hassles — weight, limited size of both your screen and keyboard, limited power — all this, and they're more expensive than their desktop equivalents, both to buy and to maintain. Having said all that, I can't live without mine. I use it at the office (I'm the lone Mac user in a sea of PCs), I use it on the bus, when I'm traveling; in short: everywhere. In this chapter, I look at some of the things you can do to keep your PowerBook running, and the tools you can use to make it run better.

Battery Life

The first thing you need if you have a PowerBook is a spare battery — nothing is worse than running out of juice at 30,000 feet. This can get expensive for 500-series PowerBook owners, but it sure is worth it. I use Conflict Catcher 3 (see Chapter 1) to run a minimal set of extensions when I boot using batteries. (OK, so I'm a lousy example — try running with as few extensions as you can; they all steal processor cycles.)

- Now Toolbox (required for NowMenus)
- RAM Doubler (see Chapter 2)
- AliasDragger™ (see Chapter 5)
- DiskDoubler™ Finder Menu (see Chapter 7)
- Finder Update (part of System 6)
- AutoDoubler™ (see Chapter 7)
- Control Strip (see Chapter 5)
- CopyDoubler™ (see Chapter 7)
- FileSaver™ (see Chapter 16)
- Now Menus (see Chapter 5)
- PBTools™ (more later in this Chapter)
- Thunder 7™ (on-the-fly spell checking)
- ATM™ (see Chapter 14)

There are a number of factors that can really drain your PowerBook's battery; here are a few conservation suggestions for when you are running on battery power:

- Virtual memory may increase your available RAM, but it is one of the fastest ways to drain your battery. If you need more RAM, install RAM Doubler, or buy the real thing.
- Avoid programs that keep your hard drive spinning; if you find that your software is constantly accessing your hard drive, consider using a RAMDisk (see Chapter 2).
- Adjust your backlighting to the minimum that still allows you to read the screen.
- Turn off AppleTalk unless you are connected.
- Turn off your modem unless you are using it, if you can. Internal modems turn themselves off when not being used.
- Use the Monitors Control Panel (or one of the video depth changing Control Strip modules) to reduce your color resolution to black and white.
- Turn down (or even better, off) your sound.
- Adjust your PowerBook Control Panel settings for better conservation.

Apple PowerBook Control Panels

Let's start with a quick look at some of the tools Apple ships (with System 7.5) for the PowerBook (see also File Assistant in Chapter 3 and Control Strip below and in Chapter 6).

Battery Recondition

This application allows those who use nickel-cadmium and nickel-hydride batteries (100 series and Duos, but not 500 series "Intelligent" batteries) to fully deplete them before recharging so as to avoid the "memory effect".

PowerBook Display

PowerBook Display (Figure 18-1) is for those with an external monitor — I use it all the time for doing presentations, so what's displayed on the big screen is what I also see on my PowerBook. Video mirroring can only be turned on when you have a monitor attached.

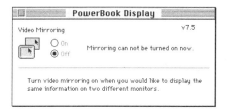

Figure 18-1: PowerBook Display Control Panel

PowerBook

The PowerBook Control Panel is the first one you should adjust when you first get a PowerBook — it allows you to have two different sets of power consumption settings — one for when you're running off the battery (Figure 18-2), and another for when you're running on A/C power. As shown in Figure 18-3, I recommend that you set your hard drive to never spin down when plugged in; hard drives live longer if they stay on all (or most of) the time.

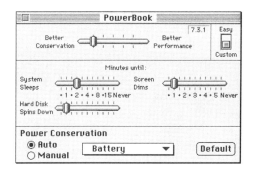

Figure 18-2: PowerBook Control Panel (battery settings)

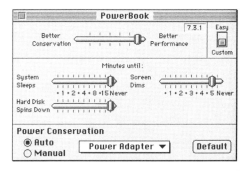

Figure 18-3: PowerBook Control Panel (A/C settings)

PowerBook Setup

I've always found the modem settings in the PowerBook Setup Control Panel (Figure 18-4) to be confusing — shouldn't the "Normal" setting also be "Compatible"? Global Village's excellent software makes things much clearer: the "Compatible" setting is for when you're using applications that do not support the Apple's Communications Toolbox (CompuServe Navigator is an example); "Normal" is for when you're using applications that support the Communications Toolbox, or when you're using an external serial device.

SCSI disk mode allows you to connect your (SCSI-equipped) PowerBook to a desktop Mac as if it were an external hard drive, providing you have a special SCSI cable made by Apple. My preference is to carry APS's SCSI Doc. This connector allows you to use an ordinary 25 to 50 pin SCSI cable for both ordinary connections and SCSI Disk Mode with the flip of a switch. The PowerBook Setup Control Panel allows you to change the SCSI address of your PowerBook's hard drive when in SCSI disk mode.

Compatible is for applications that do not support Apple's Communications Toolbox

SCSI Disk Mode allows you to connect your PowerBook as if it were a hard drive

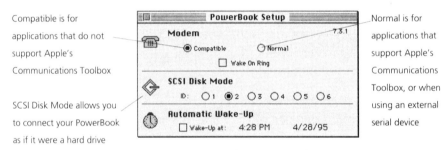

Normal is for applications that support Apple's Communications Toolbox, or when using an external serial device

Figure 18-4: PowerBook Setup Control Panel

Recommended Software

There are a number of programs that I recommend for those with PowerBooks — most of which is covered elsewhere in this book:

- RAM Doubler (see Chapter 2) is essential, especially given the high price of PowerBook RAM.
- Norton Utilities or MacTools Pro (see Chapter 16) to keep your hard drive healthy.
- Norton DiskDoubler Pro (see Chapter 7) is another utility I can't live without — my 500-megabyte internal drive is full, even when

AutoDoubler compressed.

- PowerMerge (see Chapter 3) for synchronizing files between your PowerBook and desktop Macs.
- PBTools or CPU (see below).

PBTools

VST Power Systems, Inc.
1620 Sudbury Road, Suite 3
Concord, MA 01742
Telephone: 508 287-4600
Fax: 508 287-4068
CompuServe: 72551,201
Suggested retail: $99.95

PBTools is the power users' choice for PowerBook utilities — four compact modules: PowerControl gives you control of things that affect your battery (Figure 18-5); PowerWatch allows you to track (and export) battery performance for up to four batteries; SafeSleep not only blanks your screen, but offers password protection; and PBKeys gives you configurable command keys for specific PowerBook functions. A menu bar icon shows the status of your battery, your hard drive, and AppleTalk; and a Control Strip module (see Figure 18-6) offers quick access.

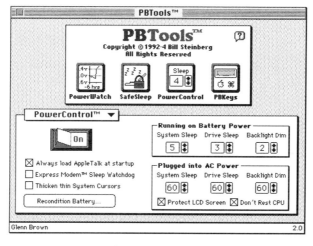

Figure 18-5: PBTools

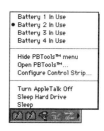

Figure 18-6: PBTools'
Control Strip

Connectix PowerBook Utilities (CPU)
Connectix Corporation
2600 Campus Drive
San Mateo, CA 94403
Telephone: 415 571-5100
Toll-free: 800 950-5880
Fax: 415 571-5195
America Online: Connectix
AppleLink: Connectix.CS
CompuServe: 75300, 1546
eWorld: RAM Doubler
Internet: support@connectix.com
Suggested retail: $99.00

CPU offers a different approach than that taken by Bill Steinberg's minimalist PBTools — this powerhouse Control Panel packs in just about every PowerBook-related utility you could want or need. Features include battery and A/C settings, configurable hot keys, a screen blanker, password security, menu bar status display, EasySync (file synchronization), modified cursors and cursor location, application switching, and more. Cursor location is especially useful for those with passive matrix screens which can be subject to cursor "submarining": a command key locates the cursor for you (all of the commercial utilities covered here can do this for you). Keyboard Power is a unique feature that allows keyboard control of your menu bar items and

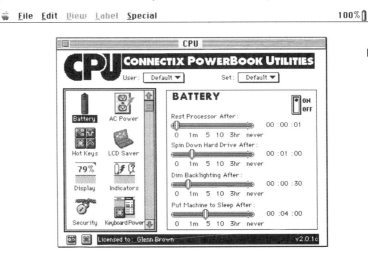

Figure 18-7: Connectix PowerBook Utilities

dialog boxes (using Windows-like underlined commands like those shown in the menu bar in Figure 18-7).

Travel Kit

One of the first things you need to make up is a travel kit for your PowerBook. Here's what I carry:

- Spare batteries and an A/C adapter.
- Essential disks: a set of System disks (with enablers), a MacTools or Norton Disk Doctor Emergency disk.
- An original AutoDoubler disk, because it occasionally needs reinstalling, and when you do, you need the original disk.
- A blank floppy or two.
- Two AppleTalk connectors and phone wire.
- Kensington lock (this $40 cable secures my 540c wherever I go; those running System 7.5 can read "About PowerBook Security" in the Software Highlights Control Panel for more details).
- Silicon Sports' WetSuit (a snug-fitting case made of wetsuit material that protects my PowerBook).
- APS SCSI Doc, along with a 3 foot 25/50 APS SCSI cable.
- One more essential, whether you travel or not: AppleCare. Repairs on a PowerBook can exceed its value otherwise.

Battery Utilities

There is no shortage of utilities available to help you with your PowerBook batteries — some of the best of what's available are on the CD-ROM included with the book.

Battery Drain
Carl Powell III
2306 Pembrook Circle S.W.
Huntsville, AL 35803
CompuServe: 76702,457
Battery Drain is freeware

Some PowerBook batteries can suffer from a "memory effect" — they remember the amount that they were recharged at; the end result is that you lose battery capacity. The cure is to fully discharge your batteries before recharging, and that's just what Battery Drain (Figure 18-8) does for you.

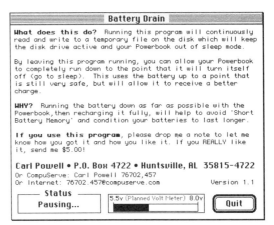

Figure 18-8: Battery Drain

BatteryAmnesia

Jeremy Kezer
143 Songbird Lane
Farmington, CT 06032-3433
America Online: JBKezer
Shareware fee: $10.00

I debated including Jeremy's stuff in Chapter 11 (Outstanding Authors), but I decided that because all of his programs (BatteryAmnesia, MyBattery, PowerBook Tweak, Threshold, Jeremy's CS Modules, Insomniac) are for the PowerBook, it made more sense to put them here.

BatteryAmnesia (Figure 18-9) is another utility for completely discharging nickel-cadmium (NiCad) and Nickel-Hydride (NiMH) batteries — it runs your PowerBook at full power until a "hard" hardware shutdown occurs.

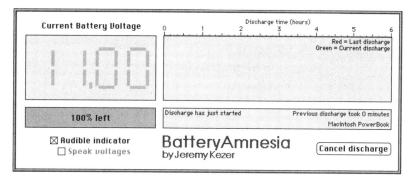

Figure 18-9: Battery Amnesia

BatteryMinder

Randall Voth
46058 Fiesta Avenue
Chilliwack, B.C. V2P 3S4
Canada
Telephone: 604 795-4746
Internet: hvoth@cln.etc.bc.ca
Shareware fee: $15.00

BatteryMinder offers much more than the name implies — this utility allows you to control almost everything that relates to the amount of juice your PowerBook draws. Preferences (Figure 18-10) allow you to mute the startup sound, force AppleTalk to load at startup, and toggle the amount of backlight. The same figure also shows a floating status display and a floating control for backlighting. Figure 18-11 shows the main menu, with controls for AppleTalk, your modem, sound, screen depth, and more. BatteryMinder also allows direct access to another of Randall's programs, Sync (see Chapter 3).

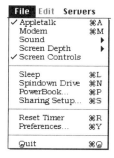

Figure 18-10: BatteryMinder prefs

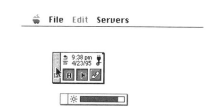

Figure 18-11: BatteryMinder options

DuoMon
Mike Blackwell
The Robotics Institute,
Carnegie Mellon University
5000 Forbes Avenue
Pittsburgh, PA 15213
Internet: mkb@cs.cmu.edu

DuoMon is freeware

This little utility (Figure 18-12) lets owners monitor the effect that various power operations have on their Duos by accurately tracking battery voltage in a graphic display that is updated every 5 seconds (the time interval can be changed).

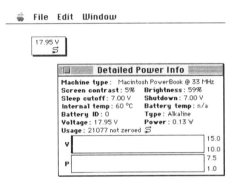

Figure 18-12: DuoMon

EMMpathy
Bill Steinberg
VST Power Systems
1620 Sudbury Road, Suite 3
Concord, MA 01742
Telephone: 508 287-4600
CompuServe: 72551,201

EMMpathy is freeware

The "smart" batteries shipped in the 500 series PowerBooks each contain an internal Energy Monitoring Module (EMM) for controlling charging and discharging. EMMpathy (Figure 18-13) detects and corrects memory corruption errors in the EMM which can occur if smart batteries are left discharged for long periods. Version 2.0 (on the CD-ROM) adds the ability to track and log multiple batteries, and an extension that automatically fixes the sleep drain calibration bug common in intelligent batteries.

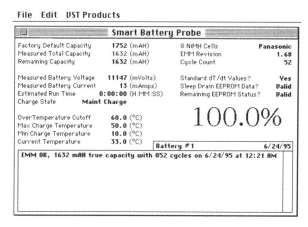

Figure 18-13: EMMpathy Smart Probe

MyBattery

Jeremy Kezer
(see BatteryAmnesia for Jeremy's address information)

Shareware fee: $10.00

MyBattery is a utility for that offers more ways to "see" what your battery is doing — with both numeric and graphic displays, including a gas gauge (see Figure 18-14), a bar graph, and a line plot; battery life estimation, support for multiple batteries, menu bar displays, CPU speed display, and battery charger status. Many features are available only to registered users, including column and line plot displays, support for multiple batteries, and menu bar displays.

The latest version (3.0, on the CD-ROM) allows you to customize your own version of the display. MyBattery can establish a link with Threshold (another of Jeremy's utilities also covered in this chapter) to set the current voltage threshold in your PowerBook's battery.

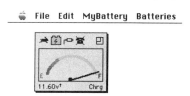

Figure 18-14: MyBattery

PowerBook Tweak
Jeremy Kezer
(see BatteryAmnesia for Jeremy's address information)

Shareware fee: $10.00

Want flexible control of your battery settings, with the ability to have the setting automatically changed to suit the application you are using? PowerBook Tweak (Figure 18-15) is the utility you need — it allows custom battery conservation settings for up to 50 applications (four in the unregistered version). PowerBook Tweak requires the latest version of Apple's Power Manager software, shipped with the 500 series PowerBooks, and included with System 7.5.

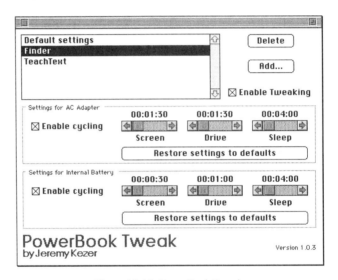

Figure 18-15: PowerBook Tweak

Threshold
Jeremy Kezer
(see BatteryAmnesia for Jeremy's address information)

Shareware fee: $10.00

One of the limitations of Apple's battery software is that the low battery warnings, which automatically dim your screen, often occur when you have lots of life left in your batteries. This is especially so if you use an external battery pack, because Apple's software cannot recognize them. The cure is Threshold (Figure 18-16), which allows you to adjust when the low battery warnings occur, with the ability to have up to three sets of battery warning thresholds, and support for external batteries.

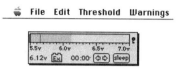

Figure 18-16: Threshold

Control Strips

One of the great new toys that Apple gave PowerBook 500 users, and now those with System 7.5 and better, is the Control Strip. This utility offers a new way for users to access information that is particularly suited for those with limited screen real estate. To make sure that those with desktop Macs don't get too jealous, the first utility in this section is one that allows them to use Control Strip modules — DeskTop Strip.

DeskTop Strip
Petur Petursson
Men & Mice
P.O. Box 7238
107 Reykjavik
Iceland
Telephone: +354 169 4938
Fax: +354 169 4991
Internet: peturp@rhi.hi.is
America Online: MenAndMice
CompuServe: 100045,2425
Shareware fee: $20.00

Men & Mice is a Mac utility software company located in Reykjavik. In 1994, they released Monitor Expander 1.0 and DeskTop Strip 1.0 (both on the CD-ROM). In the future they plan to improve the DeskTop Strip by supporting vertical strips and many other features. DeskTop Strip is written in C.

As I said, DeskTop Strip (Figure 18-17) allows the use of Control Strip modules on a desktop Mac. Actually, it goes further than that, with horizontal and vertical strips, and multiple strips, all of which offer expansion. One thing to remember is that not all Control Strip modules will work correctly with your desktop Mac (unless you're running it off of batteries). Those with PowerBooks should remember to disable Control Strip before they try DeskTop Strip, because the two conflict.

Figure 18-17: DeskTop Strip

BalloonHelpMe
Patrick McClaughry
Internet: patm@parcplace.com

BalloonHelpMe is freeware

Patrick is a software engineer at ParcPlace Systems, Inc. of Sunnyvale, California. He has programmed in Smalltalk, C, Pascal, and assembly for over 10 years and specifically for the Macintosh for about 5 years.

Balloon Help, when left on, can be a real PITA (pain in the neck). BalloonHelpMe (Figure 18-18) is a simple Control Strip module that allows you to toggle Balloon Help on and off.

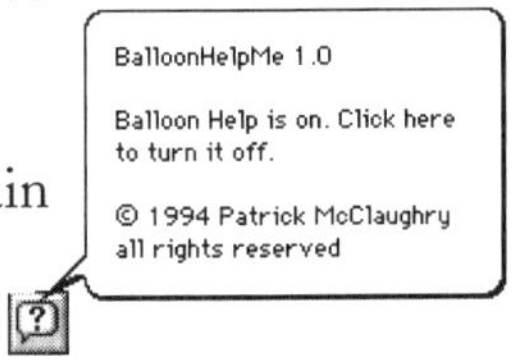

> BalloonHelpMe 1.0
>
> Balloon Help is on. Click here to turn it off.
>
> © 1994 Patrick McClaughry all rights reserved

Figure 18-18: BalloonHelpMe

BunchOApps
Patrick McClaughry
Internet: patm@parcplace.com

BunchOApps is freeware.

Here's another of Patrick's — a Control Strip module (Figure 18-19) that gives you a configurable list of recently launched applications.

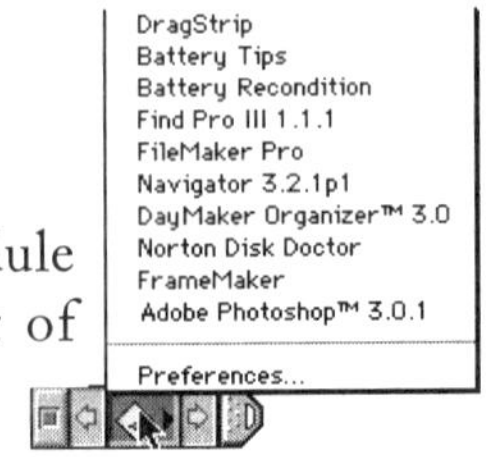

DragStrip
Battery Tips
Battery Recondition
Find Pro III 1.1.1
FileMaker Pro
Navigator 3.2.1p1
DayMaker Organizer™ 3.0
Norton Disk Doctor
FrameMaker
Adobe Photoshop™ 3.0.1

Preferences...

Figure 18-19: BunchOApps

Chris Modules

Chris Owen
27 Bishop Street #2R
New Haven, CT 06511
Internet: owen-christopher@yale.edu
Shareware fee: $10.00

This $10 collection gives you (from left to right in Figure 18-20) a clock, Control Panel access, an Express Modem module, a display of free RAM, a list of active processes, and a processor speed display.

Figure 18-20: Chris Modules

Duo Temperature Strip

Mike Blackwell
The Robotics Institute,
Carnegie Mellon University
5000 Forbes Avenue
Pittsburgh, PA 15213
Internet: mkb@cs.cmu.edu
Temperature is freeware

Temperature (in Figure 18-21) is a Control Strip module for Duo owners who want to know the temperature inside their Duos — in Celsius or Fahrenheit. PowerBook 500-series owners should stick with Jeremy's CMS (below) to get a more accurate reading.

Figure 18-21: Temperature

Jeremy's CS Modules

Jeremy Kezer
(see BatteryAmnesia for Jeremy's address information)

Shareware fee: $10.00

This is quite a collection of Control Strip modules (CSM) (from left to right in Figure 18-22): Jeremy's Application CSM (can be used as an application switcher), Battery CSM / CPU Speed CSM, Battery Time CSM (shows Apple or historical estimates of time remaining), Clock CSM, Sleep CSM,

Sound Volume CSM, and Temperature CSM (shows the internal and battery temperatures in Fahrenheit, Celsius, or Kelvin).

Figure 18-22: Jeremy's CS Modules

SoBig
Patrick McClaughry
Internet: patm@parcplace.com

SoBig is freeware

This Control Strip module (Figure 18-23) shows you the available free space on your startup disk; clicking on the module gives you display of the free space on all mounted volumes.

Figure 18-23: SoBig

More PowerBook Shareware

I suspect that the limited number of commercial applications written specifically for the PowerBook has had a positive effect on shareware developed — there sure is a lot of good material out there. Here are some more shareware utilities for your PowerBook.

BlackLock
Erik Sea
Tuffet AntiGravity
P.O. Box 61-1260
Port Huron, MI 48061-1260
AppleLink: CDA0745
CompuServe: 74170,111
Shareware fee: $5.00

Erik has been programming and tinkering with the Macintosh since 1985. Since 1987, he has been a professional Macintosh software designer, programmer, and consultant, whose code has found its way into a number of vertical and custom applications now in use by … dozens of people. Currently he is working on Macintosh-based wirephoto reception software (in C++), with time off to program his Newton and work on his Master's thesis (which involves user interface research).

Ever accidentally hit the Caps Lock key, and end up typing in all caps? This simple control panel does one thing, and does it well: it reverses the colors in your menu bar when the Caps Lock key is down, to give you a visual indicator. And, it works fine on desktop Macs, too.

Insomniac
Jeremy Kezer
(see BatteryAmnesia for Jeremy's address information)

Shareware fee: $10.00

Insomniac is a utility designed for those Macs that can "wake" themselves (the Portable, PowerBook 100, and Duos) — it allows you to schedule up to 50 wakeup events (to check your e-mail, send faxes, or whatever). For those interested, this screen shot was taken on a old Portable. Insomniac is limited to two events until registered.

Figure 18-24: Insomniac

PowerStrip
Mike Caputo
595 Lamoka Avenue
Staten Island, NY 10312
America Online: MCaputo
CompuServe: 74372,2431
Shareware fee: $10.00

Mike works as a network administrator and programmer for a Wall Street firm in Manhattan, and moonlights as a cartoon animator (his "reel" ambition — check out the icon he used for PowerStrip). He does his drawings the conventional way — on a light table — then, using a video camera hooked up to Digital Vision's ComputerEyes frame grabber, he shoots the drawings into Premier, where everything gets composited into a QuickTime movie. He's hoping to sell enough shareware to buy an AV Power Mac (any model!), but he *does* have to save for his twins' college education, too.

Here's another utility designed for the PowerBook that still manages to offer considerable functionality for desktop Macs. As you can see in Figure 18-25, PowerStrip is a configurable display of all kinds of information, including the time, date, free RAM, free disk space, AppleTalk status, printer, and mouse coordinates. PowerBook owners get even more, with the ability to display CPU speed, modem status, elapsed charging or battery time, battery voltage, and graphs of your battery level and voltage history.

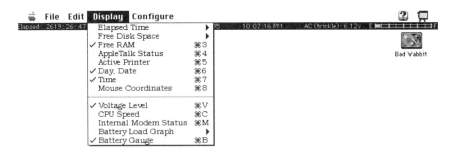

Figure 18-25: PowerStrip

Quiet Start
Tom Bridgewater
Internet: tbridgwa@cymbal.calpoly.edu

Quiet Start is freeware

Imagine this scenario: you're sitting in an important meeting, quietly taking notes on your PowerBook, when all of a sudden it crashes. Do you really want to reboot, and listen to the startup sound? Quiet Start is a great little freeware extension that silences the startup sound.

Silent Beep
Simon Bone
P.O. Box 1847
Lewisburg, TN 37091-0847
CompuServe: 70324,1340
Silent Beep is freeware

Simon is a student at Humboldt-Universität zu Berlin in Germany, but feel free to send him money or software at his U.S. address.

This is a simple sound bite with one purpose: to give you a noiseless beep sound. Just drag it into your System folder, and assign it as your beep sound (in the Sound Control Panel), and your Mac will stop beeping at you, while still allowing you to hear other sounds.

Sleep Deprivation
Mark Pilgrim
MerriMac Software Group
1130 Radnor Hill Road
Wayne, PA 19087-2203
Internet: f8dy@netaxs.com
Sleep Deprivation is freeware

Mark is a senior at Earlham College, majoring in philosophy. He will graduate by the time this book is published, and become a computer consultant or a professional computer programmer. He programs in his spare time, exclusively on the Macintosh and exclusively in C. He's been programming for 11 years, first on the Apple][e and the past 3 years on the Mac. He's a fierce advocate of free software, and releases source code with everything he releases publicly.

This freeware extension clears the screen with one of 50 cool graphic effects whenever you put your Mac to sleep.

SpinD
Bill Steinburg
America Online: BillS
CompuServe: 76703,1027

SpinD is freeware

Here's a simple Fkey from the author of PBTools. As the name implies, it allows you to spin down your hard drive to conserve your battery. See Chapter 11 for fkey installation instructions.

ToggleAT
Jon Pugh
1861 Landings Drive
Mountain View, CA 94043
Telephone: 415 691-6643
Internet: jonpugh@netcom.com

ToggleAT is freeware

Here's another fkey to help conserve your PowerBook's battery — like it says, ToggleAT allows you to toggle AppleTalk on and off.

19 Power Macs

Thanks to David Gillen for his help with this chapter.

This chapter tells you how the PowerPC chip came about, some of the differences you'll find when you upgrade from a 680x0 Mac to a Power Mac, and tips on how to optimize your new computer to get the best out of it, along with some shareware to help you. It concludes with a technical note from Connectix on the benefits of using RAM Doubler on a Power Mac.

What is a Power Macintosh?

Since 1984, all Macintosh computers have been based on the Motorola 680x0 family of processors. The first Macintosh computers used the 68000 processor, followed by computers using the 68020-, 68030-, and 68040-series of processors. Although Motorola has produced a 68060 processor, Apple decided to move away from the 680x0 family of processors in favor of a new family of processors, the PowerPC, also manufactured by Motorola.

The PowerPC processor are designed by Apple, IBM, and Motorola. It is a RISC (Reduced Instruction Set Computer), as opposed to the 680x0 chips which are CISC (Complex Instruction Set Computer). A RISC processor has fewer instructions in it, allowing the chip to be smaller and faster, while a CISC processor has to be able to perform many complex instructions, making it bigger and slower. Personal computers have traditionally used CISC processors, and RISC processors are commonly found in Unix workstations and other high-end workstations.

Apple realized it couldn't make the transition from CISC to RISC without support from its major developers, since every Macintosh application would have to be rewritten to work well with the new PowerPC processor. This commitment had not been necessary in the past since a 68040 processor could execute the same programs, for the most part, that a 68030 processor could, since the two processors were in the same family. But the PowerPC belongs to a different family of processors, so this compatibility convenience

375

does not exist. Fortunately, many developers saw the potential in the PowerPC family of processors, and Apple went ahead with its plans to migrate the Macintosh from the 680x0 to the PowerPC.

The first processor to become available for use by Apple was the PowerPC 601 processor. Even while this processor was being designed and tested, its successors were already being designed. These include the PowerPC 603 and the 603e, low-power versions of the 601, and the PowerPC 604, which is approximately one and a half times as fast as an equivalent PowerPC 601 chip at the same clock speed.

Meanwhile, in the computing world, Intel was busy producing their successor to the 80486 processor, the Pentium chip. There were a lot of comparisons between the PowerPC 601 and the Pentium chip, but these chips are very different, and the comparisons were apples and oranges. The Pentium chip is a CISC processor, and the PowerPC 601 is a RISC processor. The Pentium is near the end of a family of processors, while the PowerPC 601 is the first in a new family of processors.

In March 1994, Apple introduced three Macintosh models based on the PowerPC 601 processor: the Power Macintosh 6100, Power Macintosh 7100, and Power Macintosh 8100. Later in 1994, Apple introduced Work Group Servers based on the PowerPC 601 processor, as well as faster versions of the original three models. As this book is being printed, Apple has introduced computers based on the PowerPC 603 and 604 processors.

Apple realized that new PowerPC processors would be available in the future, so they made sure all current PowerPC-based Macintoshes could be upgraded to the new processors when they become available. This is done with both socketed processor chips (plug the new chip right on top of the old one), and in other cases, with add-on cards containing the new processor.

What's Different about a Power Macintosh?

Now that you know what a Power Macintosh is, how does it really differ from the older 680x0-based Macintosh models? The differences to users are small, but noticeable. Apple wanted the Power Macintosh to "look and feel like a Macintosh," and for the most part, it does. Apple's main goal with the design of the Power Macintosh was compatibility. But if you look close enough, you'll find some differences between the two types of Macintoshes.

"Native" versus "Emulated" versus "Fat"

First, some terminology. I mentioned already that Apple needed its developers to rewrite applications to work well on the Power Macintosh. An application that has been rewritten for the Power Macintosh is known as a *native* application, because it runs in the processor's native PowerPC (RISC) mode. But Apple didn't expect every software package to be available native for the PowerPC processor, so they designed a 680x0 emulator. Any application that has not been rewritten for the Power Mac runs in an *emulated* mode. It's called emulated because the Power Macintosh acts like it is emulating a 68020 Macintosh (no, that's not a misprint, and yes, it's a problem). Like all emulators, the 68020 emulator is not known for its speed, but the level of compatibility is extremely high. Most older Macintosh applications will run just fine on a Power Macintosh in emulated mode; they just won't be all that fast.

You might be thinking — what if I have native applications and emulated applications on my machine at the same time? How does the Power Macintosh know what to do? Do I have to manually switch between native and emulated modes? Fortunately, the answers to all of these questions are very simple. The Power Macintosh takes care of it all internally, so don't have to worry about a thing. If you run a native application, the Power Macintosh will run it in native mode. If it encounters a non-native application, it will automatically switch into emulated mode and run this application with the emulator.

So, maybe you're asking — what happens if I run a native application on a non-PowerPC Macintosh, like a Mac IIci? This also has a simple answer: the application won't run; unless the application is a *fat binary*. A fat binary is an application that contains instructions for both a 680x0 processor and a PowerPC processor. When you run a fat binary on a Mac IIci, the Mac IIci uses the 680x0 instructions, and when you run the same fat binary on a Power Macintosh 6100, the Power Macintosh will use the PowerPC instructions. This sounds like a great way to package all applications, but fat binaries take more disk space because they essentially contain two copies of the same program! If you're a 680x0 user, you may want to consider using Fat Free (below) to save some disk space.

Fat Free
Hubert Figuiere
24 rue des Filmins
92339 Sceaux
France
Telephone: 33-1-47-02-40-07
Internet: figuiere@altern.com
Fat Free is freeware.

Hubert is a 20-year-old Computer Sciences student at the Institute of Orsay. He's in his second (and last) year of studies before graduation. Hubert is a self-taught programmer, who's been programming for about three years in THINK Pascal, Metrowerks Pascal (CodeWarrior), and in C/C++ with CodeWarrior.

Fat binaries are great — they allow software to be distributed with both 680x0 and PowerPC code. What if you don't have a Power Mac, and you want to save the space wasted by the PowerPC code? Fat Free is the answer — run it (on a copy first, please) to strip the "fat" out of your applications.

Apple System Software

So now that you know what kind of programs will run on a Power Macintosh, let's look at some actual software for the Power Macintosh. We'll start with the system software.

The first Power Macintosh models came with System 7.1.2. System 7.1.2 is basically System 7.1 modified to work on a Power Macintosh. Most of the system operates in emulated mode, with a few components operating in native mode. One example of a native mode component is QuickDraw, the mechanism by which the Macintosh draws on the screen. The Macintosh spends a lot of its time doing QuickDraw-related activities, so it was very smart of Apple to make QuickDraw native.

Will earlier versions of System 7.1 work on a Power Macintosh? The answer is no. Nothing earlier than System 7.1.2 will boot the machine. And will System 7.1.2 run on a 680x0 Macintosh? The answer again is no. System 7.1.2 is for Power Macintoshes only. But what if you need a common system to operate on a Power Macintosh and an older Macintosh? Apple's answer to this is System 7.5. System 7.5 will run on a 680x0 Macintosh and a Power Macintosh because System 7.5 is fat. Well, it's fat enough. System 7.5 is still not completely native on a Power Macintosh, but more of it is native than what is in System 7.1.2. It's also a lot more stable than System 7.1.2. System 7.5 also includes a lot of little patches and bug fixes, such as System Update 3.0 and Network Software Installer 1.4.5. See Chapter 6 for a description of System 7.5 update 1.0.

But what about some of the other system components? QuickTime fans can be happy because QuickTime 2.0 is native on a Power Macintosh. But PowerTalk fans will need to wait a little longer for a completely native version of PowerTalk. Also, for you networking fans, none of Apple's network software (AppleTalk, AppleShare, MacTCP) is native.

Other Differences

So what are some of the other differences between older Macintoshes and Power Macintoshes? There are probably quite a few differences internal to the machines, but most really don't matter. But there are some differences in the Power Macintosh that may cause problems with some older applications.

One difference is how the Power Macintosh handles floating-point arithmetic. Older Macs required a special FPU (floating-point unit) chip, also known as a math coprocessor, to perform complex floating-point arithmetic. There are some applications that will not run unless an FPU is present in the Macintosh. 68030 processors require an external FPU chip on the motherboard, while some 68040 processors include an FPU right in the processor. The PowerPC processor does all of its floating-point math internally in the processor without an FPU. Some older software that requires an FPU will not run because the software is not able to find an actual FPU. Older versions of Microsoft Excel are not able to find an FPU chip, so the application uses a slower method to perform its calculations, rather than letting the PowerPC perform the instructions internally. A solution is John Neil's PowerFPU, a commercial version of his shareware program SoftwareFPU.

SoftwareFPU
John M. Neil
John Neil & Associates
P.O. Box 2156
Cupertino, CA 95015
Internet: johnneil@netcom.com
Shareware fee: $10.00

John is a 29-year-old software developer living in the San Francisco Bay area. He got his start in 1988 as a hardware engineer at Apple Computer, helping develop the Macintosh Classic, LC, si, and Power Macintosh machines, among other projects. After three years he realized that his true calling was software, not hardware (the fun/drudgery ratio is higher in software than hardware), and left to work on his own software projects. Since then he has developed three released software products (SoftwareFPU, Monopoly for MacPlay, and OTA for Digital Eclipse Software), worked on twice that number that never saw the light of day, started two software companies, and learned a whole lot about the software market and business in general.

SoftwareFPU is a Control Panel (see Figure 19-1) that allows owners of those Macs without FPUs to run software that requires one, without having to upgrade their hardware. Power Mac users should check out John's PowerFPU, which is a high-speed FPU emulator written especially for the Power Mac. See the SoftwareFPU documentation for a listing of the Macintosh models supported, and for a listing of some of the software that FPU will allow you to run.

Figure 19-1: SoftwareFPU

Another difference is the way a Power Macintosh handles memory for its applications. Older Macintoshs read the executable part of a program from the resource fork of the file, from CODE resources. These resources are only loaded as needed. If an application needs to execute a section of code that has not yet been loaded, the Macintosh reads that resource into memory and continues. This way, a bigger application can use less memory, and only load into memory those parts that are needed. On a Power Macintosh, this process is done differently. A Power Macintosh native application stores all of its code in one large section, in the data fork of the application. Assuming that Virtual Memory is off, when a Power Macintosh starts an application, it will try to load the entire program into memory all at once. You might say, "Should I care about something like this?" Yes, you should, since this is one of the major reasons that Power Macintosh native applications require more memory than their 680x0 counterparts. One way around this problem is to turn on virtual memory, which we'll discuss in the next section.

Optimizing a Power Macintosh

Apple designed the Power Macintosh with compatibility with older software as its number one priority. But there are software packages out there that don't play by all the rules. How can we optimize a Power Macintosh for greatest compatibility, but not let performance suffer? The following sections describe a number of techniques to use.

Modern Memory Manager

If you've looked in the Memory Control Panel on a Power Macintosh, it looks the same as older Macintoshes, except for one new item: the Modern Memory Manager (Figure 19-2). What exactly is the Modern Memory Manager?

According to Apple, the Modern Memory Manager is a new memory manager written specifically for the Power Macintosh. It is native, and uses

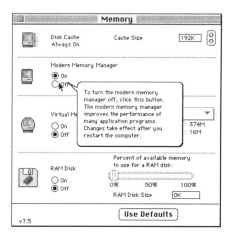

Figure 19-2: Modern Memory Manager

more advanced techniques for caching and other memory management. Any application that completely follows Apple's rules for memory management will work fine with the Modern Memory Manager turned on. The Modern Memory Manager, being native, runs faster than the old memory manager, which runs in emulation.

But, as we all know, not all applications play by all of the rules. It turns out that the new Modern Memory Manager is not as forgiving as the old memory manager. There are certain things Apple prohibited developers from doing, but they worked anyway under the older memory manager. Some of these techniques no longer work with the Modern Memory Manager. If you have an application that just won't work (it freezes or crashes randomly), the first thing to do is turn off the Modern Memory Manager. The older memory manager really isn't that slow on a Power Macintosh, and you probably won't notice a difference, except that your applications may work better, which is always a good thing.

Virtual Memory

When System 7 arrived in 1991, it brought virtual memory to the Macintosh operating system. Virtual memory is a technique used to increase the amount of memory your Macintosh has by utilizing the hard disk as psuedo-RAM.

Here's a simple example of how virtual memory works: let's say your Macintosh has 8MB of RAM. Your system takes up 2MB of RAM leaving 6MB free for your applications. As soon as you use up this 6MB, no more applications can run until you quit your existing applications. But if you turn on virtual memory, let's say, to 12MB, your Macintosh now has 10MB of RAM for applications. As soon as your Macintosh uses up the available "real" memory (the 8MB inside your Mac), it finds some memory that hasn't been used in awhile, and writes the contents of the memory to your hard disk. It then makes that memory available to another application that needs it. When another application needs some data from memory that has been written to the hard disk, some other portion of memory is written to the hard disk, and the data on the hard disk is read back into memory. This is called *swapping* and the hard disk space used is called *swap space*.

On an older Macintosh, the rule of thumb was: if you need more memory, go buy some more. Turn on virtual memory only as a last resort, or as a temporary solution, because it really slows down your Mac. Every time the

Mac needs to swap, the Mac must wait for the hard disk to write the old data and read the new data. This takes considerable time, and the higher you set virtual memory, the slower it gets, since your Mac can spend more time swapping than actually running your program.

But on a Power Macintosh, it's a different story. Remember I said above that Power Macintosh native applications are stored as one big chunk of code on your hard disk? It was done this way to make virtual memory work really well. When you turn on virtual memory on a Power Macintosh, it uses the big chunk of code as its own swap space. When you start up an application, the Power Macintosh will load a part of the application. It will read more of it from the hard disk only when it is needed. The Power Macintosh doesn't need to store the entire application in memory because it can swap the code itself. On an older Mac, when a swap needs to take place, data is first written to the hard disk, then the new data is read from the hard disk. Since an application's code never changes, a Power Mac won't have to write any data when it performs a swap; it only needs to read the new code into the same memory the old code was using.

The bottom line is that virtual memory on a Power Macintosh allows the Mac to use memory in a more effective fashion since it won't need to load the entire application into memory at once. But the question remains: how much virtual memory should you turn on? It's recommended that you turn on the minimal amount. So, if your Power Macintosh has 16MB of RAM, set the virtual memory to 17MB. This allows your Power Macintosh to take advantage of virtual memory, but it also won't spend all of its time swapping.

680x0 Code versus PowerPC Code

When you run older, non-native software on your Power Macintosh, the software will run in emulated mode. Although the emulator does a good job, it can be slow at times. Minimizing the number of emulated programs on your Power Macintosh will speed it up tremendously.

But what about all of those extensions and control panels every Mac user loves to have in the System Folder? What if they are not native? Lots of extensions and control panels are not native. Depending on what the extension of control panel does, it may be constantly running in the background monitoring something, or it could be waiting for something to happen, or it could just load at startup and never be seen again. It's the ones that are constantly running that can cause big performance hits. Whenever your Power Mac switches between executing native code and emulated code, a few things must happen internally on the Power Macintosh. These things are associated with the context switch that takes place. These things, although relatively quick, do take some time, especially if they are done often enough. Some extensions run many times each second, resulting in many context switches taking place each second. And if each context switch takes time, this will slow down your Power Macintosh.

The rule of thumb here is to minimize the number of non-native control panels and extensions. Contact the vendor or the author of the extension to see if a native version exists. There won't be a way to eliminate all context switches until Apple releases a fully native version of the system software, but it is definitely a good idea to minimize the number of them.

Want to find out if your applications are native? Here are two freeware utilities that can check your applications for PowerPC code — I Love Native! (Figure 19-3) offers unique dialog boxes (to say the least...), and PowerPCheck (Figure 19-4) displays more information. You might also want to check out the demo of Conflict Catcher 3 (Chapter 1); it, too, can identify native applications for you.

I Love Native!
Jerry Du
Dragonsoft
603 E. Minor Drive #101
Kansas City, MO 64131
Telephone: 816 943-1835
America Online: Dragonsoft
CompuServe: 74471,3403
I Love Native! is freeware

Figure 19-3: I Love Native!

PowerPCheck
Alessandro Levi Montalcini
C.so Re Umberto 10
10121 Torino Italy
Internet: Lmontalcini@pmn.it
PowerPCheck is freeware

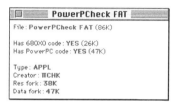

Figure 19-4: PowerPCheck

System 7.1.2 versus System 7.5

It's much easier to support a group of Macintosh users when they're all running the same software. This is one reason why System 7.5 is a good idea for all Macintosh systems. The feature set of System 7.5 is very rich, and a consistent environment across all machines is attainable with everybody running System 7.5. Plus, on a Power Macintosh, minimizing the number of context switches is a good idea, and since System 7.5 is more native than System 7.1.2, System 7.5 will run better on a Power Macintosh than System 7.1.2 will.

If you must continue to use System 7.1.2, make sure you install Apple's System Update 3.0. If you're on an Ethernet network, you should also install Apple's Network Software Install 1.4.5. These two "patches" will make your Power Macintosh more reliable.

Incompatibilities

You will find certain software packages are incompatible with a Power Macintosh. Turning off the Modern Memory Manager and turning on virtual memory to the minimal setting will give you the highest level of compatibility attainable with Apple software. But this doesn't address other compatibility problems, such as the lack of an FPU.

For software that is not compatible with virtual memory, RAM Doubler by Connectix may be a solution. It gives all the advantages of Apple's virtual memory, plus it can be more compatible with other software. (See the article at the end of this chapter on using RAM Doubler with native PowerPC applications.)

Updated Tools

Every Mac user will eventually use Norton Utilities, or a comparable product, to fix a damaged hard disk. Although these software packages work fine on a Power Macintosh, don't expect your old "System 7 Emergency Disk" to boot a Power Macintosh. You'll need to make sure you have the latest versions of these software packages that will boot a Power Macintosh.

You should also make sure your hard disk formatters are installing Power Macintosh compatible drivers. Although many emulated drivers will work fine, some older drivers take advantage of specific hardware features not found in a Power Macintosh, and can result in a hard disk that won't mount on the desktop.

Showing Off Your Power Mac

Okay, you've spent the big bucks, and upgraded to a Power Mac — what are you going to do to show off your new power to your friends (this should be considered a duty for those in mixed-platform environments). The first thing you should do is to fire up Apple's sexy new Graphing Calculator (Figure 19-5); then you might want to try Alessandro's PowerXPlorer (shown in Figure 19-6 with the settings over a fractal map).

PowerXPlorer
Alessandro Levi Montalcini
C.so Re Umberto 10
10121 Torino
Italy
Internet: Lmontalcini@pmn.it
PowerXPlorer is freeware

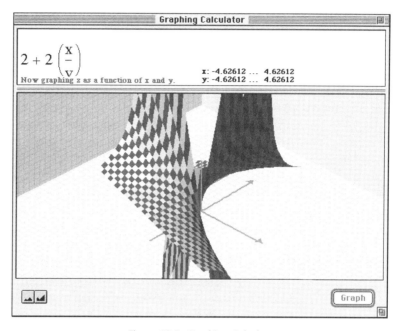

Figure 19-5: Graphing Calculator

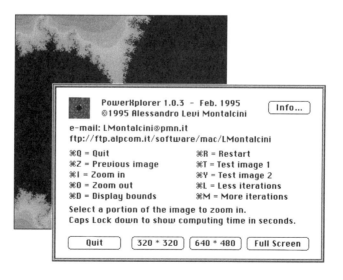

Figure 19-6: PowerXPlorer

Technical Notes: Using RAM Doubler with Native PPC Applications

The following article, provided by Connectix Technical Support, outlines some of the reasons to use RAM Doubler on a Power PC, and is reprinted with permission.

Power Mac native applications use less memory with RAM Doubler installed. By using a memory management technique known as file mapping, RAM Doubler reduces the memory footprint of all native applications. This memory savings is in addition to the doubling of memory RAM Doubler provides. With this twofold benefit, RAM Doubler is the best way to optimize Power Mac memory usage and get the most out of installed RAM. This document briefly describes the file mapping memory management technique utilized by RAM Doubler and its importance for Power Mac native applications.

Memory Usage of Power Mac Native Applications and File Mapping
RISC (PowerPC) processors are optimized to handle a smaller number of instruction types as opposed to CISC processors (680x0). Because of the faster processing speeds achieved by the reduced instruction set, programs run much faster. One minor drawback to RISC processors is that they take more instructions to perform the same amount of work (about 33%, on average). Fortunately the speed benefits far outweigh this small increase in code size. But this code size increase requires more RAM. Thus, native Power Mac applications require a larger amount of memory to perform the same function as its 680x0 equivalent. Moreover, the faster processing speed of PowerPC chips has encouraged developers to add additional features to their products. In many cases, the memory requirements for native applications grow to several times the size of their 680x0 equivalents.

These memory requirements are reduced by using the file mapping memory management technique Apple built into the Power Mac ROM. File mapping is used whenever Connectix RAM Doubler is installed or System 7 virtual memory is enabled. In fact, using one of these two products is the only way you can get file mapping's benefits.

Without file mapping, native applications load their entire code base, often several megabytes worth, into application memory. File mapping works by loading into memory only the application code being used, leaving additional application code on the hard drive to be swapped into memory as necessary. This significantly reduces the amount of memory used by native applications. To find out how much memory is being saved by file mapping, do a "Get Info" on a native application with RAM Doubler running.

RAM Doubler File Mapping Example — Microsoft Excel 5.0 for the Power Mac

The best way to illustrate the difference RAM Doubler's file mapping will make on a native application is to compare memory requirements without RAM Doubler to memory requirements with RAM Doubler installed. This example uses Excel 5.0 for the Power Macintosh. (Memory requirements for Microsoft Excel 5.0 from the Microsoft Strategic White Paper — Power Macintosh™ Technology: Microsoft Office 4.2 for the Macintosh®; Part Number 098-56876, October 1994. This document is available from Microsoft Sales Fax Service at (800) 727-3351.)

Without RAM Doubler, you cannot launching native Excel 5.0 on an 8MB Power Macintosh:

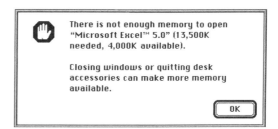

> There is not enough memory to open "Microsoft Excel™ 5.0" (13,500K needed, 4,000K available).
>
> Closing windows or quitting desk accessories can make more memory available.
>
> OK

Excel memory requirements

- 4MB of memory for the Excel default partition (can be changed by the user via "Get Info" under the system's File menu when large spreadsheets are being used).

- 6MB of memory for Excel data fork (a fixed number based on code size).

- 3.5MB of memory for the code contained in shared libraries used by Excel on the Power Macintosh (fixed number based on code size). Having code in a shared library means it is only in memory once, even when used by multiple applications.

This adds up to a grand total of 13.5MB of physical memory required to start Excel when virtual memory is off. Thus, even a Power Mac with 16MB RAM (assuming System Software uses 4MB) will not have enough memory to launch Excel 5.0. With RAM Doubler installed, you can launch native Excel 5.0 on an 8MB Power Macintosh:

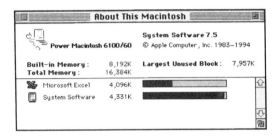

Excel 5.0 running with RAM Doubler

- 4MB of memory for the Excel default partition (can be changed by the user via "Get Info").

- All code will be "demand paged" through RAM Doubler file mapping so no memory is required in the set partition for Excel code and the shared libraries.

This adds up to a grand total of 4MB of logical memory required to boot Excel with RAM Doubler installed. By using RAM Doubler, there is a dramatic reduction in Excel 5.0 memory demands, from 13.5MB to 4 MB. Suddenly, a 16MB Power Mac has enough room to run Excel, and also additional applications as well. In addition to the memory savings, RAM Doubler doubles the amount of memory installed, providing room for more applications to be run. With the twofold benefit of file mapping and RAM expansion, RAM Doubler is the best way to optimize Power Mac memory usage and get the most out of installed RAM.

File Mapping — RAM Doubler vs. Virtual Memory
File mapping is essential to reduce memory demands of native applications. Power Mac file mapping is enabled through two

methods: Connectix RAM Doubler and System 7 virtual memory. While both provide the file mapping benefit, RAM Doubler performs faster and saves valuable hard drive space over System 7 virtual memory.

Apple Computer, as of January 1995, ships every new Power Macintosh model with virtual memory turned on to the amount of physical RAM plus one megabyte. On a 16MB configuration, for example, virtual memory will be set to 17MB. The primary benefit of virtual memory on the Power Mac is file mapping. The cost of virtual memory on the Power Mac is (1) a 10 to 15% performance penalty and (2) drive space usage equivalent to the total amount of memory (in our example, this amount is 17MB). Apple provides a document (entitled "About Virtual Memory") on the root level of the hard drive of every new Power Mac to explain file mapping and virtual memory usage to new Power Mac customers.

By using RAM Doubler instead of Apple's virtual memory on a Power Mac, the benefit of file mapping is gained without the cost of performance or hard drive usage. RAM Doubler causes no discernible performance degradation (typically about 1 to 3%) and usually requires no hard drive space to double any configuration of 8MB RAM or greater. In addition, RAM Doubler exactly doubles the amount of application memory available to run more applications. Let's look at RAM Doubler's benefits over System 7 virtual memory more closely:

- Improved performance — System 7 virtual memory slows your Power Mac's performance 250% or more than does RAM Doubler

- More hard disk space — System 7 virtual memory uses 8 to 17 megabytes more hard disk space than does RAM Doubler in standard configurations, and it gets worse as you increase the virtual memory size.

- More application space — RAM Doubler provides double the application memory, where the System 7 virtual memory configuration Apple ships provides only a megabyte of extra space (while you can up this amount, performance decreases and more hard disk space gets chewed up with System 7 virtual memory).

Compare a Power Mac with RAM Doubler installed to a Power Mac with virtual memory enabled: The RAM Doubler Power Mac is faster, has more drive space available, and exactly doubles the memory — there is no comparison.

The Information Highway

Getting On-Line

An Introduction to Network Troubleshooting

20 Getting On-Line

Now you've learned all this great stuff, and you have a CD-ROM full of shareware and demos — where do you go to get more? The answer is simple: the same place I did — on-line. Getting on-line can take many forms, from a local bulletin board, to the Internet, to one of the commercial services. In my experience, the best place to get answers to questions is on one of the commercial services, especially the MAUG® (Micronetworked Apple Users Group) areas on CompuServe. Although you can find shareware and get answers to many questions on a local BBS or on the Internet, neither offer the focused access to expert help that MAUG does.

In this chapter, I'm going to briefly cover getting on-line on America Online and CompuServe, and conclude with a group interview with some of MAUG's sysops.

America Online
America Online
8619 Westwood Center Drive
Vienna, VA 22182
Toll-free: 800 827-6364
Rates: $9.95/month for the first five hours, then $2.95/hour (software included)

With the release of version 2.5 (2.5.1 as of this writing) of their software, America Online improved its look dramatically. This service offers good software libraries and support, but the lack of *topic threading* (see CompuServe for a description) makes it second to CompuServe when it comes to technical support.

Here's a quick tour, which will take you into the software libraries, give you some idea of the interface, and what is available. After launching AOL's software and logging on, you'll be brought to the main menu (Figure 20-1). As you can see, there are all sorts of areas to explore; for now, we'll look for some software to download. After dismissing the ad, clicking on COMPUTING will take you to the Computing Menu (Figure 20-2). From there, clicking on Software Center will take you to the Macintosh Software

Global Village
PowerPort 2.5
software showing a
2400 baud connection

Click here to go to
Computing (Figure
20-2)

Figure 20-1: AOL Main Menu

Center (Figure 20-3), and selecting Search the Libraries will bring you to the dialog box shown in Figure 20-4. If you want to get there directly, try Command-5. After telling AOL about what you'd like to see, you'll get a list of files to review, and you can select those you want for immediate or later downloading. I usually tell the AOL software to Download Later (Figure 20-5), so that I can end with a FlashSession. As you can see in Figure 20-6, a FlashSession allows you to have the AOL software log off automatically after sending and receiving messages and files that you specify. Both AOL (Figure 20-7) and CompuServe offer connection to the Internet; my

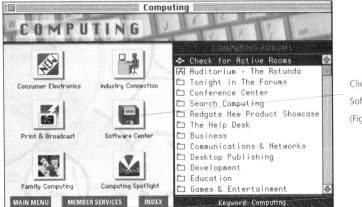

Click here to go to the
Software Center
(Figure 20-3)

Figure 20-2: AOL Computing Menu

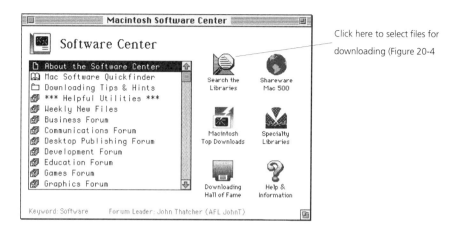

Click here to select files for downloading (Figure 20-4

Figure 20-3: AOL Macintosh Software Center

recommendation for those who wish to explore the Internet is to contact a local service provider — the connect charges are usually much lower.

I have to admit, I have not had the best of luck with America Online; I'm often unable to connect at 14400 bps, the host often disconnects (see Figure 20-8), and worst of all, the lack of topic threading makes on-line conversing tedious. In the upper right-hand corner of Figure 20-1, you can see Global Village's PowerPort Mercury software indicating a 2400 bps connection made the time I took these screen shots.

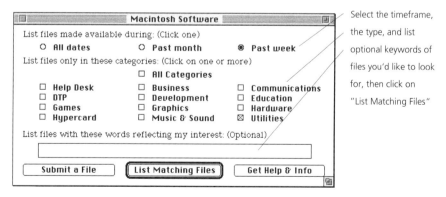

Select the timeframe, the type, and list optional keywords of files you'd like to look for, then click on "List Matching Files"

Figure 20-4: Searching for files on AOL

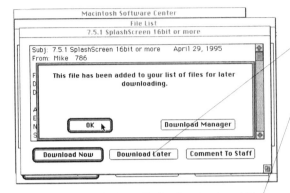

Selecting a file for downloading later allows you to have AOL run a "FlashSession", where files and messages are uploaded and downloaded, then the software automatically disconnects to save you connect charges

Figure 20-5: Selecting a file for download on AOL

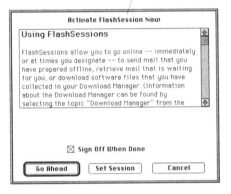

Figure 20-6: AOL FlashSession

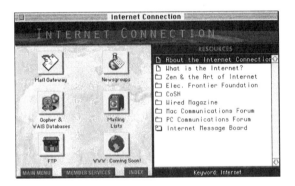

Figure 20-7: AOL Internet connection

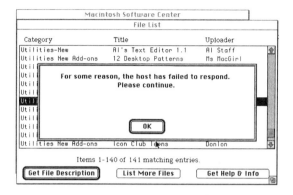

Figure 20-8: Bye-bye AOL

Macintosh CompuServe Information Manager (MacCIM)
CompuServe
5000 Arlington Center Boulevard
Columbus, OH 43220
Telephone: 614 457-8650
Toll-free: 800 848-8199

Rates: basic services (120 services) $9.95/Month (MacCIM included); Internet access: first 3 hours are free, then $2.50 per hour. Other extension services outside the basic are 8 cents per minute.

Not only is a full, working Mac version of CompuServe Information Manager on the CD-ROM, but the card inside the sleeve with the CD-ROM gives you 10 free hours of connect time if you sign up! CompuServe's libraries are second to none — no matter what your interest, there's a Forum area for you there.

MacCIM is CompuServe's graphical interface. Complete documentation for MacCIM is on the CD-ROM, so I'm going to leave it with a screen shot (Figure 20-9), and move onto the power users' tool: CompuServe Navigator.

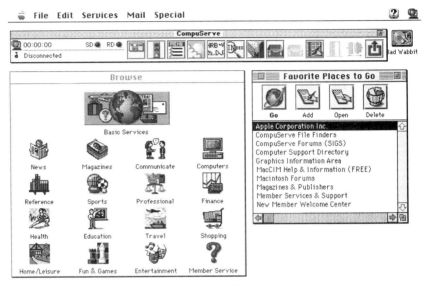

Figure 20-9: CompuServe Information Manager

CompuServe Navigator
(see MacCIM for CompuServe's address information)
Suggested retail: $50.00

It should be no secret which of the services or programs is my favorite: CompuServe, using CompuServe Navigator. This program offers an interface that isn't quite as friendly as the two programs (AOL and MacCIM) I've already mentioned, but it makes up for it big time. The biggest difference with Navigator is that the program is designed to minimize connect charges by allowing you to make selections, respond to e-mail or messages, and select files for uploading or downloading; all before you connect. Once you've made your selections, Navigator takes over, doing what you've asked it to and then disconnecting. Let's have a look and see just how it works.

Once you've loaded Navigator, select Show Preview from the Session Menu (or press Command-p). For new members, I've included a copy of my session file (with my password edited out, of course) on the CD-ROM — just add your name, password, and local access number, and you're ready to go. Figure 20-10 shows a scrolling list on the right-hand side of the screen that shows you what you've asked Navigator to do the next time you log on, and darkened icons on the left-hand side of the screen allow you to tell the

Clicking here to move Forums up or down in the listing

Click here to compact the file listing

Darkened files are Forums you have selected to have Navigator check out for you

The right side of the screen tells you exactly what Navigator will do the next time you run it

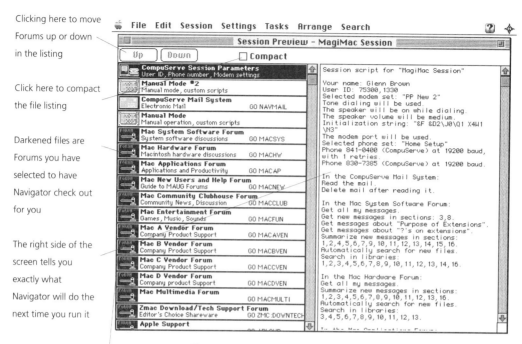

Figure 20-10: CompuServe Navigator Session Preview

Double-clicking on a forum icon allows you to tell Navigator what file libraries you're interested in (this Figure) and what messages you'd like to look at (Figure 20-13 on page 403)

Figure 20-11: Navigator file preview

software more about what you like it to do for you. Double-clicking an icon toggles its status (either you want to look in the area, or you don't); double-clicking on the description to the right of the icon lets you tell Navigator what messages and software areas you are interested in. Figure 20-11 shows my selections for the file area in MacSYS. Note that I'm only asking to see new files since that last time I looked in each area. Figure 20-12 shows my selections for the messages in the same Forum; you'll note that I read all messages in area #3 (INITs/Extensions) and area #8 (System Conflicts) — I'm a Discussion Leader for these areas. Readers who want to reach me will find me daily on CompuServe (my address is 75300,1330 or 75300.1330@compuserve.com via the Internet); I check America Online every few weeks (my AOL screen name is GlennBrown).

The message summary screen shows you messages posted since the last time you logged on. The summary pop-up allows you to read a message, get an entire thread, or anything in between

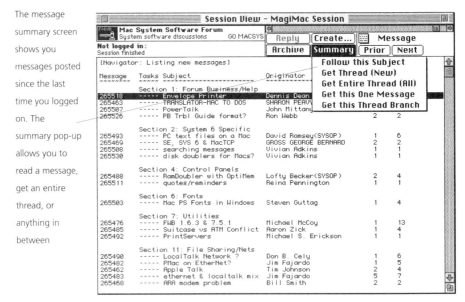

Figure 20-12: Navigator message preview

Once you've made all your selections, you can tell Navigator to run, either immediately or at whatever future time you care to specify, and it will take off, doing all you've asked of it. You can even tell it to quit or shut down after it finishes! Once Navigator is finished working on-line, it will disconnect, and you can review the session to see what interests you. If you don't automatically get the session review view, select Show Review from the Session Menu or press Command-r.

Figure 20-13 illustrates one of the most powerful features of CompuServe (for both users of MacCIM and CompuServe Navigator): topic threading. This allows you to follow discussions. Here's how it works: someone posts a message, typically asking a question. Other users read the message, and respond if they care to (reading messages without responding is known as *lurking*) — when you look at message summaries, you can select whether you want to read future messages on this topic thread, read the entire thread, or just read the latest message. Navigation through the session file is simple — just click on the Prior and Next buttons at the upper right-hand corner of the screen to move back or forward.

As Discussion Leader, I read every message posted in these two areas. You quickly learn to answer only those questions that you truly know the correct answer for.

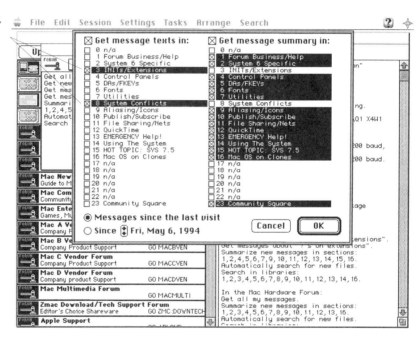

Figure 20-13: Navigator message summary

Figure 20-14 shows a typical message (for privacy reasons, I've edited out the recipient's name and user ID). You can reply to messages using the Message pop-down, or save it to a file by selecting the Archive pop-down. Figure 20-15 shows a file listing; simply double-clicking on its description tells Navigator that you'd like to download it the next time you log on.

Click here to
reply to a
message
(adding to the
thread)

Click here to create
a new message

Clicking here allows you to move forward
or backwards through your session file

Click here to
save the
message as a
text file (you
can specify the
archive file
names and
types)

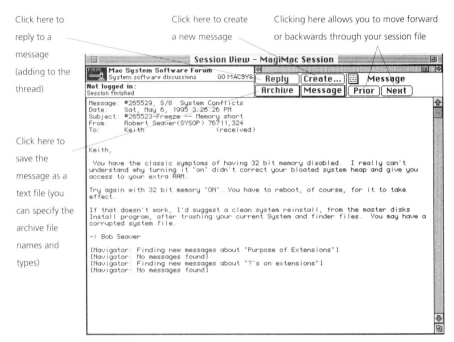

Figure 20-14: A sample Navigator message

Double-clicking
on a file name
selects it for
downloading
the next time
you run
Navigator

Figure 20-15: Selecting a file for downloading with Navigator

Some of the things I like the best about the MAUG areas on CompuServe are the level of service and the quality and the speed of the answers that users get to their questions. The interviews in this chapter show off the talents of just a few of Neil Shapiro's MAUG sysops (Neil is the head sysop of MAUG; his CompuServe address is 76703,401). These people answer hundreds of questions a week — their stamina amazes me.

Lofty Becker 76703,4054

Lofty is a 50-year-old law professor who lives in West Hartford, Connecticut — he's also one of the most active sysops when it comes to answering questions (at least in the forums that I lurk). He started programming computers at NASA in the summer of 1961, teaching himself machine language from the manual, and tracking sunspots and occasionally satellites. He subsequently took a programming course, in which one of the section men was Dennis Ritchie (later a coinventor of the C language, famous at the time for a three-line program that would bring an IBM 7090 to its knees). After college Lofty did nothing with computers until 1982, when he bought an Apple][, followed in 1984 by a Macintosh. He's written some shareware utilities in assembly language, Pascal, and C, but hasn't had much time for that recently. In his other life he teaches law at the University of Connecticut, listens to a lot of classical music, and reads as many books as his wife lets him (she has this strange view that the house should be cleaned from time to time). He's beta tested a lot of programs, and written for several Mac magazines, most often recently for *MacWEEK*.

Comment on the pros and cons of file- and disk-level compression techniques.

In theory, *driver-level compression should be completely transparent to the user and save more disk space, but would be somewhat slower since every read or write would be decompressed or compressed, respectively. File-level compression would save less disk space and be more prone to incompatibilities, but would give the user more control and be potentially faster, since the user can decide which files will or won't be compressed.*

In practice, theory holds up pretty well but not completely. For a variety of reasons some programs (particularly disk repair programs) may bypass the normal read and write mechanisms and not work properly even with driver-level compression. Moreover, the switch to System 7 has turned up some incompatibilities and problems even in noncompressing drivers, and disk drivers that do compression haven't been immune. On the other side, though you can spend a lot of time tweaking your file-level compressor, by now the vendors have had enough experience that the default settings usually work pretty well and many people can install and forget about them.

The bottom line is that nothing is as good as a bigger hard disk, but we can't always afford what we want. I'd say that these days, file-level compression should be the first choice except for people who want the absolute maximum amount of compression on their disk, or those who don't want kids or students or other uncontrollable natural forces changing the compression settings. For those people, driver-level compression is probably the way to go.

Anne Lyndon Peck 76711,140

The need to write and print law school admission essays was Anne's first excuse to buy a Macintosh (a Plus, in 1987.) She has jumped at any excuse since then to upgrade her Macintosh hardware; currently she and her husband share a IIvx and a Power Mac 7100. She has absolutely no formal background in computing beyond a college-level BASIC course, but she does have a Bachelor of Science in Architecture from the University of Virginia. She spends free moments doodling in Painter or trying (for the millionth time) to learn to program her Macintosh... and, of course, playing the newest nonviolent Macintosh game. When she's not logged on to CompuServe, or playing with her computer, or giving pep talks to her entrepreneurial husband, she spends her time raising their two young daughters. They enjoy life in the wilds of Northwest Connecticut with two cats and a collie dog.

Tell us about Netiquette (Net etiquette).

We don't allow pseudonyms in MAUG forums because people tend to "hide" behind handles and feel free to say things that are frequently much more provocative than what they really think. A person is likely to be much more thoughtful and honest about what he or she says when his or her real name is attached to a message. This kind of responsibility helps people forge friendships, and creates a real on-line community.

Try not to leave a message that just says "Thank You." Remember that people are paying to read your (great, of course) ideas, and that every message takes up a chunk of the limited forum space, too. If you want to thank someone, tell them what you're thanking them for ("Thanks for the game hint") and then add something to the conversation ("I was so proud to find a clever way to get by the monster in level 5, and then I was hit with this!")

Keep to the topic. If you feel that you're moving away from the topic, change the subject of the "thread." Most of the people who use the MAUG forums are "lurkers" who are spending money to read your messages, and if they want to read all the messages under the subject "Fabulous New Game" they may not be interested in your recipe for Grilled Swordfish Kebabs.

Remember that a message that's typed entirely in capital letters is very difficult to read. Only use your Caps Lock key when you want TO SHOUT!

Even though the CompuServe system software includes a great "thread" system that links each original message to all its replies, it's usually a good idea to include a small quote from the message that you're replying to at the top of your reply. Be sure the quotes are succinct, however; there's nothing worse than having to reread a complete message before you get to the reply.

It's hard to express nuances of emotion (such as irony, sarcasm, etc.) You can resort to using emoticons (like :-), the sideways "smiley face") or you can just take the time reread your message before you send it to made sure that the person you're sending it to couldn't possibly misinterpret it. If you see a message that makes you really angry, it's usually a good idea to stop and think before you send a hasty (and perhaps nasty) reply. Take a deep breath (or maybe even take a walk!) and come back to it later. Remember that it's OK to attack ideas ("I disagree with what you said"), but personal attacks ("I think you're a bonehead") are a no-no.

There really are very few real rules of on-line etiquette. Just remember that not everyone has a great sense of humor and some people have very thin skins. If you keep this in mind while you take the time to reread your messages before you post them, you'll be fine.

David Ramsey 76702,335

I suspect that neither David nor Lofty have a real life — these guys have been active, answering questions for as long as I can remember. David has accomplished a lot on the Mac; MacPaint 2.0 is the first I remember, and his *MacWEEK* columns were the highlight of the magazine (at least, for me).

How long have you been using the Mac and how did you get started?

I've been working with the Mac since January 1984. I got started when the company I was with at the time, the late lamented Corvus Systems, decided to add the Mac to the list of computers supported by their OmniNet network.

What is your educational background — are you formally trained, or did you teach yourself?

I have a degree in Biology and I think I took a COBOL course in college. I bought Apple II serial #478 in 1977. After that I kind of lost interest in going to medical school.

What programs or publications have you been involved with?

A few, over the years: OmniNet utilities and support for the Mac while at Corvus; MacPaint 2.0 at Apple, the application software for the MicroTV and DigiVideo boards at the ill-fated Aapps, OmniScan, OmniPage Direct, and portions of OmniPage Pro 5.0 at Caere.

What language(s) do you write in or what software tools do you use?

These days, it's all C++ (ick). I prefer Pascal and some assembly but these just aren't used much any more. On the Mac, most of my work has been in MPW, although most of MacPaint 2.0 was done in Borland Pascal (the final version was built with MPW).

What equipment you use (computer, RAM, etc.)

I have a big 90-MHz Pentium box with 16 MB, 500 MB hard disk, CD-ROM, and Matrox graphics card connected to an Apple 17" Multiple Scan monitor. All I do on that machine is play DOOM and variants thereof. My Mac is an 8100/80 with 40 MB of RAM, two 500 MB Seagates configured as a 1 GB drive array, and a 16" Apple monitor.

Do you have other interests you'd like mentioned in a bio?

I'm a competitive pistol shooter and have started collecting wristwatches.

What do you do for a living?

Programming at Caere Corporation.

Where do you live, are you married with children, how old are you, (etc.)

I live in San Jose, CA; am married to an Apple programmer, no kids. I'm 39 as of March 2, 1995.

Other than the obvious (not enough RAM installed or assigned the app) what are some of the reasons for getting an "out of memory" error message?

The most common cause of this is not having 32–bit addressing turned on on a Mac with more than 8 MB of RAM. Doing a PRAM zap will reset 24–bit addressing on Macs that support this; but it's not obvious and a lot of users panic after they suddenly seem to lose all that memory!

Also, a lot of users don't seem to realize that setting a large disk cache in the Memory Control Panel subtracts directly from system RAM.

To a lesser degree, memory fragmentation (launch three apps: A, B, and C; then quit A and C; app B now occupies a block in the middle of memory. User thinks he has free memory equal to the sum of the partitions of A and C, and he does, but he can't use it as one contiguous chunk...) causes problems for some users. The Mac's weird "fixed partition" application scheme is an artifact of a single–tasking system coerced into multitasking (sigh).

Robert Seaver 76711,324

I first "met" Bob on-line in 1991; he was one of the first supporters and beta testers for INITInfo. In the past four years, he has become one of the most active Sysops — I suspect he spends even more time on-line than I do <vbg>.

In 1981, Bob bought an Apple][for his precocious 9-year-old son, who was thrilled with the power it gave him. Within a month, he had to buy a second one, when his son realized Bob was hogging "his" machine. Though his son was more talented, Bob was more persistent, and has been enthralled with Apple computers since. Trained at Mount Sinai (New York) and Yale, he was disabled in 1985 by heart disease and had to retire from a 25-year private practice of Internal Medicine and Gastroenterology in western Massachusetts. Told by his doctors to avoid stress and go fishing, he quickly tired of the mosquitoes. He turned to computing and telecommunications as a more comfortable — if challenging — sedentary pursuit. He tempers his enforced retirement with travels by modem, beta testing, and collecting software. He joined MAUG in early 1982 (at about message number 2000) and has been a sysop for nearly four years. Having learned so much from friends and acquaintances of the on-line community, he enjoys giving back what he can even as he continues to learn more.

What questions are most frequently asked by Mac users?

The Mac is a famously easy machine to set up and operate — and across applications, consistent in appearance. This lulls people into believing it is also an easy machine to understand and master. Of course, it is anything but. Introduced to Macs at an early age in the classroom, too many people have no idea how to cope with what is, truth be told, a less than stable OS. The insatiable lust for those INITs that make the Mac so customizable leads to frequent crashes that often damage vulnerable system files… The desktop metaphor is widely admired, but poorly understood. With drives plunging in price and capacities increasing geometrically, the Mac market is plagued with the lack of inexpensive, conventional backup alternatives, leading many to tempt fate daily — and lose.

Thus, the most common questions we receive include: "My machine has crashed/frozen/locked. Why? What does Error number X mean, or 'co-processor not installed.' I have a co-processor!" *No one is happy to learn that of the many hundreds of error messages, perhaps two are of any pragmatic help to them in finding and fixing their problem.*

"I can't find my hard disk. It's lost on the desktop , (or I get a "sad Mac" or blank or blinking icon.) My life is on that disk. I have no backup, because I can't afford $800 dollars for a DAT, and I won't make 200 floppies. Help!" *Answer: The only good backup is a current, duplicate and convenient one. You can't afford NOT to buy DAT or a Removable and lots of cartridges at a cost at least that your hard drive itself. (Oddly, this is a litany no one wants to hear.)*

"My machine keeps crashing or won't boot. I 've installed a new system from a floppy. It still won't work!" *(Everyone begrudges the 20 minutes to do a clean reinstall from the master disks. This advice is made no easier by Apple's inexplicable failure to include these with late model machines — and failure to emphasize the importance of a clean reinstall in the ever more skimpy documentation included with the machine.*

"My icons keep vanishing. I get the wrong ones, or generic ones. Where are they?" *The Mac invented (or at least popularized) the desktop iconic graphic metaphor. You'd think the Desktop files would be more robust in housekeeping, and that rebuilding the desktop with the commands provided would do a better job. We constantly direct people to a good desktop deletion/rebuild utility.*

Practically no one remembers to turn on 32-bit addressing when they add more

RAM — to accommodate ever more bloated software and because most Macs are sold with half the RAM they need — and wonder why they suddenly have a 12-meg system but no memory for their applications…

And, of course, the plea: "I am hopelessly confused. Should I buy a Quadra? A Performa? Which one? A PowerMac? My salesman can't explain anything. He said the machine is upgradeable, but my friend says he heard different and I should wait for the next model due in a month." *While every computer purchaser must face decisions, Apple makes it harder by its quixotic marketing techniques, multiple channels, confusing labeling, and plethora of similar models and seemingly arbitrary (and expensive) upgrade options. Having driven their full-service dealers to all but extinction, they offer phone support that ranges from abysmal to excellent, but only if you can camp by the phone long enough to reach someone. The best models are never in stock. Buggy, problematic ones are discounted so deeply that the market is flooded with machines guaranteed to instill buyer's remorse when the cheaper, better, "fixed" version follows a week later.*

Marty Silbernik 76702,1415

Marty has been using a Mac since the day that the Mac was released, and still has an original "mint" 128K Mac as part of his collection. He's never had any formal training in computers and learned as he went starting on an Apple][in the late 70s. Over time he's acquired skills in not only the Mac platform but is becoming conversant in DOS and Windows as well.

Marty hasn't been published and doesn't program or write any code… he's just a user who got into personal computing in the early days and has built his knowledge from experience. The closest that he gets to programming is through participation in beta testing where he can help take a program from it's rough form to something that users can intuitively work with.

His primary computer, as of this publication is a Centris 650, 32 megs of RAM, a 540-meg hard drive with a CD-ROM, but since he spends a lot of time traveling, his 12 meg Duo 270c is also one of his workhorses. Outside of MAUG, Marty has been actively involved in the leadership of a number of charitable organizations over the years, as well as being involved in local government through volunteer work on governmental commissions and panels.

Marty is 45-years old, married with two children, and lives in suburban Chicago. Professionally, Marty is the Director of Market Development for a large restaurant chain.

What are the most common hardware problems on the Mac?

There are really three common hardware problems that we see, particularly from the new users. First is memory usage. Often users will have 12 or 16 megs of RAM, but the Mac will only see the first 8 megs, assigning the balance of the memory to the System. This tends to really confuse the newer user and the resolution is really simple. All they need to do is to open the Memory Control Panel and turn on 32-bit addressing and restart the machine. Once that's turned on, then the Mac can access all the RAM and the user can work much more effectively.

The second most common problem we run across is folks who use PCs or Windows machines to download files, because that's what they have at work, and then try to run that downloaded file on a Mac. And guess what — it doesn't work. There's a simple workaround that goes like this:

Downloading files onto a PC and transferring them to a Mac: You can download files onto a PC or other non-Mac machine and then transfer them to your Mac, but to get the files to behave properly as Mac files some further processing is required. That processing can most reliably be done on the Mac, though some PC programs seem to work at least well enough to get the post-processing software over.

Easiest thing to do, usually, is this:
1. *Download MACSEE.ZIP from Library 8 (Talking to PCs) of MacComm.*
2. *Download Binhex.Bin from Library 4 (Comm programs, Utilities) of MacComm.*
3. *Use MacSee to process Binhex and write it out to a 1.4 meg Mac disk.*
4. *Move Binhex to the Mac.*

Thereafter, download to the PC, move the files over to the Mac with Apple File Exchange (came with the Mac; turn off "text translation"), and process them with Binhex. If you have PC Exchange from Apple, you can shortcut part of this by downloading DOS2BH.ZIP from Library 7 (System Tools) of MacNew, UnZipping it on the PC, and then following directions (in the ReadMe file) to move BinHex over to the Mac. This last won't work, as far as we know, with Apple File Exchange or DOS Mounter.

Finally, there's one recurring question with the original PowerBook 1XX series. We get lots of messages asking "Why won't my PowerBook work on batteries?" The answer is simple — it looks like you're bugged by the ever-present chipped plastic on the ring of the tip of the power supply that plugs into the PB and blows the fuse bug... Meaning, that the black plastic insulation on that tip is cracked, shorting out the fuse on the motherboard. The only recourse is to call 800-SOS-APPL and have them pick up the PB and the power supply and fix it.

David Winograd 71333,1574

David got involved with computers when he bought his Apple][+ in the late 70's. At that point a 300-baud modem, a 40-column all-upper-case screen, and running programs from a cassette tape recorder was heaven. He was entranced by the incredible possibilities of this machine that was only limited by his imagination. He liked it even more when Apple released the 143K Disk][floppy disk drive.

David started the first themed Bulletin Board Systems in Northern NJ (using six 143k drives) and logged over 25,000 calls in the two years of its life. Then he found CompuServe, which was better. He says the Apple][forums taught him most of what he knew and soon enough he was giving back what he had learned — he found himself writing for the Apple][gs Buyers Guide with a bunch of the other MAUG Apple][people.

In 1987, he bought his first Mac, an SE/30 and it was nearly a religious experience. Once again he learned most everything he knew from MAUG and soon was able to give it back. One of the neatest things about MAUG is that you enter it a student and remain to become a teacher. The power of that has convinced him to change careers from business and financial analysis to teaching. He's now in the process of getting himself into a doctoral program in Instructional Technology which will end up with him teaching teachers how to teach using new technologies.

David currently lives in New Jersey; he's 42 years old, heavily involved in home theater and films, married for 15 years with two kids who air point and click in their sleep and a wife that is still wary of it all. They have a home AppleTalk network consisting of a PowerBook 540c, an LCIII, a IIci and two printers. They also have an Apple][gs for old time's sake.

What is your advice to users on using TrueType versus Type 1 fonts?

PostScript (Type 1) on a Macintosh was a great idea that became less great as technology marched on. The Mac was never built to use PostScript, which is a page description language, but it was the only game in town and fortunes were made finding ways to integrate it with Macintosh computers.

A PostScript font consists of two pieces, a screen font and a printer font. Just as it sounds, the screen font does no more than put the picture on your screen and the printer font sends it to the printer. For any given size of any given font, both parts had to be installed in your Mac for much to happen. Since many printers were PostScript-compatible, this made lots of sense since such a printer would either already contain the font or have it downloaded from the Mac and look great. A problem was that if you have a 12-point font and want to print in 24-point, it would look jagged and lousy. The solution was a software wonder called Adobe Type Manager (ATM) which most people consider a bit of system software but isn't … yet. What this would do is take any size printer font and allow you to use it at any other size seemingly by magic. But it wasn't a perfect solution.

I've personally had more problems with ATM conflicting with other system components than any other three extensions put together. I don't find it to crash but I do find it not to work under the simplest of circumstances. Any time Apple comes out with a new version of system software, you can bet that whatever version of ATM you're using will stop working. At least I've found that to be the case. Luckily enough Adobe has been very quick to come up with inexpensive revisions, but even so, this can be quite annoying.

Using TrueType fonts solves these problems and does it quite elegantly. TrueType is a part of Apple's system software and as such does not add another level of complexity to already complex software. A TrueType font is one piece that really isn't a picture of a letter at all; instead it's the information needed to build the letters, and if it can be done in one point size, it can be done in just about any point size. It looks good on the screen and it looks good on a printer. It doesn't conflict with anything. If you don't have or need a PostScript printer (and I don't), it's wonderful. I've tossed out most of my PostScript (also known as Type 1) fonts in favor of TrueType fonts. The downside (and you knew one was coming) is that it doesn't do as much as PostScript does — which as a page description technology also handles graphics and complete pages. But I wouldn't worry too much about that if you're an average user.

So my advice is to use TrueType fonts and eschew PostScript fonts. For most people that will be fine. If your work requires PostScript, life is still good, it's just a bit more complicated.

Rich Wolfson 74774,26

Rich is a professor at Montclair State University in the Department of Curriculum and Teaching specializing in educational technology. Montclair has just completed a special computing initiative that placed a new PowerPC or Pentium on every faculty desk. Their fully networked mixed environment enables high speed Internet access for all faculty, staff, and students from any of the over 500 workstations. Lately, a wealth of knowledge is coming from the experiences of the campus community learning to use new machines both in and out of the classroom.

Rich's first experience with Macintosh was with a 128K Mac, ImageWriter, external disk drive and carrying bag in 1985. He consumed anything written about his new machine in an effort to learn all there was. It wasn't very difficult in those days — connect to the MAUG forum on CompuServe and any problem he was having was already being discussed with a variety of solutions or workarounds. He's still there every day listening and learning.

In 1991 when the PowerBooks were introduced, he thought this was such a revolutionary product that he wrote *The PowerBook Companion*. Lately he's been spending my time getting all the Macs on campus working nicely with their new owners, setting up Internet WEB pages for the University, and helping Sharon Zardetto Aker (soon to be his wife) with her projects as well as taking care of their new house and his new sons (her old sons) who are 13 and 15. They have no less than a half dozen personal Macs in their home (Sharon's, his, the kids, at least two PowerBooks, and a house controller/fileserver) with a full network serving each room. Oh yeah, if he can squeeze it in, he and the boys race Go Karts, RC trucks and he takes an occasional hour in a Cessna to stay current.

What are the most common problems experienced by Mac PowerBook users?

Battery management is the single biggest problem area. Everyone wants to have unlimited battery life. Treat your batteries well and they'll last and work for you. That means exercise them regularly, recondition when necessary, keep your Power Manager clean with an occasional reset, use AppleTalk only when necessary, and don't shut off System Rest.

21 An Introduction to Network Troubleshooting

I am indebted to Tom Dell, Senior Editor, Network Frontiers, Inc., for writing this chapter. Networking is an area I wish to know more about, and, based on the sample that this chapter provides, I plan to read Network Frontiers' networking series. This chapter starts with an overview of network troubleshooting, covers the network-related shareware on the CD-ROM, and concludes with an interview with Dorian Cougias of Network Frontiers. Thanks guys!

Data network troubleshooting is often considered to be more difficult than desktop hardware and software troubleshooting. On the desktop you have but one machine, the argument goes, while on networks there are many computers as well as the hubs, bridges, gateways, and routers that connect them. When there is a problem, it could be anywhere! Where do you start?

One place to start is in your own head. A simple way to think of a network is not as a daunting collection of separate trouble spots, but rather as one virtual *machine*. I use machine in the classical sense here: a collection of devices employed together to perform a specific bit of work. With this concept in mind, troubleshoot the network in the same way you would probably troubleshoot a desktop computer:

1. Identify the problem.
2. Isolate the problem.
3. Correct the problem.

Network Frontiers has written a series of books for AP PROFESSIONAL detailing the application of various troubleshooting methodologies to AppleTalk networks. Needless to say, it is not possible to compress them into one chapter here. What I can do here is give you an idea of what procedures you should follow and what tools you can purchase to help you. In addition, Glenn Brown has thoughtfully collected several handy shareware utilities on the CD-ROM that you can try out immediately.

Troubleshooting Network Components

First, let's apply this idea of treating the AppleTalk network as a virtual machine to a common networking phenomenon: *ghosting*. As you've always suspected, supernatural forces do get into your network wiring... Seriously, ghosting is characterized by the sudden disappearance and reappearance of servers, workstations, and printers in the Macintosh Chooser (Figure 21-1). This is rarely caused by real ghosts.

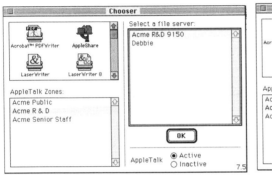 

Figure 21-1: Now you see it, now you don't. Ghosting is characterized by the sudden disappearance and reappearance of network nodes in the Macintosh Chooser.

Imagine this scenario: User "Rosemary" reports that the connection to the "Acme R&D 9150" AppleShare server in the "Acme R&D" zone is habitually severed. (Actually what she says in an accusatory tone is "your server keeps going down!" — but turning that kind of input into feedback you can use is another discussion).

For our purposes, the virtual machine we need to look at contains all the parts, both hardware and software, between the desktop Macintosh and the AppleShare server. It "looks" something like the diagram shown in Figure 21-2.

A   The missing Acme R&D 9150 AppleShare server, its system software, server software, networking driver software, and so on.

B   The Network Interface Card (NIC), in this case an Ethernet NuBus card.

C   The patch cable running from the server's NIC to the wall plate.

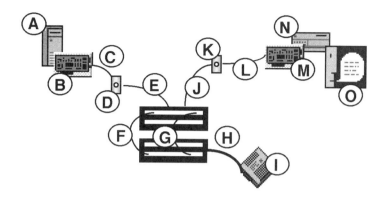

Figure 21-2: Model of a network machine

D   The wall plate and, in this case, its 10BaseT plug-in module.
E   The cabling run from the wall jack through the walls to the wiring closet (simplified).
F   The patch cable running between the cabling run's patch panel and the hub's patch panel.
G   The patch cable between the hub's patch panel and the cabling run's patch panel.
H   The patch panels themselves and the cable running between the hub's patch panel and the hub.
I   The hub itself, such as a Farallon StarController.
J   The cabling run from the patch panel in the wiring closet to the wall jack near the workstation.
K   The wall jack near the workstation.
L   The patch cord from the wall jack to the workstation's NIC.
M   The workstation's NIC, in this case let's say its an AAUI transceiver taking advantage of the newer Macintoshes' built-in Ethernet.
N   The workstation and its associated network hardware, system software, AppleShare client software, and network driver software.
O   One of the machine's most important but forgotten parts: the user. Don't forget users and the affect they have on the virtual network machine. After all, the machine was built *for* them.

Now that you have familiarized yourself with the trouble-stricken virtual machine, you can consult technical sources to determine what known causes match the symptoms for the parts in that machine.

Doing this after you've visualized what the machine looks like ensures that you won't waste time on dead ends. For instance, you might find a perfectly plausible explanation but then realize it is an explanation for a problem inherent in LocalTalk while the network is Ethernet! It also ensures that you know which technical sources to consult. It would be less than helpful to find a solution in a Farallon manual, then find out the NIC you planned to apply the solution to is made by Asanté!

In the case of ghosting, technical sources would tell you something like this:

1. One of the common causes of ghosting is having more than the recommended maximum number of nodes powered up on the network at a given time. The maximum number of recommended LocalTalk nodes is 32, for instance.

2. Another cause of ghosting is overextended network wiring runs. This basically causes a weak signal to reach the node. For LocalTalk cabling, the recommended maximum cable run is 1,000 feet. ThinNet gets you out to 600 feet. For 10BaseT over unshielded twisted pair (UTP) the maximum is 328 feet.

   Note: When I describe LocalTalk, I mean Apple's original and seldom-used shielded twisted pair (STP) wiring. What most people think of is Farallon's PhoneNET, which is an implementation of LocalTalk over voice-grade UTP wiring. Permissible lengths vary depending upon the topology in which it is employed, which is more than we need to talk about here.

3. A more interesting cause of ghosting is electrical "echoes" in the signal called reflections. These are generally caused by changes in impedance in a cable run along its length. Kinked wires will cause this, as will a change from one wire gauge to another (for example, if the cabling run is 24 American Wire Gauge (AWG) while the patch cord from the wall jack to the workstation is 22 AWG). A more acute problem occurs when cabling runs are not adequately terminated (in topologies that require it).

4. Yet another possible explanation for ghosting is electromagnetic interference. This can occur when an appliance that generates a strong

magnetic field, such as a microwave or refrigerator, is introduced next to network wiring. The field can block or decrease the strength and reliability of the network signal.

You now know what parts in the network machine could be affected and how. Now go through the parts methodically in an attempt to identify the faulty part.

The first part to check, *always*, is the user (letter **O** in Figure 21-2). In our example we have learned all we can from the user and have replicated the steps that she takes before encountering the problem. In so doing we have eliminated her as the cause of the problem.

Next, put aside the obvious. If user Rosemary is the only one experiencing this problem, you can probably rule out parts **A** through **F**. If the fault was here, other users would be seeing this problem as well. Likewise, if Rosemary is not the only one having this problem and she is able to see other devices and other devices in the same zone even though the server is missing, you can probably rule out parts **G** through **N**. Clearly the fault is occurring in the server or along its network path.

In our example, let's suppose that we have ruled out parts **A** through **F** as faulty because Rosemary is the only one experiencing this problem. Further, we interview her (part **O**) and find that sometimes she also gets the message "The printer is not on the network."

We deduce from this that the problem is resides in parts **G** through **N**. Further, since our technical sources cite mostly wiring faults as responsible for these symptoms, we narrow the problem down to parts **G** through **L**. These we inspect and find:

G   The patch cable between the hub's patch panel and the cabling run's patch panel is made of the same gauge and manufacture as the wire running through the walls. We replace it to make sure, but the problem recurs.

H   The ports on the patch panels themselves appear to be fine. All the pins are straight, unbroken and in order. We cut off a small length of cable at the cable run's block and punch down the cable again to be sure the fault doesn't reside there. Again the problem recurs.

I   The Farallon StarController we are using is "intelligent" in that it can be used with Farallon StarCommand software to generate reports about the condition of its ports. The device checks out, and when we employ another of its ports to power the suspect cabling run, the problem still recurs.

J   The cabling run from the patch panel in the wiring closet to the wall jack near the workstation cannot be examined as it is inside the walls.

K   Like the port on the cabling run's patch panel, the wall jack near the workstation is likewise undamaged. Here too we punch down the cable again. The problem still recurs.

L   The patch cord from the wall jack to the workstation's Ethernet transceiver is not made of the same gauge and manufacture as the wire running through the walls. We replace it, but the problem recurs.

At this point, we have tried everything simple. This is a good idea since the problem often is something simple. We are left, however, with part **J** untested. Here we employ a cable scanner. This device sends a radar-like signal through the cable run to detect physical defects such as the wire kink that caused our hypothetical mischief here.

Troubleshooting Network Processes

So far we have applied a simple troubleshooting methodology to tracking down and fixing what turns out to be a common *physical* network problem. Unfortunately, not everything that goes wrong with a network occurs in the wiring. It is not enough to hunt down errors in the network's connection *components*. Errors just as often occur in the network's communications *process*. Next let's look at how that process works.

AppleTalk delivers data from one node to another through *transmission paths* including both software and hardware components that are part of a layered model of design that closely follows the International Standards Organization (ISO) Open Systems Interconnect (OSI) model.

For each layer of the model that AppleTalk uses, *protocols* exist. A protocol is a formalized set of procedural rules for the exchange of information and the interactions between the network's interconnected nodes. Protocols specify how the networking software or hardware is to implement the functions that each layer provides. These protocols also tell the software or hardware how to interact with the layer above and below it (Figure 21-3).

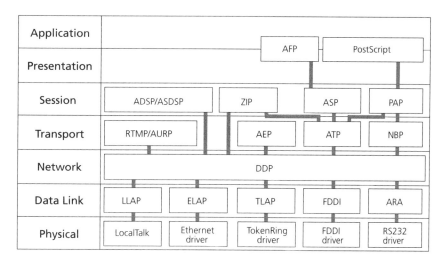

Figure 21-3: The OSI model and the AppleTalk protocols that fall within each layer

Here's an example of how this model looks in action. In Figure 21-4, user "Dorian" is printing directly to a shared network LaserWriter (without Background Printing selected in the Chooser).

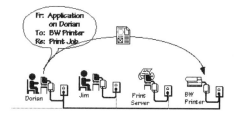

Figure 21-4: User Dorian prints to a networked laser printer

When user Dorian sends a command to an application to print a document, the application uses QuickDraw and the Font Manager to convert the document into the PostScript commands and draw the document to the communications port. The Print Manager will activate the currently selected print driver and load it into memory. The driver then will call the AppleTalk Manager to contact the printer. All of this happens in the upper layers of the OSI model.

Next, AppleTalk uses the *Name Binding Protocol (NBP)* to confirm the name and address of the currently selected printer (Figure 21-5). Because the Macintosh keeps track of the last device selected, user Dorian could have selected the printer in the Chooser hours or even days before the print job was issued by the application. Since the information is stored in memory, the print manager has to call NBP to ensure that the printer is still using the same name and network number.

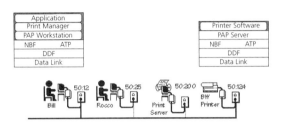

Figure 21-5: NBP confirms the address of the currently selected printer

Once the NBP address has been established, AppleTalk's *Printer Access Protocol (PAP)* will attempt to open a connection with the printer (Figure 21-6). PAP is a client of the *AppleTalk Transaction Protocol (ATP)* and also uses the *Datagram Delivery Protocol (DDP)*. Notice, too, as Figure 21-6 illustrates, that PAP is *asymmetrical*. The PAP code in the workstation is different from the PAP code in the printer.

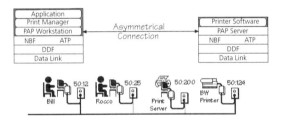

Figure 21-6: PAP attempts to open a connection with the currently selected printer

The print driver within the user's Macintosh will receive an answer from the printer that it is the selected LaserWriter and that it is ready to receive a print job. Once a connection has been opened to the printer, PAP uses ATP transactions to transfer the data.

As the file is being transferred to the printer and converted into a physical document, the workstation and the printer maintain a constant dialog. This dialog (Figure 21-7) is illustrated on the user's screen.

> **user: Dorian Cougias; document: 05 Network Services; status:**
> **processing job**

Figure 21-7: The print transaction dialog

If the printer is busy and a workstation requests to print a job, a "wait" dialog is returned to the workstation while PAP continually attempts to connect to the printer. When the printer finishes a print job, it politely sorts through all print request jobs to find the ones coming from the workstations that have been waiting the longest time for a connection. Once a connection has been established with a printer, the process of sending data proceeds.

Here PAP's data transfer phase is put into play. This phase has two functions:
- It transfers data between the sender and the printer
- It detects and disconnects half-open connections (generated when the sender bombs, hangs, etc.)

The data transfer model used by PAP is referred to as *read-driven*. When the printer wants to read data from the other end it uses a PAP Read call to the sender's ATP responding socket. In order to prevent duplicate delivery of data to the printer, all ATP data transfer transactions use ATP's *exactly once* mode and attach a sequence number to each transaction. This ensures that the printer doesn't get any duplicate information.

In Figure 21-8, the printer and workstation are sending transactions. The printer has requested a transaction and the workstation has responded within the given time. All is as it should be.

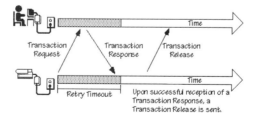

Figure 21-8: The printer requests data and the workstation responds in a given time period

Figure 21-9 illustrates what would happen if a request was not met with a response. In this case the packet did not get to the printer. The printer frantically sends off other transaction requests until the appropriate response is received.

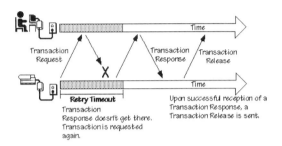

Figure 21-9: A request fails to get a response

While the process of sending data is going on, PAP is also monitoring the transaction to ensure that one of the connections does not close down. The connection can close down for any reason: bad software could crash the workstation, a file that sends "offending commands" to the printer could crash the printer, or the file could take up too much memory for the printer to handle and therefore crash both the workstation *and* the printer. If either side of the PAP connection discovers that the other side has ceased operation, the connection will be closed.

When you know how this network communications process is supposed to work, you can more easily figure out what is happening when it *doesn't* work.

Again, this chapter is not the place to go into the details of all this. What you should take away from the previous few pages is the idea that troubleshooting AppleTalk networks involves viewing them *holistically* (like a machine) and addressing both their *components* and *processes*. This is easy to do if you equip yourself with the right tools.

Network Troubleshooting Tools

Here are a few of the best and best-known commercial networking tools:

Apple Support Professional
Apple Computer, Inc.
20525 Mariani Avenue
Cupertino, CA 95014-6299
Toll-free: (800) 745-2775
Demo Kit of software and tutorials available at no charge

This is a complete CD-based package of Apple software, tutorials, white papers, technical notes, and support (and some third-party information as well). It is a great source of troubleshooting solutions. Contact Apple Computer, Inc. at (800) 745-2775 for information.

Inter•Poll
Apple Computer, Inc.
(see above for address information)
Toll-free: (800) 776-2333

Arguably the best known and certainly one of the earliest AppleTalk network management tools, this application gives you a sortable list of network nodes, their system types, node numbers, socket numbers, and network or zone numbers.

LANsurveyor
Neon Software, Inc.
3685 Mt. Diablo Blvd., Suite 203
Lafayette, CA 94549
Toll-free: (800) 334-NEON
Fax: (510) 283-6507
Internet: sales@neon.com
Suggested retail: $395 (5 zone), $695 (unlimited zones)

This network mapping software lets you scan your network for all of its visible devices and services, then draw a diagram of what it finds. It can also be used to measure the response times of various nodes and to query nodes for their Simple Network Management Protocol (SNMP) data. Finally, it can also be used to automatically alert network administrators of network trouble events.

LocalPeek/EtherPeek
The AG Group, Inc
2540 Camino Diablo Suite 200
Walnut Creek, CA 94596
Toll-free: 800 466-2447
Fax: 510 937-2479
Internet: ftp.aggroup.com or www.aggroup.com
Suggested retail: $495 (LocalPeek), $795 (EtherPeek)

This software captures data packets from LocalTalk or Ethernet network segments which can then be analyzed to find specific AppleTalk problems. It also includes an alarm function that can warn network administrators of potential problems. It can be used with most major network protocols and can gather statistics in real time.

NetMinder LocalTalk/Ethernet
Neon Software, Inc.
(see LANsurveyor for address information)
Toll-free: 800 334-NEON
Suggested retail: $395 (NetMinder LocalTalk), $695 (NetMinder Ethernet)

These applications capture protocol data, generate network transaction statistics, and calculate network bandwidth.

NetWORKS
Caravelle Networks Corp.
210 Colonnade Road South, Suite 301
Nepean, ON K2E 2L5
Canada
Toll-free: 800 363-5292
Fax: 613 225-4777
Suggested retail: $499 (25 device licence)

This software console provides the network administrator with a problem early-warning system for AppleTalk networks by diligently polling network nodes for errors.

PentaScanner

MicroTest, Inc.
4747 North 22nd st.
Phoenix, AZ 85016
Toll-free: 800 526-9675
Suggested retail:$3495 (super injector), $4595 (2-way injector)

This hardware is one of many Time Domain Reflectometer (TDR) devices that can electronically test your network's cabling for physical defects and damage.

RouterCheck

Neon Software, Inc.
(see LANsurveyor for address information)
Toll-free: 800 334-NEON
Suggested retail: $649.00

This application lets troubleshooters gather information on various networked routers through SNMP agents. It can be used to check router configurations, monitor router efficiency, and notify network administrators of router trouble.

Saber LAN

Saber Software Corp.
5944 Luther Lane, Suite 1007
Dallas TX 75225
Toll-free: 800 338-8754
Fax: 214 361-1882
Internet: sabersoftware@notes.compuserve.com
Suggested retail: $299 and $59 per node

Formerly called GraceLAN, this is a robust remote software management and network monitoring system that can provide information on a great many configuration variables on networked workstations. Often it permits network administrators to solve problems users are having without getting up from their desks, sometimes before the users even know about them!

Skyline/Satellite
The AG Group, Inc.
(see LocalPeek for address information)
Toll-free: 800 466-2447
Suggested retail: $795.00

A new and long-awaited network monitoring package, this software allows the troubleshooter to record and analyze network traffic patterns over time. The main product is Skyline, a centralized traffic analysis console. Satellite is a traffic collection tool that can be run on the same desktop as is Skyline or on remote nodes.

Network-Related Software

There are a number of network-related programs on the CD-ROM, in addition to those covered here. Be sure to check out Maurice Volaski's ChooserUser and LaserWriter Lockout (Chapter 11), the 21-day demo of Casady & Greene's Snap Mail (Commercial Demos), SpaceServer, the companion program to Hugo Diaz's SpaceAlert (Chapter 16) that allows you to find free space on servers without having to mount its volumes first, and Jan Bruyndonckx's The Red Queen (Chapter 11), a utility that speeds network file access by compressing data before it is sent over your network.

Announce 1.1
Tad Woods
T & T Software
920 Quail Lane
Salem, VA 24153
Fax: 703 389-0889
America Online: Tad Woods
CompuServe: 70312,3552
Internet: tandtsw@roanoke.infi.net
Shareware fee: $39.00

Announce (Figure 21-10) is a simple network utility that allows you to send messages to other users. Features include the ability to send the same message to many users or to send several different messages at the same time, saving groups of users, and support for multiple zones.

Figure 21-10: Announce

AutoBoot 1.3 / Keep It Up 1.2
Karl Pottie
Mac Support
University Hospitals of Leuven, Belgium
Internet: Karl.Pottie@uz.kuleuven.ac.be
Shareware fee: AutoBoot $20.00

Karl is a 27-year-old Computer Science graduate who does Macintosh support and consulting. He has been programming the Mac for 4 years. Mac programming is only a hobby, though AutoBoot made him some nice pocket money. Developing AutoBoot was very time consuming, because his development system is the same as his test system and he also couldn't use a debugger. Imagine having to crash your system every few minutes to see if your changes have worked :-). He uses THINK C, THINK Pascal, and recently switched to Metrowerks CodeWarrior.

Figure 21-11: AutoBoot

These two programs work in tandem to keep your Macs running: AutoBoot (Figure 21-11) will reboot your Mac after a System crash, and Keep It Up (Figure 21-12) monitors your applications to ensure they are running, and attempts to relaunch them if they have crashed. AutoBoot can also maintain a log file, to help you identify problem machines.

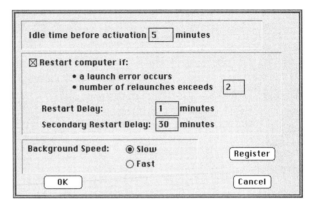

Figure 21-12: Keep It Up

Folder Watcher

Joe Zobkiw, President
TripleSoft, Macintosh Software Development
172 Charles St., Suite A
Cambridge, MA 02141-2118
Telephone: 919 782-3230 (voice/fax)
America Online: AFL Zobkiw
CompuServe: 74631,1700
Internet: zobkiw@world.std.com
Shareware fee: $20.00

Folder Watcher (Figure 21-13) is a background application that can keep track of the contents of an unlimited number of folders on your Macintosh, a remote Mac, or a server. If the contents of any of these change, Folder Watcher will notify you by displaying an alert dialog box, playing a sound, writing to a log file, executing an AppleScript script, or some combination of these actions.

Figure 21-13: Folder Watcher Controls

MailSlot

Tim Bitson
AnalySYS Software
P.O. Box 35967
Tucson, AZ 85740-5967
America Online: TBitson
Shareware fee: $10.00

Figure 21-14: MailSlot Setup

MailSlot (Figure 21-14) is a simple e-mail system for use on Macs running System 7. It basically monitors a shared folder, and notifies you when someone places a file in that folder.

NetDragMover

Don Winsby
Typotronics Inc.
2001 S. Hanley, Suite 200
St. Louis, MO 63144
Shareware fee: $39.00

Don has been coding for 17 years, using AppleScript, BASIC, HP-SPL, and NewtonScript. Typotronics is a prepress service provider specializing in the catalog, financial, and advertising markets. Their latest adventure is designing interactive CDs by way of their new company "38North" (check your Mac Map 39° 38'N lat 90° 11' long, you'll find St. Louis). Their plant's creative and production departments rely heavily on Macs. Don's favorite periodicals are *MacWEEK, MacTech,* and *New Media;* his favorite Mac authors are Scott Knaster and Bruce Tognazzini.

NetDragMover is actually two droplets written in AppleScript. They are particularly useful for service bureaus and prepress shops, where files are often moved from machine to machine and modified prior to printing, leaving the old version of the file on the first machine. When a folder is needed from a remote volume, mount the volume and drop the folder onto the GetFolder droplet. The folder and its contents are moved to the destination (that is, they are copied, and then the source files are deleted). ReturnFolder is the companion script that does the reverse operation.

NetSecurity Guard

MR Mac Software
P.O. Box 2547
Del Mar, CA 92014
Telephone: 619 453-2845
Internet: MrMac@mrmac.com
Support: nsgsupport@mrmac.com
Suggested retail: $259.00

Network Security Guard (Figure 21-15) is an AppleTalk-based utility that can scan multiple zones and compile security reports on the servers it finds. It can help monitor all Macs on a network with file sharing turned on or with Guest access enabled, provide a "password crack" report which identifies easily guessed passwords, and provide a list of other possible security violations.

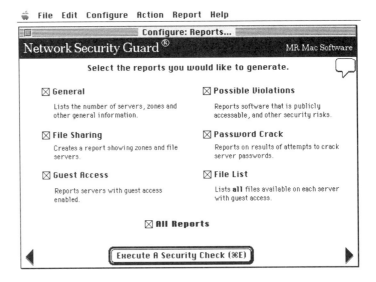

Figure 21-15: Network Security Guard

Interview: Dorian J. Cougias

Networking Consultant/Trainer/Author.

How long have you been programming and how did you get started?

A better question would be how long have I been building networks, and when did I get started? I've been building networks since I left the Army's Special Forces I guess in '89 or '90, but since I can't even remember what I did a couple of weeks ago, the dates are a bit fuzzy. The guy who would really know used to work for CE Software, his name is Bob Brown. He sort of "rescued me" from the military and helped me get my first couple of consulting gigs at McDonnell-Douglas in St. Louis, building networks for the AI lab and others. He's got some great "Dorian Started Here" stories. He probably knows the dates too. I still owe him a few more beers for helping me out back then.

Anyway, my first "job" in the Mac world was a part-time gig I did working for a service bureau in St. Louis. I linked them electronically to Calgon Vestal (the industrial soap folks). I would get their data across the wire, wrote a small program to translate their markup language to Rich Text Format for page layout, and then created their negatives off a Linotronic 100. For a while I moved between dealers and after that I designed a couple of more things at McDonnell Douglas.

To answer the programming question, all I know how to program is HyperCard, and I learned a lot of that from Rob Diamont, a guy I worked with in St. Louis. I think he's at Ernst & Young now. My programming ability is pretty cheesy at best. All I know how to do is hack something out and give it to real programmers like Lee Buck at SDU Consulting or Randy Matamoros at Bear River. Those are the real programmers.

What is your educational background — are you formally trained, or did you teach yourself?

At first, getting started was a lot easier, because LocalTalk was still called AppleTalk, and these guys at a then-not-well-known company called Kinetics had or were, just coming out with a device called the FastPath router. Not much to AppleTalk networking back then. Dave Kosiur was just starting a journal called Connections, *and he and others like Kee Nethery and Dan Magorian were available by phone or e-mail. I learned by doing and screwing things up.*

And when (notice I say when because that's more accurate than "if") I didn't know something, the world's biggest brain was right down the street at Apple. His name is Sam Wood. Sam was the guy who gave me the most technical help from Apple. Sam is actually one of the 24 or so reasons that Apple is still in business. The other 23 or so reasons are the rest of the field SEs (service engineers) around the country like Jesse Stein, Rich Park, Andy Brownell, Don Oehlert, Curtis Juliber and others. They've been my biggest help throughout my career.

What programs have you written (or been involved in the development of)?

Believe it or not, I actually did write a program which had a HyperCard front end and lots of back end XCMDs from Lee Buck and gang. It was while I worked with a consulting/VAR firm called Hawkey & Associates in Chicago. The program was called FullFile. It was a very small, very interesting utility application for document management in a production environment. For what it did, it was great. We showed it at Seybold and got a pretty good response. The biggest problem was with the marketing manager they gave us. My co-conspirator on the project, Darien Kruss, and I couldn't even believe that it was the same product the marketing manager was talking about when he introduced it to clients. I remember one time when I turned around to Darien during a "speech" this marketing guy was giving, and very quietly said "great product — who's going to go out and build it?" and then found out that it was supposedly about the product we wrote. That pretty much killed any chance of the product being accepted by clients. I don't think whatever that guy was talking about will ever get built.

What language(s) do you write in?

How about instead of asking what languages I write in, asking about what networking languages I speak? I am pretty fluent in AppleTalk, Apple's networking language. I'm also conversant in IPX/SPX, Novell's language. Then there's TCP/IP and IBM's SNA.

What software tools do you use?

Boy, this is a good question. Here's a list of my "top tools that I can remember this week," because I guess I'm a network tool fanatic. Many were already mentioned earlier in the chapter. They are listed in alphabetical order so as not to anger any vendor by showing priority.

ArcServe	*NetMinder Ethernet*
CheckNET	*NetMinder LocalTalk*
EtherPeek	*NetWORKS*

Excel	*Retrospect*
FastTrack Schedule	*RouterCheck*
FileWAVE	*SaberLAN*
Inter•Poll	*Server Manager*
LANsurveyor	*Server Tools*
LocalPeek	*Skyline/Satellite*

Please describe the equipment you use (what computer, how much RAM, etc.).

My computer is a PowerBook 520c, with a 500MB drive from APS and 36MB of RAM. I need that much RAM to do packet capturing (and play war games at the same time).

What is your favorite piece of software?

My favorite piece of software is FastTrack Schedule from AEC Software. Why? Because it seems that nobody in the world seems to know how to write and conduct a project plan that works. *And writing a simple plan in FastTrack usually makes me look like some genius or something. I love that. Being seen as smart without having to* be *smart.*

Do you have other interests you'd like mentioned in a bio?

I love playing darts and I suck at golf, but love it. I don't suck at darts. If you ever meet my wife, ask her about our first date and the infamous dart game…

What do you like to do when you're not programming?

Since I don't program much, anything. Just kidding. How about when I'm not building networks? Usually I'm out building networks with my clients across the country. Which means that I'm in strange and wonderful cities like Dallas, New York, Minneapolis, Los Angeles, Boston, etc. While out and about I like to go to great restaurants. My favorites are the No Name in Boston, Skyline Chili in Cincinatti, Due's Pizza, Lou Mitchell's, and Mr. Beef in Chicago, the Butcher Block in Dallas, and a little Fish and Chips place in Pasadena CA.

What do you do for a living (if not programming)?

Hmmm, some people say I build networks. Others say I write books. Others say I'm a trainer. I sort of run a company called Network Frontiers. Somebody called me a "visionary" or "thought leader" the other day.

I tell people I'm the guy they pay to come in and look at their network and say

"Damn, I've never seen that *before." And then of course I fix the problem. The other thing I do for a living is listen to the computer folks within a company, debabelize what they are saying, and explain it to upper management in words they can understand (usually short words with lots of picture language). Yep, I guess those two things are what I really do for a living.*

Where do you live, are you married with children, how old are you?

I live in San Francisco, two blocks from work (with a great coffee shop being the half-way point between work and home). I live pretty much about a block from the water. We work about a half a block from the water. My wife is a pretty darned good chef, which is why my waistline looks the way it does. I'm around 35 I think. I can't remember. That was a long time ago.

How did Network Frontiers get started?

We, the unwilling led by the unknowing, chartered a course to God-knows-where because we couldn't get real jobs. Seriously though, Network Frontiers was started from within the Network Consulting and Training group of Bear River. We had a different work ethic than they did. We were usually in before them and usually left after them, and decided that we'd be better off on our own. My old partners at Bear River would tell people about my "forward approach" to doing business that people "shouldn't worry about him. He used to eat at a place called Mr. Beef every day." I don't know exactly what that meant, but in Berkeley eating beef was supposedly bad for you. Oh well.

What products has your company released?

We wrote CE Software's certification program, and have written Apple's new networking certification program. We've released around seven incredibly well-received network training classes, and by the end of this year will have written about six books (most being published by good ol' AP Professional).

How big is your company (how many people do you employ, annual sales, whatever)?

I'll tell you what I tell everyone else about our company's size: We are as big as we need to be to get the job done. Why have masses when you can have the best? Works for Special Forces (Green Berets) to send a dozen guys into a country to overhaul the whole system, why not for us? We aren't overthrowing a country, just a few MIS departments.

What are the top questions your tech support people field, and more important, what are the answers?

1. What's AppleTalk, and what's the difference between AppleTalk, LocalTalk, and Ethernet?

   Seriously, we get that all the time. So I'll give you the same answer that Gurshuran Sidhu, Father of AppleTalk, gave me the first time I asked it (although I can't impart his world-famous accent here): AppleTalk is not a cable. AppleTalk is a networking system. LocalTalk is AppleTalk running on a single pair of twisted pair cable. It runs at roughly 230 Kbits, and uses dynamic addressing. EtherTalk is AppleTalk running on any 802 standard cabling (from thick, to thin, to 10BaseT, to Cat5, through Fiber), using AARP to form a link between Ethernet's hardware encoded addressing scheme to AppleTalk's dynamic addressing scheme. It runs at either 10Mbps or 100Mbps.

2. Why do I need to back up, or (in a different tone), why do I need to practice restoring my server?

   The answer is that there are two kinds of people, those who have lost data, and those who haven't had their computer for very long. If you don't back up, you are going to be pretty sorry some day. And if you don't practice restoring your data every so often, you're backups won't be worth much. As my friend Craig Isaac over at Dantz says, "To go forward you must back up." I like that. Cheezy, but I like it.

About networking...

Networking itself has radically changed since the time that I entered the business. The problem is that Macintosh networks haven't really changed as much as the rest of the networks.

Network designs in large corporations with multitudes of computers have gotten very complex. I was at a client site the other day and was working out their networking numbering strategy among their 42 buildings in the Bay area, their 15 different locations across the States, and then their networking locations in five other countries. This client has around 80 different network locations. They have a pretty good sized staff, with a great education behind them and a lot of network management tools and utilities with a budget to match. Now before you say "wow, they ought to because they are so massive", let me put this into perspective for you.

I also have a client, a school system in the States. They have a total of 86 sites, even more sites than this large corporation. Their 86 sites are part of a much larger (total of 207 sites) structure. They have a total of around 6 full-time people to manage those 86 sites. And the tools are pretty wimpy compared to the job. Yes, they now have LANsurveyor and RouterCheck, but that's about it. We are getting the administrators to that point wherein they can put in Skyline/Satellite, but right now they don't even know what a packet does, much less how it affects what they are trying to do. Why have they grown to such a large proportion without growing their support staff? I can see two reasons. One is that everyone thinks "Networking a Macintosh is plug and play." The other is that there isn't someone out there jumping up and down and making their administrators get "certified." Hopefully with Apple's new certification program, and all of the vendors backing it, that will change.

Another case in point is a major military operation with thousands and thousands of Macintoshes. They want to throw "AppleTalk off the network because it is chatty and causes problems." And yet, the AppleTalk administrators out there hardly know routing tables, the difference between RTMP and AURP, and how to check for cabling problems. They have no budget for training and have no real AppleTalk tools in place to manage the system. Of course AppleTalk is going to give them troubles! The point is you can't install a big system without installing a program and people to manage the system.

In short, the rest of the world is building massive networks with great management tools. And we Macintosh people are building massive networks that aren't managed well at all.

Where I think that networking utilities are going is in the right direction. They are growing up and giving us tools to manage distributed systems. They are getting more in depth. What has to happen before these systems can grow any farther and give us what we need, is that we, the network designers and administrators, will have to grow up as well. We will have to become far better trained so that we can understand these tools and understand what they can offer and where they can take us. Once we begin telling the tool makers what kinds of tools we need, both the tool makers and we networking staff will be in a better situation.

Appendices

Glossary
Conflicts Listing
Sources
The Hardware and Software Used
About the CD-ROM

Glossary

16-bit color: Capable of showing 65,535 colors at one time; this is the color level that QuickTime is best at.

24-bit addressing: Prior to System 7, the Mac could address only 8 megabytes of memory at one time (see 32-bit addressing).

24-bit color: Capable of showing 16.7 million colors at one time; even if quick math indicates that the number exceeds the number of pixels on most screens, it is still the best for high-end graphics work.

32-bit addressing: Ever since System 7, Macs have been capable of addressing more than 8 megabytes of RAM at one time.

8-bit color: Capable of showing 256 colors at one time; this is the level used by most Macs.

ADB: Apple Desktop Bus; the means Apple uses to connect mice and other pointing devices.

AIFF: Audio Image File Format; a sound file format.

alias: An icon created in System 7 (or better) that points to a file, document, application or hard drive.

ARA: AppleTalk Remote Access; the software Apple provides to allow easy connection of two remote Macs.

archival compression: Compression that occurs while a file is being stored off-line.

archive: A file stored off-line, usually compressed.

BBS: Bulletin Board System; a computer or computers set up using modems to answer calls from other computers. Local BBS are a great way to get started telecommunicating — most offer areas with messages, files, and new friends to talk to.

benchmark: A standard test performed to determine relative performance.

beta testing: The process of testing a prerelease version of a software program to ensure that most of the bugs are out before the program is released. Bugs that make it past beta testing into the release version are often referred to as "undocumented features." External beta testing is also known as slave labor.

BinHex: A means of encoding a Macintosh program file as text so that it can be transmitted to those who don't have direct access to the file itself. A number of the programs on the CD-ROM were sent to me by authors over the Internet. I downloaded them from CompuServe, and used Compact Pro (also on the CD-ROM) to decode them.

bitmapped font: A font format used by earlier Macs, which describes fonts using a a grid of dots. Bitmapped fonts print "jaggy," unless you have three times the print size installed (i.e., to prevent 12-point Chicago from printing jaggy, you need to have 36-point Chicago installed). TrueType and PostScript fonts have almost entirely replaced bitmapped fonts.

BNDL resource: The part of a file that tells the Mac operating system which application should be opened when you double-click on a document, commonly called the "bundle bit."

cdev: The programmers' name for a Control Panel device (the name was more commonly used under System 6).

CISC: Complex Instruction Set Computing. The way a 680x0 works.

Control Panel: A control panel is a small program (known pre-System 7 as cdevs) that can be accessed through the control panel item in the Apple Menu. Most, but not all, control panels also include extension code.

data caching: The ability to set aside a small amount of RAM to speed data access times.

differential backup: A hard drive backup that updates all files that have changed since the last full backup.

DPI: Dots per inch, the measurement of the density of a printer (LaserWriters are available in 300 and 600 dpi, Imagesetters typically deliver from 1200 to 2540 dpi).

driver level compression: This is compression performed at the disk level, which is usually transparent to the user; Stacker is an example.

em dash: The typographers' term for a dash the width of an "m" character (created by Shift-Option-hyphen) — used to separate thoughts or ideas, as in this sentence.

en dash: The typographers' term for a dash the width of an "n" character (created by Option-hyphen); used to separate numbers (i.e., 25–26).

encryption: A means of scrambling computer information so that it is unreadable unless decrypted.

EPS: Encapsulated PostScript; a file format that includes a PostScript description of a graphic.

extension: A small file that loads at startup time to extend the functionality of the operating System. Since System 7, extensions have loaded from their own folder within the System folder.

fat binary: A file that includes code for both PowerPCs and 680x0 Macs.

fkey: Function keys, a resource that can be activated by a Shift-Command-number keystroke (see Chapter 11 for instruction on how to install an fkey).

FPU: Floating Point Unit; a math chip. An FPU is built into the 68030 and 68040 (but not the 680LC40).

fragmentation: The operating system writes data to your hard drive wherever it can find room. This often means that files are not written contiguously (in one place), but may be fragmented (pieces of the file are written in different locations on your hard drive). See *optimization.*

freeware: Software that the author retains the rights to, but releases without asking for compensation.

full backup: A complete backup of all designated files on a hard drive.

IDE: Integrated Drive Electronics, a standard for hard drive controllers predominant in the PC marketplace, which Apple has now used in some of its low-end Macs.

incremental backup: A hard drive backup that updates all files that have changed since the last backup.

INIT: The programmers' term for an extension, also used prior to System 7.

jaggies: The stair-stepped look of bitmapped graphics.

ligature: A special character that replaces two or three letters — used because some character combinations look better when modified (such as fl).

lossless compression: Compression that reduces the size of a file without any loss of data when the file is expanded.

lossy compression: A method of compressing graphics files where the values of similar colors which are next to each other are averaged. Small amounts of lossy compression can result in acceptable proofing graphics; excessive lossy compression results in "banding" (gradient fills that have distinct bands of color).

MDB: Master Directory Block; the part of your hard drive that stores the locations of information on your hard drive. Also referred to as the *Volume Information Block.*

MMU: Memory Management Unit; can be a separate chip, but is built into the 68030, 68040, and PowerPC Macs.

modal dialog box: An unmovable dialog; one that beeps if you click outside of it (most file selection and System message dialog boxes are modal). Prevents all other action until; acted on or dismissed.

on the fly compression: A technique where files are compressed upon closing and decompressed when you open them.

open files count: The table within the System heap that keeps track of how many files your Mac has open at any given time.

optimization: The process of defragmenting your hard drive. See *fragmentation.*

orphaned alias: An alias that points to a file which has since been deleted.

pica: A measurement used by typographers — there are 12 points to a pica, and 6 picas to an inch.

PMMU: Paged Memory Management Unit. For the 68020-equipped Mac IIs, the 68851 PMMU was an option; an MMU is built into the 68030, 68040, and PowerPC computers.

point: A typographer's measurement equaling 1/72 of an inch — see pica.

postcardware: Shareware where the author asks that you send a postcard from your home town instead of payment.

PostScript: Adobe's page-description language.

QuickDraw: The method Apple uses to render graphics on-screen.

QuickTime: Apple's format for screen movies.

resource compression: Compression of the resources within a file.

RIP: Raster Image Processor, the hardware in an imagesetter that converts your pages into high-resolution output.

RISC: Reduced Instruction Set Computing. What Power Macs use (and what PowerPCs are).

root level: The top, or first level, of your hard drive, obtained by double-clicking the drive icon.

SCC: Serial Communication Controller; an integrated circuit (IC) on your Mac's logic board that handles serial communications (i.e., printers, modems).

segmenting: Files that are too large for one diskette can be split or segmented into pieces that will fit onto floppies. Compression software provides for the re-creation of the original file when all of the segments are copied onto another drive.

shareware: Software where the author allows you to try the software before paying for it. After a reasonable evaluation period, if you use the software, you are obligated to pay the fee.

System heap: The memory area that the System uses to load fonts, desk accessories, extensions, and control panels.

TIFF: Tagged Image File Format; a picture compression format.

TLA: Three-Letter Acronym (there are way too many of these...).

VIA: Versatile Interface Adapter; an integrated circuit (IC) on your Mac's logic board that handles the mouse, keyboard, and floppy drives.

VIB: Volume Information Block; the part of your hard drive that stores the locations of information on your hard drive. Apple now refers to this as the *Master Directory Block* (MDB).

B Conflicts Listing

It is amazing how fast any listing of conflicts goes out of date (believe me, I know); this may give you a start at tracking down some of your problems. If you want a more up-to-date list, consider buying Teknosys Help! (Chapter 12), and subscribing to their quarterly updates.

AltWDEF	vs.	Microphone II	AltWDEF does not work with Microphone II; the fix is to exclude MicroPhone II.
AltWDEF	vs.	QuickMail	AltWDEF 1.4 conflicts with QuickMail (QuickMail menus show up but no windows do).
AutoDoubler 1.0.6	vs.	PC Exchange 1.0	Fixed with 1.0.7 or better of AutoDoubler.
AutoDoubler 1.02	vs.	DiskExpress II 2.0.7	When running System 6.0.x, AutoDoubler 1.02 and DiskExpress II 2.07 conflict— this was fixed with AutoDoubler 1.0.3.
Big Thesaurus 1.0c	vs.	Microphone II 3.0	Big Thesaurus 1.0c conflicts with Microphone II 3.0.
Big Thesaurus 2.0.1	vs.	Word 6.0	An error may occur in Word if you select text for a search in Big Thesaurus
Boomerang	before	Directory Assistance	Boomerang should load before Directory Assistance; the fix is to upgrade to Directory Assistance II (part of Norton Utilities 2.0) and Super Boomerang 3.02 (part of Now Utilities).
CEToolbox	before	ClickChange 1.0.5	CEToolbox should load before ClickChange.
CEToolbox	before	StuffIt SpaceSaver 1.0.2	You will need to configure SpaceSaver to load after CEToolbox in order to use them both.

CEToolbox 1.4	vs.	SmartAlarms 3.0.3	With CEToolBox 1.4 and earlier, and SmartAlarms 3.0.3 or earlier, SmartAlarms would show up once, and then disappear from the menu; the fix is to upgrade to CEToolBox 1.5 or later, or to upgrade to SmartAlarms 3.0.4.
CEToolbox 1.4	vs.	Spelling Coach Pro	CEToolbox 1.4 and earlier versions conflicted with Spelling Coach Pro (Coach would call the wrong DA); the fix is to upgrade to CEToolbox 1.5 or later.
ClickChange 1.0.4	vs.	QuicKeys 2 2.0	QuicKeys 2 clicks in the wrong place when ClickChange dubl-arrows are enabled; the fix is to upgrade to ClickChange 1.05 and QuicKeys 2.1 or better.
ClickChange 1.0.4	vs.	QuicKeys 2.0	The fix is to upgrade to ClickChange 1.0.5 and QuicKeys 2.1 or better.
ClickChange 1.0.5	vs.	Cursor Animator	ClickChange has conflicts with anything which tries to change one of the standard cursors (arrow, watch, I-beam, cross, plus), such as SunDesk, Personality, and Cursor Animator. The fix is to turn those features off.
Cmdr. Dialog][	vs.	Easy Envelopes+	Cmdr. Dialog][conflicts with Easy Envelopes+.
Coach Pro 4.0.1	vs.	Word 6.0	An error may occur in Word if you select text for a search in Coach Pro.
Directory Assistance	vs.	Dialog View 2.5.2	Dialog View will not run in the presence of Norton Directory Assistance.
Disk Express II 2.0.7	vs.	System 7.1	The conflict is resolved with version 2.1.0 and better.
Disk Express II 2.1.0	vs.	Crash Barrier	The conflict is resolved with version 2.1.1.
Disk Express II 2.1.1	vs.	Staircase	With both installed, status dialog buttons do not work.

Disk Express II 2.1.1	vs.	Norton Disk Light 2.0	These two conflict, resulting in System freezes during optimization. The fix is to disable Disk Light.
DiskDoubler 3.0.1	vs.	ResEdit 2.1	DiskDoubler 3.01 conflicts with ResEdit 2.1; fixed in version 3.1 of DiskDoubler.
DiskDoubler 3.7.2	vs.	DeskWriter 2.2	Versions of DiskDoubler prior to 3.7.3 conflicted with DeskWriter 2.2. Fixed with version 3.7.3 of DiskDoubler.
DiskExpress II 2.0.4	vs.	System 7	The conflict is resolved with version 2.0.7c and better.
DiskLight 1.0	vs.	After Dark	DiskLight 1.0 conflicts with After Dark; the fix is to upgrade to version 2.0 of DiskLight (part of Norton Utilities for the Mac 2.0).
DiskLight 1.0	vs.	Rival 1.1.4	Rival 1.1.4 and DiskLight 1.0 conflict under System 6.0.7 (MultiFinder).
DiskLight 1.1	vs.	Canvas 3.0.4	DiskLight versions 1.0 and 1.1 caused Canvas to crash; fixed with version 2.0 of DiskLight.
DiskLight 1.1	vs.	Expert Color Paint	Norton DiskLight versions 1.0 and 1.1 causes Expert Color Paint to crash, especially during file operations; fixed with version 2.0 of DIskLight.
DOS Mounter	before	DT-Launch	DOS Mounter should load before DT-Launch.
DOS Mounter 2.0	vs.	DiskFit	DOS Mounter 2.0 conflicts with DiskFit; the fix is to upgrade to version 2.04 or better of DOS Mounter.
Easy Alarms 1.5	before	INITPicker 2.0.2	INITPicker 2.02 cannot display or control the Easy Alarms Extension 1.5 by Essential Software, because it does not recognize INIT resources of type appe; the fix is to Load Easy Alarms Extension before INITPicker 2.02 at startup.

Empower 4.0	vs.	QuickMail DA 2.5	Empower 4.0 prevents QuickMail DA 2.5 from loading; the fix is to upgrade to Empower 5.0 or better.
Escapade 1.3.1	vs.	Snap Mail	Old versions of Escapade can cause a crash when opening a log item in Snap Mail's Delivered Mail Log; upgrading to Escapade 1.3.2 or better fixes this problem
Exposure	vs.	ScreenShot	Exposure conflicts with ScreenShot (they both do basically the same thing, so just use one).
Exposure Pro	vs.	ScreenShot	Exposure Pro conflicts with ScreenShot (they both do basically the same thing, so just use one).
Greg's Buttons 3.1.2	vs.	Word 6.0	Later versions of Greg's Buttons do not conflict with Word.
Hand-Off II 2.2	and	INITPicker 2.0.2	You cannot access the original name of an alias of INITPicker 2.02 via the Control Panels menu with SuperMenus, which is a part of Hand-Off II 2.2, under System 7. The fix is to rename the INITPicker 2.02 alias. SuperMenu does not like file names that begin with a null character.
Hand-Off II 2.2.1	vs.	AutoDoubler 1.0.6	If AutoDoubler, Hand-Off II, and System 7 filesharing are all activated, Hand-Off II will cause a system crash; the fix is to upgrade to Hand-Off II 2.2.5 or better.
Hand-Off II 2.2.1	vs.	QuarkXPress 3.1	Hand-Off II 2.2.1 conflicts with QuarkXPress 3.1; the fix is to upgrade to Hand-Off II 2.2.5 or better.
Hard Disk ToolKit 1.0	vs.	FastBack Plus	Hard Disk Toolkit 1.0 had problems with Fastback Plus that were fixed with HDT version 1.1.
HeapTool 1.2	vs.	Tempo II	Versions of HeapTool earlier than 1.4 conflict with Tempo II; the fix is to upgrade to HeapTool 1.4.

Icon-It! 2.0	vs.	Double Helix 3.0	Icon-It! 2.0 conflicts with Double Helix 3.0.
INIT Manager 1.0	vs.	Remv INIT	INIT Manager 1.0 conflicted with Remv INIT (PLI's Syquest mounting software); the fix is to upgrade to INIT Manager 1.1 or better.
INIT Manager 1.0	vs.	Tempo II Plus	INIT Manager 1.0 conflicted with Tempo II Plus; the fix is to upgrade to INIT Manager 1.1 or better.
INITPicker 2.0.2		Tempo II	You need to disable INITPicker 2.0's BombGuard incompatibility detection preference when using Tempo II, because BombGuard will disable it; the fix is to upgrade to Tempo II Plus.
INITPicker 2.0.2	and	SuperMenu	You cannot access the original name of an alias of INITPicker 2.02 via the Control Panels menu with SuperMenu, which is a part of Hand-Off II 2.2, under System 7; the fix is to rename the INITPicker 2.02 alias (SuperMenu does not like file names that begin with a null character).
INITPicker 2.0.2	before	AutoDoubler	Under System 7, extensions may not load after AutoDoubler during startup when INITPicker 2.02 is installed; the workaround is to position AutoDoubler to load last at startup in the INITPicker 2.02 list.
INITPicker 2.0.2	vs.	ClickChange 4.0.3	The last INIT being loaded will run twice if INITPicker's Bombguard feature is turned on. This corrupts MenuFonts, so you'll have to either make sure MenuFonts is followed by at least one other extension, or turn off INITPicker's Bombguard feature.

Last Resort 1.0	before	Rival 1.1.6	If Rival versions 1.1.6 or earlier load before Last Resort 1.0, you will experience a System crash at startup; the fix is to either load Last Resort before Rival or upgrade to Rival versions 1.1.8 or higher.
LaunchINIT	vs.	MacRecorder 1.0	LaunchINIT and MacRecorder are incompatible; the result can cause damage to your System file.
LifeGuard	before	QuicKeys	LifeGuard should load after QuicKeys.
MacDraw Pro	vs.	GreatWorks 1.0	The Claris Translators shipped with MacDraw Pro prevent GreatWorks from loading; the fix is to upgrade to version 2.0 of GreatWorks.
MacEKG	before	Rival 1.1.6	Mac EKG should load before Rival 1.1.6; the fix is to upgrade to Rival 1.1.8 or better.
MacEKG	before	Rival 1.1.6	If Rival versions 1.1.6. or earlier load before MacEKG, it will not load at startup; the fix is either to load Rival after Mac EKG or upgrade to Rival version 1.1.8 or higher.
MacPassword	before	INITPicker	MacPassword should load before INITPicker.
MacPassword 3.8.5	vs.	QuickMail DA 2.5	When running System 6.0.5, MacPassword 3.8.5 prevents QuickMail DA 2.5 from loading; the fix is to upgrade to MacPassword 3.8.7 or better.
MacTools 7.2	vs.	Pyro! 3.0	MacTools 7.2 contains a bug that can cause a crash when Pyro! 3.x is installed (or possibly without Pyro! 3.x), when the Undelete Files menu item is chosen and then the Save Deletes button is clicked; the fix is to upgrade to MacTools Deluxe.
MasterJuggler	before	ClickChange 1.0.5	Loading MasterJuggler before ClickChange allows ClickChange to play sounds at startup.

MasterJuggler	before	Magic Menu 3.0.3	If you are using System 7, then this needs to load before Magic Menu, or you may get Get Info windows when using Magic Menu.
MasterJuggler	before	MenuFonts	MasterJuggler should load before MenuFonts.
MasterJuggler	vs.	myDiskLabeler 2.9.1	MasterJuggler conflicts with myDiskLabeler 2.9.1; the fix is to upgrade to myDiskLabeler III.
MasterJuggler	vs.	QuickEnvelope DA	MasterJuggler conflicts with QuickEnvelope DA.
MasterJuggler	vs.	Suitcase II	MasterJuggler conflicts with Suitcase II (this is not a problem; they both serve the same purpose, so choose the one you want to use).
MasterJuggler 1.5.2	vs.	FileMaker Pro 1.0	The fix is to upgrade to MasterJuggler 1.5.3 or better.
MasterJuggler 1.5.8	before	hierDA	MasterJuggler must load before hierDA
MasterJuggler 1.5.8	vs.	Moire	All versions are incompatible (crash at startup).
Maxima	vs.	INITPicker 2.0	Maxima conflicts with INITPicker 2.0.
MenuChoice	before	TrashAlias	MenuChoice must load before TrashAlias.
MenuExtend 1.0	vs.	Helium	Incompatible (system crashes).
MenuFonts	before	Thunder 7	Thunder 7 must load after the MenuFonts INIT under System 7 (otherwise the Mac beeps incessantly in any application that contains a font menu).
MenuFonts 4.0	vs.	Hand-Off II 2.2.1	MenuFonts 4.0 and Hand-Off II 2.2.1 conflict—it is impossible to select fonts on MenuFonts' submenus when Hand-Off's AutoDrop feature is on; the fix is to upgrade to version 4.03 or better of MenuFonts.

MenuFonts 4.0	vs.	HyperCard 2.1	HyperCard 2.1 cannot run in color (it complains that it lacks the memory to run) with MenuFonts 4.0—this was fixed with version 4.03 of MenuFonts.
Møire	vs.	PrePrint	Møire should be shut off when printing separations from Aldus PrePrint.
Møire	vs.	Tempo II	Versions of Møire earlier than 3.0 conflict with Tempo II; the fix is to upgrade to Møire 3.0 or better.
MultiClip	before	Suitcase II	MultiClip should load before Suitcase II.
MultiClip 2.0	vs.	CAT 2.0.4a	MultiClip 2.0 conflicts with CAT 2.04a.
Now Menus 4.0.1	vs.	Word 6.0	With Now Menus 4.0.1 installed, the undo and repeat commands may not work in Word.
Now Profile 4.0.1	vs.	Complete Undelete	Now Profile 4.0.1 is not compatible with Complete Undelete; the fix is to upgrade to Now Profile 4.0.1p.
Now Toolbox 4.0	vs.	Freehand 3.1	Now Toolbox version 4.0. had some problems with Aldus Freehand; the fix is to upgrade to version 4.0.1 or better of Now Toolbox.
Now Toolbox 4.0	vs.	QuarkXPress 3.1	Now Toolbox version 4.0 had some problems with QuarkXPress; the fix is to upgrade to version 4.0.1 or better of Now Toolbox.
NowMenus	before	ScreenShot	NowMenus should load before Screen Shot (Screen Shot wants to be the last extension to load); otherwise, selecting Control Panels with NowMenus will not work properly.

NowMenus 2.0	vs.	TouchBASE 1.0	NowMenus 2.0 had some problems with TouchBASE 1.0 (Super Boomerang's direct open would open the desk accessory at the wrong time); the fix is to upgrade to NowMenus 2.03 or better.
NowMenus 3.0.1	vs.	Excel	NowMenus causes problems for Excel working under non-MultiFinder environments.
NowMenus 3.0.1	vs.	Spelling Coach Pro	NowMenus conflicts with Spelling Coach Pro.
NowMenus 3.0.1	vs.	Suitcase II 1.2	NowMenus 3.01 conflicts with earlier versions of Suitcase II; the fix is to upgrade to Suitcase II 1.2.10 or better.
NowMenus 3.0.2	before	Suitcase 2.0	Now Menus should load before Suitcase 2.0 just the same as it did before Suitcase II 1.2.x, although if you're under System 7, and you're not using Suitcase II to load desk accessories which have submenus, it doesn't matter.
NowMenus 4.0	vs.	Canvas	NowMenus 4.0 conflicted with palette-type menus in Canvas; the fix is to upgrade to version 4.0.1 or better of NowMenus.
NowMenus 4.0	vs.	FileMaker Pro	NowMenus 4.0 conflicted with palette-type menus in FileMaker Pro; the fix is to upgrade to version 4.0.1 or better of NowMenus.
NowMenus 4.0	vs.	MacWrite II	NowMenus 4.0 conflicted with palette-type menus in MacWrite II; the fix is to upgrade to version 4.0.1 or better of NowMenus.
NowMenus 4.0	vs.	MenuFonts	NowMenus 4.0 had some problems with MenuFonts; the fix is to upgrade to version 4.0.1 or greater of NowMenus.

NowMenus 4.0	vs.	Microsoft Mail	NowMenus 4.0 had some problems with Microsoft Mail; the fix is to upgrade to version 4.0.1 or greater of NowMenus.
NowMenus 4.0	vs.	Microsoft Word	Compatibility and menu display difficulties with Microsoft Word have been resolved by excluding NowMenus 4.0.1 from Word automatically.
NowMenus 4.0	vs.	Microsoft Works	NowMenus 4.0 had some problems with Microsoft Works; the fix is to upgrade to version 4.0.1 or greater of NowMenus.
NowMenus 4.0	vs.	Nisus	NowMenus 4.0 had some problems with Nisus; the fix is to upgrade to version 4.0.1 or greater of NowMenus.
NowMenus 4.0	vs.	Persuasion 3.1	NowMenus 4.0 conflicted with palette-type menus in Aldus Persuasion; the fix is to upgrade to version 4.0.1 or better of NowMenus.
NowMenus 4.0	vs.	PopChar	NowMenus 4.0 had some problems with PopChar; the fix is to upgrade to version 4.0.1 or greater of NowMenus.
NowMenus 4.0	vs.	Timbuktu	NowMenus 4.0 had some problems with Timbuktu; the fix is to upgrade to version 4.0.1 or better of NowMenus.
NowMenus 4.0	vs.	TypeIt4Me	NowMenus 4.0 had some problems with TypeIt4Me; the fix is to upgrade to version 4.0.1 or greater of NowMenus.
NowMenus 4.0.1	vs.	Thunder 7	NowMenus 4.0 had some problems with Thunder 7; the fix is to upgrade to version 4.0.1 or greater of NowMenus.

NowMenus 4.0.1	vs.	Virex	NowMenus 4.0 had some problems with Virex; the fix is to upgrade to version 4.0.1 or greater of NowMenus.
OmniPage Direct 2.0	vs.	ATM 3.8.1	OmniPage Direct 2.0 conflicts with ATM 3.8.1 on Power Macs.
OmniPage Pro 5.0	vs.	ATM 3.8.1	OmniPage Pro 5.0 conflicts with ATM 3.8.1 on Power Macs.
On Cue 1.3	vs.	Virex 1.5.1	On Cue and Virex 1.51 conflict; the fix is to upgrade to Virex version 1.52 or better.
On Cue II 2.0		Navigator 3.1	On Cue II conflicts with CompuServe Navigator (Navigator crashes on startup if On Cue II is loaded); the fix is to upgrade to On Cue II 2.01.
On Cue II 2.0.1	before	INITPicker 2.0.2	On Cue II 2.01 and INITPicker 2.02 conflict—if both are active, your System will hang on loading the last INIT; the fix is to load On Cue II before INITPicker.
ON Location 1.0	vs.	Hand-Off II	ON Location version 1.0 conflicted with Hand-Off II; the fix is to upgrade to ON Location 1.02.
OptiMem 1.5.6f	vs.	Word 6.0	Word may hang in low memory circumstances; the fix is to upgrade to OptiMem 1.5.6g or better
Pop-Keys	vs.	Dark Castle	Pop-Keys conflicts with Dark Castle.
Pop-Keys	vs.	LaunchKey	Pop-Keys conflicts with LaunchKey.
PopChar 1.7	vs.	Type Reunion 1.0.1	PopChar 1.7 and the Adobe Type Reunion 1.01 INIT conflict when running System 6.0.5. (PopChar 1.7 works fine with ATR 1.01 when running on System 6.0.7 or System 7, but not on System 6.0.5); the fix is to upgrade to PopChar 1.91.
PopChar 2.5.1	vs.	QuicKeys 2.1.1	If PopChar 2.5.1 is loaded, QuicKeys' PasteEase extension pastes in random locations.

PopChar 2.7.1	vs.	Word 6.0	PopChar may fail to display the selected font in the Font list on the Formatting toolbar. At this point, there is no workaround.
Pyro!	vs.	PrePrint	Pyro! should be shut off when printing separations from Aldus PrePrint.
Pyro! 4.0	before	Mirror 1.1	Pyro! 4.0 should load before Mirror versions 1.0 and 1.1.
QuicKeys	before	TypeIt4Me	QuicKeys should load before TypeIt4Me.
Shortcut 1.0.1	vs.	The Curator 1.0.5	Shortcut 1.0.1 conflicts with The Curator 1.05 (in Show Catalog, Shortcut removes any way to exit that mode); the fix is to upgrade to Shortcut 1.5 or better.
SimAnt Cheater 1.1	vs.	QuicKeys 2.1.1	SimAnt Cheater conflicts with QuicKeys.
Smart Alarms 3.0.2	vs.	Excel 2.2	Smart Alarms 3.0.3 corrects problems with Microsoft Excel version 2.2.
Smart Alarms 3.0.2	vs.	HyperCard 2.0	Smart Alarms 3.0.3 fixes problems with HyperCard 2.0.
Smart Alarms 3.0.3	vs.	CEToolbox	Smart Alarms 3.0.4 fixes the menu conflicts that occurred with CEToolbox. Importing Reminders from text or database files now imports the date and advance warning correctly even if a minimum number of fields are used.
Smart Alarms 3.0.3	vs.	Theorist	Smart Alarms 3.0.4 fixes the creator type conflict with Theorist.
Smart Alarms 3.0.4	vs.	Spelling Coach Pro	Smart Alarms conflicts with Spelling Coach Pro (it contributes to the auto opening of the wrong DA when Spelling Coach Pro is set to Auto Open); the fix is to upgrade to Smart Alarms 3.0.6.

Spelling Coach Pro	vs.	CEToolbox	There was a problem with Spelling Coach auto-opening in Microsoft Word with earlier versions of CEToolbox installed; this is fixed with version 1.5.1 of CEToolbox.
Spelling Coach Pro 3.1a	vs.	FullWrite Professional 1.1	Spelling Coach Pro 3.1a conflicts with FullWrite Professional 1.1. Setting up Coach to be always open helps but it still crashes on occasion.
Spot On 1.8	vs.	Maxima 2.0.2	Versions of MacPeak's Spot-On Formatter earlier than 1.8 conflicted with Maxima 2.02; the fix is to upgrade to Spot On 1.8 or better.
Startup Manager 4.0	vs.	Maxima	Startup Manager 4.0 has problems with the stutter restart generated by Maxima; the fix is to upgrade to Startup Manager 4.01 or better.
Startup Manager 4.0	vs.	Virtual	Startup Manager 4.0 has problems with the stutter restart generated by Virtual; the fix is to upgrade to Startup manager 4.01 or better.
Stepping Out II 2.0.2	vs.	AlarmsClock	Stepping Out II 2.02 prevents AlarmsClock from displaying its time in the menu bar.
Stretch 1.0	vs.	Excel 4.0	Stretch conflicts with Excel 4.0.
StuffIt SpaceSaver 1.0.2	vs.	FolderBolt1.0.2b	Versions of FolderBolt earlier than 1.0.2c will not work properly with StuffIt SpaceSaver.
StuffIt SpaceSaver 1.0.2	vs.	Virex3.8.2	Virex (3.8.2 and earlier) can cause your Macintosh to lock up when the Finder is trying to load. You may also find that even if you get past the Finder that you may have problems in other applications. The fix is to update to Virex 3.8.3, which is fully compatible with StuffIt SpaceSaver.
StuffIt SpaceServer 3.5	before	General Controls	If StuffIt SpaceServer loads after General Controls when running System 7.5.1, files become invisible.

StuffIt SpaceServer 3.5	vs.	System 7.5.1	Unmounting removable volumes will lock up your Mac.
Suitcase II	before	ClickChange 1.0.5	If you are using alternate ClickChange windows and don't want to crash in Smart Alarms' Appointments DA, you should make sure that the Suitcase II INIT loads before the ClickChange INIT. Loading Suitcase II before ClickChange allows ClickChange to play sounds at startup.
Suitcase II	before	MenuFonts	Suitcase II should load before MenuFonts.
Suitcase II	vs.	myDiskLabeler	Suitcase II conflicts with myDiskLabeler 2.9.1; the fix is to upgrade to myDiskLabeler III.
Suitcase II 1.2.6	vs.	QuarkXPress 3.0	QuarkXPress 3.0 had some problems with Suitcase II 1.2.6's Power User option; the fix is to upgrade to Suitcase II 1.2.8 or better.
Suitcase II 2.1.1	vs.	Snap Mail	Old versions of Suitcase will cause a start-up error (-109); upgrading to Suitcase II 2.1.2 or better fixes the problem
Super Boomerang 2.0.3	vs.	GreatWorks 1.0	The Super Boomerang (2.03) Rebound feature conflicted with the main open dialog in GreatWorks; the fix is to upgrade to Super Boomerang 3.0 or better.
Super Boomerang 3.0.2	before	Directory Assistance II 2.0	Super Boomerang 3.02 should load before Directory Assistance II.
Super Boomerang 3.0.2	vs.	DeltaGraph Pro 2.0.1	Super Boomerang 3.02 conflicts with DeltaGraph Pro 2.01.
Super Boomerang 3.0.2	vs.	Excel 4.0	Super Boomerang 3.02 does not show in Excel 4.0's Open dialog box.
Super Boomerang 3.0.2	vs.	Maxima	Super Boomerang 3.02 does not work properly with Maxima ram disks.

Super Boomerang 4.0	vs.	FileMaker Pro	Super Boomerang 4.0 had some problems with FileMaker Pro; the fix is to upgrade to version 4.0.1 or greater of Super Boomerang.
Super Boomerang 4.0	vs.	Freehand	Super Boomerang 4.0 had some problems with Aldus Freehand; the fix is to upgrade to version 4.0.1 or greater of Super Boomerang.
Super Boomerang 4.0	vs.	MasterJuggler	Super Boomerang 4.0 had some problems with MasterJuggler; the fix is to upgrade to version 4.0.1 or greater of Super Boomerang.
Super Boomerang 4.0	vs.	QuarkXPress	Super Boomerang 4.0 had some problems with QuarkXPress; the fix is to upgrade to version 4.0.1 or greater of Super Boomerang.
Super Boomerang 4.0	vs.	WordPerfect	Super Boomerang 4.0 had some problems with WordPerfect; the fix is to upgrade to version 4.0.1 or greater of Super Boomerang.
Super Boomerang 4.0.1	vs.	Wipe Info	Super Boomerang 4.0.1 crashed when using Norton Utilities' Wipe Info; the fix is to upgrade to version 4.0.1p or greater of Super Boomerang.
Super Boomerang 4.0.1	vs.	Word 6.0	Re-launching may not function correctly; the fix is to upgrade to a later version of Now Utilities.
SuperClock! 3.5	vs.	PageMaker	Versions of SuperClock! earlier than 3.5 conflict with PageMaker; the fix is to upgrade to SuperClock 3.9 or better.
SuperDisk!	vs.	FileSaver 1.1	There are some problems with versions 1.0 and 1.1 of Norton FileSaver that can cause problems when running SuperDisk! (and AutoDoubler)—these were fixed with version 2.0 of FileSaver.

SuperDisk! 1.7.3	vs.	DiskTop 4.0.1	Files compressed with version 1.73 of SuperDisk! and copied with DiskTop 4.01 will be truncated and thus usually ruined—this was fixed with version 1.8 of SuperDisk.
SuperDisk! 1.7.3	vs.	WriteNow 2.2	SuperDisk! 1.73 and WriteNow 2.2 were incompatible — fixed with SuperDisk 2.0 and WriteNow 3.0.
SuperMenu	vs.	HAM 1.0	SuperMenu conflicts with the submenus generated by HAM.
System 7.5.1	vs.	MacTools Trashback	MacTools TrashBack needs to be updated to at least version 4.0.2 to work with System 7.5.1.
System 7.5.1	vs.	RAM Doubler 1.5.1	With file sharing enabled, files on CD-ROMs may disappear; the fix is to upgrade to version 1.5.2 of RAM Doubler (the updater is on the CD-ROM).
System 7.5.1	vs.	SpeedyFinder7 1.5.9i	SpeedyFinder7 does not load under System 7.5.1. No a big deal: this version was set to expire March 15, 1995.
Talking Moose 3.0	vs.	After Dark 2.0	After Dark 2.0 had some problems playing sounds with Talking Moose 3.0; the fix is to upgrade to After Dark 2.0u (or better) and Talking Moose 3.10 or better.
Talking Moose 3.0	vs.	DiskDoubler	Talking Moose 3.0 conflicted with DiskDoubler (selecting a pop-up menu in the DD preferences dialog will cause a crash when you click the OK button); the fix is to upgrade to Talking Moose 3.0.1 or better.
Thunder 7 1.0.5	vs.	Nisus 3.0.6	Thunder 7 1.0.5 does not work within Nisus 3.0.6.
Thunder 7 1.0.5	vs.	WriteNow 3.0	Thunder 7 has problems with WriteNow 3.0; the fix is to add the WriteNow compatibility module (available from Baseline or on-line services such as CompuServe).

TMON	before	Hand-Off II 2.2.1	TMON should load before Hand-Off II.
TurboMouse	before	INITPicker	The Kensington ADB TurboMouse INIT needs to load before INITPicker; this allows you to invoke the INITPicker Startup window when using the TurboMouse.
Type Reunion	vs.	Accountant, Inc.	There is a conflict between Accountant, Inc. and Adobe Type Reunion. When Type Reunion is loaded, Accountant, Inc. is unable to access the payroll tax tables from the pop-up menu. The fix is to hold down the Shift key after double-clicking on Accountant, Inc. to keep Type Reunion from modifying the menus.
Type Reunion	vs.	Boomerang 2.0	Adobe Type Reunion and Boomerang 2.0 conflict; the fix is to either turn off Keep CODE in SysHeap in Boomerang's Preferences Dialog or increase the System heap size.
Type Reunion	vs.	MenuFonts	Adobe Type Reunion conflicts with MenuFonts.
Type Reunion	vs.	MultiMaster	Adobe Type Reunion conflicts with MultiMaster.
Type Reunion	vs.	Navigator 3.0.4	Navigator 3.04 does not run properly with Adobe Type Reunion installed (the Archive dropdown displays font attributes, instead of your archives). The workaround is to hold down the Shift key while booting Navigator (this disables ATR); the fix is to upgrade to version 3.1 of Navigator.
Type Reunion	vs.	PopChar 1.5	Adobe Type Reunion conflicts with PopChar versions 1.4 & 1.5; the fix is to upgrade to version 2.52 of PopChar.

Type Reunion	vs.	WYSIWYG Menus	Adobe Type Reunion conflicts with WYSIWYG Menus (they both try to do the same thing).
Type Reunion 1.0	vs.	SuperDisk! 1.7	Type Reunion 1.0 conflicts with SuperDisk 1.7; the fix is to upgrade to Type Reunion 1.01 or better.
Type Reunion 1.0	vs.	UltraPaint 1.0	Adobe Type Reunion conflicts with UltraPaint, preventing the pop-up menus (in gradient fill, for example) from working correctly.
Type Reunion 1.0.1	vs.	StuffIt Lite	Versions of ATR earlier than 1.0.2 will cause StuffIt Lite to quit unexpectedly.
TypeIt4Me	before	ProSwitch	TypeIt4Me should load before ProSwitch.
TypeIt4Me	before	Stepping Out II	TypeIt4Me should load before Stepping Out II.
TypeIt4Me 4.4.1	vs.	Thunder 7 1.5.5	TypeIt4Me conflicts with Thunder7.
Wallpaper 1.0.2	vs.	THINK C Debugger 5.0.2	Wallpaper 1.0.2 and the THINK C 5.02 Debugger conflict; the fix is to upgrade to Wallpaper 1.0.3 or better.
WindowList 1.3	vs.	WDEF	WindowList 1.3 and WDEF conflict.
WYSIWYG Menus	before	Magic Menu 3.0.3	You will need to rename WYSIWYG Menus to load before Magic Menu in order to use them both.
WYSIWYG Menus	before	TOM√INIT II	WYSIWYG Menus should load before TOM√INIT II.
WYSIWYG Menus 2.0	vs.	MacWrite II	WYSIWYG Menus 2.0 doesn't work with MacWrite II, which does its own menus; the fix is to upgrade to WYSIWYG Menus 2.0.3 or better.
WYSIWYG Menus 3.0	vs.	NowMenus 3.0	If you have folders named Text, Style, Font, or Size in your Apple Menu Items folder, WYSIWYG Menus mistakes the resultant menu for an actual Text style menu; the workaround is to add a space to the folder name; the fix is to upgrade to version 3.02 of Now Utilities.

WYSIWYG Menus 3.0.1	vs.	Word 5.0	WYSIWYG Menus 3.0.1 has some problems with Word 5.0; the fix is to upgrade to WYSIWYG Menus 3.0.2 or better.
WYSIWYG Menus 3.0.2	vs.	Acta 7	Acta and WYSIWYG conflict. The fix is to add Acta 7 into WYSIWYG's exclude list (by hitting the Exclude... button in the WYSIWYG Control Panel).
WYSIWYG Menus 4.0.1	vs.	Word 6.0	Some fonts may not display correctly in Word; the fix is to upgrade to a later version of Now Utilities.

C

Sources

This Appendix gives a complete listing of the authors and manufacturers of the software covered in this book. Thanks to David Hannon of AP PROFESSIONAL for fact-checking the list for me. Before starting with the list, I can think of no better place to describe Bill Baldridge's VendorDA (Figure C-1). Color and monochrome versions of this wonderful resource are on the CD-ROM.

VendorDA
Bill Baldridge
FourArts™
P.O. Box 936
Riverdale, MD 20738-0936
Shareware fee: $10.00

Bill is a 47-year-old "kid" with three computers in his house, and three cars in his garage in "historic" Riverdale, Maryland. Bill bought his first Macintosh in September 1984, and has been a fan ever since. The concept for VendorDA came about when he was Director of Software Services for a non-storefront Apple dealer in 1992; he has carefully nurtured the product into what it is today through a lot of grunt work, contributions from others, and just plain old phone and e-mail contacts with hundreds of developers and vendors. His ultimate goal is to produce a true standalone database with editable fields, e-mail addresses, product info and more.

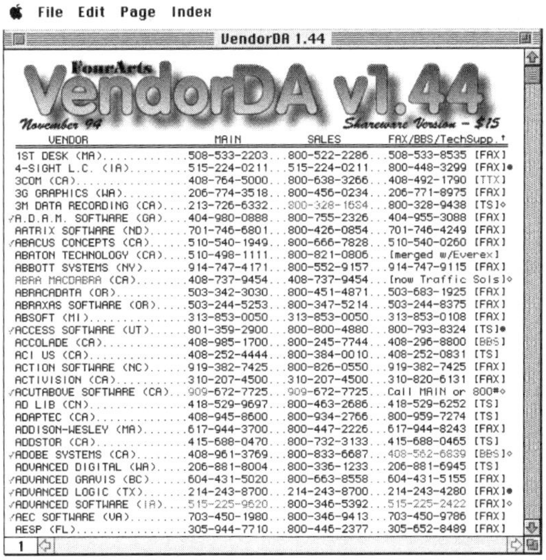

Figure C-1: VendorDA

Abbott Systems Inc.
62 Mountain Road
Pleasantville, NY 10570-9802
Telephone: 800 552-9157
Fax: 914 747-9115
CanOpener (suggested retail: $125.00)
Rescue TXT (suggested retail: $79.00)

Adobe Systems
1585 Charleston Road
P.O. Box 7900
Mountain View, CA 94039
Telephone 415 961-4400
Adobe Type Manager (suggested retail: $39.95)

The AG Group, Inc
2540 Camino Diablo Suite 200
Walnut Creek, CA 94596
Toll-free: (800) 466-2447
Fax: 510-937-2479
Internet: ftp.aggroup.com or
www.aggroup.com
LocalPeek/EtherPeek (suggested retail: $495/ $795)
Skyline/Satellite (suggested retail: $795.00)

Aladdin Systems
165 Westridge Drive
Watsonville, CA 95076
Telephone: 408 761-6200
Fax: 408 761-6206
AOL/AppleLink: ALADDIN
CompuServe: 75300,1666
eWorld/GEnie: AladdinSys
Internet: aladdin@well.com
StuffIt Deluxe (suggested retail: $129.00)

ALSoft Inc.
22557 Westfield, Suite 122
Spring, TX 77373
Telephone: 713 353-4090
Support: 713 353-1510
Fax: 713 353-9868
Disk Express II (suggested retail: $89.95)
MasterJuggler (suggested retail: $69.95)
Power Utilities (includes both of the above; suggested retail: $129.00)

Alysis Software Corp.
1231 31st Street
San Francisco, CA 94122
Telephone: 415 928-2895
Fax: 415 928-2896
America Online: Alysis
CompuServe: 75300,3011

America Online
8619 Westwood Center Drive
Vienna, VA 22182
Toll-free: 800 227-6364 x5257

Jason Anderson
Beyond Midnight Software
P.O. Box 471
Devonport, TAS 7310
Australia
Internet:
jason_ga@postoffice.utas.edu.au
4-Matter (shareware fee: $10.00)
EjectDisk (freeware)
PictSize (freeware)
Volume FKey (freeware)

Apple Computers
20525 Mariani Avenue
Cupertino, CA 95014-6299
(408) 996-1010
Apple File Assistant ($58.95) (Apple no longer provides list prices; this price is from MacZone.)
Inter•Poll
Apple Support Professional Demo Kit of software and tutorials available at no charge

APS Technologies
6131 Deramus
Kansas City, MO 64120
Telephone: 816 483-6100
Support: 800 334-7550
Fax: 816 483-4541

Roger D. Bates
P.O. Box 14
Beaverton, OR 97075
Telephone: 513 591-9223
America Online: RogerB2437
DiskDup+ (shareware fee: $25.00)
RamDisk+ (shareware fee: $35.00)

Ross E. Bergman
Internet: hyjinx@isr.harvard.edu
RAM Doubler 1.5.2 Indicator Patch
(freeware)

Berkeley Systems, Inc.
2095 Rose Street
Berkeley, CA 94709
Telephone: 510 549-2300
Fax: 510 849-9426
America Online: BrklySystm
AppleLink: D0346
CompuServe: 75300,1376

eWorld: BSI
Internet: mactech@berksys.com
After Dark (suggested retail: $49.99)

Brian Bezanson
Manta Software Corporation
1289 129th Avenue NE
Blaine, MN 55434
Telephone: 612 754-8140
CompuServe: 76711,550
Bring Finder to Front (freeware)

Tim Bitson
AnalySYS Software
P.O. Box 35967
Tucson, AZ 85740-5967
America Online: Tbitson
Auto Shutdown (freeware)
MailSlot (shareware fee: $10.00)

Mike Blackwell
The Robotics Institute
Carnegie Mellon University
5000 Forbes Avenue
Pittsburgh, PA 15213
Internet: mkb@cs.cmu.edu
DuoMon (freeware)
Temperature (freeware)

Mason L. Bliss
18 Beach Street
Middleton, MA 02346
Internet:
mason@acheron.middleboro.ma.us
Basic Black (freeware)

Simon Bone
P.O. Box 1847
Lewisburg, TN 37091-0847
CompuServe: 70324,1340
Silent Beep (freeware)

Tom Bridgewater
Internet: tbridgwa@cymbal.calpoly.edu
Quiet Start (freeware)

Jan Bruyndonckx
Salvialei, 23
B-2540 Hove
Belgium
AppleLink: WAVE.BEL
Jack in the Trash (Postcardware)
MenuMail (shareware fee: varies)
Mithrandir (Postcardware)
Red Queen (shareware fee: $1.00 per Mac)
SuperApple and Color SuperApple (Postcardware)
WindowWarp (shareware fee: $25.00)

Peter S. Bryant
Ethos Software
P.O. Box 11235
Zephyr Cove, NV 89448
America Online: BryantPS
CompuServe: 74071,3536
Open Files (shareware fee: $10.00)

EJ Campbell
EJ Enterprises
4096 Sutherland Drive
Palo Alto, CA 943093
America Online: EJC3
Ultra Recorder (shareware fee: $5.00)

Mike Caputo
595 Lamoka Avenue
Staten Island, NY 10312
America Online: Mcaputo
CompuServe: 74372,2431
PowerStrip (shareware fee: $10.00)

Caravelle Networks Corp.
210 Colonnade Road South, Suite 301
Nepean, ON K2E 2L5
Canada
Toll-free: (800) 363-5292
Fax: (613) 225-4777
NetWORKS (suggested retail: $499/25 device licence)

John Carlsen
CompuServe: 74766,1164
Finder Preferences 7 (freeware)

Casa Blanca Works, Inc.
148 Bon Air Center
Greenbrae, CA 94904
Telephone: 415 461-2227
Fax: 415 461-2249
Drive7 (suggested retail: $89.95)
DriveCD (suggested retail:$79.95)

Casady & Greene
22734 Portola Drive
Salinas, CA 93908-1119
Telephone: 408 484-9228
Fax: 408 484-9218
AppleLink: D0063
America Online: CasadyGreene
CompuServe: 71333,616
Conflict Catcher 3 (suggested retail $64.95; upgrade $29.95)

Samuel Caughron
Samat Software
9600 East 150 Highway
Kansas City, MO 64149
America Online: MRCAUGHRON
CompuServe: 76354,3302
Victoire! (shareware fee: $15.00)

Charles River Analytics Inc.
55 Wheeler Street
Cambridge, MA 02138
Telephone: 617 491-3474
Fax: 617 868-0780
America Online: OpenSesame
AppleLink: OPENSESAME
Internet: sesame@cra.com
Open Sesame (suggested retail: $99.00)

Coco Chen
Dragonsoft
603 E. Minor Drive #101
Kansas City, MO 64131
Telephone: 816 943-1835
America Online: Dragonsoft
CompuServe: 74471,3403
EZ Floppy Eject (Postcardware)

Stuart Cheshire
29C Escondido Village
Stanford, CA 94305
Telephone: 415 497-2399
Internet: cheshire@cs.stanford.edu
WriteThrough (freeware)

Kerry Clendinning
P.O. Box 26061
Austin, TX 78755-0061
AppleLink: KerryC
CompuServe: 76424,2214
HeapTool (shareware fee: $13.50)

MenuChoice (shareware fee: $15.00)
PrintChoice (shareware fee $14.00)

CompuServe
5000 Arlington Center Boulevard
Columbus, OH 43220
Telephone: 614 457-8650
Toll-free: 800 848-8990
CompuServe Information Manager is on the CD-ROM
CompuServe Navigator (suggested retail: $50.00)

Connectix Corporation
2655 Campus Drive
San Mateo, CA 94403
Telephone: 415 571-5100
Toll-free: 800 950-5880
Fax: 415 571-5195
America Online: Connectix
AppleLink: Connectix.CS
CompuServe: 75300, 1546
eWorld: RAM Doubler
Internet: support@connectix.com
CPU (suggested retail: $99.00)
Maxima (suggested retail: $99.00)
Ram Doubler (suggested retail: 99.00)
Virtual (suggested retail: $99.00)

Mike Conrad
Night Light Software
P.O. Box 2484
Oak Harbor, WA 98277-6484
America Online: NL Software
CompuServe: 73457,426
AutoMenus Pro (shareware fee: $15.00)
QuickFormat (shareware fee: $15.00)

Mark Crutchfield
P.O. Box 6456
Kingwood, TX 77325
America Online: MarkC23041
Warp7Utilities (shareware fee: $12.00)

Paul Cunningham
Performance Data
P.O. Box 1923
Mango, FL 33550-1923
America Online: TKS Paul
CompuServe: 75020,3540
TaskMan (freeware)

Brian Cyr
415 Long Hill Avenue
Shelton, CT 06484
America Online: Cyrano B
Internet: bcyr%mother@utrcgw.utc.com
SunBlock (shareware fee: $5.00)

Dantz Development Corporation
4 Orinda Way, Building C
Orinda, CA 94563
Telephone: 510 253-3000
Fax: 510 253-9099
Tech Support: 510 253-3050
America Online: Dantz
AppleLink: DANTZ
CompuServe: 72477,1322
DiskFit Direct (suggested retail: $49.00)
DiskFit Pro (suggested retail: $125.00)
Retrospect (suggested retail: $249.00)
Retrospect Remote (suggested retail: $449.00)

Dawson Dean
Software Publishing
654 Blair Avenue
Piedmont, CA 94611
America Online: DawsonDean
Internet: dawson@cs.cornell.edu
File Kit (shareware fee: $15.00)
Key Tools (shareware fee: $15.00)

Hugo Diaz
32 Whites Avenue #6608
Watertown, MA 02172-4351
Telephone: 617 924-8768
America Online: HugoD
SpaceAlert (shareware fee: $15.00)

Jerry Du
Dragonsoft
603 E. Minor Drive #101
Kansas City, MO 64131
Telephone: 816 943-1835
America Online: Dragonsoft
CompuServe: 74471,3403
7Tuner (shareware fee: $15.00)
I Love Native! (freeware)

Dubl-Click Software
20310 Empire Avenue, Suite A102
Bend, OR 97701
Telephone: 503 317-0355
Fax: 503 317-0430
ClickChange (suggested retail: $89.95)
Icon Mania (suggested retail: $69.95)
MenuFonts (suggested retail: $69.95)

Brian Durand
Aurelian Software
922 W. Buena #3W
Chicago, IL 60613
Telephone: 312 857-7110
America Online: BriDurand
StartUpLog (freeware)

Henrik Eliasson
Sunnerviksgatan 15 A
S-418 72 Göteborg
Sweden
Internet:
henrik_eliasson@macexchange.se
CD Menu (shareware fee: $10.00)

Dave Ely
Palace Productions
4567 West 159th Street
Lawnsdale, CA 90260
America Online: Ely.D
CompuServe: 72170,2373
Internet: david_ely@qm.symantec.com
DirtyDesk (freeware)

Tobias Engler
Môhrendorferstr. 6
91056 Erlangen
Germany
CompuServe: 100317,545
Internet: te@syrinx.franken.de
KillDF (freeware)
Refresh (freeware)

Riccardo Ettore
67 rue de la limite
1970 Wez.-Oppem
Belgium
CompuServe: 72277,1344
TypeIt4Me (shareware fee: $30.00)

Richard E. Fiegle
P.O. Box 5062
Kokomo, IN 46904-5062
America Online: Rfigleaf
CompuServe: 76350,761
Line Up (shareware fee: $10.00)
MacUpdate (shareware Fee: $5.00)

Hubert Figuiere
24 rue des Filmins
92339 Sceaux
France
Telephone: 33-1-47.02.40.07
Internet: figuiere@altern.com
Fat Free (freeware)

FWB Incorporated
1555 Adams Drive
Menlo Park, CA 94025
Telephone: 415 325-4FWB
Fax: 415 833-4653
Hard Disk Toolkit (suggested retail: $199.00)

Jean-Pierre Gachen
Résidence Beaucastel
4, avenue François Mauriac
F-64200 Biarritz
France
Fax: +33-59 22 18 20
CompuServe: 76667,3075
Internet: jpg11@calvacom.fr
AutoClock (freeware)

Rick Genter
Useful Software Corporation
12 Page Street
Danvers, MA 01923-2825
Telephone: 508 774-8233
America Online: Useful
CompuServe: 73163,2142
Filename Mapper (shareware fee: $10.00)

David Giandomenico
4 Waverley Drive
Camberley, Surrey GU15-2DL
England
CompuServe: 100016,1053
Once Daily (freeware)
Quit All Applications (freeware)

Bill Goodman
Cyclos
P.O. Box 31417
San Francisco, CA 94131-0417
CompuServe: 71101,204
Compact Pro (shareware fee: $25.00)

Jon Gotow
St. Clair Software
2025 Mohawk Road
Upper St. Clair, PA 15241
America Online: StClairSW
CompuServe: 72330,3455
Internet: gotow@ansoft.com
Default Folder (shareware fee: $10.00)
Sleeper (shareware fee: $10.00)

Justin Gray
Alysis Software Corp.
1231 31st Street
San Francisco, CA 94122
Telephone: 415 566-2263

America Online: Alysis
CompuServe: 75300,3011
Safety Belt (freeware)

Jim Hamilton
2904 Jubilee Trl.
Austin, TX 78748
America Online: JimH16
CompuServe: 71640,235
Internet: hamilton@io.com
BundAid (freeware)

Kevin Hardman
c/o Nivek Research
108 Kramer Court
Cary, NC 27511
Internet:
symbionts@hardman.pdial.interpath.net
Symbionts (shareware fee: $20.00)

Laurence Harris
1100 W. NC Highway 54 BYP, Apt 29-J
Chapel Hill, NC 27516-2826
Telephone: 919 933-9595
America Online: Lharris
CompuServe: 76150,1027
Alias Director (shareware fee: $10.00)
File Buddy (shareware fee: $25.00)

Richard Harvey
P.O. Box 118332
Carrollton, TX 75011
America Online: Banana6000
Extension Kit (shareware fee: donation)

C.K. Haun
RavenWare Software
22045 McClellan Road
Cupertino, CA 95014
AppleLink: C.K.HAUN
CompuServe: 75300,1001
GEnie: C.Haun1
AETracker (Fredware)

Michael Hecht
SAS Institute Inc.
SAS Campus Drive
Cary, NC 27513
Internet: hecht@vnet.net
About (freeware)

Brian Hutchison
CompuServe: 70421,3557
Internet: brian@harpo.ampr.ab.ca
Pledge (freeware)

Insanely Great Software
126 Calvert Ave. E.
Edison, NJ 08820
Telephone: 908 548-5107
America Online: AdamStein
CompuServe: 71140,2051
Desktop Remover (freeware**)**
*Mac Life Insurance (shareware fee:
$29.95)*
On Location (suggested retail: $129.95)

Jonathan Jacobs
2374 Euclid Heights, Blvd. #407
Cleveland Heights, OH 44106-2745
Telephone: 216 368-3574 (lab)
Internet: jxj24@po.cwru.edu
Kill FinderZooms (freeware)
WhoAmI? (freeware)

John Jeppson
CompuServe: 76174,2007
HellFolderFix (freeware)

Mitchell Jones
P.O. Box 354
Temple City, CA 91780
Fax: 818 287-3067
America Online: MitchJones
CompuServe: 76506,753
Internet: mjones@netcom.com
Snitch (shareware fee: $5.00)

Jump Development Group, Inc.
1228 Malvern Avenue
Pittsburgh, PA 15217-1141
Telephone: 412 681-2692
America Online: JumpDevgrp
AppleLink: RThornton
CompuServe: 71321,1527
OptiMem (suggested retail: $129.00)

Jeremy Kezer
143 Songbird Lane
Farmington, CT 06032-3433
America Online: JBKezer
BatterAmnesia (shareware fee: $10.00)
Insomniac (shareware fee: $10.00)
*Jeremy's CS Modules (shareware fee:
$10.00)*
MyBattery (shareware fee: $10.00)
*PowerBook Tweak (shareware fee:
$10.00)*
Threshold (shareware fee: $10.00)

Berrie Kremers
Remise 4
4207 BC Gorinchem
The Netherlands
Internet: Berrie.Kremers@kub.nl
Quit It (shareware fee: $15.00)

David Lambert
Dejal Userware
P.O. Box 33-1011
Takapuna, Auckland 1309
New Zealand
CompuServe: 100033.2435
Internet: dejal@iconz.co.nz
5-6-7 INIT (freeware)
Beep FKey (freeware)
Dejal Desktop Utilities (shareware fee: $15.00)
Dejal File Utilities (shareware fee: $10.00)
Dejal Sound Library (shareware fee: varies)
Dejal Text Utilities (shareware fee: $20.00)
Dejal's Quoter Fkey (Donationware)
MacCheckers (freeware)
Message Fkey (freeware)
Say It FKey (freeware)
Shutdown FKey (freeware)
SimCity Bank (freeware)
SndCataloguer (shareware fee: $9.95)
SndCollector (freeware)
SndConverter Lite (shareware fee: $9.95)
SndConverter Pro (shareware fee: $25.00)
SndPlayer (shareware fee: $15.00)
SndRecorder (freeware)
Vol Setter FKey (freeware)
{ Wrap } FKey (freeware)

Leader Technologies
4590 MacArthur Blvd., Suite 550
Newport Beach, CA 92660
Telephone: 714 757-1787
Fax: 714 757-1777
Technical Support: 505 822-0700
America Online: LeaderTech
PowerMerge (suggested retail: $129.00)

Olivier Lebra
8, rue Paul Bounin
06100 Nice
France
Telephone: (+33) 93 98 40 91
Internet: olebra@ifaedi.insa-lyon.fr
AutoCat (shareware fee: $10.00)

Jim Lewis
Golden Gate Graphics
2137 N. Candis Avenue
Santa Ana, CA 92706-2422
Telephone: 714 542-5518
America Online: JimXLewis
CompuServe: 71650,2373
theTypeBook is on the CD-ROM, contact Rascal Software at 805 255-6823 for information on the commercial version

Jacques Lövi
Rue des Romains, 50
L-2444 Luxembourg
Luxembourg
CompuServe: 100477,2436
Blind Monitors (shareware fee: $10.00)

John Mancino
Decision Maker's Software, Inc.
1910 Joslyn Place
Boulder, CO 80304
Fax: 303 449-6207

America Online: JGCMAN
CompuServe: 70337,2143
Internet: mancino@decismkr.com
SwitchBoot (freeware)
TattleTech (shareware fee: $15.00)

Hugues Marty
19 rue Franc
3100 Toulouse France
Internet: hugues@isoft.fr
ProcessWatcher (freeware)

Patrick McClaughry
Internet: patm@parcplace.com
BalloonHelpMe (freeware)
BunchOApps (freeware)
SoBig (freeware)

Cliff McCollum
Blue Globe Software
P.O. Box 8171
Victoria, B.C. V8W 3R8
Canada
CompuServe: 76170,601
Internet: cmccollu@sol.uvic.ca
Alias Zoo (shareware fee: $15.00)

Ken McLeod
Apple Computer, Inc.
Internet: ken@cloudbusting.apple.com
(preferred)
AppleLink: THE.CLOUD
eWorld: TheCloud
Icon Wrap II (freeware)
MacEnvy (freeware)
Scrolling (freeware)

MicroMat Computer Systems
8934 Lakewood Drive #273
Windsor, CA 95492

Telephone: 415 898-6227
Toll-free: 800 829-6227
Support: 415 898-2935
Fax: 415 897-3901
America Online: MicroMat
AppleLink: MicroMatComp
CompuServe: 71333,166
eWorld: MicroMat
Drive Tech (suggested retail: $59.95)
MacEKG (suggested retail: $150.00)
TechTool (freeware)

MicroTest, Inc.
4747 North 22nd st.
Phoenix, AZ 85016
Toll-free: (800) 526-9675
PentaScanner (suggested
retail:$3495/super injector, $4595/2-way
injector)

Alessandro Levi Montalcini
C.so Re Umberto 10
10121 Torino
Italy
Internet: Lmontalcini@pmn.it
ShareDisk (shareware fee: $25.00)

MR Mac Software
P.O. Box 2547
Del Mar, CA 92014
Telephone: 619 453-2845
Internet: MrMac@mrmac.com
Support: nsgsupport@mrmac.com
NetSecurity Guard (suggested retail:
$259.00)

Natural Intelligence, Inc.
725 Concord Ave.
Cambridge, MA 02138
Telephone: 617 876-7680 x1203
Toll-free: 800 999-4649
Fax: 617 492-7425
America Online: ChrisEvans
Internet: evans@natural.com
DragStrip (suggested retail: $59.95)

John M. Neil
John Neil & Associates
P.O. Box 2156
Cupertino, CA 95015
Internet: johnneil@netcom.com
SoftwareFPU (shareware fee: $10.00)

Neon Software, Inc.
3685 Mt. Diablo Blvd., Suite 203
Lafayette, CA 94549
Toll-free: (800) 334-NEON
Fax: (510) 283-6507
Internet: sales@neon.com
LANsurveyor (suggested retail: $395/5 zone, $695/unlimited zones)
NetMinder LocalTalk/Ethernet (suggested retail: $395/$695)
RouterCheck (suggested retail: $649.00)

Now Software, Inc.
921 S.W. Washington St. Suite 500
Portland, OR 97205-2823
Telephone: 503 274-2800
Fax: 503 274-0670
America Online: Now
AppleLink: NowSoftware
CompuServe: 71541,170
eWorld: NowSoft
Internet: support@nowsoft.com
Now Utilities (suggested retail:$89.95)

Fabrizio Oddone
C.so Peschiera 221
10141 Torino
Italy
Internet: gspnx@di.unito.it
CDIconKiller (freeware)
ChunkJoiner (shareware fee: $5.00)
DarkShutDown (shareware fee: $5.00)
Disk Charmer (shareware fee: $10.00)
FaberFinder (shareware fee: $5.00)
Folder Icon Cleaner (shareware fee: $5.00)
Font Control (shareware fee: $5.00)
Forward Delete (freeware)
SetupPartitions (shareware fee: $10.00)
μSim (freeware)

Herb Otto
America Online: Herbo
CompuServe: 72257,1133
BugOff (freeware)

Chris Owen
27 Bishop Street #2R
New Haven, CT 06511
Internet: owen-christopher@yale.edu
Chris Modules (shareware fee: $10.00)

Luc Pauwels
Katholieke Universiteit Leuven
Centre for Computational Linguistics
Maria-Theresiastraat 21
B-3000 Leuven
Belgium
Telephone: +32-16-285092
Fax: +32-16-285098
Internet: Luc.Pauwels@ccl.kuleuven.ac.be
Prefs Cleaner (shareware fee: $15.00)

David Davies Payne
Glendower Software Limited
12 Grosvenor Terrace
Wadestown, Wellington
New Zealand
Internet: dave.davies-
payne@strongbow.otago.ac.nz
SwitchBack (shareware fee: $30.00)

Petur Petursson
Mice & Men
P.O. Box 7238
107 Reykjavik
Iceland
Fax: +354-169-4991
America Online: MenAndMice
CompuServe: 100045,2425
Internet: me-registrations@rhi.hi.is
DeskTop Strip (shareware fee: $20.00)
Monitor Expander (shareware fee:
$25.00)

Mark Pilgrim
MerriMac Software Group
1130 Radnor Hill Road
Wayne, PA 19087-2203
Internet: f8dy@netaxs.com
Sleep Deprivation (freeware)

Robert Polic
c/o SyQuest Technology
47071 Bayside Parkway
Fremont, CA 94538
America Online: RedPat
Internet: D6055@applelink.apple.com
SCSIProbe (freeware)

François Pottier
4 rue Colette
94210 La Varenne

France
Internet: pottier@dmi.ens.fr
Décor (shareware fee: $10.00)
Disk Wizard (shareware fee: $10.00)

Karl Pottie
Mac Support
University Hospitals of Leuven, Belgium
Internet: Karl.Pottie@uz.kuleuven.ac.be
Keep It Up 1.2
Shareware fee: AutoBoot $20.00

Carl III Powell
2306 Pembrook Circle S.W.
Huntsville, AL 35803
CompuServe: 76702,457
Battery Drain (freeware)
Password Key (shareware fee: $20.00)
The Timekeeper (shareware fee: $5.00)

PrairieSoft Software, Inc.
P.O. Box 65820
West Des Moines, IA 50265
Telephone: 515 225-3720
Fax: 515 225-2422
America Online: PrairieSft
AppleLink: PRAIRIESOFT
CompuServe: 72662,131
eWorld: PrairieSft
DiskTop (suggested retail: $49.95)

Jon Pugh
1861 Landings Drive
Mountain View CA 94043
Internet: jonpugh@netcom.com
AppleTalk On (shareware fee: $5.00)
Jon's Commands (freeware)
Show Sizes II (shareware fee: $20.00)
ToggleAT (freeware)

Alex Rampell
1186 North Ocean Way
Palm Beach, FL 33480
America Online: LOTTSIM
Volume/DS Screensaver (shareware fee: $10.00)

John Rawnsley
Mathematics Institute
University of Warwick
Coventry, CV4 7AL
United Kingdom
Printer Defaults (freeware)

Eberhard Rensch
Spitalhofstr. 3
D-94032 Passau
Germany
CompuServe: 100010,604
LogSpy (shareware fee: $5.00)
UnFinder (shareware fee: $5.00)

Paul Reznick
1535 S. Marie
Westland, MI 48185-3874
America Online: Przeznik
CompuServe: 72154,2710
Go Gestalt (freeware)

Melissa Rogers
P.O. Box 20723
San Jose, CA 95160
America Online: AFLBear
Trash Chute (freeware)

Leonard Rosenthol
Aladdin Systems
165 Westridge Drive
Watsonville, CA 95076
Telephone: 408 761-6200

Fax: 408 761-6206
AOL/AppleLink: ALADDIN
CompuServe: 75300,1666
eWorld/GEnie: AladdinSys
Internet: aladdin@well.com
AliasDragger (freeware)
Disk Rejuvenator (freeware)

Dave Rubinic
1315 Pieffers Lane
Oberlin, PA 17113-1016
America Online: DaveR9
Internet: udrubini@mcs.drexel.edu
Easy Errors (freeware)

Saber Software Corp.
5944 Luther Lane, Suite 1007
Dallas TX 75225
FAX 214-361-1882
Internet:
sabersoftware@notes.compuserve.com
Toll-free: (800) 338-8754
Saber LAN (suggested retail: $299 and $59 per node)

John A. Schlack
406 Newgate Court, Apt. A1
Andalusia, PA 19020
America Online: John40
CompuServe: 70252,143
Attributes (shareware fee: $15.00)
Chronograph (shareware fee: $15.00)
Padlock (shareware fee: $5.00)

David Schooley
200 26th Street NW N-203
Atlanta, GA 30309
America Online: Dschooley
Internet: schooley@ee.gatech.edu
EPS Fixer (shareware fee: $10.00)

Art A. Schumer
Evergreen Software, Inc.
15600 NE 8th Street, Suite A3126
Bellevue, WA 98009
Telephone: 206 483-6576
America Online: ArtSchumer
CompuServe: 76004,557
MacPassword (shareware fee: $49.00)
MacSnoop (shareware fee: $25.00)

Daniel Schwartz
Articulate Systems Inc.
600 West Cummings Park Suite 4500
Woburn, MA 01801
Internet: dan@cs.brandeis.edu
SpeedSwitch (Jerryware)

Erik Sea
Tuffet AntiGravity
P.O. Box 61-1260
Port Huron, MI 48061-1260
AppleLink: CDA0745
CompuServe: 74170,111
BlackLock (shareware fee: $5.00)

Shepherd's Pi Software
3408 S. Rusk Street
Amarillo, TX 79109
America Online: Rbuckwheat
CompuServe: 75264,3431
GumShoe (shareware fee: $15.00)

Scott Silverman
SilverWARE (formerly CRA.Z Software)
P.O. Box 6379
Haverhill, MA 01831
Telephone: 508 521-5262
America Online: Silverwre
AppleLink: Silverware
CompuServe: 74007,2303

eWorld: Silverman
PrintOne (freeware)

Hugh Sontag
Qdea
6331 Hilton Court
Pine Springs, MN 55115
Internet: Qdea@eworld.com
Synchronize! (registration fee: $29.95)

Jim Speth
Internet: speth@end.com
DiskSweeper (Work-at-Home-ware)

Bill Steinberg
VST Power Systems
1620 Sudbury Road, Suite 3
Concord, MA 01742
Telephone: 508 287-4600
CompuServe: 72551,201
Bootman™ (freeware)
EMMpathy (freeware)
SpinD (freeware)

Steve Stockman
Sonflower Softworks
219 S. Barrington Ave. #3
Los Angeles, CA 90049-3324
Telephone: 310 440-3933
America Online: SonflowrSw
CompuServe: 76507,2646
eWorld: SonflowrSw
Notify (shareware fee: $10.00)

Dave Sugar
3718 Norburn Road
Randallstown, MD 21133
Internet: udsugar@king.mcs.drexel.edu
Find Stuff (PostcardWare)

David P. Sumner
1009 Walters Lane
Columbia, SC 29209
INIT-Scope (shareware fee: $15.00)

Symantec
10201 Torre Avenue
Cupertino, CA 95014
(orders to:)
Symantec Fulfillment Center
Attn: Order Admin.
P.O. Box 10849
Eugene, OR 97440-2849
Telephone: 408 253-9600
Customer Service: 800 441-7234
Tech Support: 503 465-8420 (free for 90 days)
America Online: keyword: SYMANTEC
CompuServe: GO SYMANTEC
MacTools Pro (suggested retail: $149.95)
Norton DiskDoubler Pro ($109.00)
Norton Utilities for the Mac ($149.95)
Suitcase ($79.00)

Alex Tang
Internet: altitude@umich.edu
Miguel Cruz (original author)
65 Oakwood Street
San Francisco CA 94110
Internet: mnc@netcom.com
FLUT (freeware)

Teknosys, Inc.
3923 Coconut Palm Drive, Suite 111
Tampa, FL 33619
Telephone: 800 873-3494
Fax: 813 620-4039
AppleLink: TEKNOSYS
CompuServe: 73237,2370
Help! (suggested retail: $149.00)

Michael Thies
Fachbereich Informatik
Universitaet-Gesamthochschule
Paderborn
Germany
Internet: thiesana@uni-paderborn.de
sAVe the Disk (freeware)

Robert Thornton
Jump Development Group, Inc.
1228 Malvern Avenue
Pittsburgh, PA 15217-1141
Telephone: 412 681-2692
America Online: JumpDevgrp
AppleLink: Rthornton
CompuServe: 71321,1527
Bail (freeware)

Trilobyte Software
6982 Devon Drive
Middletown, OH 45044
Telephone: 513 777-6641
Fax: 513 779-7760
America Online: Trylobyte
AppleLink: flying.phone
CompuServe: 73740,2472

UltraDesign Technology Ltd.
5/39 St.George's Square
London SW1V 3QN
England
Telephone: +44 171 931 0010
Fax: +44 171 630 9105
AppleLink: ULTRA.TEC.UK
eWorld: UltraTec
ftp: ftp.demon.co.uk/pub/mac/ultratec
Internet: find@ultratec.demon.co.uk
UltraFind (shareware fee: $38.00)

Visionary Software
1820 SW Vermont, Suite A
Portland, OR 97219-1945
Telephone: 503 246-6200
Fax: 503 452-1198
LifeGuard (suggested retail: $79.95)

Maurice Volaski
8201 Henry Ave Apt J23,
Philadelphia, PA 19128-2216
America Online: fluxsftwre
Internet: volaski@contra.med.buffalo.edu
Beep Saver (freeware)
ChooserUser (freeware)
CommentKeeper (freeware)
FCB Inspector (freeware)
LaserwriterLockout (freeware)
Mac Identifier (freeware)
Movies in the Dark (freeware)
SmartKeys (freeware)
TrashAlias (freeware)

Randall Voth
46058 Fiesta Avenue
Chilliwack, BC V2P 3S4
Canada
Telephone: 604 795-4746
Internet: hvoth@sfu.ca
or: hvoth@cln.etc.bc.ca
BatteryMinder (shareware fee: $15.00)
Synk (shareware fee: $5.00)

VST Power Systems, Inc.
1620 Sudbury Road, Suite 3
Concord, MA 01742
Telephone: 508 287-4600
Fax: 508 287-4068
PBTools (suggested retail: $99.95)

Marty Wachter
2107 Sulgrave Avenue
Baltimore, MD 21209
America Online: AFA Marty
Internet: mrw@falconmicro.com
MacErrors (Boloware)

James W. Walker
3200 Heyward Street
Columbia, SC 29205
America Online: JWWalker
CompuServe: 76367,2271
Internet: walkerj@math.scarolina.edu
Dialog View (shareware fee: $10.00)
PrintAid (freeware)

Dan Walkowski
140 Pasito Terrace #512
Sunnyvale, CA 94086
Internet: walkowsk@taurus.apple.com
TrashMan (shareware fee: $10.00)

Jonas Walldén
Rydsvagen 252 c:11
S-582 51 Linkoping
Sweden
Telephone: +46-13-176084 (voice/fax)
AppleLink: sw1369
Internet: jonasw@lysator.liu.se
PowerScan (shareware fee: $10.00)

Mike Weasner
2567 Plaza Del Amo #209
Torrance, CA 90503-7329
America Online: MWEASNER
AppleLink: MWEASNER
CompuServe: 70307,243
ExAminer (shareware fee: $10.00)

Mark R. Weinstein
#5 Johns Canyon Road
Rolling Hills, CA 90274
QuikFloppy (shareware fee: $10.00)

Andrew Welch
Ambrosia Software, Inc.
P.O. Box 23140
Rochester, NY 14692
Telephone: 716 427-2577
Fax: 716 475-9289
America Online: AmbrosiaSW
AppleLink: Ambrosia.SW
CompuServe: 73424, 1226
Apeiron (shareware fee: $15.00)
Big Cheese Key (shareware fee: $10.00)
Bomb Shelter (freeware)
Chiral (Shareware fee: $15.00)
ColorSwitch (shareware fee: $10.00)
Discolor (freeware)
Easy Envelopes+ (shareware fee: $15.00)
Eclipse (shareware fee: $10.00)
FlashWrite][(shareware fee: $15.00)
Maelstrom (shareware fee: $15.00)
Oracle (shareware fee: $10.00)
Snapz (shareware fee: $10.00)
To Do! DA (shareware fee: $15.00)
Wacky Lights (freeware)
µLife (freeware)

Robert Wiebe
Systems Research Group
20-8451 Ryan Road
Richmond, B.C. V7A 2E8
Canada
CompuServe: 70262,342
Shdred It (shareware fee: varies)
Don Winsby
Typotronics Inc.
2001 S. Hanley, Suite 200

St. Louis, MO 63144
NetDragMover (shareware fee: $39.00)

Bill Woody
In Phase Consulting
337 West California #4
Glendale, CA 91203
Telephone: 818 502-1424
Internet: woody@alumni.cco.caltech.edu
Clipboard Master (freeware)

Tad Woods
T & T Software
920 Quail Lane
Salem, VA 24153
Fax: 703 389-0889
America Online: Tad Woods
CompuServe: 70312,3552
Internet: tandtsw@roanoke.infi.net
Announce (shareware fee: $39.00)

Working Software Inc.
P.O. Box 1844
Santa Cruz, CA 95061-1844
Telephone: 408 423-5696
Technical Support: 408 423-5696
Toll-free: 800 229-9675 (US and Canada)
Fax: 408 423-5699
America Online: WorkingSW
CompuServe: 76004,2072
Internet: Info@working.com
Toner Tuner (suggested retail:$24.95)
Working Watermarker (suggested retail:
$49.95) (both products are available
together for $64.95)

Joe Zobkiw
TripleSoft, Macintosh Software
Development
172 Charles St., Suite A
Cambridge, MA 02141-2118
Telephone: 919 782-3230 (voice/fax)
America Online: AFL Zobkiw
CompuServe: 74631,1700
Internet: zobkiw@world.std.com
Cleaning Lady (freeware)
Folder Watcher (shareware fee: $20.00)

D Tools: Hardware & Software Used

Here are some of the toys I used to put this thing together:

Hardware

My home machine is a Quadra 700, with 20 megabytes of RAM, a 540-megabyte Fujitsu internal hard drive, DayStar QuadraCache (128K), and 2 megabytes of VRAM attached to a Apple 17" Color Monitor; my second screen is a Sigma Designs 19" L-View monitor. Attached to it are a CD Technology Porta-Drive CD-ROM and an APS 230-megabyte MicroOptical Drive; I use Monster SCSI cables and an APS Active Terminator to tame SCSI. I connect to the outside world with a Supra 14400 bps fax/data modem, and I print to an Apple LaserWriter Select 310 (at the office I also use an HP 1200 C/PS).

As I started the book, I upgraded my Duo 230 to a PowerBook 540c/12/500 with a PowerPort Mercury 19200 bps internal fax/data modem (thanks to Gail Bartlett of Apple Canada). I used to connect the Duo to my Quadra with AppleTalk; I now use an APS SCSI Doc to connect my 540c in SCSI mode. Other Macs used include an SE/30 8/80, and a Portable 2/40. My friend Chris Fortin at Apple Canada lent me a QuickTake 150 to take the pictures in this chapter.

Software

Where to start? I guess the beginning is a good place. My connection to the outside world was the MAUG area on CompuServe; I connect there using CompuServe Navigator 3.2.1p1. I used CompuServe to contact the authors (including those on America Online and on the Internet), to download all the great shareware on the CD-ROM, and to send files to Steve Bobker for technical editing (thanks again, Steve!). For my weekly foray, I used version 2.5.1 of America Online's software. Once I started contacting shareware authors, I set up a little database using FileMaker Pro 2.1v3 (Figure D-1) to keep track of things. My original intent was to use Panorama, which I think is more powerful, but their copy-protection scheme prevented me from using it on the road.

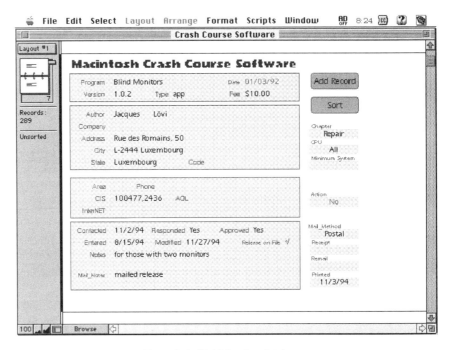

Figure D-1: FileMaker Pro database

I started writing using Microsoft Word 5.1a, then briefly upgraded to 6.0 (I moved back to 5.1a when the problems with 6.0 became apparent). I'm now using 6.0.1, which addresses most, but not all, of 6.0's problems. I've identified a number of conversion problems between the versions that have Microsoft Technical Support baffled. The most interesting is where opening and resaving a 5.1 document in 6.0 or 6.0.1 results in some graphics being rescaled horizontally 3271%!

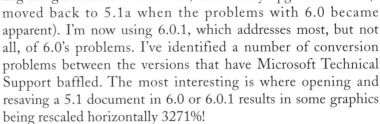

The icons were drawn in Aldus Freehand 4.0, and saved as EPS files. I used Ambrosia's Snapz 1.0 to capture screens, which I converted to grayscale and cropped in Adobe Photoshop 3.0.1. Page layout was done in QuarkXPress 3.31, with Sonar

Bookends Xtension doing the indexing. The typefaces used are from the Adobe Caslon and Adobe Frutiger families.

Every day, I use Leader Technologies' PowerMerge 2.0.5 to merge files between my 540c and Quadra; with weekly backups to my APS 230 MO with Dantz Retrospect 2.1. I used Norton Disk Doctor 3.0 to keep my hard drives in shape; it has saved my bacon more times than I care to admit.

For system software, I started with 7.1, then graduated to 7.5, and now 7.5.1. Active extensions include Conflict Catcher 3, which recently replaced Now Startup Manager 5.0.1; RAM Doubler 1.5.2, AliasDragger, DiskDoubler, Microsoft OLE Extension, and SCSI Manager 4.3. Active Control Panels include After Dark 3.0, AutoDoubler, CopyDoubler, FileSaver, MacTools DriveLight 4.0, Now Menus 5.0.1, PowerKey 2.0.1, APS PowerTools Drive Controls 3.0.6, Daystar's QuadControl 2.3, Snapz 1.0, Thunder 7 1.5.5, ATM 3.8.2, and MenuFonts 4.5. On my PowerBook, I also run Global Village's PowerPort software version 2.5, Control Strip, and PBTools 2.0.

E About the CD-ROM

There's tons of good stuff on the CD-ROM, thanks to the generosity of the shareware authors and the companies who provided demos. There are three main folders; Shareware by Chapter, Commercial Demos, and CompuServe. Here's what's in them:

Shareware by Chapter

Ch 01 Loading Extensions
ExAminer 1.4
Extension Kit™
IconWrap II 1.2
INIT-Scope 2.1
Symbionts 2.5

Ch 02 Memory
About 1.0.3
MODE32 7.5
RamDisk+ 3.2.4
RAMDoubler 1.5 .2 Indicator
SpeedSwitch '040
UnFinder
WriteThrough

Ch 03 Backup
AutoCat™ 1.7
AutoCat™ 1.7 FR
AutoClock 1.4.4
Chronograph 1.1.1
Disk Wizard 2.0
MacUpdate 3.2.5
SwitchBack 2.5.1
Synchronize! 3.2.9
Synk 1.0.6

Ch 04 System 6
Bootman
FCB Inspector 1.1
HeapTool
HellFolder
SwitchBoot 1.1

Ch 05 System 7
7Tuner 1.7
7Tuner 1.7 Patch 1.1
Alias Director 3.5.2
AliasZoo 2.0.5
CommentKeeper 1.0
Desktop Remover
Finder Preferences 7, v2
KillFinderZooms 1.2
MenuChoice 2.1
PowerShare 1.1
Trash Chute
TrashAlias 1.1.1
TrashMan 4.0.5
Warp7Utilities v1.3

Ch 06 System 7.5
AETracker
AliasDragger
JonsCommands 1.3.5
Mac Identifier 1.1.1
WhoAmI? 1.0.1

Ch 07 Compression
Compact Pro 1.5.1

Ch 08 Diagnostics
CountPatches
EasyError 1.11
Go Gestalt 1.5
MacEnvy 2.1
MacErrors 1.2.1 Fat
MacSnoop™ 1.5.5
Open Files 2.0
ProcessWatcher 1.1
Snitch 2.0
Speedometer 4.0.1
TattleTech 2.1.4

Ch 09 Protection
Basic Black 1.4.1
Basic Black 1.4.1f
Bomb Shelter 1.0.1
BugOff 1.3.1
DiskLocker 1.3
Eclipse 2.2.0
KillDF 1.1
MacLifeInsurance 2.0.1
MacPassword 4.1.1
Padlock 1.0
Password Key 3.0.3
ShredIt 2.4
Sleeper 1.1.4
StartupLog 2.0.1
SunBlock 2.2
Umbra™ 1.2

Volume/DS Screensaver

Ch 10 Shareware Utilities
AppleTalk On
Auto Shutdown 1.1
AutoMenus Pro 1.5
Bail 2.0.2
Bring Finder to Front
CD Menu 1.3.1
Clipboard Master 2.0
Décor 2.6.1
Décor 2.6.1F
Key Tools 1.0.1
Line Up 2.1
LogSpy 1.0
Notify 3.02
Once Daily 1.1
Quit All Applications
Quit It 1.2.3
RefreshFKEY
Scrolling 7.0.1
TaskMan 1.1
Timekeeper 1.1
TypeIt4Me 4.4.1 (fat)
Ultra Recorder 2.0
Victoire! 1.0.3

Ch 11 Outstanding Authors
Alessandro Montalcini
ShareDisk 2.1
Control Panels & Extensions
  AfterDark Modules
  Async Family 1.14
  B-Panel 1.17
  Blood 2.0.2
  Depth&Volume 1.0
  DragAnyWindow 3.1 FAT
  KeyClicks 1.0.3
  MenuBall 2.0.2
  NoDesktopCleanup 1.1.3

Ch 11 (continued)

PowerClicks 1.1.1
QuickRedraw 2.01
ResumeToFinder 2.0
Shutdown Delay 2.1
Startup Player 1.0.3
For Power users Only
Attributor 1.1.1 FAT
cdevEloper FKEY 1.0
CheckOpen 1.1.2
CountPixels FKEY 1.0
DBugR 1.2.1
Global Search 1.03
Set Startup 1.3
SoundSet FKEY 1.0
Trapper 1.0.4
KeyQuencer 1.2.1
List Files 2.5 FAT
ShareDisk Info
Utilities
CalConvert 1.2.1 FAT
Erritor 1.1
LoopSound 1.0
Macro Editor 1.2.1 FAT
MediaSizer 1.3.2 FAT
PowerPCheck 2.1 FAT
PowerXplorer
SimpleText Color Menu 2.0
SoundCase 1.01 for 7.1
Verifile 1.2.3 FAT
Ambrosia
OPEN ME FIRST!
Ambrosia Software Licence
Apeiron 1.0.1
Big Cheese Key 1.2.1
Bomb Shelter 1.0.1
Chiral 1.0.0
ColrSwitch 2.3.0
Discolor 1.0.2
Easy Envelopes+ 2.6.0

Eclipse 2.2.0
FlashWrite][1.1.0
INITs, the System Heap, and You
Maelstrom 1.4.1
Oracle 2.1.0
Snapz 1.0.0
Swoop 1.0.0
The Ambrosia Times 2.3
To Do! 3.2.1 DA
Wacky Lights 1.0.1
µLife 1.0.1
Dejal Userware
Dejal Desktop Utilities
DrawDesktop
AltFromMain Folders
AltOrMan Folders
AltToMain Folders
AltClipboard
AltClipboard FKEY
Clipsize? FKEY
Hide Menubar FKEY
LockHD4Session
Privacy FKEY
Volume
Dejal File Utilities
Create Suitcase 1.1
Deleter 1.1
New Suitcase 1.1
Resource Leech 1.1
Dejal Freeware
5-6-7 INIT
Beep FKEY
Greetings INIT
MacCheckers
Message FKEY
Say It FKEY
SimCity Bank
SndCollector
Snd Recorder
Vol Setter FKEY

Ch 11 (continued)
{Wrap} FKEY 1.1
Dejal Sound Library
Dejal Text Utilities
TextMerge 2.0
TextSplitter 2.0
Dejal's Quoter FKEY 1.6
SndCataloguer 1.3
SndConverter 1.3
SndConverter Lite 1.3
SndConverter Pro 2.2
SndPlayer 2.2
Fabrizio Oddone
CDIconKiller 1.3.3
ChunkJoiner 2.0.1
DarkShutdown 2.1
Disk Charmer 2.3
FaberFinder 4.1.3
Folder Icon Cleaner 1.1.3
Font Control 1.1.1
Forward Delete 1.1.2
SetupPartitions 1.0.5
µSim 1.0b5
Jan B's stuff
Color SuperApple
Jack in the Trash
MenuMail
Mithrandir
SuperApple
The Red Queen 1.2
WindowWarp
Jason Anderson
4-Matter 1.6.0
EjectDisk 1.0.3
PictSize 1.1
Volume FKEY 1.1
Maurice Volaski
Beep Saver 1.1
ChooserUser 1.2.1
CommentKeeper 1.0

FCB Inspector 1.1
LaserwriterLockout 1.2
Mac Identifier 1.1.1
Movies in the Dark 1.0
SmartKeys 2.1
TrashAlias 1.1.1

Ch 13 Files
Attributes 1.21
Bund Aid
Cleaning Lady 1.0
Default Folder 2.5.4
Dialog View 2.1.4
DirtyDesk 1.0.1
File Buddy 3.1.1
File Kit 1.1
Filename Mapper 1.ov1
Find Stuff 1.0.4
Folder Icon Cleaner 1.1.3
Gumshoe 1.0.3p1
Pledge 1.0
PowerScan 2.0.7
Prefs Cleaner 1.1
Safety Belt
UltraFind™ 2.0B.(Fat)

Ch 14 Fonts
Carpetbag 1.4.3
EM Fonts Patchers
Font Control 1.1.1
FontClerk 5.0
HideFonts
theTypeBook 3.26

Ch 15 Printing
EPS Fixer 1.52
PrintAid 1.4
PrintChoice 1.4
Printer Defaults 1.3.2
PrintOne 1.0.1

Ch 16 Hard Drives

Disk Bug Checker 1.1
Disk Rejuvenator™
sAVe the Disk
ShowSizes 2.2.3
SpaceAlert 2.0.2
SpaceServer 2.0

Ch 17 Hardware

Blind Monitors 1.0.2
DiskDup+ 2.6.1
DiskSweeper
EZ FloppyEject
FLUT .94a
MonitorExpander 1.0.1
QuickFormat! 8.0
QuikFloppy 1.0.1
TechTool 1.0.7

Ch 18 PowerBooks

Battery Drain
Battery Amnesia 1.4.0
BatteryMinder 2.1.1
BlackLock
Control Strips
  BalloonHelpMe 1.0.1
  BunchOApps 1.0b3
  Chris Modules 1.3
  Duo Temperature Strip
  Jeremy's CS Modules 1.4.2
  SoBig 1.0b1
Desktop Strip 1.2
DuoMon 1.2
EMMpathy 2.0
Insomniac 1.0.3a
My Battery 3.0.1
PowerBook Tweak 1.0.3a
PowerStrip 3.5.1
Quiet Start 1.3
Silent Beep 2.0

Sleep Deprivation 1.1
SpinD Fkey 1.0
Threshold 1.0.5a
ToggleAT 4.0

Ch 19 Power Macs

Fat Free 1.2
I Love Native 1.1 (680x0)
I Love Native! 1.1p (PPC)
PowerPCheck 1.2.1 FAT
PowerXplorer 1.0.3
SoftwareFPU 3.03

Ch 20 Getting On-Line

MCC Session

Ch 21 Networking

Announce 1.1
AutoBoot 1.4.1
Folder Watcher
Keep It Up 1.2
MailSlot 1.1t
NetDragMover 1.4
Network Security Guard 3.0

Appendix D: Sources

Vendor DA 1.44
VendorDA (B&W)
VendorDA (Color)

Commercial Demos

Aladdin
DropStuff w/EE™ 3.5.2
StuffIt Expander 3.5.2 Installer
StuffIt Lite™ 3.5

Berkeley
After Dark 3.0b Updater
Expresso Demos

Casady & Greene
CC 3.0.1 Demo
Crystal Crazy Demo
Glider PRO 1.0.1 Demo
Snap Mail demo

Charles River Analytics
Open Sesame 1.1.2c Patcher
Open Sesame demo

Claris
Macintosh Trial Applications
Amazing Animation Trial
BrushStrokes Trial
Claris Organizer Trial
ClarisDraw Trial
ClarisImpact Trial
FileMaker Pro Trial
MacProject Pro Trial
MacWrite Pro Trial
Retrieve It! Trial
Power Mac Trial Applications
ClarisDraw Trial Power Mac
ClarisImpact Trial Power Mac
ClarisWorks Trial Power Mac
MacWrite Pro Trial Power Mac

CompuServe
MacCIM 2.4.1

Connectix
CPU 2.0.4 Demo
Mac Memory Guide 6th Edition
Mode 32 7.5
QuickCam 1.0.2 Updater
QuickCam Demo
RAM Doubler 1.5.2 Updater
RAM Doubler Demo

Dantz
DiskFit Demo
Retrospect Demo
Retrospect Remote Demo
Retrospect 2.1 Updater

Dubl-Click
CCS Demo Calcs
ClickChange 2.0 Demo
ClickChange-E
Icon Mania! Demo
Icon Mania!-E 1.02
MenuFonts 4.5E

Jump Development
OptiMem 2.1.1 Demo
OptiMem 2.1.1 Update

Lind
EMMpathy 2.0
Lind BU500
PBTools 1.2
PBTools™ 1.1 Update

MicroMat

DriveTech™ Demo
MacEKG 2.0.6 Demo
MicroMat & CompuServe
MicroMat Catalog
Other MicroMat Products
TechTool 1.0.7

Natural Intelligence

DragStrip 1.0.1 Updater
DragStrip™ Demo

Now Software

Now Contact 3.0.1
Now Up-To-Date 3.0.1
Now Utilities™ 5.0.1

PrairieSoft

DateBook 1.0
Disktop 4.5.2 Demo
DiskTop ToolKit
InTouch 2.0.7 Updater
InTouch Fixer

Symantec

AutoDoubler 2.0.2 Patcher
CopyDoubler™ 2.0.2 Updater
NUM Speed Disk 3.0 -> 3.1 Updater
Suitcase 2.1.4p3 Update

Teknosys

Help! Demo

Trilobyte

ARA Commander 2.0.2 Demo
MasterFinder 1.3 68k
MasterFinder 1.3 FAT
PowerBar Pro 2.0.1
PowerBar Pro 2.0.1 updater

Visionary Software

FTF Pro 1.5.1 Installer
LifeGuard™ 1.0.2 Demo

Working Software

Spellswell™ 7 Demo
The Findswell™ Demo
The QuickLetter™ Demo
Toner Tuner™ Demo
WaterMaker Demo
Writeswell Jr.

Index

501

E

F

N

About the CD-ROM

The enclosed CD-ROM alone would be worth the price of *Macintosh Crash Course*. It includes over 290 shareware and freeware applications, 52 commercial demos, and a dozen updaters. Here's a sample of what you'll find on the CD-ROM, which is packed with over 170 megabytes of software:

Chapter 01 Loading Extensions: Symbionts
Chapter 02 Memory: MODE32 7.5
Chapter 03 Backup: Disk Wizard
Chapter 05 System 7: 7Tuner
Chapter 06 System 7.5: Alias Dragger™
Chapter 07 Compression: Compact Pro
Chapter 08 Diagnostics: Speedometer
Chapter 09 Protection: Volume/DS Screensaver
Chapter 10 Shareware Utilities: TypeIt4Me
Chapter 11 Outstanding Authors: Alessandro Montalcini's Sharedisk
(25 programs for $25.00!); all of Ambrosia Software's great share
ware, including their latest: Apeiron and Swoop; Fabrizio Oddone's
Disk Charmer; and Jan Bruyndonckx's The Red Queen.
Chapter 13 Files: File Buddy and UltraFind
Chapter 14 Fonts: the TypeBook
Chapter 15 Printing: PrintChoice
Chapter 16 Hard Drives: SpaceAlert
Chapter 17 Hardware: TechTool
Chapter 18 PowerBooks: PowerBook Teak
Chapter 19 PPC: I Love Native
Chapter 21 Networking: Network Security Guard

Commercial Demos

Aladdin: **StuffIt Lite**™
Charles River Analytics: **Open Sesame**™
Claris: Macintosh Trial Applications of all their current applications
Dantz: **Retrospect**™
Jump Development: **OptiMem**™
MicroMat: **DriveTech**™
Natural Intelligence: **DragStrip**™
Now Software: **Now Utitlities**™
PrairieSoft: **Disktop**™
Teknosys: **Help!**™
Trilobyte: **PowerBar Pro**™
Working Software: **Toner Tuner**™
A full working version of CompuServe's compuServe Information Manager
(MacCIM™)

For a complete listing of the CD-ROM contents by chapter, please see Appendix E.